DAF 31, 32, 33, 44, 46, 1961-76

By Kenneth Ball

and the Autobooks Team of Technical Writers

DAF 750 1961-63
DAF Daffodil 1961-67
DAF 33 1967-74
DAF 44 1966-75
DAF 46 1975-76

Autobooks

Autobooks Ltd. Golden Lane Brighton BN1 2QJ England

The AUTOBOOK series of Workshop Manuals is the largest in the world and covers the majority of British and Continental motor cars, as well as all major Japanese and Australian models. For a full list see the back of this manual.

CONTENTS

ISBN 0 85147 605 8

First Edition 1973
Second Edition, fully revised 1974
Third Edition, fully revised 1976

752

Printed and bound in Brighton England for Autobooks Ltd by G. Beard & Son Ltd C

ACKNOWLEDGEMENT

We wish to thank DAF Motors (GB) Ltd for their co-operation and also for supplying data and illustrations. Considerable assistance has also been given by owners, who have discussed their cars in detail, and we would like to express our gratitude for this invaluable advice and help.

FIG 1 : 1   A cutaway view of the 746 cc engine

The connecting rod big-ends have removable caps and plain bearings. The small-ends are fitted with bush bearings. The gudgeon pins are a press fit in the pistons and are retained by circlips.

The steel cylinder barrels are spigoted into the crankcase assembly and the separate cylinder heads are spigoted to the barrels. Each cylinder and head assembly is retained to the crankcase by four studs. The overhead valves are pushrod operated through rockers carried on a rocker shaft mounted on the cylinder head. The valve seats are shrunk-in inserts. Valve to rocker clearances are set by means of adjusters at the pushrod ends of the rockers. The pushrods are enclosed by pushrod cover tubes.

A single downdraught carburetter is mounted on the top of the engine and the intake manifold incorporates an exhaust gas heated hot spot. Closed crankcase ventilation is provided and this is described in **Section 1 : 21**. The crankcase breather is piped to the air cleaner. Ducts which surround the exhaust pipes carry pressure air from the cooling system and provide the source of warm air for the heating system which is described in **Chapter 4**.

The engine lubrication system is shown diagrammatically in **FIG 1 : 3**. The gear pump takes oil from the sump through a gauze strainer. Oil pressure is limited by a relief valve. Pressure oil is fed to the camshaft bearings and to the main bearings. The connecting rod big-end bearings are pressure fed by oil transferred from the main bearings through passages drilled in the crankshaft. The overhead valve gear is lubricated by pressure oil which is transferred to the hollow pushrods through passages drilled in the tappets and oil drains from the valve gear down the tubular covers which encloses the pushrods. An aircooled oil cooler is provided. This is of 'doughnut' shape and is mounted round the hub of the cooling impeller. The lubrication circuit incorporates an oil cooler bypass valve and this allows cold oil to bypass the cooler.

There are three mounting points for the engine; one at the front and two at the rear.

Never carry out repairs or adjustments to the engine without making sure that the Variomatic selector lever is in the neutral position.

1 : 2 Maintenance

Engine oil level:

Check the oil level with the engine cold and with the vehicle standing on a level surface. Remove the dipstick, wipe it clean and replace it fully; remove and note the oil level which should be neither below the MIN mark nor above the MAX mark. Top up as may be necessary but never overfill by bringing the level above the MAX mark. The difference between the MIN and MAX marks is equivalent to 1 pint (.6 litres).

Use the same oil as that already in the engine. An SAE 20 or 10W30 oil may be used the whole year round but if the ambient temperature is consistently above 86°F (30°C), the engine should be filled with SAE 30 or 30W40 oil.

CHAPTER 1

THE ENGINE

1 :1 Description

B74 engines of 746 cc capacity are fitted to DAF 31, 32 and 33 models. B85 engines of 844 cc capacity are fitted to DAF 44 and 46 models.

These aircooled, four-stroke, horizontally opposed two-cylinder engines are identical in principle and have exactly the same features. The 844 cc capacity engine is a longer stroke version of the 746 cc capacity engine. The cylinder bore dimension of both engines is the same. Arising from the difference in stroke, the engines, in certain respects, are not dimensionally equal and reference to **Technical Data** in the **Appendix** will provide information regarding the main dimensional differences.

A partially cutaway illustration of the 746 cc capacity engine is shown in **FIG 1 :1** and a fully exploded view of the 844 cc engine is shown in **FIG 1 :2**. The two-throw crankshaft runs in two plain bearings. These are carried in a two-piece crankcase which is split vertically fore and aft. Each half of the wet sump is integral with a crankcase half. The camshaft, which is located centrally below the crankshaft and also runs in plain bearings, is driven by helical gearing from the front end of the crankshaft. The drive spindle of the oil pump is driven from the forward end of the camshaft onto which it is keyed. A skew gear which is mounted on the forward end of the crankshaft in front of the camshaft drive gear, drives the vertically mounted distributor drive shaft. An eccentric on this shaft operates the diaphragm type fuel pump by means of a short pushrod. The flywheel is spigoted and bolted to the rear end of the crankshaft. A ring gear with which the starter motor pinion engages, is incorporated on the forward periphery of the flywheel. The flywheel carries the pivoted shoes of the centrifugal drum type clutch. On 746 cc engines fitted to DAF 31 models, the forward end of the clutch shaft is piloted into the crankshaft. On 746 cc engines fitted to later DAF 31 models, to all DAF 32 and 33 models and all 844 cc engines, the clutch shaft is piloted in a ballbearing which is carried in the hub of the flywheel. This design difference is referred to in **Chapter 5** and is illustrated in **FIG 5 :1**. The pulley for the generator belt drive is carried on the hub of the cooling impeller and is attached to the crankshaft by a single bolt. The impeller and cooling system is described in **Chapter 4**.

INTRODUCTION

This do-it-yourself Workshop Manual has been specially written for the owner who wishes to maintain his car in first class condition and to carry out his own servicing and repairs. Considerable savings on garage charges can be made, and one can drive in safety and confidence knowing the work has been done properly.

Comprehensive step-by-step instructions and illustrations are given on all dismantling, overhauling and assembling operations. Certain assemblies require the use of expensive special tools, the purchase of which would be unjustified. In these cases information is included but the reader is recommended to hand the unit to the agent for attention.

Throughout the Manual hints and tips are included which will be found invaluable, and there is an easy to follow fault diagnosis at the end of each chapter.

Whilst every care has been taken to ensure correctness of information it is obviously not possible to guarantee complete freedom from errors or to accept liability arising from such errors or omissions.

Instructions may refer to the righthand or lefthand sides of the vehicle or the components. These are the same as the righthand or lefthand of an observer standing behind the car and looking forward.

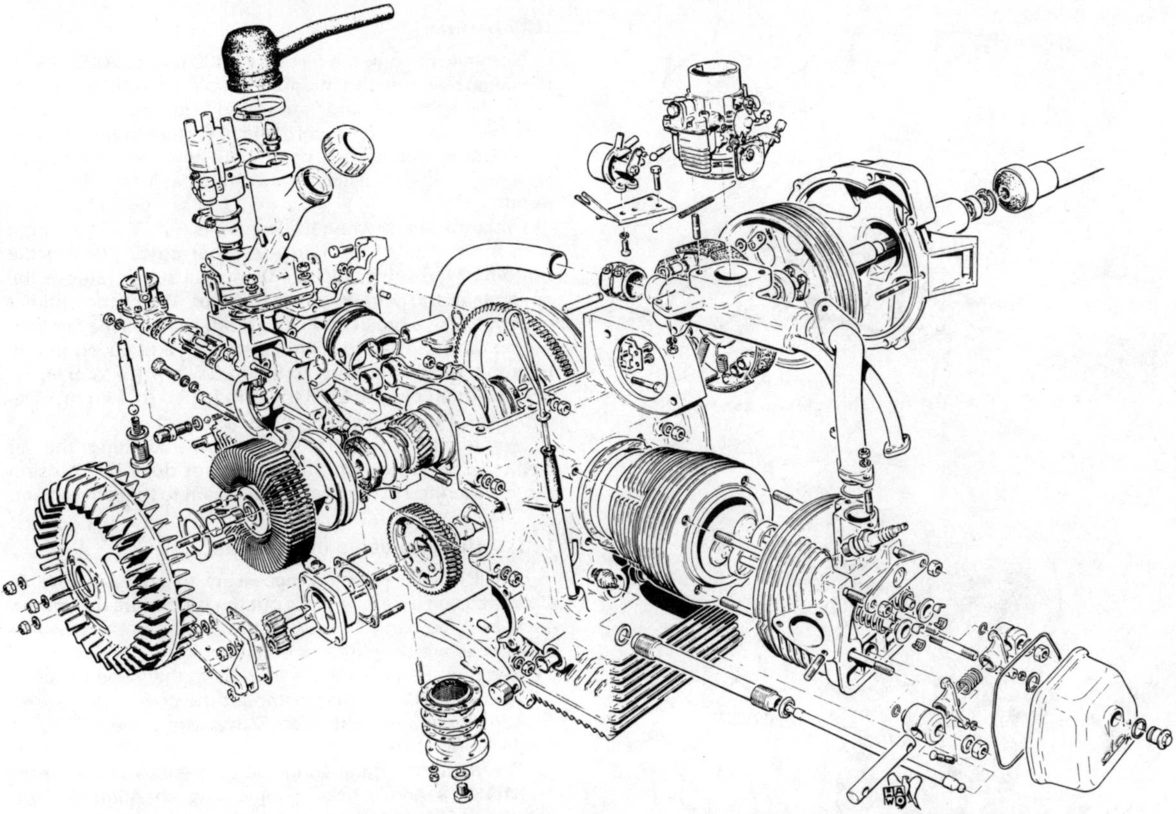

FIG 1:2 An exploded view of the 844 cc engine

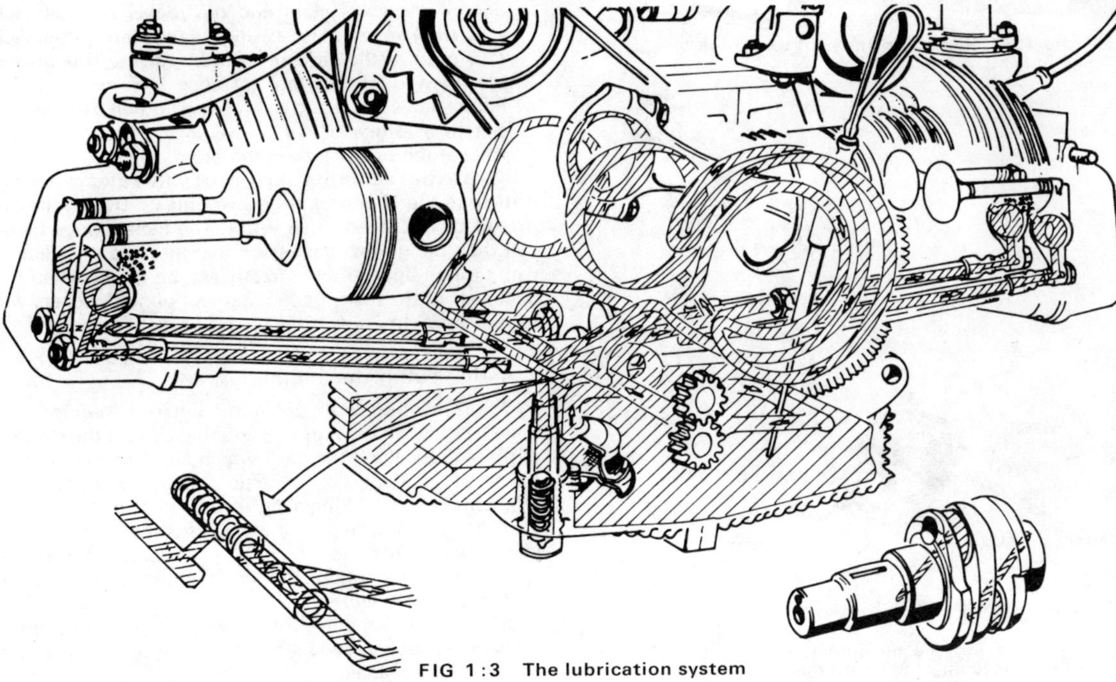

FIG 1:3 The lubrication system

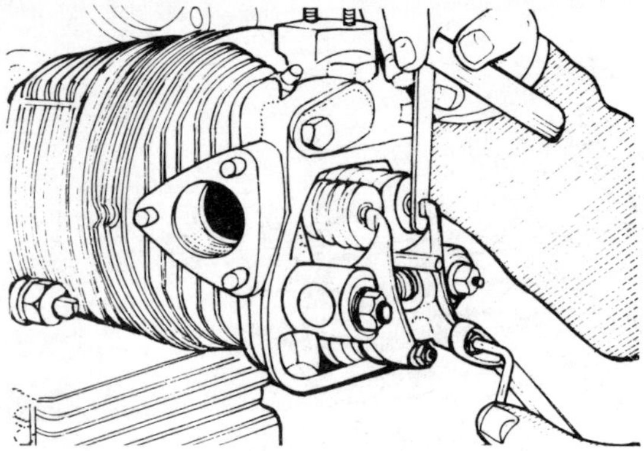

FIG 1:4 Adjusting valve clearances

FIG 1:5 Removing the heat exchangers

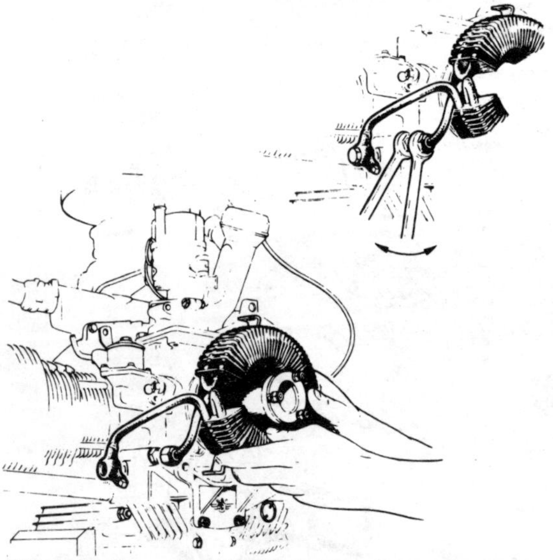

FIG 1:6 Removing the oil cooler, holding the union nipple whilst loosening the union nut

Oil changes:

Normally change the oil every 3300 miles (5000 km). If the car is being driven in unfavourable conditions such as short distance running, stop/start running, city traffic, very cold weather or in particularly dusty terrain, an extra oil change should be made between two normal oil changes or, in the case of low mileage, at least every three months.

Drain the sump when the engine is hot. The drain plug is in the centre of the gauze strainer cover plate in the bottom of the sump. After draining the sump, remove the coverplate and withdraw the strainer. Wash the strainer in petrol. Use a brush and not a cloth as fibres may remain on the gauze. After refitting the strainer and cover, torque tighten the retaining nuts to 5.1 to 6.5 lb ft (.7 to .9 kg m) and the drain plug to 25.3 to 29 lb ft (3.5 to 4 kg m). The capacity of the sump is $3\frac{1}{2}$ pints (2 litres).

Maintenance of the fuel system (including the air cleaner), the distributor, the generator drive belt tension etc. is described in the chapters relevant to that equipment.

1:3 Adjusting valve clearances

It will not be normally necessary to adjust the valve clearances on a routine basis but the procedure can, when necessary, be carried out with the engine in the car. The clearances are set with the engine cold.

1 Remove the cap nut which retains the valve cover to the cylinder head and dismount the cover and gasket. Turn the engine until both valves are closed (TDC of the firing stroke).
2 The method of adjusting the clearances is shown in **FIG 1:4** and a ring spanner and an Allen key are required in addition to a set of feeler gauges.
3 Loosen the locknut and, with the Allen key, make the adjustment necessary to give a clearance between the end of the valve stem and the rocker of .004 inch (.10 mm) in the case of inlet valves and .006 inch (.15 mm) in the case of exhaust valves. Tighten the locknut and recheck the clearance.
4 Fit the valve cover and gasket and tighten its retaining nut to a torque of 4.4 to 5.8 lb ft (.6 to .8 kg m). Repeat the procedure on the other cylinder.

Note that accurate setting of valve clearances is not possible if the valve stem end of the rocker is pitted or cratered with wear. The feeler gauge blade will then bridge the depression and the actual clearance will, though apparently correctly set, be greater than the thickness of the feeler gauge. Fitment of new rockers will be necessary to correct this defect.

1:4 Removing the engine

Before starting work, refer to 'Hints on Maintenance and Overhaul' in the **Appendix** and clean off the exterior of the engine along the lines which are described in that article under item 1 of 'Practical suggestions to solve problems'. Have a lifting sling ready and also, if access to an official engine repair stand cannot be arranged, an improvised cradle into which the engine can be lowered.

1 Remove the bonnet, bumper and grille as described in **Chapter 12**. Note, however, that in the case of DAF 31, 32 and 33 models (rear bonnet hinges) the bonnet need not be removed if a cantilever type engine lifting trolley is available.

2 Disconnect the battery and engine earth cables. Identify and disconnect the wiring from the generator and starter motor terminals. Disconnect the LT lead to the ignition coil. Disconnect the electrically operated Variomatic valve on DAF 33 models.
3 Refer to **Chapter 2**, **Section 2:5** (DAF 31, 32 and 33 models) or to **Section 2:6** (DAF 44 and 46 models) and uncouple the carburetter choke and throttle control cables. Remove the feed pipe to the fuel pump.
4 Refer to **Chapter 6** and disconnect the vacuum hoses which connect with the Variomatic drive unit.
5 Refer to **Chapter 2** and remove the silencer attaching bolts from the exhaust pipes. Slacken off the engine mounting nuts and bolts but do not remove them yet.
6 Check that everything linking the engine unit to the frame has been disconnected, uncoupled or removed.
7 Arrange a suitable lifting sling and take up the weight of the engine. Remove the engine mounting nuts and bolts and lift the engine upwards and forwards out of the car. Withdraw the propeller shaft.

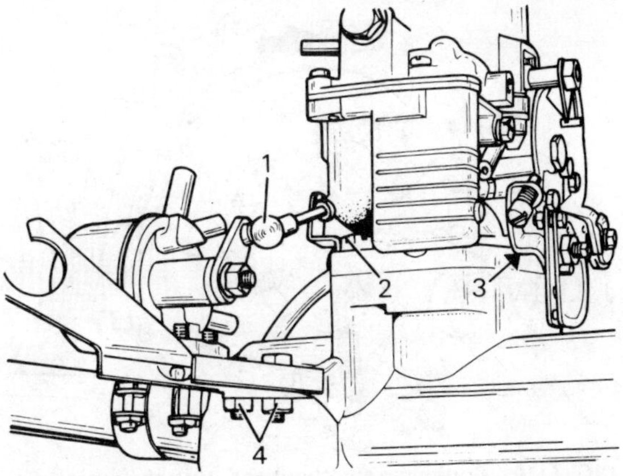

FIG 1:7 Removing the vacuum control valve assembly

Key to Fig 1:7 1 Ball joint 2, 3 Carburetter nuts 4 Control valve bolts

1:5 Dismantling the engine

If the operator is not a skilled automobile engineer, it is suggested that he will find much useful information in 'Hints on Maintenance and Overhaul' which is included in the **Appendix** at the end of this manual and that he should read it before proceeding to dismantle the engine.

1 Drain and discard the oil from the sump if this was not done earlier. Remove the ignition coil Remove the impeller shroud screen, the impeller and the engine cowling as described in **Chapter 4**.
2 Remove the exhaust heat exchangers and the engine front support bar (see **FIG 1:5**).
3 Refer to **Chapter 11**, **Section 11:3** and remove the starter motor. Refer to **Chapter 11**, **Section 11:4** and remove the generator.
4 Remove the oil cooler (see **FIG 1:6**) and oil cooler bypass valve (see **FIG 1:31**) as described in **Section 1:10**.
5 Disconnect the pump to carburetter fuel pipe and remove the fuel pump as described in **Chapter 2**, **Section 2:4**. Withdraw the pushrod which operates the pump from the crankcase. Remove the air cleaner as described in **Chapter 2**, **Section 2:8**.
6 Disconnect the leads from the sparking plugs. Refer to **Chapter 3** and remove the distributor. Dismount the oil filler pipe by removing four retaining nuts (collect the bracket from the forward lefthand stud) and withdraw the distributor drive shaft as described in **Section 1:11**.
7 Refer to **Chapter 6**, **Section 6:5**, disconnect the vacuum control valve linkage (see **FIG 1:7**) and remove the vacuum control valve.
8 Remove the carburetter as described in **Chapter 2**, **Section 2:5** (DAF 31, 32 and 33 models) or **Section 2:6** (DAF 44 and 46 models).
9 Remove the hot spot piping and dismount the intake manifold (see **FIG 1:8**) as described in **Section 1:18**. Remove the heat exchanger crossbrace shown in **FIG 5:2**.
10 Refer to **Chapter 5**, **Section 5:2** and remove the clutch housing. Refer to **Chapter 5**, **Section 5:3** and remove the clutch shaft pilot ballbearing with a

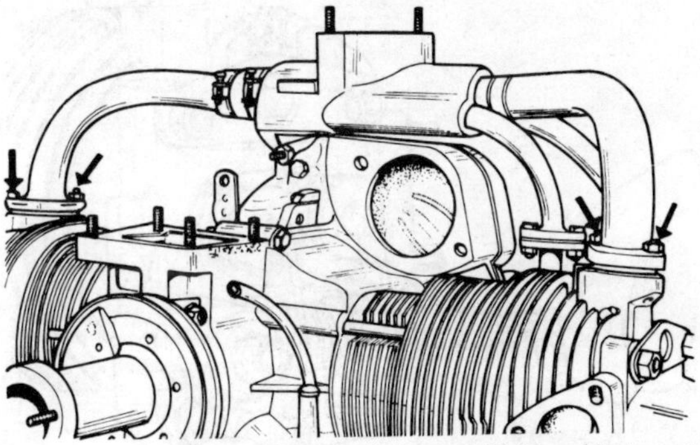

FIG 1:8 Bolts retaining the inlet manifold and hot spot pipe

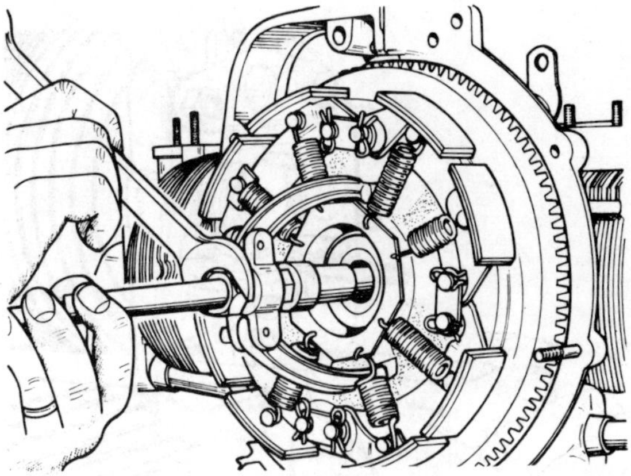

FIG 1:9 Removing pilot bearing from flywheel with a puller tool

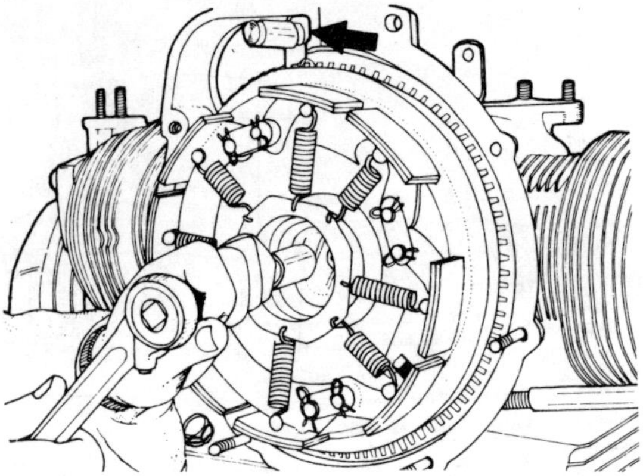

FIG 1:10 Removing the flywheel, with the restraining device shown arrowed

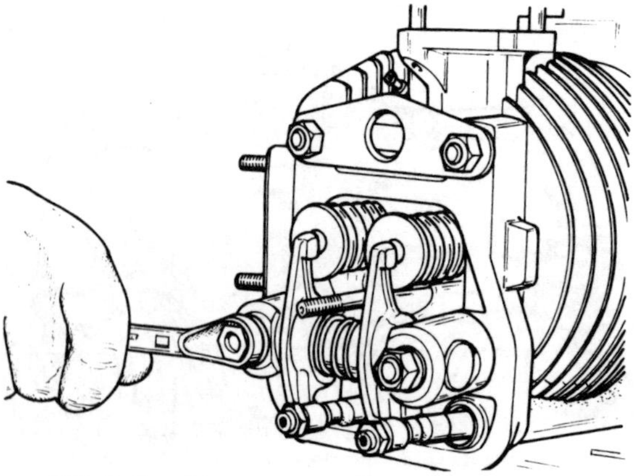

FIG 1:11 Removing the rocker shaft assembly

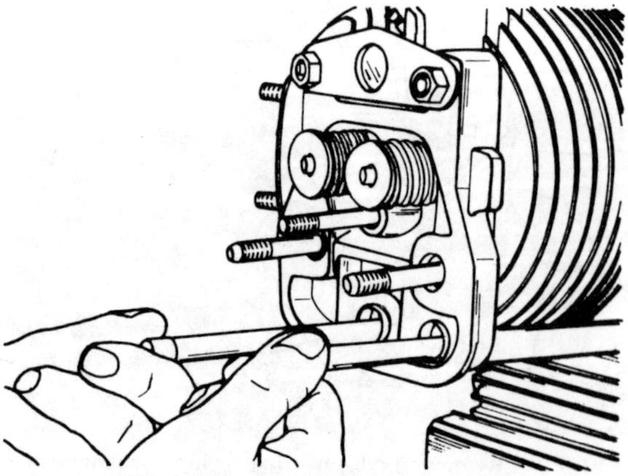

FIG 1:12 Removing the pushrods

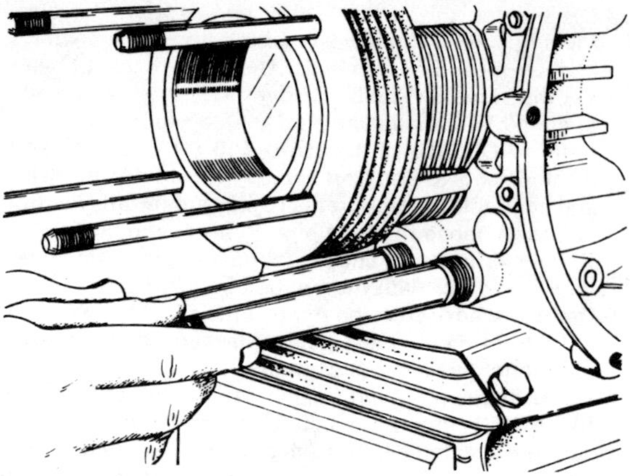

FIG 1:13 Removing the pushrod tubes

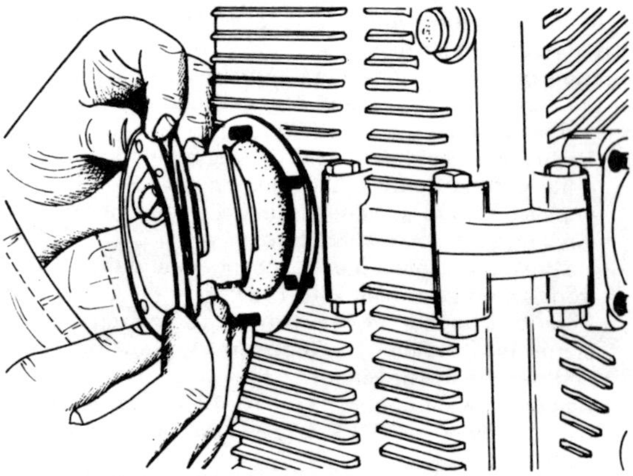

FIG 1:14 Removing the oil strainer

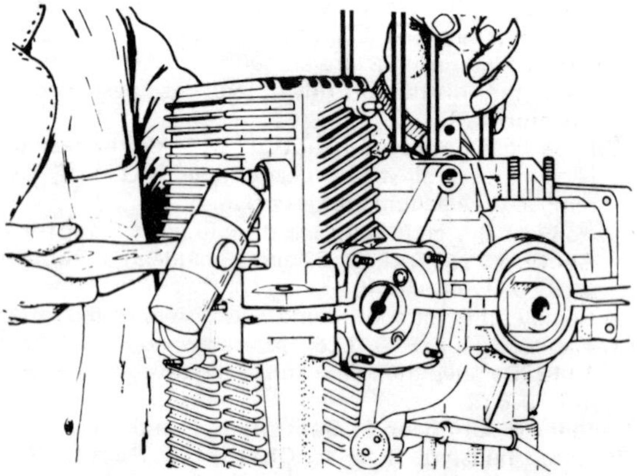

FIG 1:15 Splitting the crankcase

suitable puller as shown in **FIG 1:9**. Note that this operation is not applicable to engines fitted to early DAF 31 models.

11 Block the flywheel with tool No. 2-99-535002 which is shown arrowed in **FIG 1:10**. Remove the bolt which retains the impeller and pulley hub to the crankshaft and collect its washer. Note that, on 746 cc engines, the hand cranking ratchet is integral with the head of this bolt. Remove the hub.
12 Remove the flywheel as described in **Section 1:13**.
13 Remove the rocker shaft assemblies (see **FIG 1:11**), pushrods (see **FIG 1:12**), cylinder heads (see **FIG 1:18**) and pushrod tubes (see **FIG 1:13**) as described in **Section 1:6** and ensure that all components are identified to their respective cylinders.
14 Identify each cylinder barrel in relation to the crankcase and remove the barrels as described in **Section 1:7**.
15 Refer to **Section 1:8** and remove the pistons. Identify each to its cylinder.
16 Dismount the front mounting bracket. Remove the oil pump assembly and oil pressure relief valve as described in **Section 1:9**.
17 Remove the six retaining nuts and withdraw the sump oil strainer cover, the strainer (see **FIG 1:14**) and the two gaskets.
18 Remove the crankcase bolt nuts, remove the bolts and split the crankcase as shown in **FIG 1:15**.
19 Refer to **FIG 1:16**. Lift out the camshaft and sealing cup and withdraw the tappets.
20 Refer to **FIG 1:17** and lift out the crankshaft and connecting rod assembly. Collect the front oil seal. Remove the connecting rods from the crankshaft as described in **Section 1:15** and identify them to their respective crankpins.

1:6 Cylinder head and valve gear

Removal:

Turn the crankshaft until the piston of the cylinder which is being worked on is at TDC of the compression stroke. Both valves will now be closed and there will be no valve spring load on the rockers and pushrods. Remove the two nuts which retain the rocker shaft, lift off the rocker shaft assembly and, if they are fitted, collect the nylon seals from beneath the rocker shaft pillars. Withdraw the pushrods.

Mark the cylinder heads, cylinder barrels and the crankcase to identify their relative positions. Remove the remaining two cylinder head retaining nuts, collect the lifting bracket, lift off the cylinder head and withdraw the pushrod cover tubes.

Refitment:

Refitment of the cylinder head and valve gear is the reverse of the removal procedure.

Stretch the convolutions at both ends of the pushrod cover tubes by a small amount so that, when the cylinder head is fitted, they will be slightly compressed. Position the cylinder head and guide the pushrod cover tubes into their locations as shown in **FIG 1:18**. Install the lifting bracket and fit (finger tight only) its two cylinder head nuts. Blow through the pushrods with compressed air before fitting them.

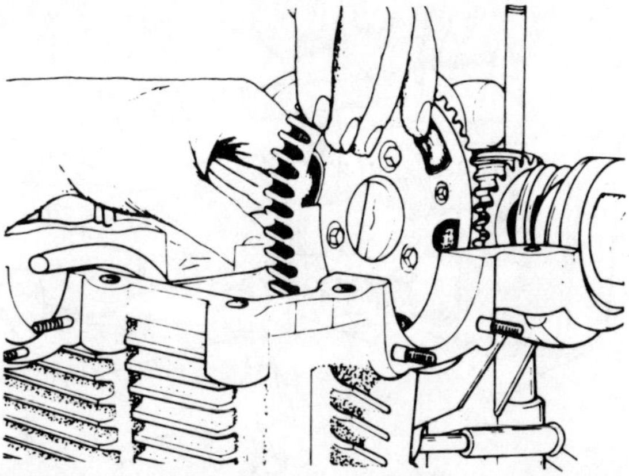

FIG 1:16 Lifting out the camshaft assembly and sealing cup

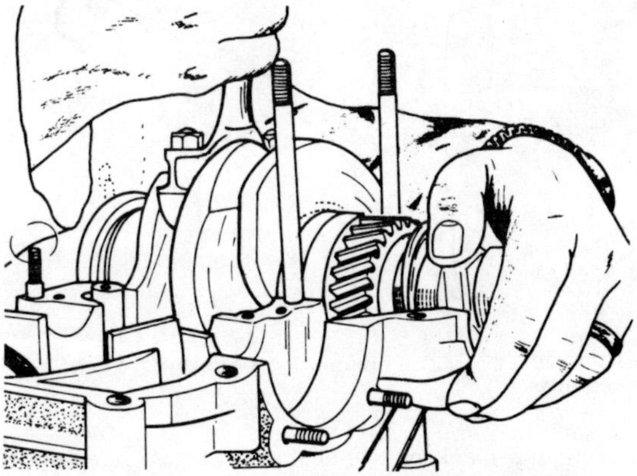

FIG 1:17 Removing the crankshaft assembly

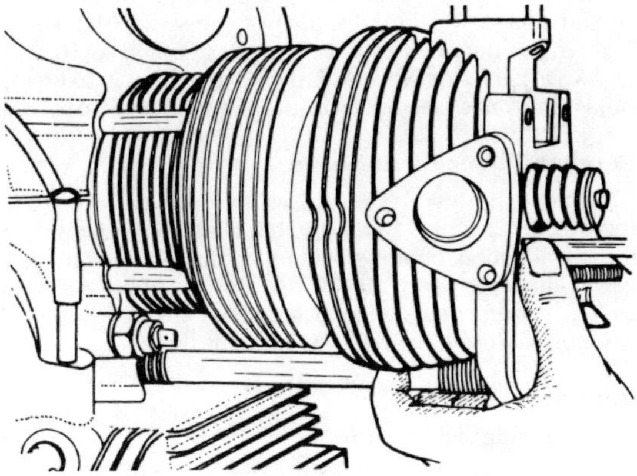

FIG 1:18 Removing a cylinder head

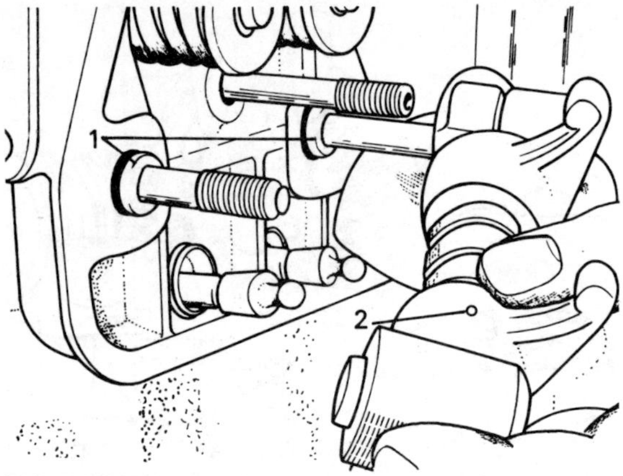

FIG 1:19 Removing the rocker shaft assembly, showing the stud seals 1 and the oil hole 2

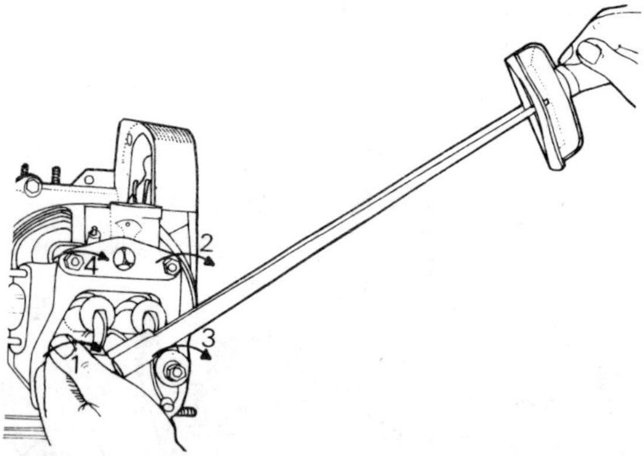

FIG 1:20 Correct sequence of tightening of cylinder head nuts

Turn the crankshaft until the piston of the cylinder which is being worked on is at TDC of the compression stroke. Refer to **FIG 1:19** and ensure that the nylon seals (if fitted) are in position and that the oil hole in the exhaust rocker is not obstructed. Fit the rocker shaft assembly and its two retaining nuts.

Torque tighten the cylinder head nuts in three stages and, at each stage, in the sequence shown in **FIG 1:20**. Tighten the nuts first to 5 lb ft (.7 kg m) then to 10 lb ft (1.4 kg m) and finally to 14.5 to 16.3 lb ft (2 to 2.25 kg m) Adjust the valve clearances as described in **Section 1:3**.

Servicing the cylinder head:

Remove the cylinder head as described earlier. Use tool No. 2-99-535011 or a suitable block of hard wood in the combustion chamber between the bench and the valve heads to hold the valves closed while the split collets, spring collars and valve springs are removed.

Later engines have oil seals fitted to the inlet valves.

Valves:

Valve dimensions are given in **FIGS 1:21** and **1:22** for 746 cc engines and in **FIGS 1:23** and **1:24** for 844 cc engines. Examine the valve head faces for pitting and burning and their stems for distortion or wear. Stem wear should not exceed .003 inch below the original diameter. Dimensions which are not included in **FIGS 1:21** or **1:22** are quoted in **Technical Data**. Valves which are too pitted to clean up on grinding to their seats may be refaced by machining but the amount of metal which may be removed is limited. This is particularly so if the valve seat has also to be salvaged by refacing.

Valve springs:

Check the valve springs for their ability to apply their functional load. Reject the springs if their load figures are less than the figures given in **Technical Data** by more than 5 or 6%. If the car has done a considerable mileage, it will be advisable to fit new springs irrespective of their load figures.

Valve seats:

Valve seat dimensions are given in **FIGS 1:21** and **1:22** for 746 cc engines and in **FIGS 1:23** and **1:24** for 844 cc engines. Examine the seats for pitting and burning. Seats which are too pitted or burned to clean up on valve grinding may be refaced. The amount of metal which may be removed is limited if the valves are also being refaced. It will normally be possible to salvage the seats for use at least with new valves.

If the seats will not salvage by refacing, they may be machined out and new inserts shrunk in. The facilities required will necessitate the work being entrusted to a competent garage.

Valve guides:

Examine the guides for excessive wear. The clearance between the valve stems and guides when new was .001 to .002 inch (.03 to .057 mm) for inlet valves and .0015 to .0025 inch (.04 to .067 mm) for exhaust valves. An acceptable maximum would be .006 inch (.17 mm) for an engine which has done a considerable mileage and it may be possible, by fitting new valves, to restore the clearance to this figure. Excessive wear will dictate the fitment of new guides.

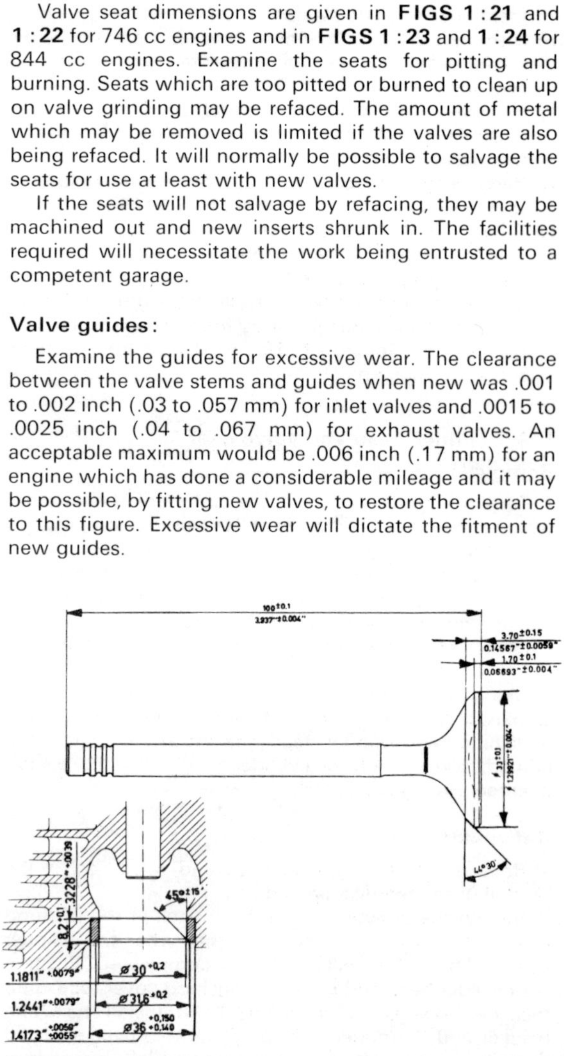

FIG 1:21 Inlet valve and seat dimensions, 746 cc engines

Sparking plug threads:

The threads in the cylinder head should be cleared of carbon with a tap. If a tap is not available, use an old sparking plug with cross-cuts down the threads.

Decarbonizing and valve grinding:

Avoid the use of sharp tools and scrapers which could damage the surfaces of the combustion chambers and passages. Remove all traces of carbon deposits from the combustion chambers, inlet and exhaust ports with worn emery cloth and paraffin. Remove the carbon deposits from the crowns of the pistons. Grind the valves to their seats using a suction type valve grinding type tool and, on completion, ensure that all traces of grinding paste are removed from the valves and the seats.

Rockers and rocker shafts:

Check the rocker shaft and rocker bush diameters against the dimensions given in **Technical Data**. Excessive wear can be corrected by rebushing the rockers. Excessive wear or cratering of the radiused end of the rocker cannot readily be rectified and, if this has occurred, a new rocker should be fitted. Ensure that the oil hole in the exhaust rocker (2 in **FIG 1:19**) is not obstructed.

Assembly:

Assembly of the valves to the cylinder head is the reverse of the dismantling sequence. Assemble the rockers to their shafts with their bearing surfaces wetted with engine oil and ensure that the spacing spring is not omitted.

Refitment of the cylinder head is described earlier in this section.

1:7 Cylinders

Removal:

Check that the relative positions of the cylinder head, cylinder barrel and crankcase have been marked. Remove the cylinder head as described in **Section 1:6**. Withdraw the cylinder barrel and, as it comes clear of the piston, be prepared to prevent the piston and connecting rod from swinging onto the crankcase. Remove the cylinder gasket.

Refitment:

Ensure that the crankcase face is clean and fit a new cylinder barrel gasket. Wet the piston rings, piston skirt and barrel bore with engine oil. Check the alignment marks and start the barrel onto the studs and over the top land of the piston. Position the piston ring gaps out of line with each other, apply a piston ring clamp and slide the barrel over the rings. Remove the clamp and push the barrel fully home. Fit the cylinder head as described in **Section 1:6**.

Servicing the cylinder barrels:

Wash off the cylinder bores first in paraffin and then in petrol. Scrape away any ring of carbon from the top of the bore.

If a cylinder bore has been damaged by piston scoring or by fracture of a piston ring or if, due to wear, the

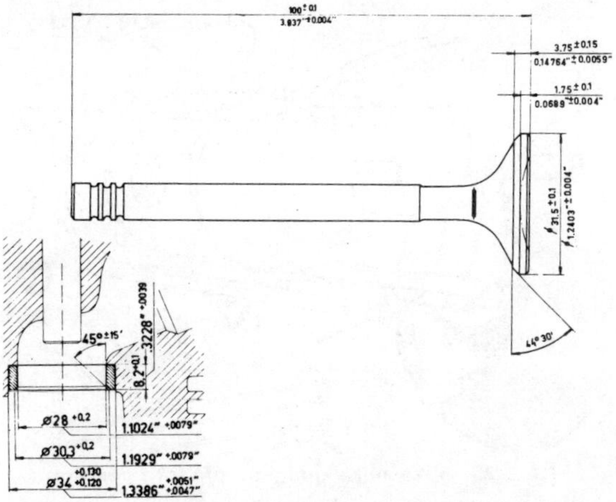

FIG 1:22 Exhaust valve and seat dimensions, 746 cc engines

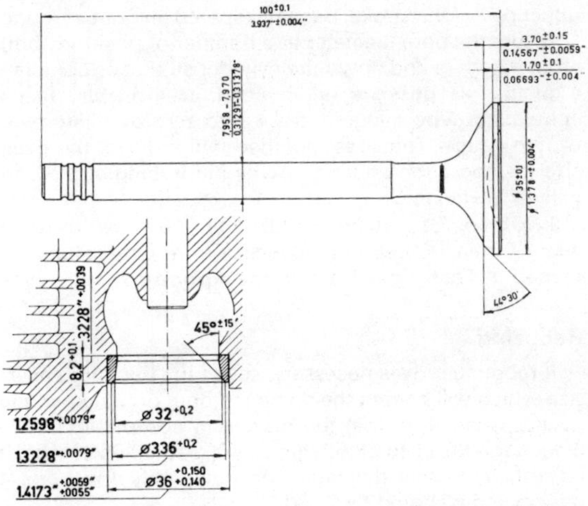

FIG 1:23 Inlet valve and seat dimensions, 844 cc engines

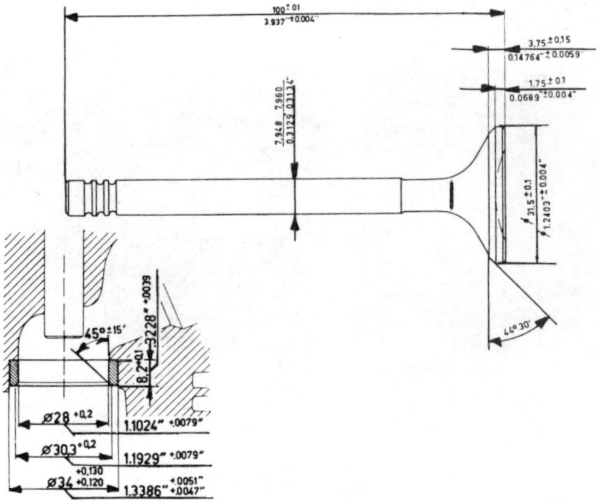

FIG 1:24 Exhaust valve and seat dimensions, 844 cc engines

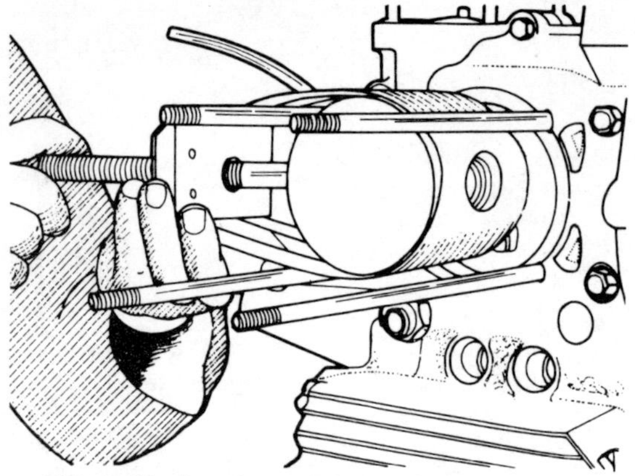

FIG 1:25 Pressing a gudgeon pin into position

cylinder requires reconditioning, reboring or honing will have to be carried out. Bores normally wear most at the upper part of the stroke, become tapered and out of round. Measure the bore diameter at a number of positions both around and up and down the cylinder so that as complete a picture as possible is obtained. If available, use a comparator type gauge and set it to zero by micrometer or ring gauge. The sizes recorded will indicate the oversize to choose for a rebore or whether honing of the bore will be adequate.

Two gradings of standard, .50 mm (.0197 inch) oversize and 1.0 mm (.0394 inch) oversize bore dimensions are quoted in **Technical Data** in the **Appendix**.

Reboring:

If reboring proves necessary, select the minimum oversize which will correct the damaged bore or the taper and ovality wear. Note that the maximum acceptable rebore diameter is 86.51 to 86.52 mm (3.4059 to 3.4063 inch). If refinishing to this diameter will not rectify the bore, a new cylinder should be fitted.

Following a rebore, ensure that all machining swarf, grinding dust, etc. is removed from the cooling fins.

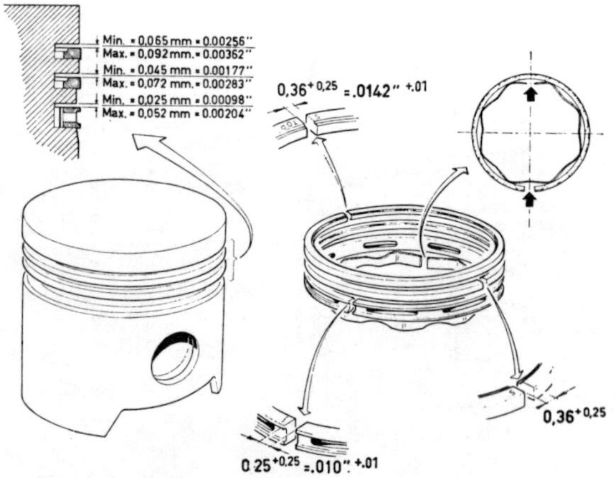

FIG 1:26 Piston ring gap and clearance dimensions. Also shown are piston rings of the 're-ring' type

Honing:

If wear is not excessive and if any scoring which may be present is not deep, a cylinder bore may be refinished by honing to an extent which will not give an unacceptable excessive clearance with a new piston.

Pistons:

The selection of a piston to suit a standard and an oversize cylinder bore is described in **Section 1:8**.

1:8 Pistons and rings

Piston removal:

Gudgeon pin axial movement is limited by an expanding type circlip at each end. These circlips register in grooves in the gudgeon pin bore of the piston. Using suitable pliers, remove the circlips. Press out the gudgeon pin. **FIG 1:25** shows the type of press screw tool which should be used when doing this. Collect the gudgeon pin and ensure that, when the pin clears the connecting rod, the rod does not fall onto the crankcase. Identify the piston to the cylinder to which it was fitted.

Piston fitment:

If the original pistons are being installed, ensure that each is refitted to the cylinder from which it was removed.

Check that the compression rings have been fitted the correct way up with TOP towards the crown of the piston. Lubricate the connecting rod small-end bore, the gudgeon pin and the gudgeon pin bore of the piston with engine oil. Position the gudgeon pin and screw press tool as shown in **FIG 1:25** and, **with the arrow on the crown of the piston pointing towards the front of the engine,** press the gudgeon pin into position. Fit new retaining circlips and ensure that they are correctly seated in their grooves.

Servicing the pistons:

Remove the pistons as described earlier in this Section. Remove the piston rings using, if access to one is available, a ring expanding tool. If a ring expanding tool is not available and the original piston and its rings are to be refitted, leave the rings in position and wash off the complete piston and ring assembly as a unit. It is probable however, that new rings will be fitted to a piston which is serviceable and that it will be of no consequence if, in removing the rings without the use of a ring expanding tool, they are broken. Care must be taken not to damage the lands of a piston which is to be refitted.

With the rings removed, clean all deposits from the ring grooves using a soft brush and paraffin. Remove carbon deposits from the crown of the piston. Avoid the use of sharp tools and scrapers which could damage the surface Use worn emery cloth and paraffin and, finally, wash off in petrol.

Check the widths of the piston ring grooves. The minimum and maximum groove to ring clearance is shown in **FIG 1:26** and is also given in **Technical Data**. If the ring grooves are excessively worn, new pistons should be fitted even if, in other respects they appear serviceable.

Pistons rings are described later in this Section. Use a piston ring expanding tool as shown in **FIG 1:27** to fit the rings. Fit the oil control ring first, working from the crown of the piston and follow with the compression rings. **Ensure that the compression rings are fitted the correct way up with TOP towards the crown.** Turn the rings until the gaps are spaced an equal distance apart.

Standard and oversize pistons:

There are two gradings (as there are for cylinder barrel bores) for standard pistons and for .50 mm (.0197 inch) and 1.0 mm (.0394 inch) oversize pistons. Diameters and gradings for all piston sizes are given in **Technical Data** in the **Appendix**.

The minimum desired mean piston clearance with the cylinder bore is .045 mm (.0018 inch) and scrutiny of the piston and cylinder bore diameters and gradings will indicate that a standard size piston of 'blue' grading will be required for use in a standard size 'blue' graded cylinder bore and similarly for oversize pistons and cylinder bores. Equally, the 'red' grading of a standard or oversize piston will be required for use in a corresponding 'red' graded standard or oversize cylinder bore.

From the measured diameters of the refinished cylinder barrels, pistons of the appropriate oversize and grading for each cylinder may now be selected and obtained.

Piston gudgeon pin bores are graded 'black' and 'white'. The diameter tolerances which correspond with these gradings are given in **Technical Data.**

Piston rings:

Pistons which are serviceable may, to correct excessive oil consumption, be re-installed after being fitted with a 're-ring' set of piston rings. These rings differ from standard rings in that, as shown in **FIG 1:26**, the top inner diameters of the compression rings are stepped (standard rings are parallel in section) and the oil control ring is provided with an expander spring. **Note that the gap in this spring must be fitted diametrically opposite the oil control ring gap as shown in FIG 1:26.**

From engine No. 850 AK-130102 a modified piston is used using a different type of oil control ring. This is a three piece assembly consisting of two rails and an expander. The old type of oil control ring must not be used on the modified piston but the latest oil control ring can be used on earlier pistons. The rails are fitted on each side of the expander with their gaps 3 to 5 cm on opposite sides of the coloured ends of the expander, after fitting both colours on the expander must be visible.

If oversize piston(s) are being fitted, ensure that the correct oversize rings are obtained to suit.

The desired compression ring gap is the same at .36 to .61 mm (.0142 to .0242 inch) for re-ring, standard and for oversize rings. This also applies at .25 to .50 mm (.010 to .020 inch) to all oil control rings. Ring gaps should be measured by placing a piston (without its rings) well down the bore of the cylinder and pressing a ring down onto it and using feeler gauges.

1:9 Oil pump

The oil pump is a gear pump of conventional design. The upper pump gear is driven by the dog on the end of its shaft engaging in a slot in the forward end of the camshaft. Oil is drawn from the sump through a gauze strainer. The pressure oil gallery connects with a pressure relief valve through which excess pressure oil is returned to the sump.

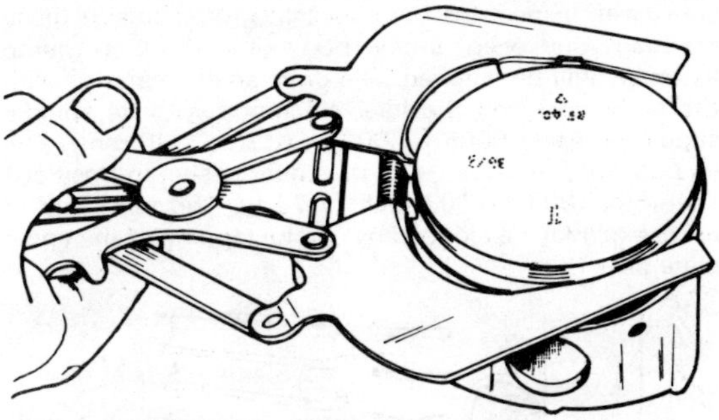

FIG 1:27 Piston ring spreader tool

Oil pump removal:

Reference to **FIG 1:2** will show that the front cover of the pump is also the engine front mounting bracket. When, in operation 16 of the engine dismantling procedure described in **Section 1:5** the engine front mounting bracket was removed, the oil pump body and gears were exposed as shown in **FIG 1:28**.

The pump body is retained to the crankcase by the four nuts which attach the mounting bracket and, following removal of the bracket, the remainder of the assembly can be prized from the crankcase as shown in **FIG 1:28**. Gaskets are fitted between the rear face of the pump body and the crankcase and the rear face of the mounting bracket and the pump body.

Oil pump fitment:

Use new gaskets. Coat both sides of the oil pump body gasket sparingly with sealing compound and fit it over the studs. Align the drive spindle dog with the slot in the camshaft and push the pump body fully home. Coat both sides of the oil pump cover (mounting bracket) gasket sparingly with sealing compound and fit the cover. Torque tighten the four nuts to 6.5 to 8 lb ft (.9 to 1.1 kg m).

Servicing the oil pump:

Clean off old gasket and jointing compound material from the pump body, the mounting bracket and the

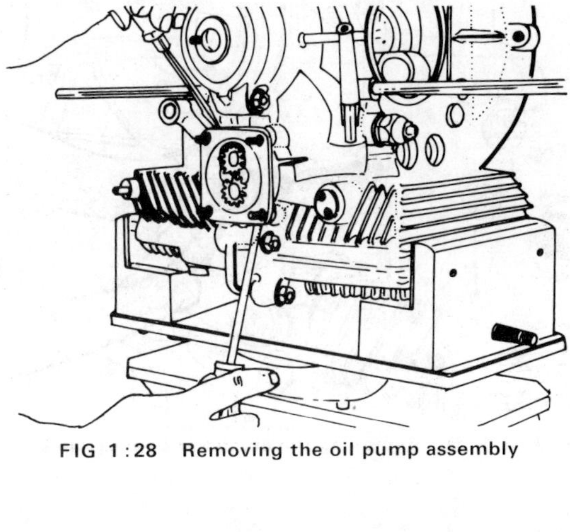

FIG 1:28 Removing the oil pump assembly

crankcase. Inspect the body recesses for scores. If these are many and deep, a new body or a complete pump assembly will be required. The drive shaft clearance with the body bore and the idler clearance with its spindle should be each .0005 to .0015 (.012 to .036 mm). The end play of the gears (with the cover gasket in position) should be .003 to .007 inch (.072 to .168 mm) and, if excessive, may be reduced by careful lapping of the cover plate face.

FIG 1:29 The oil pressure relief valve, showing the ball and spring

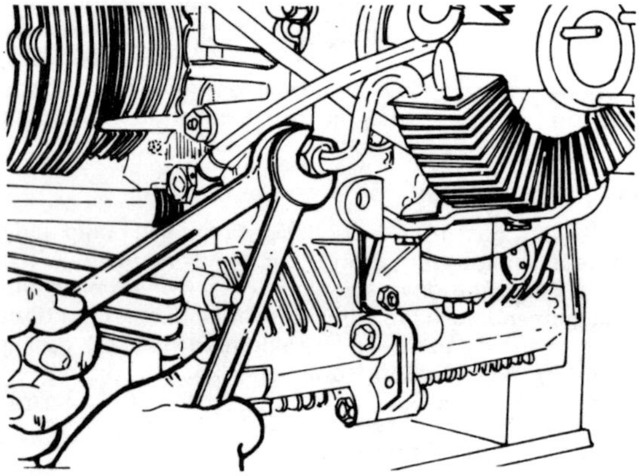

FIG 1:30 Disconnecting the oil cooler feed line whilst holding the union nipple

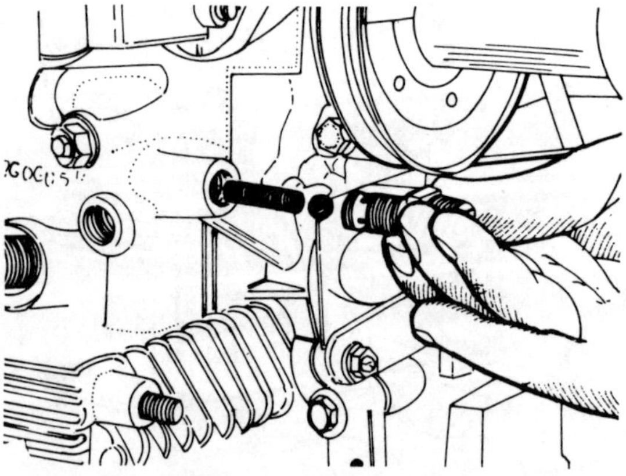

FIG 1:31 Removing the oil cooler bypass valve

Oil pressure relief valve:

The components of the relief valve which is located in the sump are shown in **FIG 1:29**. The valve is not adjustable. The ball and spring may be withdrawn after removing the retaining plug. On reassembly, torque tighten the plug to 40 to 43.5 lb ft (5.5 to 6 kg m).

1:10 Oil cooler

The location of the 'doughnut' shaped aircooled oil cooler is shown in **FIG 1:2**. It comprises a length of finned piping which is curved and bent back upon itself. The cooler is surrounded by the impeller which draws ambient air through its fins before it passes, as pressure air, to the engine cowling. A bypass valve is incorporated between the oil pump and the cooler. As the temperature of the oil rises, it circulates through the cooler.

Oil cooler removal:

Access to the cooler requires removal of the impeller shroud screen, the impeller and the engine cowling as described in **Chapter 4**.

Refer to **FIG 1:30** and, using a second spanner to hold the bypass valve union, uncouple the oil cooler feed connection. Note the method of wire locking the return line banjo. Cut the wire locking and remove the banjo retaining bolt. Remove the bolts from the two bracket fins and dismount the cooler.

Oil cooler fitment:

This is the reverse of the removal procedure. Refer to **FIG 1:30** and hold the bypass valve union body with one spanner while tightening the feed line connection with another. Use new washers on the banjo connection. The thin copper/asbestos washer fits between the crankcase and the banjo and the thick copper/asbestos washer between the banjo and its retaining bolt head. Torque tighten this retaining bolt to 14.5 lb ft (2 kg m) and wire lock it.

Bypass valve:

Following removal of the oil cooler, the bypass valve union may be removed and, as shown in **FIG 1:31**, the ball and spring may be withdrawn.

1:11 Distributor drive

The distributor drive shaft is vertical and is driven by a skew gear mounted forward of the camshaft drive gear at the front end of the crankshaft. An eccentric on the distributor drive shaft operates the fuel pump through a short pushrod.

Removal:

Dismount the ignition coil and the distributor as described in **Chapter 3**. Dismount the oil filler pipe by removing four retaining nuts and collect the bracket from the forward lefthand stud. Remove the fuel pump as described in **Chapter 2**, **Section 2:4** and withdraw its pushrod.

Remove the distributor drive retainer (this is shown resting in the distributor drive shaft slot in **FIG 1:32**) and withdraw the shaft as shown in **FIG 1:32**.

Fitment:

This is described in **Section 1:19** at operation 11 of the engine assembly procedure and must be followed, after fitting the distributor, by timing the ignition as described in **Chapter 3**.

1:12 Impeller hub and generator drive pulley

This component is spigoted to the front of the crankshaft, driven by a dowel and retained by a single bolt. On 746 cc engines the starting handle rachet is integral with the head of this bolt. The generator belt drive pulley is rivetted to a flange and studs at the forward end carry the impeller. The outer diameter at the rear provides a surface on which the front oil seal runs.

Removal of the hub is described in operation 11 of the engine dismantling procedure which is described in **Section 1:5**. Fitment is described in the engine assembly procedure and is covered in operation 10 of **Section 1:19**.

1:13 Flywheel

The flywheel carries the functional parts of the centrifugal clutch and it will be necessary to refer to **Chapter 5** for aspects of the flywheel which are not covered in this Section.

The flywheel is spigoted and dowelled to the rear end of the crankshaft and attached to it by four set bolts which are locked by tab washers. Except on early 746 cc engines, the clutch shaft pilot bearing is carried in the hub of the flywheel and located by an expanding circlip. On early 746 cc engines the clutch shaft passes through the web of the flywheel and is piloted in a plain bearing which is located in the tail of the crankshaft.

A ring gear with which the starter motor pinion engages is spigoted and shrunk onto the forward periphery of the flywheel.

Flywheel removal:

Refer to **Chapter 5**, **Section 5:2** and remove the clutch housing. Except on early 746 cc engines, use a suitable puller (see **FIG 1:9**) and withdraw the clutch shaft pilot ballbearing from the hub of the flywheel. With suitable pliers as shown in **FIG 1:33**, remove the circlip. Untab the locking of the four retaining set bolts. Refer to **FIG 1:5** and, with the flywheel blocked with tool No. 2-99-535002 withdraw the four bolts. Lift off the flywheel and clutch assembly.

Flywheel fitment:

This is the reverse of the removal sequence. Fit new tabwashers, torque tighten the retaining bolts to 18 to 19.5 lb ft (2.5 to 2.7 kg m) and bend up the tabs to lock them. Except on early 746 cc engines, fit the circlip and, using tool No. 3-99-535320, install the clutch shaft pilot ballbearing.

Servicing the flywheel:

Refer to **Chapter 5** for information regarding the clutch components. If the ring gear teeth are damaged, it may be possible to salvage them by welding and reprofiling. This work should be entrusted to a specialist.

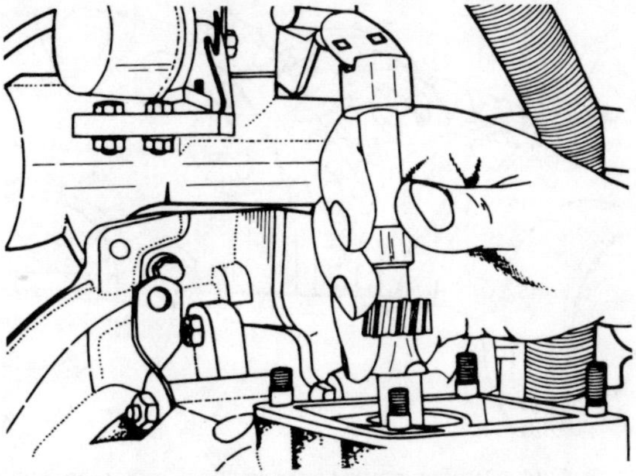

FIG 1:32 Removing the distributor drive shaft

1:14 Crankcase, sump and oil strainer

This is a two-piece assembly and half the sump is integral with each crankcase half. The division is central and vertical. The two halves of the crankcase are not separately renewable and, in the event of one half becoming unserviceable, a complete new crankcase will be required.

Removal of the pressure relief valve is described in **Section 1:9**. Removal of the oil cooler bypass valve is described in **Section 1:10**. Removal of the oil strainer, separating the two halves of the crankcase and removal of the camshaft and the crankshaft assembly are covered in operations 17, 18, 19 and 20 of the engine dismantling procedure which is described in **Section 1:5**.

Wash off the crankcase and sump halves with paraffin. Carefully clean off old sealing compound from the joint faces and from the camshaft sealing cup location. Clean off old gasket and jointing material from the oil strainer faces. Do not use sharp tools or scrapers which could damage any of the faces. Flush the oilways and blow them through with compressed air. Finally wash off the casings with petrol, dry them with compressed air and pass clean engine oil into all the oilways. Check the position of the open end of the oil pump suction pipe. The distance

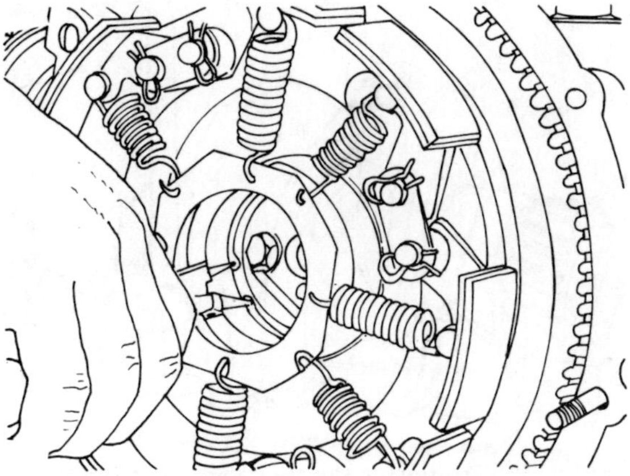

FIG 1:33 Removing the flywheel hub circlip, except on early 746 cc engines

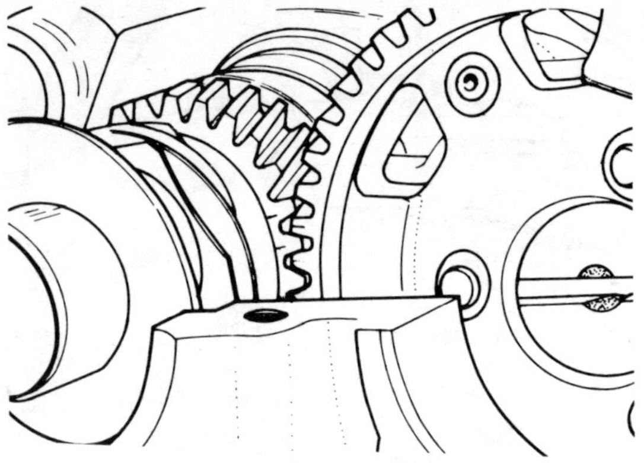

FIG 1:34 Timing marks on camshaft and crankshaft gears

between the end of the pipe and the outside face onto which the oil strainer assembly fits should be $\frac{9}{16}$ inch (14 mm).

Discard the two gaskets from the oil strainer and cover assembly. Clean off old gasket and jointing compound from the faces of the oil strainer and cover. Use a brush and petrol to clean the oil strainer gauze.

1:15 Connecting rods

Removal of the crankshaft and connecting rod assembly is described in **Section 1:5**. Rods may be removed without completely dismantling the engine as removal of the cylinders allows access to the cap retaining bolts or nuts.

Connecting rods and their caps are marked and they must be reassembled as marked. Identify the rods to the crankpins to which they are fitted, remove and discard the cap retaining bolts (in the case of 746 cc engines) or retaining nuts (in the case of 844 cc engines), separate and remove the caps and rods from the crankpins. Wash off the caps and rods.

If a big-end bearing has failed, an exchange replacement rod should be obtained. The big-end bearing diameter (whether standard or undersize) which is required will depend upon whether it has been necessary to regrind the crankpin(s) and, before obtaining replacement rods, the crankshaft should be examined and refinished if necessary. Refer therefore to **Section 1:17** which covers the crankshaft before obtaining the rods. Do not, under any circumstances, file the rod faces in an endeavour to reduce the diameter of the big-end bearing.

If the small-end bush is excessively worn, it may be machined out and a bush fitted and the bore refinished to standard size. If the small-end has worn to an extent that makes this salvage necessary it is hardly likely that the big-end bearings will be genuinely serviceable and it will be prudent to install replacement rods rather than carry out this salvage.

Refer to **Technical Data** in the **Appendix** for diameters and clearances of both the big-end and the small-end. Note that although the connecting rods for 746 cc engines are shorter than those for 844 cc engines, all other dimensions and tolerances are common. When obtaining replacement parts, ensure that those for the appropriate engine are supplied.

New retaining bolts or nuts must be used when assembling rods to the crankshaft. Check that the caps are the correct way round and, if the original rods are being refitted, that they are fitted to their original crankpins. Torque tighten cap retaining bolts (746 cc engines) to 20 to 22 lb ft (2.8 to 3 kg m) or cap retaining nuts (844 cc engines) to 25.3 to 27.5 lb ft (3.5 to 3.8 kg m).

1:16 Camshaft and tappets

The camshaft is located below the crankshaft and is driven from its front end by 1:2 ratio helical gearing. To achieve timing of the gears on assembly, one tooth on the camshaft gear and two teeth on the crankshaft gear are marked as shown in **FIG 1:34**.

The camshaft runs on two plain bearings and axial movement is controlled at the forward bearing between the web of the drive gear hub and the face of the thrust shoulder which is integral with the shaft. Both bearings are pressure lubricated. Camshaft journal and bearing diameters and tappet to tappet guide clearance figures are given in **Technical Data** in the **Appendix**.

The forward end of the camshaft is slotted to take the oil pump drive spindle dog and the oil pump consequently runs at camshaft speed, half engine speed. A sealing cup (see **FIG 1:35**) is located in the bore of the rear bearing clear of the camshaft rear journal. This cup must be effectively fitted as described in **Section 1:19** to preclude oil leakage to the flywheel and clutch assembly.

Two cams, one inlet and one exhaust, only are incorporated on the camshaft. Each, through tappets and pushrods, operates the inlet and exhaust valve rockers respectively of both cylinders. The valve timing is identical for 844 cc engines and the 746 cc engines which are installed in DAF 33 models. The valve overlap of engines fitted to DAF 31 and 32 models is slightly less than that of later 746 cc engines. Valve timing data is quoted in **Technical Data** in the **Appendix**.

Tappets are mushroom headed and are pressure lubricated. They are drilled to allow pressure oil to pass intermittently (when each tappet is not on lift) to hollow pushrods and so to the overhead valve gear. Tappets cannot be withdrawn until the camshaft has been

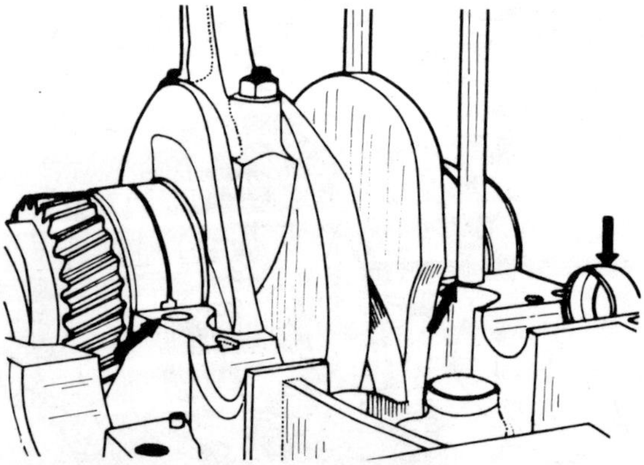

FIG 1:35 Positioning the crankshaft with the dowels entering the holes in the main bearing and the oil holes in the bearings exactly in line with the face of the case

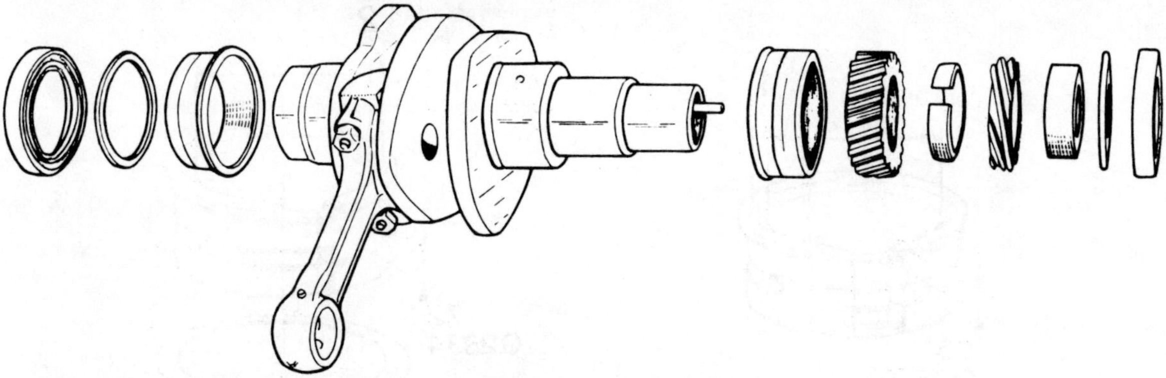

FIG 1:36 An exploded view of the crankshaft assembly

removed. The point in the engine dismantling sequence at which the camshaft can be removed is at operation 19 of **Section 1:5** and is shown in **FIG 1:16**.

1:17 Crankshaft and main bearings

The components of a crankshaft assembly are shown in **FIG 1:36**. Except for the crankshaft throw which is 32.5 mm (1.2795 inch) in the case of the 746 cc engine and 36.75 mm (1.4469 inch) in the case of the 844 cc engine, crankshaft dimensions for the two capacities of engine are identical.

Refer to **FIG 1:36**. From left (the rear of the crankshaft) to right, the components are: the rear oil seal, the rear oil thrower, the rear main bearing, the crankshaft (with one connecting rod installed), the front main bearing, the camshaft drive gear, the split spacer ring, the distributor drive shaft gear, the outer spacer ring, the front oil thrower and the front oil seal which, as described in **Section 1:12**, runs on the outer diameter of the impeller hub. The camshaft drive gear and the distributor drive shaft gear are keyed to the crankshaft and the gap in the split spacer ring allows this component to clear the single key.

The dowel which can be seen in **FIG 1:36** in the forward face of the crankshaft, drives the impeller hub. A similar dowel in the rear face of the tail of the crankshaft, drives the flywheel. The impeller hub and the flywheel are both spigoted to the crankshaft. Dowels in the crankcase engage each main bearing to prevent them from rotating and to ensure that the oil feed passages in the crankcase align with the oil feed groove in the outer diameter of each main bearing.

Crankshaft removal:

Removal of the crankshaft requires the engine to be completely dismantled and the crankcase split. The procedure is described in **Section 1:5**. If the connecting rods were not removed at an earlier stage, the bearing caps and rods are then removed as described in **Section 1:15**.

Crankshaft refitment:

Assemble the connecting rods to the crankshaft. The crankshaft and connecting rod assembly may then be fitted to the crankcase as described in the engine assembly sequence described in **Section 1:19**.

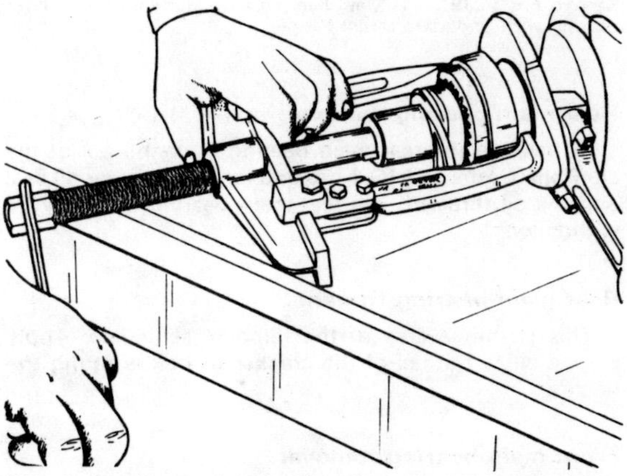

FIG 1:37 Removing the distributor worm wheel, split spacer ring and crankshaft gear

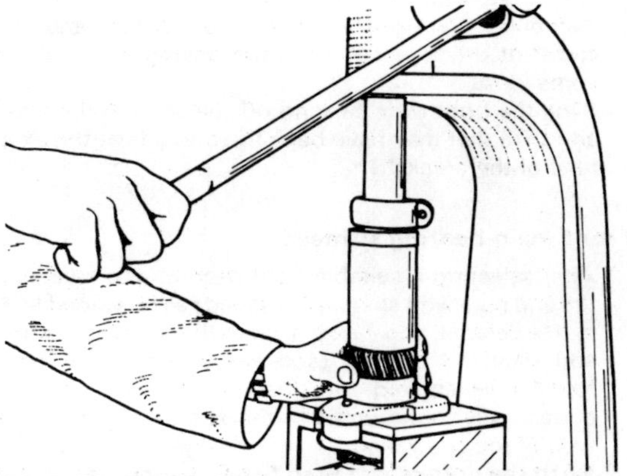

FIG 1:38 Pressing the crankshaft gear on the crankshaft with the timing mark facing forwards and the crankshaft web firmly supported

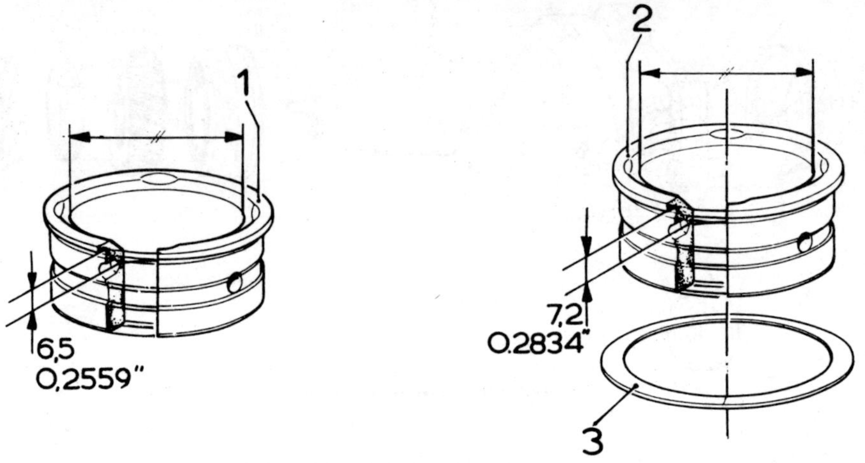

FIG 1:39 Main bearing dimensions

Key to Fig 1:39 1 Main bearing with standard thrust flange 2 Main bearing with undersize thrust flange 3 Shim for main bearing with undersize thrust flange

Rear main bearing removal:

To remove the rear main bearing from the tail of the crankshaft, refer to **FIG 1:36** and remove the rear oil seal and the oil thrower. The rear main bearing can now be withdrawn.

Rear main bearing fitment:

This is the reverse of the removal sequence. Apply engine oil to the tail of the crankshaft before fitting the bearing.

Front main bearing removal:

1 Refer to **FIG 1:36**. The front oil seal will have come away loose and will have been collected when the crankshaft was removed at operation 20 of **Section 1:5**, the engine dismantling procedure.
2 Remove the front oil thrower and the distance ring.
3 Using a suitable puller in conjunction with adaptor No. 2-99-535016 (see **FIG 1:37**), remove the distributor drive gear, the split spacer ring and the camshaft drive gear. Collect the driving key if it has come loose.
4 Slide the front main bearing off the shaft and collect any shim that may have been fitted to adjust the axial float of the crankshaft.

Front main bearing fitment:

1 After selecting a suitable front bearing and adjusting the end play with shims (if required) as described later in this Section, apply engine oil to the bearing location and slide the bearing (and any shims which were found to be required) into position. Ensure that it is the correct way round with the thrust flange next to the web of the crankshaft.
2 **With the crankshaft web firmly supported** on the bed of a press as shown in **FIG 1:38**, fit the key if it came out of position. With the camshaft drive gear the correct way round (with the marks on the timing teeth towards the front as shown in **FIG 1:34**), line up the keyway and, with a suitable adaptor, press the gear into position.
3 Fit the split spacer ring and, still supporting the web of the crankshaft, press the distributor drive gear into position.
4 Fit the distance ring with the internal chamfered side towards the rear of the crankshaft. Fit the front oil thrower. Fitment of the front oil seal is described as part of the engine assembly sequence in **Section 1:19**.

Servicing the crankshaft:

If there has been a big-end failure, the relevant crankpin must be examined for damage and for transfer of metal to its surface. The oilway to the crankpin must be checked to ensure that it is unobstructed. Damaged or worn crankpins may be salvaged by regrinding provided that the crankpin diameter is not reduced by more than about .025 inch (.60 mm) or an exchange replacement crankshaft may be obtained.

Main journal and crankpin diameters and desired clearances are given in **Technical Data** in the **Appendix**.

Crankshaft axial float:

The main bearing flanges take axial thrust. The axial float should be .004 inch (.10 mm) minimum to .012 inch (.30 mm) maximum. If the float is outside these limits, it may be adjusted by installing a front main bearing with an undersize flange (2 in **FIG 1:39**) in conjunction with a shim (3 in **FIG 1:39**) of a thickness which will bring the axial float within the range quoted earlier. The shim is installed on the forward side of the flange between the flange and the crankcase. It will be appreciated that a bearing with an undersize flange in conjunction with a shim of .70 mm (.0275 inch) is equivalent to a bearing with a standard flange (1 in **FIG 1:39**).

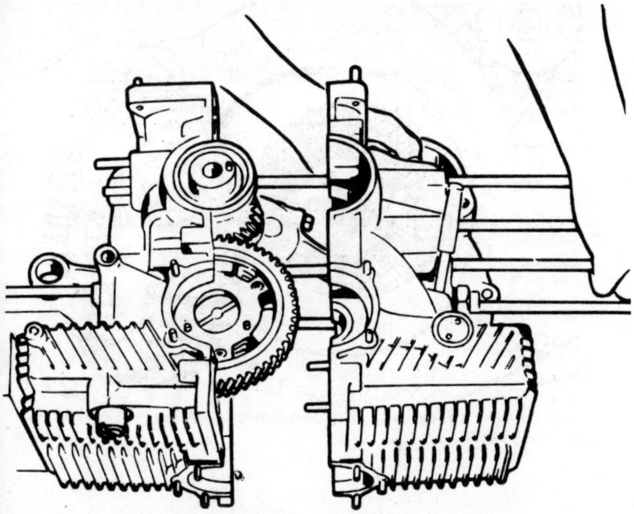

FIG 1:40 Assembling the crankcase halves

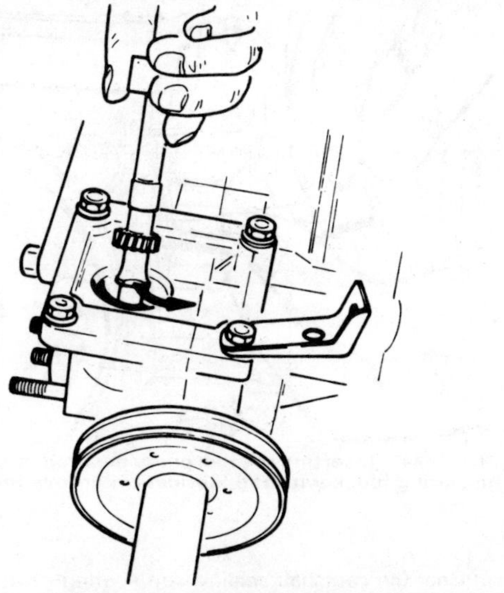

FIG 1:41 Inserting the distributor drive gear with the flat part of the shaft facing the crankcase joint

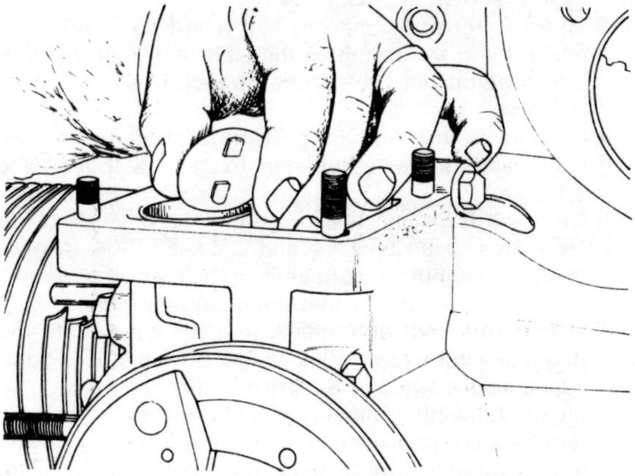

FIG 1:42 Fitting the distributor drive gear retainer

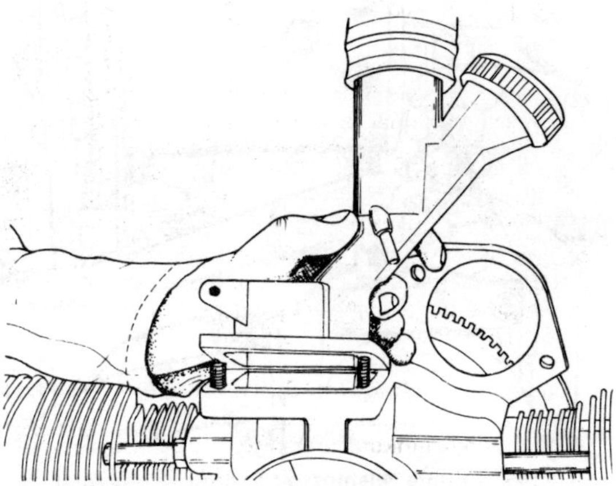

FIG 1:43 Installing the oil filler pipe

1:18 Intake manifold

Removing the manifold:

1 Referring to **FIG 1:8**, remove the nuts and spring washers which attach each intake pipe to its cylinder.
2 Remove the nuts and bolts which attach the hot spot feed and return pipes to the exhaust.
3 Remove the bolt which attaches the assembly to the crankcase and lift off the manifold.
4 Loosen the clamp which retains the righthand intake pipe in the hose joint and remove the pipe. Separate the hose from the manifold by loosening the remaining clamp.

Servicing the manifold:

Wash off the manifold internally and externally, check for cracks and remove any deposits from the joints and from the carburetter face. Check the condition of the hose joint for the righthand intake pipe and renew this if there is any signs of deterioration.

Fitting the manifold:

This is the reverse of the removal sequence. Use new joint gasket rings and leave the final tightening of the hose joint on the righthand intake pipe until last. Torque tighten the bolt which attaches the assembly to the crankcase to 13.5 to 15.2 lb ft (1.9 to 2.1 kg m) and the inlet pipe nuts to 8.7 to 10 lb ft (1.2 to 1.4 kg m).

1:19 Assembling the engine

1 Assemble the connecting rods to the crankshaft as described in **Section 1:15**. Apply a thin coat of sealing compound to the joint faces of the crankcase and position the crankshaft assembly into the lefthand half. Make sure that the dowels fully engage the holes in the main bearings and that the oil holes in the bearings align with the crankcase joint face as shown in **FIG 1:35**.

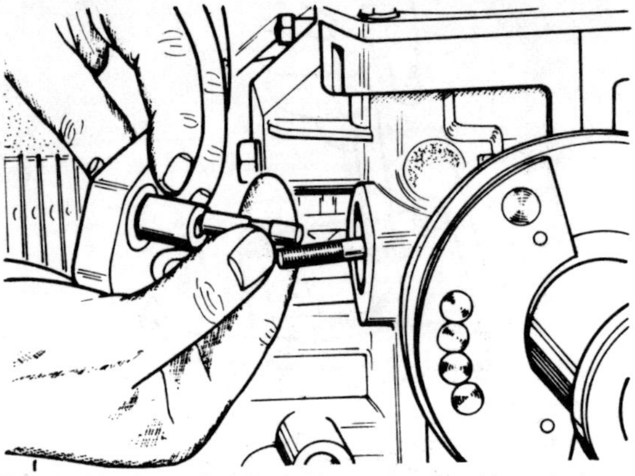

FIG 1:44 Inserting the fuel pump pushrod into the heat insulating block with the lubrication groove innermost

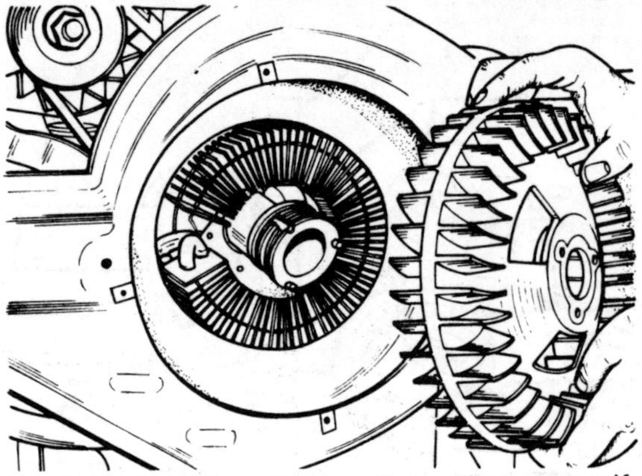

FIG 1:46 Installing the impeller, using new self-locking nuts

2 Coat the camshaft sealing cup sparingly with sealing compound and position it as shown in **FIG 1:35**. Fit the tappets and install the camshaft with the marked tooth between the two marked teeth of the crankshaft gear as shown in **FIG 1:34**.

3 Fit the righthand crankcase half (see **FIG 1:40**) and, while doing so, introduce the front and rear oil seals into position but leave them projecting slightly from the case.

4 Fit nuts to the four long studs of both crankcase halves and torque tighten them to 21 to 22 lb ft (2.9 to 3.1 kg m).

5 Drive the front and rear oil seals into position using tools Nos. 2-99-535244 and 2-99-535004 respectively. Tap lightly on both ends of the crankshaft with a soft-faced hammer to seat the main bearings.

6 Using a dial indicator, check that the crankshaft end play does not exceed .012 inch (.30 mm). If it does, adjust as described in **Section 1:17**.

7 Fit the remaining crankcase bolts and nuts (fit new tabwashers under camshaft bearing boss nuts) and torque tighten $\frac{1}{4}$ inch bolts to 5 to 6.5 lb ft (.7 to .9 kg m), $\frac{5}{16}$ inch bolts to 13.5 to 15.2 lb ft (1.9 to 2.1 kg m) and $\frac{3}{8}$ inch bolts to 21 to 22.5 lb ft (2.9 to 3.1 kg m). Lock the tabwashers.

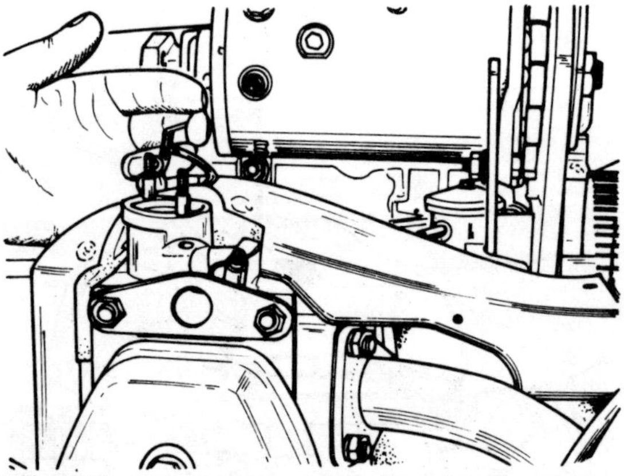

FIG 1:45 Toggle clamps attaching front and rear cowlings

8 Fit the oil strainer and cover assembly as described in **Section 1:14**. Fit the oil pump (see **FIG 1:28**) and its cover and the oil pressure relief valve as described in **Section 1:9**.

9 Fit the pistons (see **FIG 1:27**) cylinders and cylinder heads as described in **Sections 1:8, 1:7** and **1:6** respectively. Adjust the valve clearances as described in **Section 1:3**.

10 Fit the flywheel and clutch assembly as described in **Section 1:13**. Install the impeller hub and, with the flywheel blocked as shown in **FIG 1:5**, torque tighten the attachment bolt to 58 lb ft (8 kg m). With a dial gauge, check that the hub runout does not exceed .008 inch (.20 mm).

11 Turn the crankshaft until the piston of the lefthand cylinder is on TDC of the compression stroke (both valves closed and the pulley timing mark aligned with the crankcase joint) and insert the distributor drive shaft with the flat portion on the shaft facing the crankcase joint (see **FIG 1:41**). Fit the distributor drive gear retainer as shown in **FIG 1:42**. Fit the coil and sparking plugs.

12 Fit the filler pipe gasket sparingly coated with sealing compound on both sides and install the pipe (see **FIG 1:43**) with the oil cooler mounting bracket under the forward lefthand nut. Connect the oil return hose to the filler pipe nipple.

13 Coat both sides of the fuel pump gaskets lightly with sealing compound. To fit the pump, introduce the pushrod into the heat insulating block with the lubrication groove innermost, then fit the block and gaskets on the mounting studs as shown in **FIG 1:44**. Fill the rocker arm cavity about three quarters full with an approved grease and then install the fuel pump.

14 Fit the generator belt on the drive pulley and install the oil cooler (see **FIG 1:6**). Attach the oil return line with a thick copper-asbestos joint washer between the banjo bolt head and the banjo, and a thin copper-asbestos washer between banjo and crankcase. Tighten the banjo bolt to a torque of 14.5 lb ft (2 kg m)

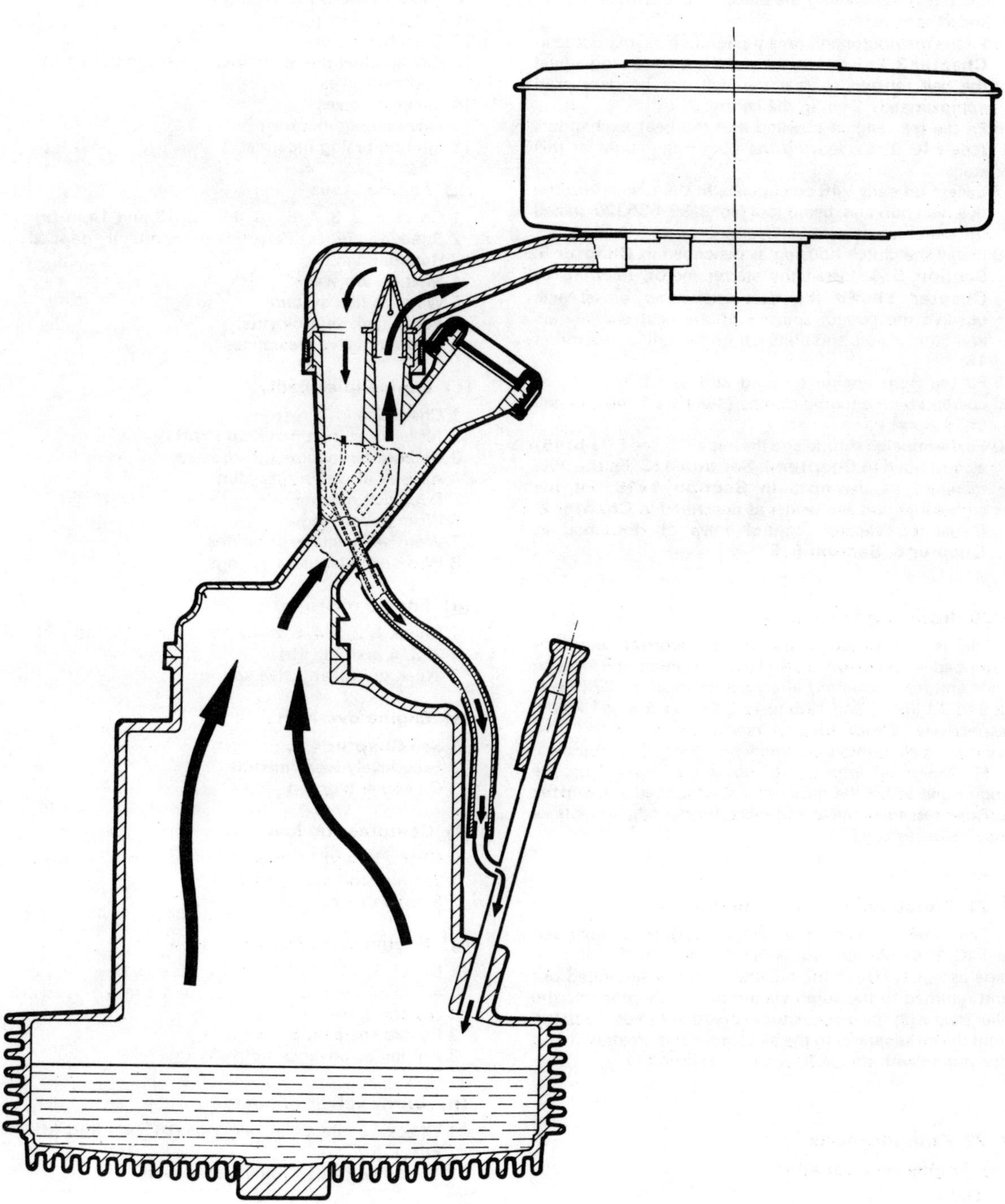

FIG 1:47 Crankcase breathing system

and additionally secure it with wire. Tighten the feed line nut while holding the union nipple with an open-ended spanner.

15 Fit the distributor and time the ignition as instructed in **Chapter 3**. Proceed to install the generator and adjust the belt tension so that the belt can be depressed approximately 1 cm in the centre.

16 Fit the rear engine cowling and the heat exchangers (see **FIG 1:5**), leaving the nuts finger-tight at this stage.

17 Except on early 746 cc engines, fit the circlip into the flywheel hub and, using tool No. 3-99-535320, install the clutch shaft pilot ballbearing.

18 Install the clutch housing as described in **Chapter 5, Section 5:4**. Install the starter motor, referring to **Chapter 11**. Fit the heat exchanger crossbrace, observe the correct spacing of the heat exchangers and tighten nuts and bolts left finger tight at operation 16.

19 Fit the front engine cowling and attach to the rear cowling by the toggle clamps (see **FIG 1:45**). Install the support bar.

20 Fit the impeller shroud and the impeller (see **FIG 1:46**) as described in **Chapter 4, Section 4:3**. Fit the inlet manifold as described in **Section 1:18**. Fit the carburetter and air cleaner as described in **Chapter 2**. Install the vacuum control valve as described in **Chapter 6, Section 6:5**.

1:20 Installing the engine

This is the reverse of the engine removal sequence described in **Section 1:4**. Torque tighten the engine front and rear mounting attachments to 21 to 22.5 lb ft (2.9 to 3.1 kg m) and 13.5 to 15.2 lb ft (1.9 to 2.1 kg m) respectively. Check that all pipes, electric cables and wiring and all controls are firmly and correctly connected.

Fill the sump with oil to the correct level. Run the engine and adjust the carburetter as described in **Chapter 2**. Road test the vehicle and make further adjustments as may be necessary.

1:21 Closed crankcase ventilation

The closed crankcase ventilation system is illustrated in **FIG 1:47**. An oil trap is incorporated in the oil filler pipe assembly. Oil in the breather gases is separated out and returned to the sump via a pipe which connects the filler pipe with the dipstick tube. Breather fumes are piped from the oil separator to the air cleaner and are drawn into the engine with the air flow to the carburetter.

1:22 Fault diagnosis

(a) Engine will not start

1 Defective coil
2 Faulty distributor capacitor (condenser)
3 Dirty, pitted or incorrectly set contact breaker points
4 Ignition cables faulty
5 Water on sparking plug leads
6 Battery discharged
7 Faulty or jammed starter motor
8 Sparking plug leads cross-connected
9 Vapour lock in fuel piping
10 Defective fuel pump
11 Overchoking or underchoking
12 Blocked fuel pump strainer or carburetter jet(s)
13 Leaking valves
14 Sticking valves
15 Valve timing incorrect
16 Ignition timing incorrect

(b) Engine stalls

1 Check 1, 2, 3, 4, 5, 10, 11, 12, 13 and 14 in (a)
2 Sparking plug(s) defective or incorrectly gapped
3 Retarded ignition
4 Mixture too weak
5 Water in fuel system
6 Petrol tank vent blocked
7 Incorrect valve clearances

(c) Engine idles badly

1 Check 2 and 7 in (b)
2 Air leaks at inlet manifold joint(s)
3 Carburetter incorrectly adjusted
4 Air leak at carburetter joint
5 Over-rich mixture
6 Worn piston rings
7 Worn valve stems or guides
8 Weak exhaust valve springs

(d) Engine misfires

1 Check 1, 2, 3, 4, 5, 8, 10, 12, 13, 14, 15 and 16 in (a); 2, 3, 4 and 7 in (b)
2 Weak or broken valve springs

(e) Engine overheats

1 See **Chapter 4**
2 Excessively weak mixture
3 Oil cooler blocked

(f) Compression low

1 Check 13 and 14 in (a); 6 in (c); and 2 in (d)
2 Worn piston ring grooves
3 Scored or worn cylinder bores

(g) Engine lacks power

1 Check 3, 10, 11, 12, 13, 14, 15 and 16 in (a); 2, 3, 4 and 7 in (b); 6 and 7 in (c); and 2 in (d). Also check (e) and (f)
2 Fouled sparking plugs
3 Automatic advance not working

(h) Burnt valves or seats

1 Check 13 and 14 in (a); 7 in (b); and 2 in (d). Also check (e)
2 Excessive carbon round valve seats

(j) Sticking valves

1 Check 2 in (d)
2 Bent valve stem
3 Scored valve stem or guide
4 Incorrect valve clearance

(k) Excessive cylinder wear

1 Check 11 in (a)
2 Lack of oil
3 Dirty oil
4 Piston ring(s) broken
5 Badly fitting piston rings
6 Connecting rod bent

(l) Excessive oil consumption

1 Check 6 and 7 in (c) and check (k)
2 Ring gaps too wide
3 Oil return holes in pistons choked with carbon
4 Scored cylinders
5 Oil level too high
6 External oil leaks

(m) Crankshaft or connecting rod failure

1 Check 2 in (k)
2 Restricted oilways
3 Worn journal or crankpin
4 Loose big-end cap
5 Extremely low oil pressure
6 Bent connecting rod

(n) High fuel consumption (see **Chapter 2**)

(o) Engine vibration

1 Loose generator
2 Engine mountings loose or ineffective
3 Impeller out of balance
4 Misfiring due to mixture, ignition or mechanical faults

NOTES

CHAPTER 2

THE FUEL SYSTEM

2:1 Description

Fuel supply:

The fuel tank which is at the rear of the vehicle is fitted with either a fuel level warning light or a fuel gauge transmitter unit.

A mechanically operated diaphragm type pump draws petrol from the fuel tank and delivers it to a single carburetter at a pressure of 1 to 2 lb/sq inch (.07 to .14 kg/sq cm). The delivery pressure of a fuel pump can be adjusted and the procedure is described in **Section 2:4**. The fuel pump is actuated from an eccentric on the camshaft and all fuel pumps incorporate a gauze type filter. Pumps are covered in **Section 2:4**.

Carburetter, DAF 31, 32 and 33 models:

The 746 cc engines fitted to these models are provided with a single Solex 34 PICS carburetter. This is a downdraught type carburetter with a manually operated choke. An accelerating pump is incorporated but fuel supply via the pump is cut off during high-speed driving. Adjustment and servicing of the carburetter is covered in **Section 2:5**. The vacuum control valve which is linked with the carburetter is covered in **Chapter 6**, **Section 6:5**. The intake manifold incorporates an exhaust heated hot spot.

Carburetter, DAF 44 and 46 models:

A single Solex 40 PICS carburetter is fitted to the 844 cc engine. This is a downdraught type. It differs from the Solex 34 PICS fitted to the 746 cc engine in size and in detail design but has the same features including an accelerating pump and a manually operated choke. There are variants of the 40 PICS carburetter fitted to DAF 44 and 46 models and details of the variant fitted at different chassis numbers are given in **Technical Data** in the **Appendix**. Adjustment and servicing of the Solex 40 PICS carburetters is covered in **Section 2:6**. The vacuum control valve which is linked to the carburetter is covered in **Chapter 6**, **Section 6:5**. An exhaust heated hot spot is incorporated in the intake manifold.

Air cleaners:

All models are provided with an air cleaner mounted above the carburetter. The cleaner incorporates a disposable element and the servicing procedure is described in **Section 2:8**.

Engine breather fumes on all models are consumed by the engine by piping the breather gases to the body of the cleaner.

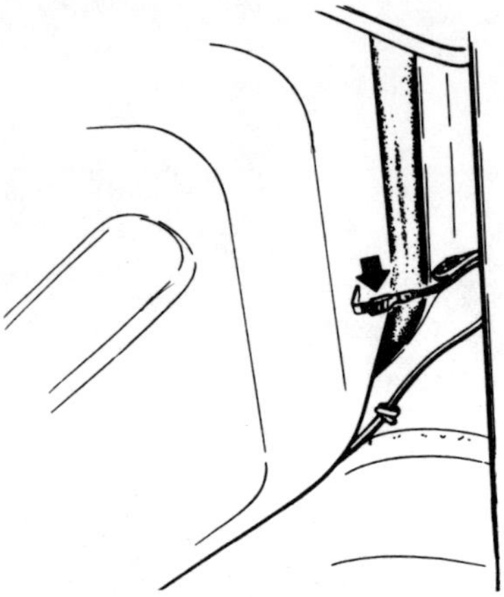

FIG 2:1 Location of fuel tank earthing connection

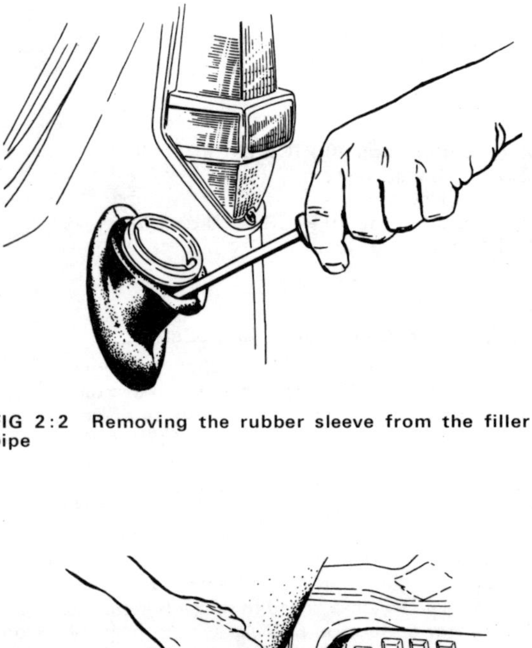

FIG 2:2 Removing the rubber sleeve from the filler pipe

FIG 2:3 Method of removing the fuel tank

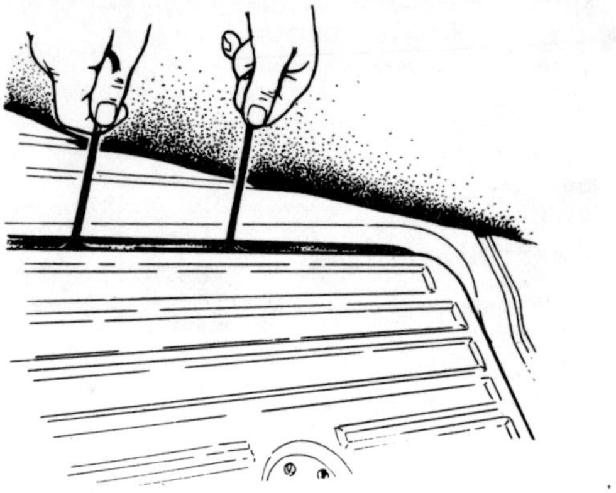

FIG 2:4 Fitting new fuel tank rubber moulding with aid of draw cord

Fuel octane rating:

It is recommended that fuel of the following rating is used:

DAF 31, 32 and 33 models	88 octane
DAF 44 and 46 models	90 octane

2:2 Maintenance

Carburetter:

Maintain the correct slow-running setting at all times. With a fully warmed up engine and **with the Variomatic selector lever in neutral**, this should be 700 to 750 rev/min in the case of DAF 31, 32, 33 and 44 models without exhaust emission control. The adjustment procedure is described in **Section 2:6**.

Access to the gauze filter in the fuel inlet of the carburetter is described in the relevant carburetter Section and it is good practice to withdraw and clean this occasionally.

Air cleaner:

A new element should be fitted every 12,500 miles (20,000 km). In dusty terrain the filter should be renewed more frequently. In extreme conditions this might be as frequently as every 5000 to 6000 miles (8000 to 10,000 km). The procedure for changing an element is described in **Section 2:8**.

At ambient temperatures of above 20°C (68°F), the lever on the intake of the air cleaner must be turned to the 'Summer' position.

Fuel pump:

No routine maintenance is called for but it is good practice to clean the gauze filter occasionally. Access to it is described in **Section 2:4**.

2:3 Fuel tank

Removal of the fuel tank for cleaning, if there is an excessive amount of sediment or if water has inadvertently gained access into the tank, is undertaken on early models by opening the car boot, pushing back the floor mat, disconnecting the fuel line and draining the tank.

Remove the warning light sending unit, if fitted. Disconnect wire on top of tank.

Disconnect the earthing wire (see **FIG 2:1**) and remove the rubber sleeve from the filler pipe as shown in **FIG 2:2**. Then prise out the tank as shown in **FIG 2:3**. Refit the tank by following the removal operations in reverse. If required, a new rubber moulding can be fitted as shown in **FIG 2:4**. Insert a suitable draw cord in the moulding, position the tank in the body opening and pull the lip of the moulding over the edge of the tank.

On the DAF 44 drain the tank by syphoning the fuel through the filler neck. Remove the exhaust pipe from the two rear suspension points. Detach the two supporting straps at the rear, and push the tank forward to clear the filler neck from the body aperture, and lower the tank a little to disconnect the two cables from the sender unit. Remove the tank sender unit (see **FIG 2:5**).

On DAF 46 models drain the tank as described for the DAF 44, remove the cover in the boot and disconnect the sender unit cables. Support the tank and remove the four retaining screws. Disengage the filler neck and disconnect the fuel hoses. Remove the tank.

A special tool 4-99-267021 is required to remove the sender unit.

2:4 Fuel pump, models 31, 32, 33 and 44

Description:

The same type of pump is fitted to all 746 cc and 844 cc engines. The model of pump fitted to early 746 cc engines differs slightly in that the fuel outlet pipe is a right angled elbow and emerges from the side of the outlet boss in the upper section. The outlet pipe on pumps fitted to later 746 cc engines and to 844 cc engines is straight and emerges from the top of the outlet boss. A cross-section through this type of pump is shown in **FIG 2:6**. Both models of pump are identical in function and, in the event of a replacement for the earlier type being required, the later type may be fitted. The pump fitted to the DAF 46 differs in appearance but can be treated in a similar manner.

The pump is mounted on the crankcase. It is a mechanically operated diaphragm type and is actuated through a short pushrod (not shown in **FIG 2:6**) by an eccentric on the camshaft. An insulation block which is fitted between the pump and the crankcase forms a guide for the pushrod.

Refer to **FIG 2:6**. The pushrod is in contact with rocker arm button 1. The rocker 2 pivots on pin 3. The forked inner end of the rocker pulls down rod 5 (which is integral with the diaphragm assembly) and draws down the diaphragm assembly 6 against the pressure of spring 8. This movement of the diaphragm assembly draws fuel through the gauze filter 11 and the inlet valve 9 into the pump chamber 15. The pumping stroke is performed by spring 8 acting upon the lower side of the diaphragm assembly and fuel is delivered through the outlet valve 10 to the carburetter via outlet pipe 14. Fuel delivery pressure is dependent only upon the load applied by spring 8 and, by varying the number of the gaskets fitted between the insulation block and the crankcase, small adjustments can be made to the delivery pressure. Increasing the number of gaskets will, by decreasing the effective load of the spring, reduce the fuel pressure. The diaphragm stroke depends upon the amount of undelivered fuel in the pump chamber. If the chamber is full, the rocker will reciprocate idly and the forked arm will not actuate rod 5.

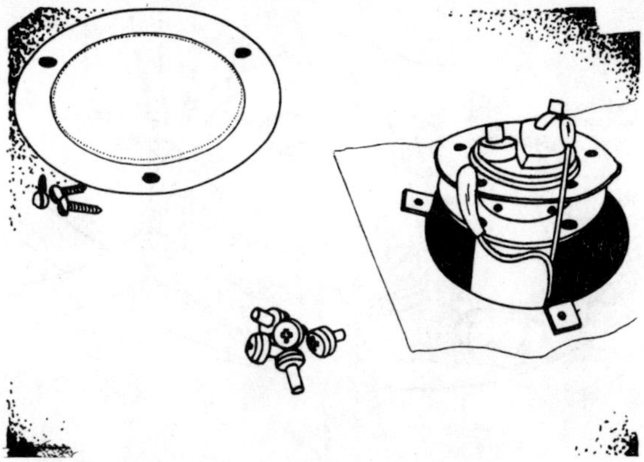

FIG 2:5 Fuel tank sending unit and cover plate, DAF 44

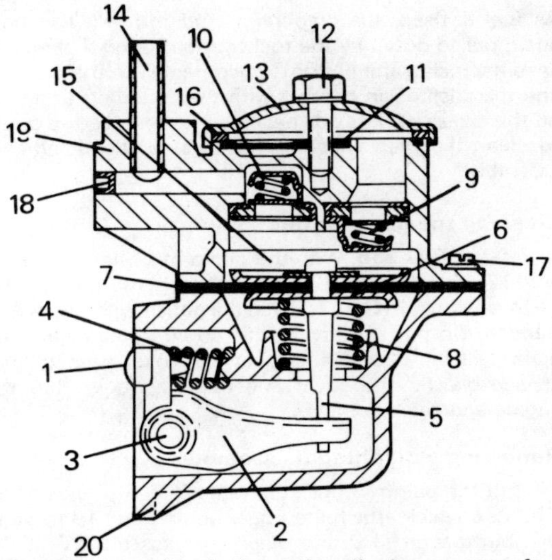

FIG 2:6 A sectional view of a diaphragm type fuel pump

Key to Fig 2:6 1 Rocker arm button 2 Rocker 3 Pivot pin 4 Rocker spring 5 Diaphragm assembly rod 6 Diaphragm assembly 7 Gasket(s) 8 Diaphragm spring 9 Inlet valve 10 Outlet valve 11 Gauze filter 12 Cover retaining bolt 13 Cover 14 Outlet pipe 15 Pump chamber 16 Cover gasket 17 Screw 18 Plug 19 Upper body 20 Lower body

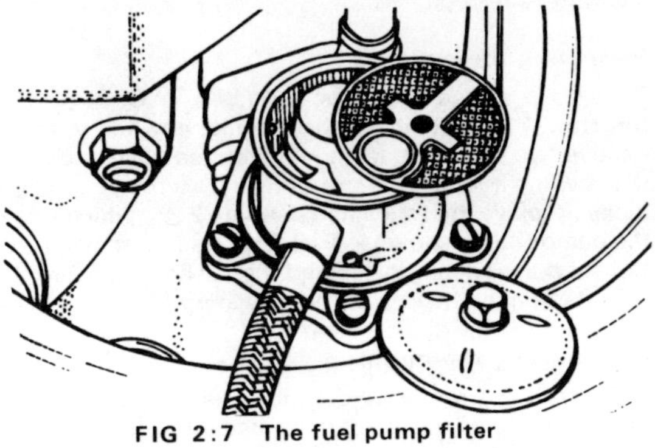

FIG 2:7 The fuel pump filter

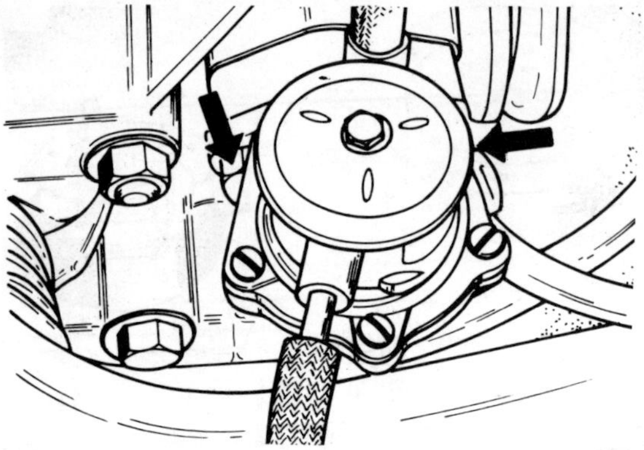

FIG 2:8 Location of the fuel pump retaining nuts

FIG 2:9 Removing the fuel pump

As fuel is used, the diaphragm and rod will rise until again pulled down by the rocker arm. Spring 4 serves to keep the rocker arm button 1 in contact with the pushrod and the pushrod in contact with the actuating eccentric on the camshaft. It is not necessary to remove the pump to clean the gauze filter or to change the diaphragm assembly.

Cleaning the gauze filter:

Refer to **FIG 2:6**. With the pump in position, remove bolt 12, lift off cover 13 and withdraw the gauze filter 11 as shown in **FIG 2:7**. Clean the gauze with petrol and a brush. Do not use rag as this could contaminate the gauze. Fit the filter. Check that the cover gasket 16 is serviceable. Fit the cover and retaining bolt. Run the engine and check for leaks.

Renewing a diaphragm assembly:

With the pump in position, remove five screws 17 in **FIG 2:6** which attach the upper pump body 19 through the joint gasket(s) 7 and diaphragm assembly 6 to the lower pump body 20. Lift off the upper section of the pump. Turn the engine until the diaphragm is in its highest position. Turn the diaphragm assembly through 90 deg. to disengage rod 5 from the fork of rocker 2 and lift out the diaphragm assembly. Collect the gasket(s).

Fit the new diaphragm assembly. Reassembly is the reverse of the dismantling sequence. Check and, if necessary, adjust the pump delivery pressure as described later in this Section.

Removing the pump:

Remove the generator as described in **Chapter 11, Section 11:4**. Remove the engine cowling clamps, remove two screws attaching the front cowling and press the cowling aside with a screwdriver. Disconnect the fuel pipes. Remove the two nuts (see **FIG 2:8**) which retain the pump and, as shown in **FIG 2:9**, dismount the pump. Collect the insulating block and the pushrod. Discard the gaskets from both sides of the insulating block.

Dismantling the pump:

Remove the pump as described earlier. Remove the gauze filter and the diaphragm assembly as described earlier. Refer to **FIG 2:6**. Remove the circlip from the rocker pivot pin 3. Withdraw the rocker and collect spring 4.

Inspecting the pump:

Refer to **FIG 2:6**. Check the conditions of gaskets 7 and 16. Neither the inlet nor the outlet valve can be serviced and, if a valve spring is broken, a valve seat worn or if a valve is not showing that it is seating fully, a complete new upper pump body must be fitted. Check the diaphragm assembly 6. If the car has covered a considerable mileage, it will be prudent to fit a new diaphragm assembly irrespective of the apparent condition of the original.

Assembling the pump:

Position the rocker and insert the pivot pin. Fit the retaining circlip and ensure that it is correctly seated in its groove. Fit the rocker spring. Fit the diaphragm assembly and its spring. Fit the upper pump body and the joint gasket(s). Fit the gauze filter and the top cover as described earlier. Install the pump as described later and check the fuel pressure. If necessary, adjust the pressure as described later in this Section.

Fitting the pump:

This is the reverse of the removal sequence. Use a new gasket on each side of the insulating block. Fill the space round the rocker with grease.

Pressure adjustment:

Insert a T-piece pipe on the delivery side of the pump and connect a suitable pressure gauge. Run the engine through a range of rev/min and note the gauge reading. The pressure should be between 1 and 2 lb/sq inch (.07 to .14 kg/sq cm). Adjustment is made by adding or removing gaskets fitted between the insulation block and the crankcase. Adding gaskets will reduce the fuel pressure and vice versa.

2:5 Solex type 34 PICS carburetter

Cross-sections through a Solex 34 PICS type carburetter are shown in **FIG 2:10**. This is a downdraught

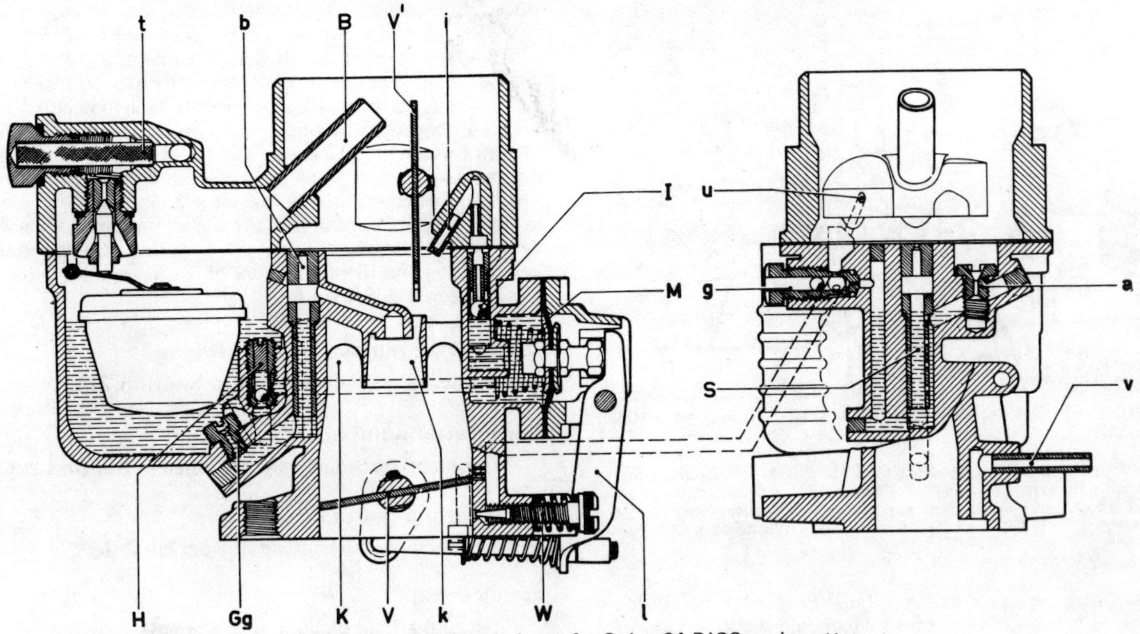

FIG 2:10 Sectional view of a Solex 34 PICS carburetter

Key to Fig 2:10 a Air-correction jet b Compensating orifice Gg Main jet i Pump discharge nozzle g Pilot jet H Pump inlet valve I Pump discharge valve K Main venturi k Secondary venturi l Pump lever M Pump diaphragm S Emulsion tube u Pilot jet air bleed W Volume control screw B Float chamber vent tube t Fuel strainer V Throttle valve V¹ Choke valve v Vacuum line connection

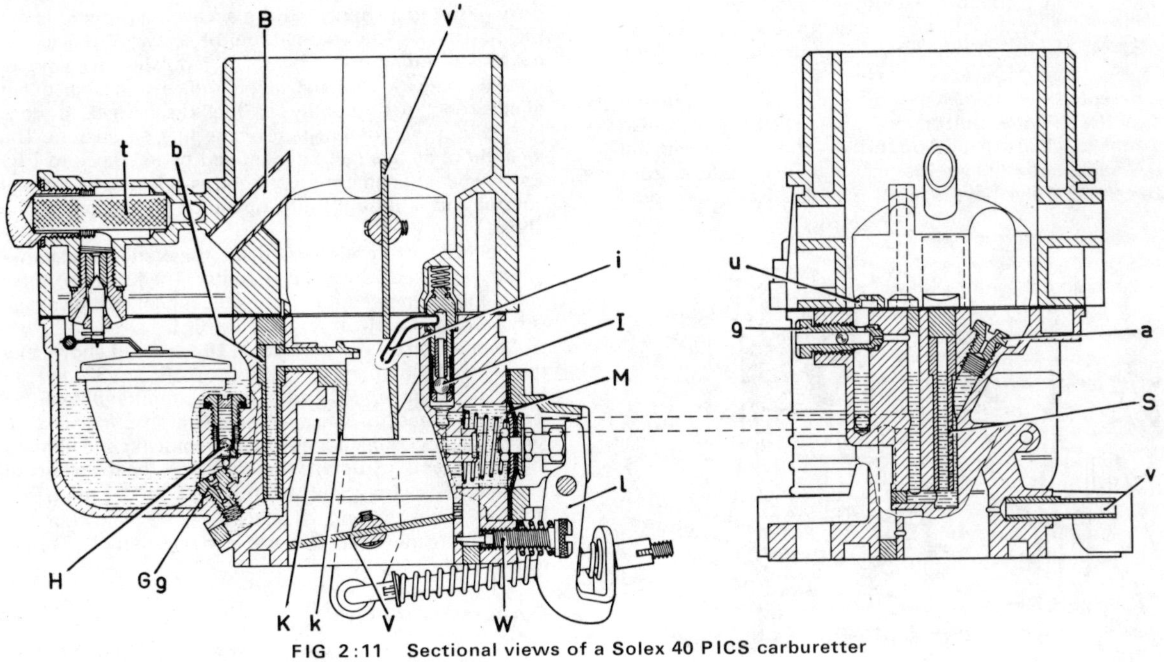

FIG 2:11 Sectional views of a Solex 40 PICS carburetter

Key to Fig 2:11 a Air-correction jet b Compensating orifice Gg Main jet i Pump discharge nozzle g Pilot jet H Pump inlet valve I Pump discharge valve K Main venturi k Secondary venturi l Pump lever M Pump diaphragm S Emulsion tube u Pilot jet air bleed W Volume control screw B Float chamber vent tube t Fuel strainer V Throttle valve V¹ Choke valve v Vacuum line connection

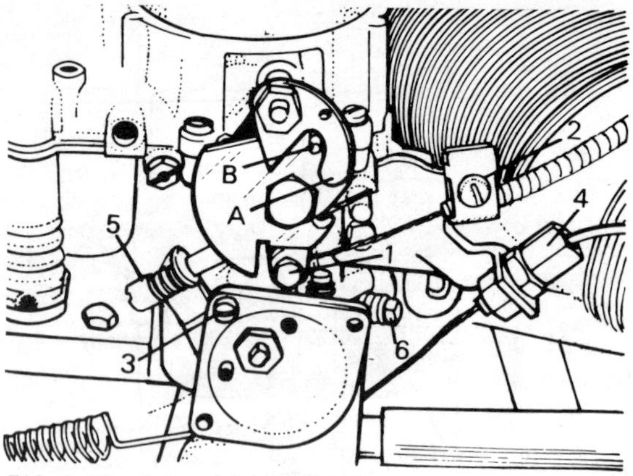

FIG 2:12 **Adjustment points on the Solex 40 PICS carburetter**

Key to Fig 2:12 A Notch B Pin 1 Choke cable attachment screw 2 Clamp clip for choke outer cable 3 Throttle cable attachment screw 4 Throttle outer cable tensioner 5 Throttle stop screw 6 Volume control screw

type with an accelerating pump. Fuel enrichment for starting is brought in by manually operated choke. During high-speed driving, the fuel supply via the accelerating pump is cut off by closure of the pump discharge valve I. Volume control screw W allows the mixture to be set. This screw regulates the flow of fuel discharged from the idling orifice. Adjustments to the screw affects only the quantity of fuel discharged and not the quality or composition of the fuel/air mixture.

34 PICS carburetters are fitted to DAF 31 and 32 models. 34 PICS-2 carburetters are fitted to the DAF 33. These carburetters are not interchangeable. They have different venturi diameters and certain jets are of different sizes. Details of venturi diameters and jet sizes are given in **Technical Data** in the **Appendix**. It should be noted that DAF 31 and 32 models manufactured before 23rd December 1964 have size 45 pilot jets while cars produced after that date have size 47 pilot jets. The location of all jets can be identified by reference to **FIG 2:10**.

Comparison between **FIGS 2:10** and **2:11** which shows cross-sections through the 40 PICS type carburetter fitted to early DAF 44 models will indicate that, although these carburetters differ in size and in minor design feature, they are very similar. Removal, refitment and servicing procedures are common between the two types and are described in **Section 2:6**.

The vacuum control valve for the Variomatic transmission is linked to the carburetter controls. The function of this valve and the adjustment of the linkage is covered in **Chapter 6, Section 6:5**.

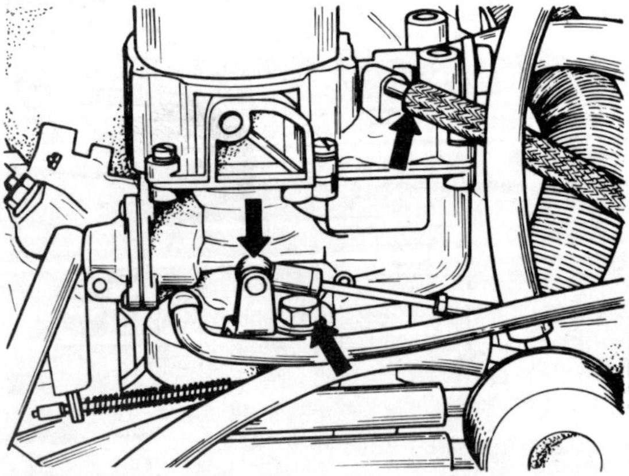

FIG 2:13 **Removing the carburetter after disconnecting the fuel feed pipe, the vacuum control connecting rod and the carburetter retaining nuts, as indicated by the arrows**

Carburetter removal and refitment:

The procedures are described in **Section 2:6**.

Carburetter adjustments:

Adjustment procedures are described in **Section 2:6**.

Cleaning the gauze filter:

This operation is described in **Section 2:6**.

Jet cleaning:

Refer to the final paragraph of **Section 2:6**.

2:6 Solex type 40 PICS carburetter

Cross-sections through a Solex 40 PICS are shown in **FIG 2:11**. This is a downdraught type and incorporates an accelerating pump. The function of this pump is to inject additional fuel during acceleration. During high-speed driving, the fuel supply via the accelerating pump is cut off by valve I. The volume control screw W provides a means of setting the mixture. It regulates the flow of fuel discharged from the idling orifice and adjustment affects only the quantity of fuel discharged. It does not control the composition of the fuel/air mixture. The location of all jets can be identified by reference to **FIG 2:11**. Fuel enrichment for starting is selected by manual control and is brought into operation by closure of the choke valve V^1.

The vacuum control valve for the Variomatic transmission is linked with the carburetter. The function of this valve and the procedure for the adjustment of the linkage is covered in **Chapter 6, Section 6:5**.

Comparison between **FIGS 2:10** and **2:11** shows that the 34 PICS carburetter fitted to DAF 31, 32 and 33 models and the 40 PICS carburetter, although different in size and in design detail, are identical in principle and, since the procedures for adjusting, removing and refitting the two types of carburetter are the same, the remainder of this Section is also applicable to the 34 PICS carburetter. If the engine is running, all adjustments to the carburetter should be made **with the Variomatic selector lever in neutral**.

Carburetter removal:

1 Remove the air cleaner as described in **Section 2:8**.
2 Refer to **FIG 2:12**. Disconnect the choke inner cable by loosening screw 1 and uncouple the choke outer cable by loosening clamp screw 2 and pulling the outer cable through the clamp clip.

3 Disconnect the throttle inner cable by loosening screw 3.

4 Disconnect the fuel feed pipe from the carburetter. Uncouple the vacuum control valve linkage at the carburetter (see **FIG 2:13**).

5 Remove the nuts which retain the carburetter to the manifold, lift off the carburetter and discard the joint gasket.

Carburetter refitment:

This is the reverse of the removal sequence. Use a new joint gasket. Adjust the choke and throttle cables as described later. Adjust the vacuum control valve linkage as described in **Chapter 6, Section 6:5**.

Choke cable adjustment:

Refer to **FIG 2:12**. With the dashboard choke control knob pushed fully in, pin B must engage in the notch A. Adjustment is made by loosening screw 1, positioning the choke inner cable so that it is just slack and retightening screw 1. If necessary, the choke outer cable may be repositioned in the clamp clip after loosening screw 2.

Throttle cable adjustment:

To enable the carburetter throttle valve (V in **FIGS 2:10** and **2:11**) to be visible, the following procedure requires the air cleaner to be dismounted.

Refer to **FIG 2:12**. Adjust the cable tensioner 4 until the throttle cable is just slack. Depress the accelerator pedal fully and adjust the pedal stop until the throttle valve is in a vertical position.

Slow-running adjustment:

With the Variomatic selector lever in neutral, start the engine and run until normal operating temperature is reached. Refer to **FIG 2:12**. Turn out the volume control screw a few turns and then turn back slowly until the best running speed is obtained. With a screwdriver, adjust the throttle stop screw 5 until the required idling speed of 700 to 750 rev/min is achieved. Anti-pollution control versions 875 to 925 rev/min (see **Section 2:9**).

Volume control adjustment:

With the Variomatic selector lever in neutral, the engine at normal operating temperature and the slow-running speed correctly set, turn the volume control screw 6 in **FIG 2:12** (W in **FIGS 2:10** and **2:11**) out a few turns. Now turn the screw slowly inwards (clockwise) until the best quality of slow-running is achieved. Reset the slow-running as described earlier.

Accelerating pump:

The stroke of the pump is factory set and no attempt should be made to adjust it. The pump diaphragm may, after considerable mileage, require to be renewed.

Cleaning the gauze filter:

The thimble type gauze filter (t in **FIGS 2:10** and **2:11**) is located between the fuel inlet to the carburetter and the float valve. Access is by removing the hexagonal retaining plug. Clean the filter with petrol and a brush. Do not use rag as this could contaminate the gauze.

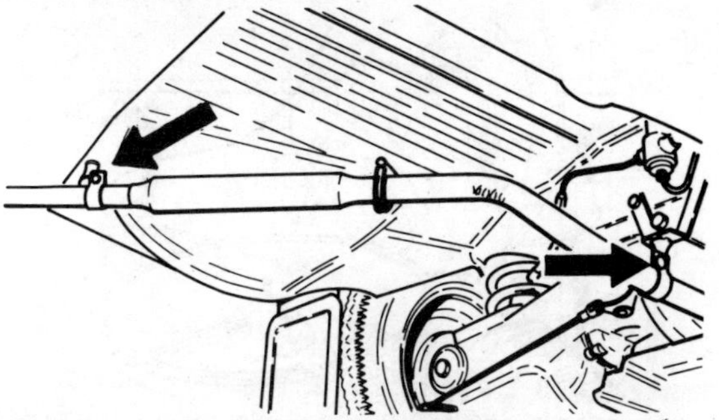

FIG 2:14 Exhaust tail pipe and resonator, showing locations of attaching bolts

Jet cleaning:

Do not clean the jets or orifices with anything other than compressed air. Calibration can be ruined if wires or probes are used in attempting to clean them. On no account should jet or orifice sizes be altered from their factory calibrations. Jet sizes are quoted in **Technical Data** in the **Appendix** for all series of carburetters and, should a jet be damaged, refer to this information and obtain a replacement of the correct size for the relevant carburetter.

2:7 Exhaust system

The silencer is mounted transversely across the rear of the engine below the clutch housing. Exhaust gases pass into the silencer at three connections, one from the inlet manifold hot spot and one from each of the heater system heat exchangers. A single exhaust tail pipe leads to the rear of the vehicle.

To renew the exhaust assembly, the car should preferably be over a pit or on a hoist. First remove the tail pipe complete with resonator (see **FIG 2:14**). Release the tail pipe mounting brackets and its connection at the silencer. Referring now to **FIG 2:15**, remove the bolts and nuts 1 to 7 and withdraw the silencer. Proceed to remove the bolts and nuts 8 to 14 to remove the heat exchangers.

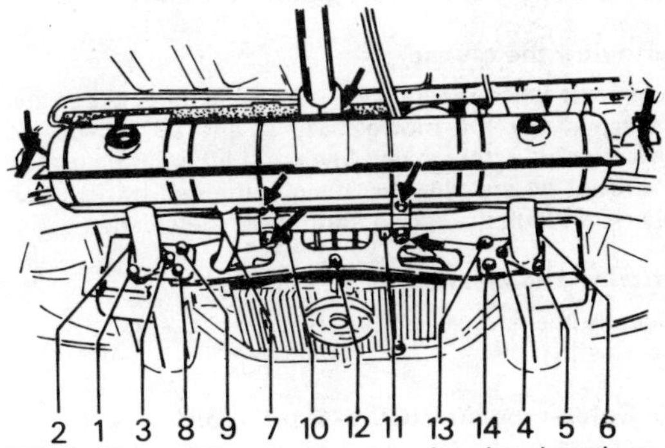

FIG 2:15 Exhaust silencer, showing locations of attaching bolts

Key to Fig 2:15 1, 2, 3, 4, 5 and 6 Flange nuts and bolts 7 Hot spot pipe connection 8, 9, 10, 11, 13 and 14 Crossbrace attachments 12 Crossbrace

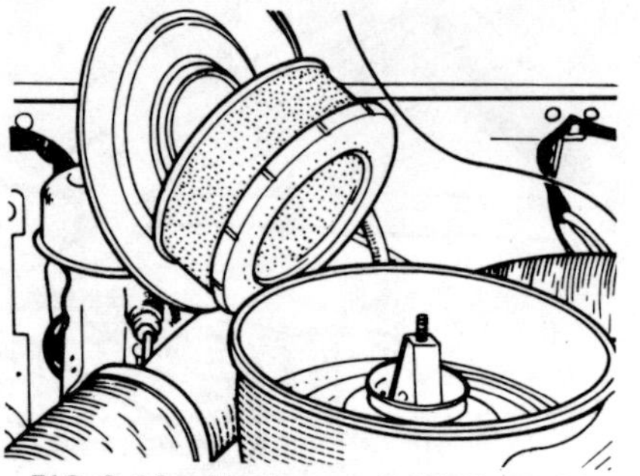

FIG 2:16 Air cleaner, DAF 31, 32, 33

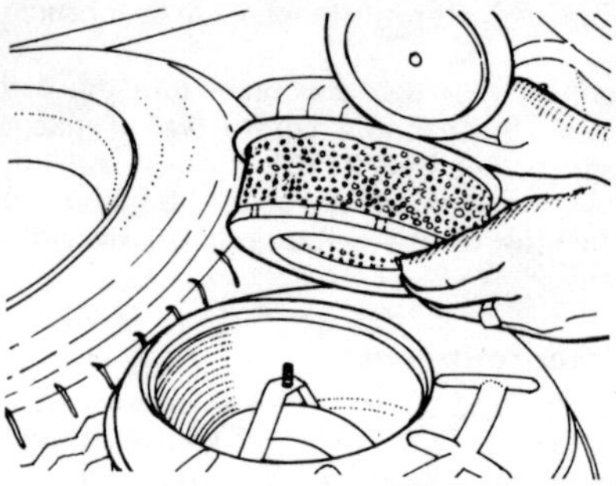

FIG 2:17 Air cleaner later models

Assembly follows the same procedure in reverse. Locate the heat exchangers on the engine and fit the bolts and nuts 8 to 14, but only to finger tightness. Fit the silencer and secure with the bolts and nuts 1 to 7, then tighten the remaining fasteners. Note that if a later type of silencer is employed to replace an earlier one the hot spot pipe needs also to be of a later type. Also when fitting the tail pipe and resonator make sure that the cupped discs of the tail pipe hanger brackets are not located too close to the floor of the car, otherwise damage to the brake and vacuum lines may occur.

2:8 Air cleaner

The air cleaner fitted to these models is mounted above the carburetter. The element is a disposable type and should be renewed at the mileage intervals recommended in **Section 2:2**. The crankcase breather pipe is connected to the air cleaner canister. A valve in the intake duct to the cleaner allows heated or unheated intake air to be selected on a seasonal basis.

Element renewal:

The cleaner fitted to DAF 31, 32 and 33 models is not interchangeable with that fitted to later models. The filter element renewal procedure is however the same for both types.

Remove the nut from the centre of the canister cover, lift off the cover and withdraw the element. **FIGS 2:16** and **2:17** illustrate this stage. Fit the replacement element, refit the cover and tighten the retaining nut.

Removing the cleaner:

On both types, uncouple the pipes connected to the cleaner canister. On **models 31**, **32** and **33**, loosen the clamping bolt with a screwdriver and lift off the cleaner. On **model 44** and **46** cars, remove the canister support bracket, unhook the spring and lift off the cleaner.

Refitting the cleaner:

This is the reverse of the removal sequence in each case.

2:9 Solex type 40 PICS-5-6 anti-pollution carburetters

This type of carburetter has been fitted to meet European emission control standards. It is manufactured to close tolerances, tested, and adjusted at the works and it is inadvisable to alter the settings.

It is similar in all respects to the carburetters already described, and the instructions given can be used as necessary.

The main modification is the incorporation of a solenoid operated pilot jet shut-off valve, which is closed in the non-energised position. Its operation can be checked by switching the ignition on and off and listening for the noise made as the solenoid core moves. The internal passages are also different to enable a by-pass screw to be incorporated.

Adjustment requires the use of an exhaust gas analyzer and if necessary the car should be taken to an agent with the necessary equipment available.

2:10 Fault diagnosis

(a) Insufficient fuel delivered

1 Air vent to fuel tank restricted
2 Fuel pipe blocked
3 Air leak between pump and tank
4 Pump filter requires cleaning
5 Pump diaphragm defective
6 Pump valves sticking or seating badly
7 Fuel vapourizing in pipeline due to heat

(b) Excessive fuel consumption

1 Carburetter requires adjustment
2 Fuel pipe leaking
3 Carburetter jet loose
4 Dirty air filter element
5 Excessive engine temperature
6 Idling speed too high
7 Brakes binding
8 Tyres under-inflated
9 Car overloaded

(c) Idling speed too high

1 Rich fuel mixture
2 Throttle control sticking
3 Incorrect slow-running adjustment
4 Worn throttle valve
5 Air leak at throttle spindle

(d) No fuel delivery

1 Float valve stuck
2 Tank vent blocked
3 Pump defective
4 Pipeline obstructed
5 Pipeline broken or disconnected

CHAPTER 3

THE IGNITION SYSTEM

3 : 1 Description

The distributors fitted to all models incorporate both centrifugal and vacuum operated variable timing. As engine speed increases, centrifugal action of rotating weights pivoting against the tension of small springs, advances the ignition timing by progressively advancing the contact breaker cam relative to the distributor driving shaft. The vacuum control unit is connected by small-bore piping to the carburetter. At high degrees of vacuum, it advances the ignition timing but under load, at reduced intake depression, the unit progressively retards the ignition timing.

Refer to **Technical Data** in the **Appendix** for information on distributor types.

3 : 2 Maintenance

Contact breaker points:

When the points are fully open, the contact breaker gap should be .016 to .020 inch (.4 to .5 mm). This points gap dimension is the same for all models irrespective of the make or type of distributor which is fitted.

Check the points gap regularly and, if necessary, adjust to within the limits specified. The procedure for adjustment of the gap is described in **Section 3 : 4**.

Distributor lubrication:

Ensure that, when lubricating the distributor, the contact breaker points are kept free from oil or grease. If they should become accidently contaminated, clean them with trichlorethylene.

Every 6000 miles (10,000 km), soak the felt pad under the rotor arm with oil. Remove the spring clip which retains the movable point, lift off the point and apply a smear of grease to the pivot post. Refit the point and its spring clip. Apply a smear of grease also to the cam. Again, be careful not to over-lubricate, otherwise the lubricant may reach the contact points resulting in burning and difficult starting.

Sparking plugs:

Maintenance of sparking plugs is covered in **Section 3 : 6**.

3 : 3 Ignition faults

If the engine runs unevenly, set it to idle at about 1000 rev/min and, taking care not to touch any metal part of the sparking plug leads, remove and replace each lead from its plug in turn. Doing this to a plug which is firing properly will cause the engine to stop completely

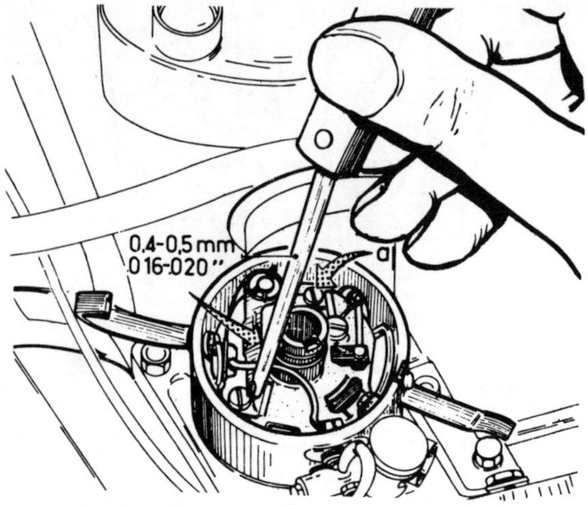

FIG 3:1 Adjusting the contact breaker points gap, DAF 31, 32

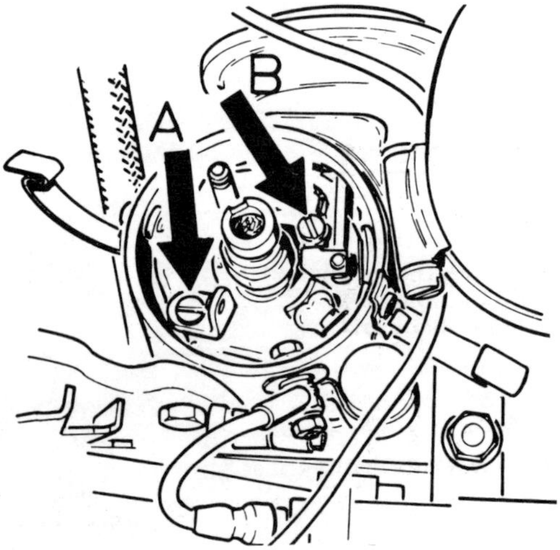

FIG 3:2 The fixed point retaining screws A and B

FIG 3:3 Adjusting the contact breaker points gap, later models

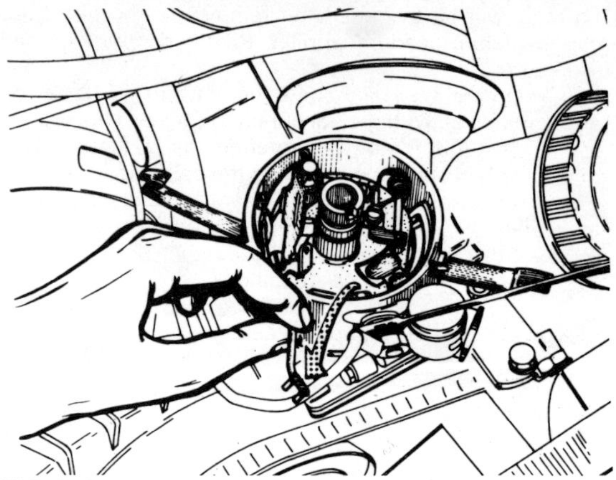

FIG 3:4 Disconnecting the contact breaker point lead after removing the distributor cap

Remove the lead from each plug in turn and pull back the insulator. Hold the lead so that the metal end is about $\frac{1}{8}$ inch (3 mm) from the cylinder head and turn the engine with the starter. A strong regular spark confirms that the fault lies with the sparking plug which should be serviced as described in **Section 3:6** or a new plug fitted.

If the spark is weak and irregular, check the condition of the lead and, if it is perished or cracked, renew it. If no improvement results, check that the distributor cap is clean and dry, that the carbon brush at its centre can be moved freely against its internal spring and that there is no 'tracking'. 'Tracking' which will show as a thin black line between the electrodes or to a metal part in contact with the cap cannot be rectified except by fitting a new cap.

If the contact breaker points are in good condition, clean and correctly set (as described in **Section 3:4**) but there is no spark, refer to the relevant wiring diagram in the **Appendix**, use a suitable voltmeter with its negative connected to a good earth and the ignition switched on, and check that there is voltage throughout the LT circuit. A 0 to 10 voltmeter will be suitable for this test. Correct the faulty cable, loose connection or defective ignition switch.

If the LT circuit is in order, the coil or capacitor must be suspect and can best be checked by substitution.

3:4 Distributor

Bosch distributors are fitted to all engines. These distributors are not all of the same type and, although the technical data may, in certain cases be the same, spare parts are not necessarily interchangeable. It is essential therefore that, when obtaining replacement parts, the parts being obtained are checked to ensure that they are identical with the parts being discarded.

Contact breaker points:

Two procedures are given for setting the points gap. Each is particularly applicable to the model(s) stated. In the event of the other type of distributor having been fitted, it will be evident, after removal of the distributor cap, which procedure applies to the distributor being worked on.

Adjustment may be made either with the aid of a cam angle meter or with less accuracy by feeler gauges. The former method is to be preferred, as a feeler gauge measures between high spots on the points instead of the true point opening, whereas the cam angle or dwell angle measures the number of degrees the distributor cam rotates from the instant that the contact points close to the instant when they open again.

If using feeler gauges in the absence of the preferred instrument, the wire type is advised, after used points have first been trued up with a contact stone. Care must be taken to hold the gauge accurately in line with the point opening to get as precise a measurement as possible.

If the contacts are to be removed and either renewed or cleaned and refitted, first check the moving contact spring tension with a small spring balance. The reading must be taken just as the contact points separate and should be within the specified limits of 400 to 500 g (14 to 18 oz). If otherwise another breaker lever must be used.

New parts must be fitted if on examination the contact points are seen to be excessively worn or burnt. Contacts showing a greyish colour and which are only slightly pitted need not be renewed. If still serviceable, clean them with a fine contact stone. Do not use emery cloth or sandpaper. All roughness need not be removed, merely remove scale or dirt. If the contact points are excessively burnt or pitted a new assembly should be fitted. It is usual for contact point sets for Bosch distributors to be supplied as complete assemblies with the breaker lever spring tension and point alignment adjusted at the factory. Only the point opening or dwell angle require adjustment after fitting.

Points gap setting, models 31 and 32:

Unclip the distributor cap, push it to one side, remove the dust shield and lift off the rotor arm. Turn the crankshaft until the points are fully open. Refer to **FIG 3:1**. Loosen both the screws which retain the fixed point and turn the adjuster screw a until the points gap is .016 to .020 inch (.4 to .5 mm) measured with feeler gauges. Retighten both the fixed point attachment screws and check that the gap is within limits. Refit the dust shield, the rotor arm and the distributor cap. Check the ignition timing as described in **Section 3:5**.

Points gap setting, other models:

Unclip the distributor cap, push it to one side, and remove the rotor arm. Turn the crankshaft until the points are fully open. Loosen screw A in **FIG 3:2**. Insert a screwdriver as shown in **FIG 3:3** between the projections on the carrier plate and the slot in the fixed point and adjust the points to .016 to .020 inch (.4 to .5 mm) measured by feeler gauge by turning the blade of the screwdriver. Tighten screw A and check that the gap is within limits. Refit the rotor arm and distributor cap. Check the ignition timing as described in **Section 3:5**.

Renewing the points:

The procedure for the renewal of the breaker points is substantially the same for all distributors although the component parts are not identical.

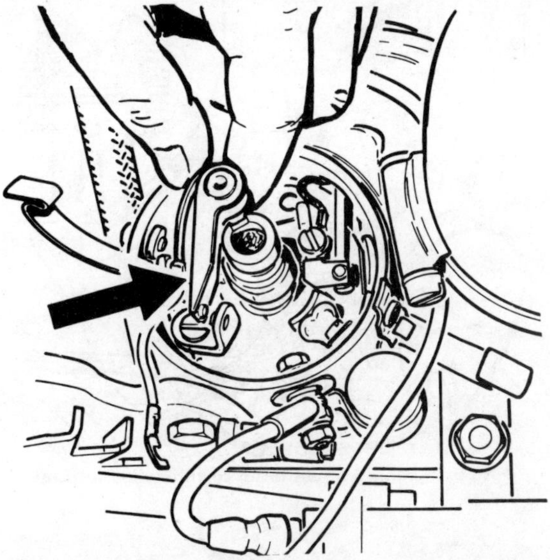

FIG 3:5 Removing the spring clip and the movable breaker point assembly

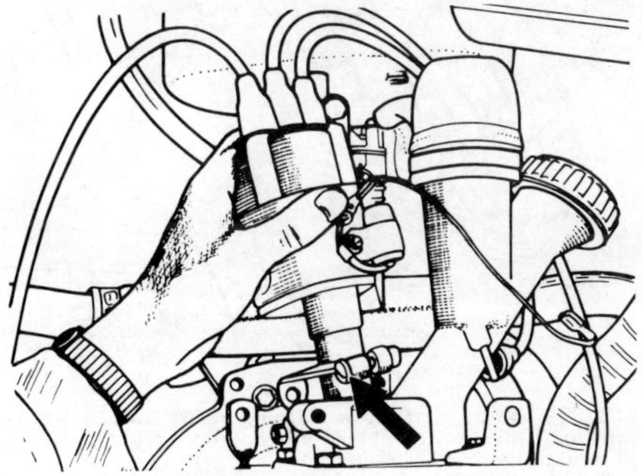

FIG 3:6 Removing the distributor, the arrow showing the clamping screw

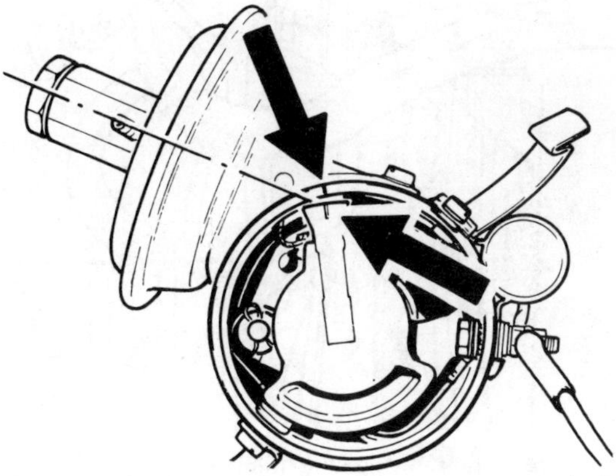

FIG 3:7 Timing marks on the rotor arm and the distributor body

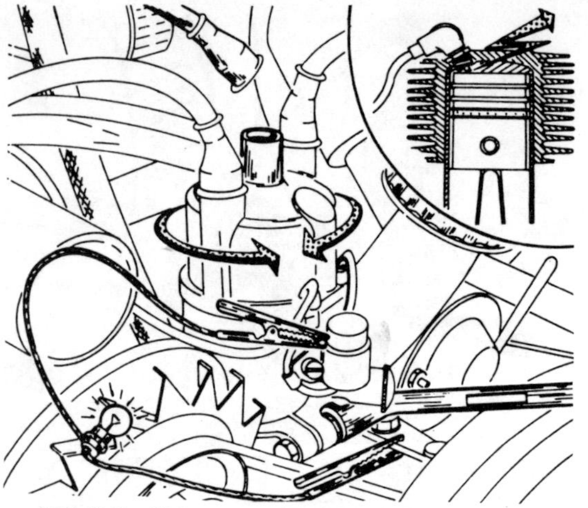

FIG 3:8 Using a test lamp to time the ignition

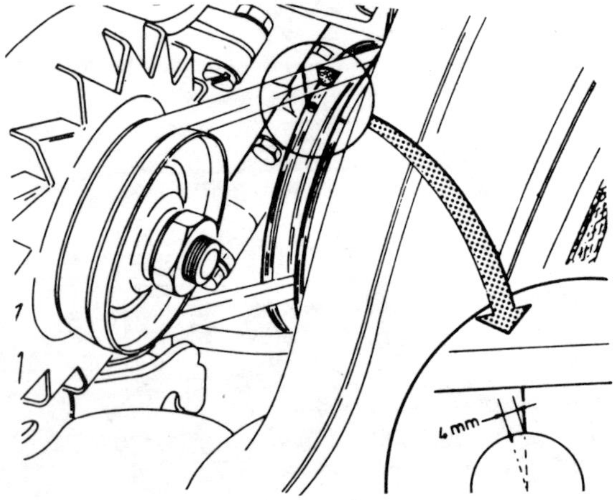

FIG 3:9 Crankshaft pulley timing mark, DAF 31, 32, 33 Ignition timing with exhaust emission control—5° ATDC (5 mm on crankshaft pulley)

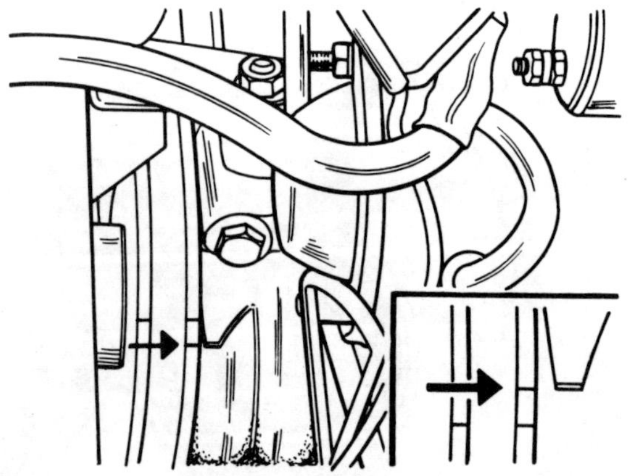

FIG 3:10 Crankshaft pulley timing mark, DAF 44 set at 6° BTDC. Inset: Position of marks for 5° ATDC (5 mm on crankshaft pulley)

Remove the distributor cap and the dust shield if one is fitted. Remove the rotor arm and disconnect the breaker point wire (see **FIG 3:4**). Slide off the spring clip and lift out the movable point (see **FIG 3:5**). Removing the two retaining screws A and B in **FIG 3:2** and withdraw the fixed point.

Installation of the new points is the reverse of this sequence. Ensure that the new points are an exact match of the type which were removed. Set the points gap as described earlier.

Removing and refitting the distributor:

Provided that the distributor clamping screw which is arrowed in **FIG 3:6** is not loosened, the distributor can be dismounted and refitted without disturbing the ignition timing. To dismount the distributor, remove the nut and bolt which retains the clamping plate to the crankcase, disconnect the cables from the sparking plugs, the LT wire from the distributor body and the vacuum pipeline from the vacuum timing control. Lift off the unit complete with the clamping plate.

Refitting the distributor is the reverse of this sequence and must be followed by checking the ignition timing as described in **Section 3:5**.

Defective distributor:

A defective distributor should be exchanged for a factory reconditioned unit.

3:5 Timing the ignition

Turn the crankshaft to bring the piston of the **lefthand** cylinder onto its firing stroke (both valves closed). Align the moving with the stationary timing mark. The stationary timing mark position depends upon the engine type and is specified at the end of this Section. Align the marks on the distributor rotor arm and the distributor body as shown in **FIG 3:7**. When the distributor is installed, the vacuum advance unit centre line will be approximately parallel with the crankcase joint. Install the distributor and fit the nut and bolt which retains the clamp plate to the crankcase.

Set the points gap as described in **Section 3:4**. Connect a test lamp between earth and the terminal on the side of the distributor body and remove the coil HT lead from the centre of the cap as shown in **FIG 3:8**. Switch on the ignition. Loosen the distributor clamping screw. The required position of the distributor is determined by turning its body until the contact breaker points just open. This is the point at which the test lamp just lights. Tighten the distributor clamping screw, turn the crankshaft through two full revolutions and confirm that, when the test lamp lights up, the timing marks coincide. If they do not, the position of the distributor must be readjusted.

The timing marks

The moving timing mark is on the periphery of the crankshaft pulley. The stationary mark for DAF 31, 32 and 33 models is shown in **FIG 3:9** and is 4 mm (.157 inch) from the crankcase joint. For DAF 44 models it is 6 mm (.236 inch) from the mark on the crankcase (see **FIG 3:10**). On engines with European emission control, turn the engine clockwise until the mark on the pulley is 5 mm after the vertical joint of the crankcase halves.

3:6 Sparking plugs

Maintenance:

About every 3000 miles (5000 km), clean the plugs and reset the electrode gaps. It is recommended that a new set of plugs should be fitted every 6000 miles (10,000 km).

Sparking plugs should be torque tightened to 11 to 14.5 lb ft (1.5 to 2.0 kg m).

Sparking plug types and electrode gaps:

Model(s)	*Make and type*	*Electrode gap*
31 and 32	Autolite AE32p	.032 to .035 inch (.8 to .9 mm)
33	Bosch W.200.T35	.032 to .035 inch (.8 to .9 mm)
44	Bosch W.175.T1	.032 to .035 inch (.8 to .9 mm)
	or equivalents.	

3:7 Fault diagnosis

(a) Engine will not fire

1 Battery discharged
2 Distributor points dirty, pitted or maladjusted
3 Distributor cap dirty, cracked or 'tracking'
4 Distributor cap centre brush not contacting rotor arm
5 Faulty cable or loose connection in LT circuit
6 Defective rotor arm
7 Defective coil
8 Broken contact breaker moving point spring
9 Contact breaker points stuck open

(b) Engine misfires

1 Check 2, 3, 5 and 7 in (a)
2 Weak contact breaker moving point spring
3 HT cable(s) cracked or perished
4 Sparking plug(s) oiled up
5 Sparking plug(s) loose
6 Sparking plug (s) defective
7 Sparking plug gap(s) incorrectly set
8 Ignition timing incorrectly set

(c) Detonation with correct fuel

1 Centrifugal advance mechanism defective
2 Vacuum advance mechanism defective
3 Vacuum pipe blocked
4 Excessively weak mixture

NOTES

CHAPTER 4

COOLING AND HEATING

THE COOLING SYSTEM

4:1 Description

The engine is cooled by the circulation of air from a specially designed blower or impeller attached to and driven by the pulley hub on the crankshaft. The engine cylinders are finned to increase the area of cooling surface and the air is directed to the engine by cowling. Further cooling is provided by the external oil cooler over which the air propelled by the impeller passes. The air flow is also directed through separate ducting and heating arrangements to provide warm air to the interior of the car as required and as described later.

FIG 4:1 shows diagrammatically the cooling air circulation. Ambient air (A) is drawn into the front and rear eyes of the impeller. The rear entry air passes over the oil cooler fins. Air (B) delivered from the periphery of the impeller is ducted across the fins of the cylinder (C) and also across the exhaust heated fins (D) which provide the heated air (E) for the interior of the car or, when heated air is not required, is spilled (F) out of the vehicle.

4:2 Maintenance

No routine maintenance is required on the air cooling system. Depending upon operating conditions, it may be occasionally necessary to remove the cowling and clean mud, flies and other traffic debris from the impeller and from the finning of the cylinders and the heat exchanger. This should not be required at other than fairly long mileage intervals.

4:3 The impeller

The purpose of the impeller is to force cooling air over the cylinder fins. To provide an efficient flow and to direct the air, the cylinders are enclosed in cowlings. As a secondary purpose, the impeller also provides pressure air to the car's heating system which is covered later.

The impeller (see **FIG 4:2**) is attached to the impeller and generator drive pulley hub by three self-locking nuts and, through this assembly, is driven by the crankshaft. The impeller and the drive assembly are also included in **FIG 1:2**.

Removing the impeller:

1 Remove the bumper and grille as described in **Chapter 12, Sections 12:3** and **12:4**. In the case of DAF 44 and 46 models, remove the bonnet as described in **Chapter 12, Section 12:2**. The rear hinged bonnet of the DAF 31, 32 and 33 models should be left in position.

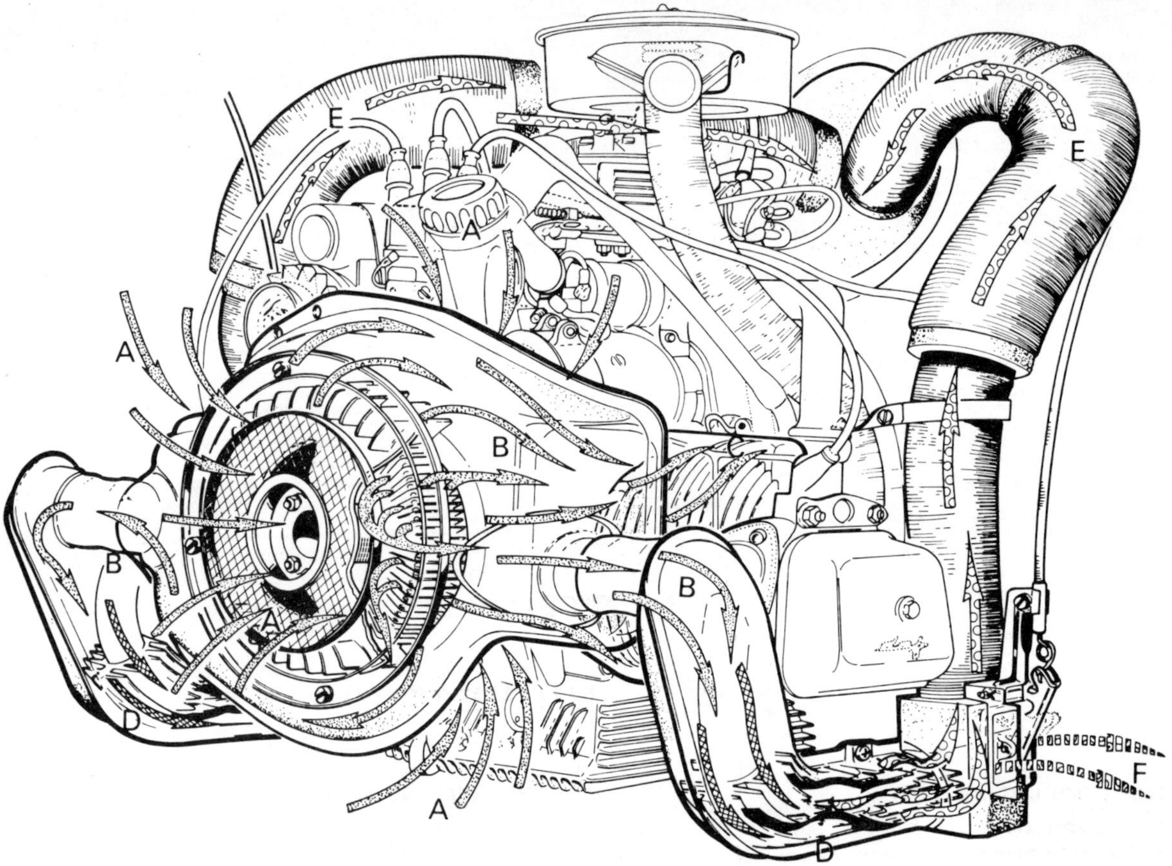

FIG 4:1 Cooling and heating flow diagram

Key to Fig 4:1 A Ambient air B Pressure air C Air flow over cylinder fins D Air flow over heat exchanger fins E Warm air to interior of vehicle F Warm air spilled to ambient when not required for heater system

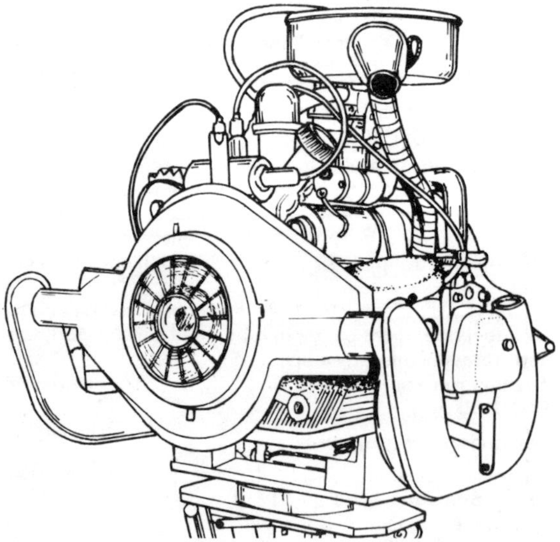

FIG 4:2 A view of the engine showing the impeller and screen

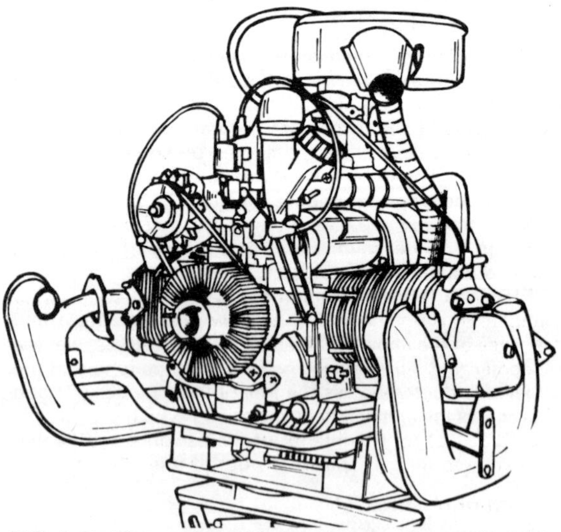

FIG 4:3 The engine with the impeller removed, showing the three retaining studs

2 Remove the impeller shroud screen. It is not necessary to remove the impeller shroud or other cowlings.

3 Remove and discard the three self-locking nuts which attach the impeller to its hub. Dismount the impeller (see **FIG 4:3**) and collect the shims which are fitted between it and the hub.

Refitting the impeller:

This is the reverse of the removal sequence. Check that the impeller does not foul the shroud. The axial position of the impeller can be adjusted by adding or removing shims. Use **new** self-locking nuts and torque tighten them to 8.7 to 10 lb ft (1.2 to 1.4 kg m).

THE HEATING SYSTEM

4:4 Description

A proportion of the air delivered by the impeller mounted at the front of the engine is forced to the interior of the car through heat exchanger ducts at each side of the engine, where the air is heated as it flows over the finned sections of the jacketed exhaust pipes shown in the

FIG 4:4 Heating and ventilation controls, DAF 44 and 46

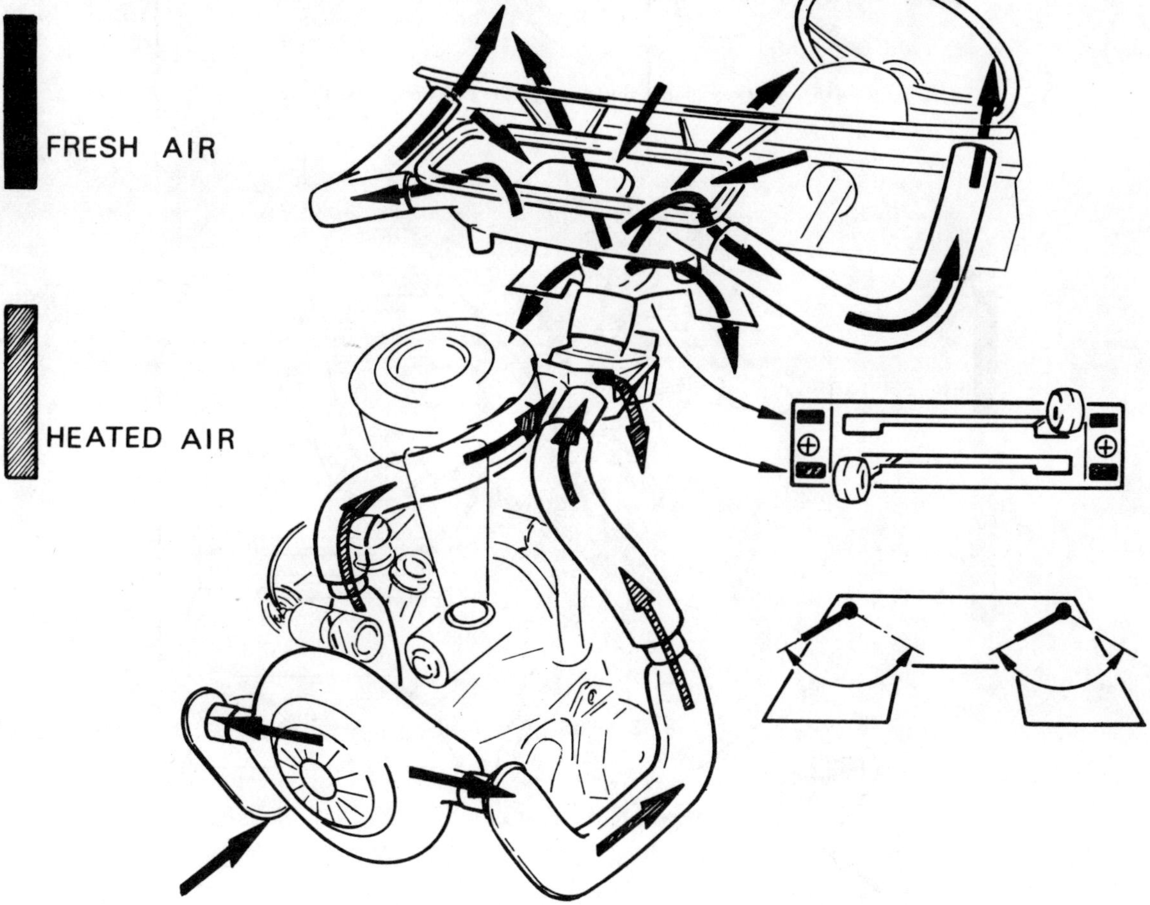

FIG 4:5 Air flow diagram with controls positioned as shown

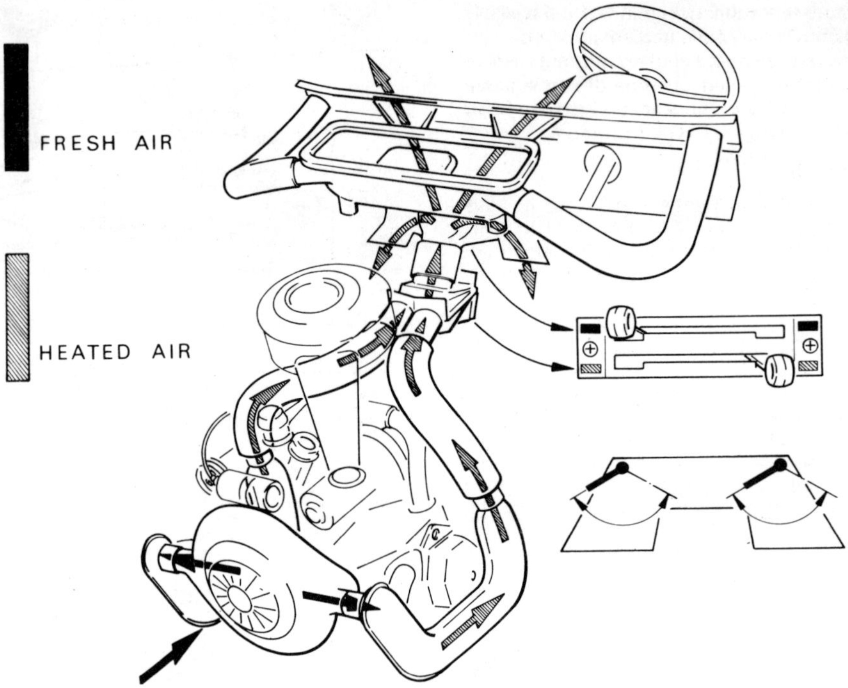

FIG 4:6 Air flow diagram with controls positioned as shown

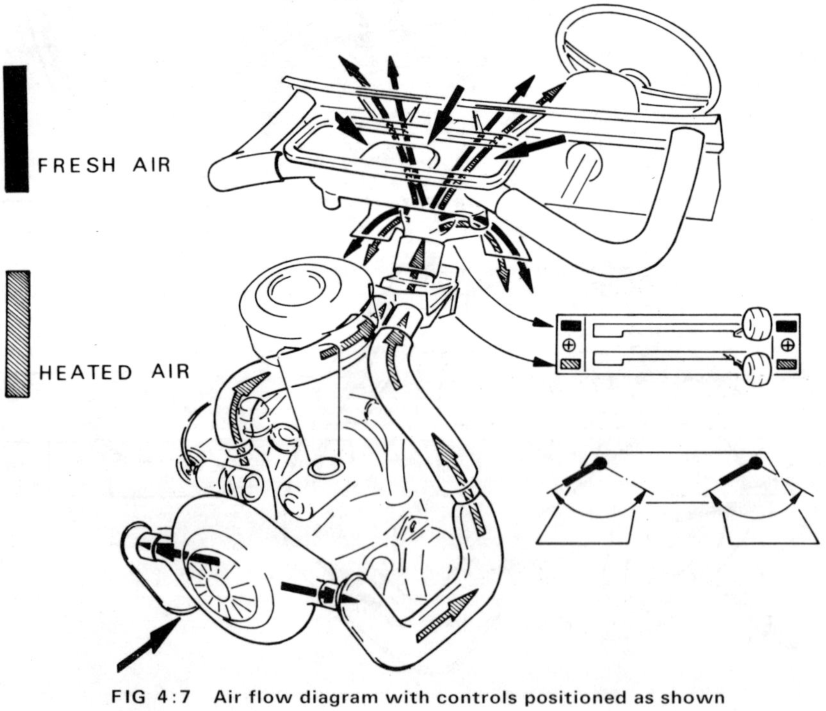

FIG 4:7 Air flow diagram with controls positioned as shown

cutaway section of a heat exchanger included in **FIG 1:1**. The general direction of flow of the heated air is shown in **FIG 4:1** in relation to the engine cooling airflow. Heated air when not required is spilled overboard at the valve boxes which are integral with the heat exchangers on DAF 31, 32 and 33 models (see **FIGS 1:1** and **4:1**) or at a separate valve box on DAF 44 and 46 models as shown in **FIG 4:5**.

Control levers for the adjustment of heating and ventilation are provided in a panel in the centre of the dashboard (see **FIG 4:4**). DAF 31 models (except for the LE model) have one dashboard lever, which is in effect a heat on/off control which operates the spillbox valve. Two levers are provided on all other models. The heater control is the lower lever, which when moved from left to right provides a warm air flow into the interior (see **FIGS 4:5**, **4:6** and **4:7**). The warm air can be directed on to the windscreen or into the interior, as desired, by means of the two levers on the distribution chamber (see **FIG 4:8**) under the dashboard. When these levers are moved to the lowest position all the warm air flows into the interior of the car, while in the uppermost position the air is directed on to the windscreen. The second (upper) lever in the centre of the dashboard is for ventilation. Fresh air is introduced into the car by moving this lever from left to right. The air flow can be divided between interior and windscreen as required by means of the two levers on the distributor chamber.

On DAF 44 cars there is a swivelling air vent (see **FIG 4:9**) at either end of the dashboard. These vents can be adjusted both horizontally and vertically, enabling fresh air to be directed on to the side windows and the corners of the windscreen. The window can thus be demisted in a minimum of time. When fresh air is introduced for ventilation the air vents can be used to help to direct the air into the interior of the car.

4:5 Operating adjustments

An exploded view of the heating and fresh air distribution system is shown in **FIG 4:10**. The dashboard control levers operate the spillbox valve and the fresh air valve (if fitted) through Bowden type flexible cables. Renewal or adjustment of the cables may be required to ensure that a valve is fully open or fully closed when its dashboard lever is in the appropriate fully left or fully right position.

Operating cable renewal:

Referring to **FIG 4:11**, disconnect the cable A at the fresh air valve in the valve duct of the drain trough, remove the control panel attaching screws and lift out the panel. Disconnect the cable at the brake vacuum valve and remove the cables from the heat control lever (see **FIG 4:12**).

Disconnect both ends of the relevant cable inner wire by loosening the screws and withdrawing the wire from the swivels. Remove the nut or clip which retains the cable outer casing at both ends. Release the cable support clips and withdraw the cable assembly.

Fitment is the reverse of this sequence. Adjust the control as described in the next paragraph.

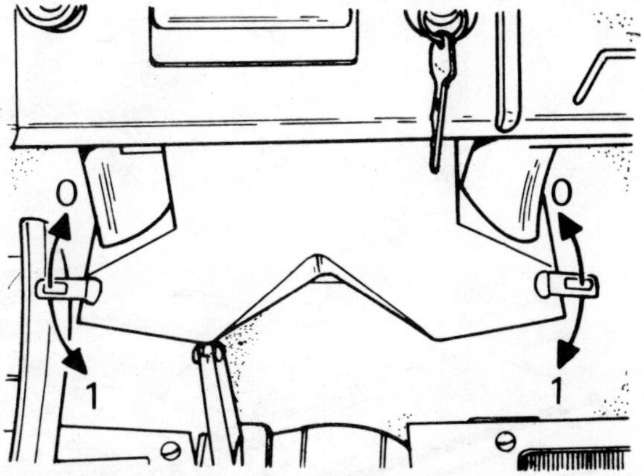

FIG 4:8 Distribution chamber and controls

Operating cable adjustment:

With the heater dashboard control lever at the righthand end of its travel (heat on), loosen the screw which clamps the cable inner wire to the spillbox valve lever and set the lever so that the valve is in the 'no spill' position. Tighten the cable wire clamp screw. Tension the cable outer casing if necessary.

The ventilation control (upper lever if fitted) is adjusted similarly.

4:6 Fault diagnosis

(a) Corrosion

1 Cooling air polluted (e.g. by salt)

(b) Overheating

1 Impeller shroud screen blanked off (e.g. by leaves, paper, etc.)
2 Debris in cylinder barrel or head fins
3 Faulty ignition timing
4 Tight engine
5 Choked exhaust system
6 Excessively weak mixture
7 Binding brakes

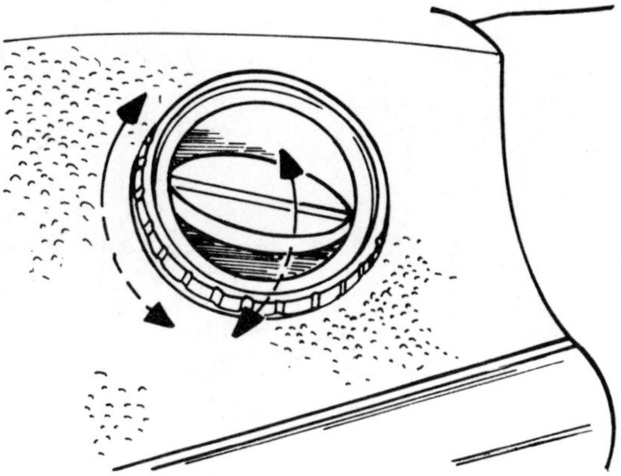
FIG 4:9 Swivelling air vent, DAF 44

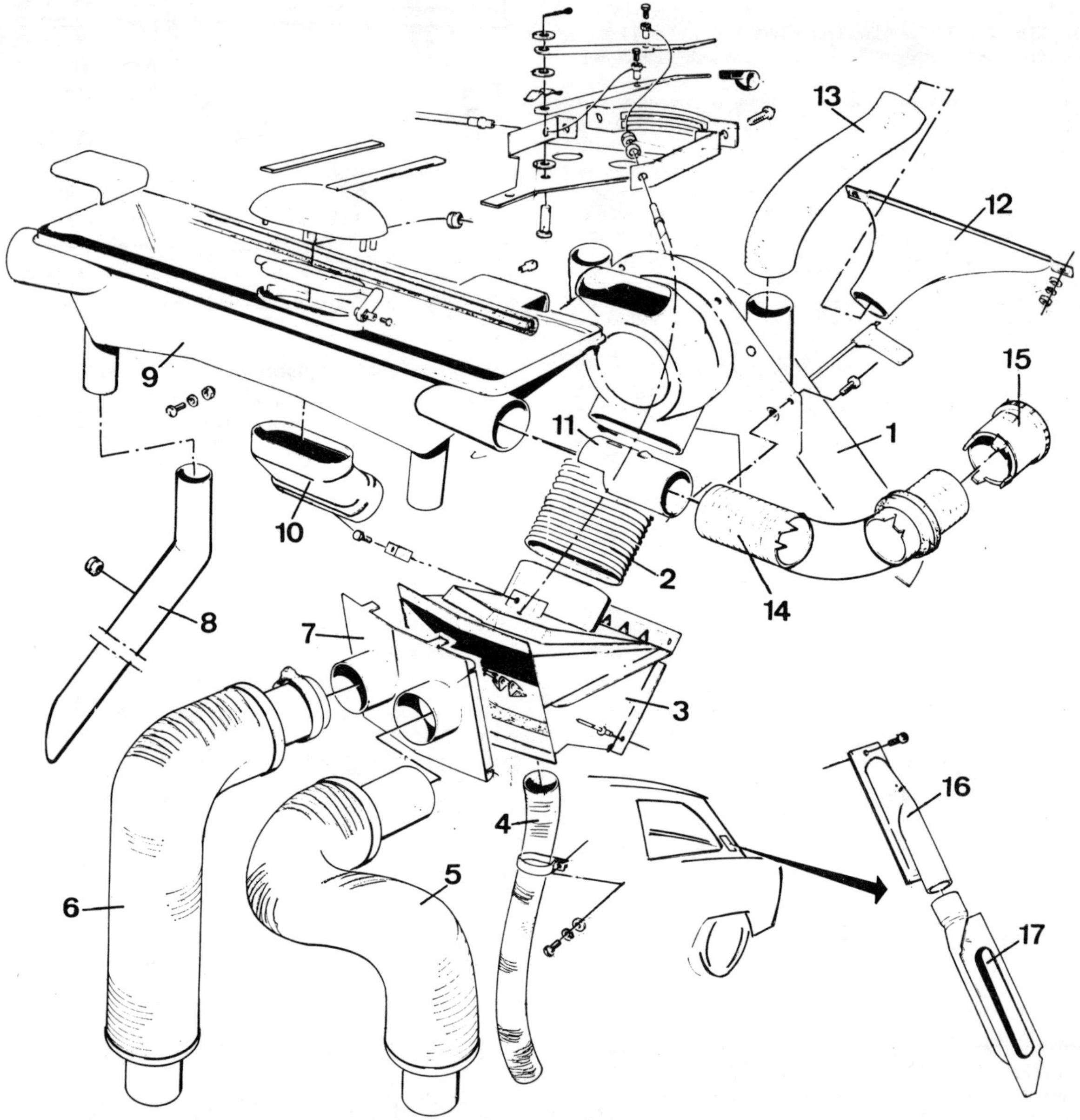

FIG 4:10 An exploded view of the heating and ventilation connections, DAF 44

Key to Fig 4:10 1 Distribution chamber 2 Flexible duct 3 Spillbox 4 Flexible pipe 5 and 6 Flexible duct (hot air) 7 Spillbox front cover 8 Drain pipe 9 Trough 10 Fresh air duct 11 Joint pipe 12 Nozzle 13 and 14 Flexible duct 15 Swivelling vent 16 and 17 Rear vent

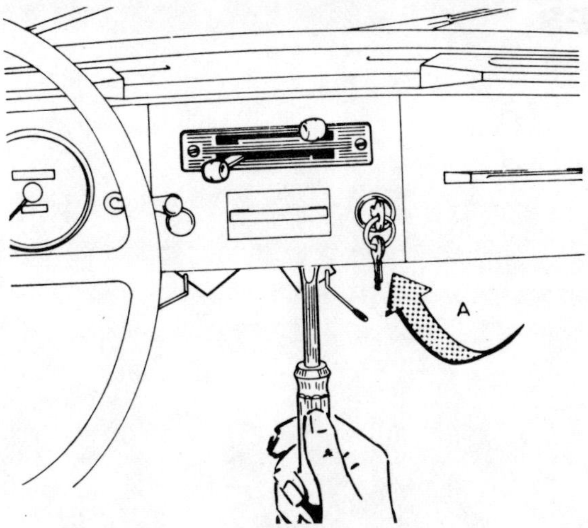

FIG 4:11 Removing the control panel

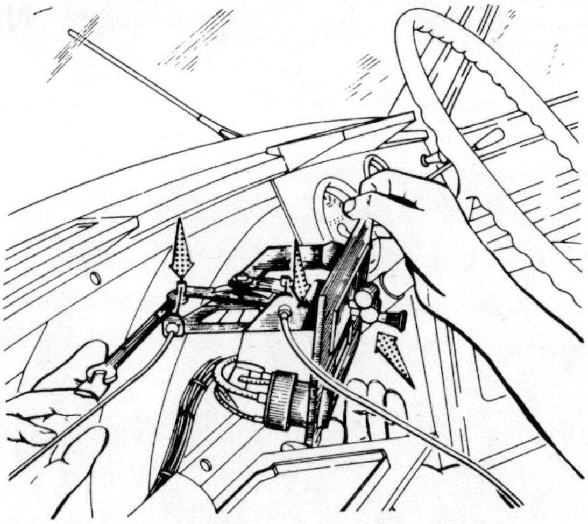

FIG 4:12 Withdrawing the lever assembly

NOTES

CHAPTER 5

THE CLUTCH

5:1 Description

The centrifugal clutch is completely automatic and does not require any action on the part of the driver of the vehicle.

FIG 5:1 shows cross-sections through the three variants of design of clutches which are fitted to models covered by this manual. The upper cross-sections show the design which is applicable to earlier DAF 31, 32 and 33 models. The forward end of the clutch shaft is piloted in a plain bearing in the end of the crankshaft. The clutch shoes each have a radially disposed pull-off spring. The central cross-sections show the design which is applicable to later DAF 31, 32 and 33 models and to earlier DAF 44 models. The forward end of the clutch shaft is piloted in a ballbearing in the hub of the flywheel. The clutch shoes each have a radially disposed pull-off spring as in the earlier design. The bottom cross-sections illustrate the basic design of the clutch which is fitted to later DAF 44 and 46 models. The clutch shaft is again piloted in a ballbearing in the hub of the flywheel but the clutch shoes have cross-connected pull-off springs and each of the four springs serves to retract two shoes.

Operation:

As engine speed is increased, the shoes pivot outwards under the influence of centrifugal force and the friction linings on the shoes engage the internal diameter of the clutch drum and progressively cause it to rotate. The drum then drives the clutch shaft and transmits engine torque via a propeller shaft to the Variomatic transmission. Reference to **FIG 5:1** will show that four of the clutch shoes are, in relation to the direction of rotation of the flywheel, trailing (these are the primary shoes) and four are leading (these are the secondary shoes). The illustrations also show that the trailing primary shoes either have weaker (longer) radial springs or on the later design, that the cross-connected springs engage the trailing shoes closer to their pivot points and thus exert less pull-off moment than the other ends of the springs exert on the leading shoes with which they are cross-connected. This arrangement of two strengths of springs in the earlier design or two magnitudes of moment in the later design results in two stages of clutch engagement and disengagement.

The primary shoes on vehicles without exhaust emission control begin to engage at between 800 to 1000 rev/min. The secondary shoes, having to overcome either stronger springs or greater spring moment, begin to engage later than the primary shoes. Engagement of secondary shoes occurs at an engine speed of between 1900 and 2200 rev/min.

On vehicles with exhaust emission control the clutch begins to engage between 975 and 1175 rev/min and is fully engaged between 2100 and 2300 rev/min.

As the vehicle slows down, the centrifugal effect gradually reduces until the centrifugal force on first the

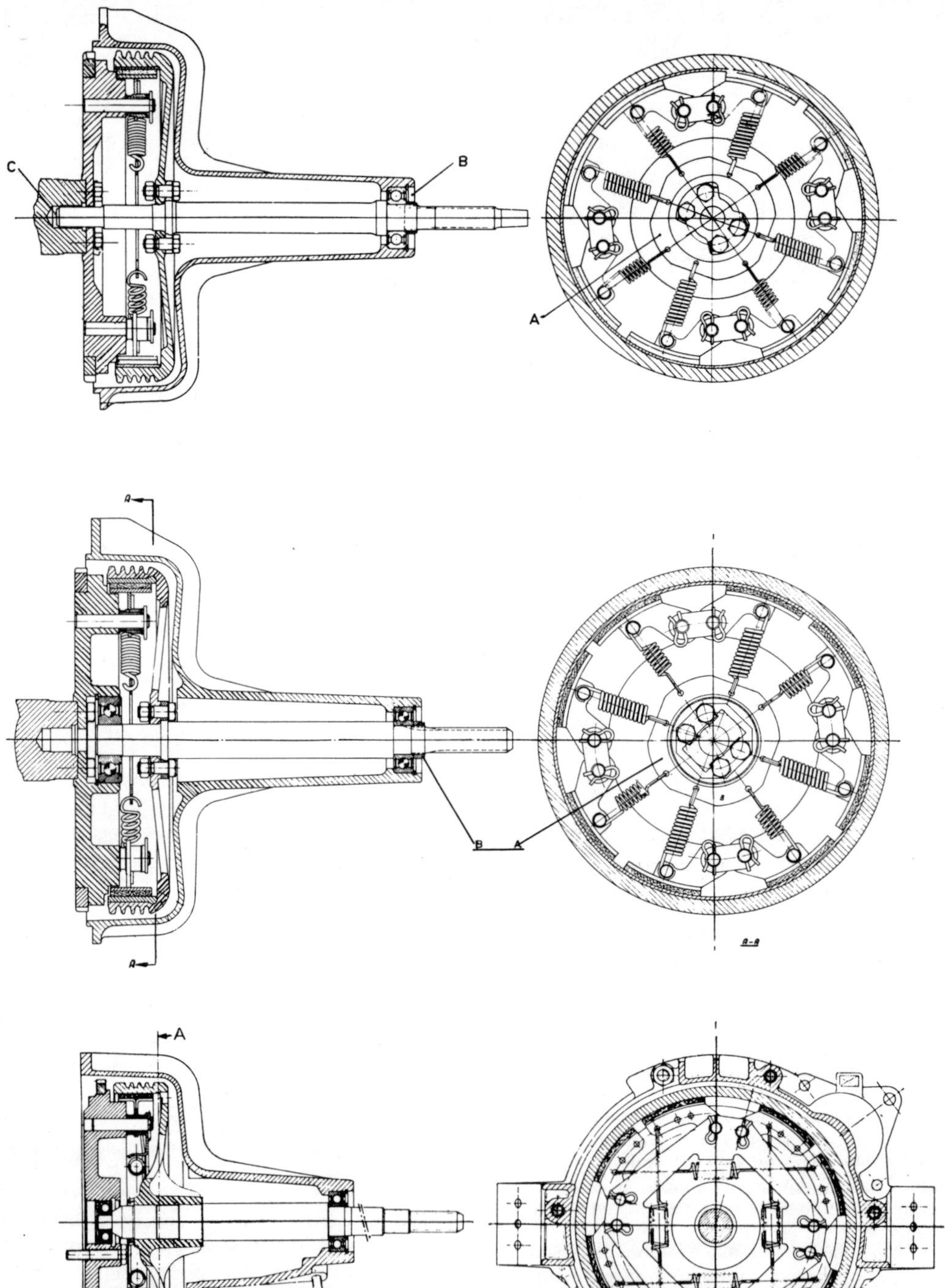

FIG 5:1 Variations in clutch design which are referred to in the text

Key to Fig 5:1 A Anchor plate B Clutch housing bearing C Space behind plain pilot bearing secondary and then the primary shoes, can no longer oppose the pull-off spring load and the clutch disengages in two stages.

Maintenance:

The clutch requires no routine maintenance.

5:2 Removing the clutch

Although the operations are not identical for all clutches, the following procedure is applicable to all models and, where relevant differences occur, the appropriate reference is given.

1 Remove the engine as described in **Chapter 1, Section 1:4**.

2 Refer to **FIG 5:2** and remove the heat exchanger cross-brace.

3 Remove the nuts and bolts which attach the clutch housing to the engine and withdraw the clutch housing assembly. It will be necessary in obstinate cases to use special tool 3-99-535640 together with a slide hammer to perform this operation. **FIG 5:3** shows this tool in use on a later model clutch housing assembly.

4 The clutch shoes are carried on the flywheel and it will normally be acceptable to service these and the associated components without removing the flywheel. If, however, it is required to remove the flywheel, refer to **Chapter 1, Section 1:13**.

5:3 Servicing the clutch

Remove the clutch housing as described in **Section 5:2**.

Dismantling and reassembling radial spring clutches:

Identify the positions of the long and short springs on the anchor plate and note that, as shown in **FIGS 1:10** and **1:33**, the long springs hook inwards and the short springs hook outwards. Note also that the long springs are fitted to the trailing shoes and the short springs to the leading shoes.

Extract the eight spring clips, remove the four bridge plates, note the position of the pivot post outer washers, ease the shoes from the pivot posts and unhook the springs from the shoes and anchor plate. Note the position of the inner washers.

Assembly is the reverse of this sequence. If clutch shoes are of different colours, **ensure that shoes of like colour are assembled opposite to each other**. Lubricate the pivot posts with Molykote paste A or Molykote 321R (spray).

Dismantling and reassembling cross-connected spring clutches:

Extract the eight spring clips and lift off the bridge plate. Note how the springs are cross-connected. In each case one end is connected close to the pivot point of a trailing shoe and its other end to the furthest point from the pivot of a leading shoe. Note the position of the pivot post outer washers. Remove the shoes and springs. Note the position of the inner washers.

Assembly is the reverse of this sequence. Lubricate the pivot posts with Molykote paste A or Molykote 321R (spray).

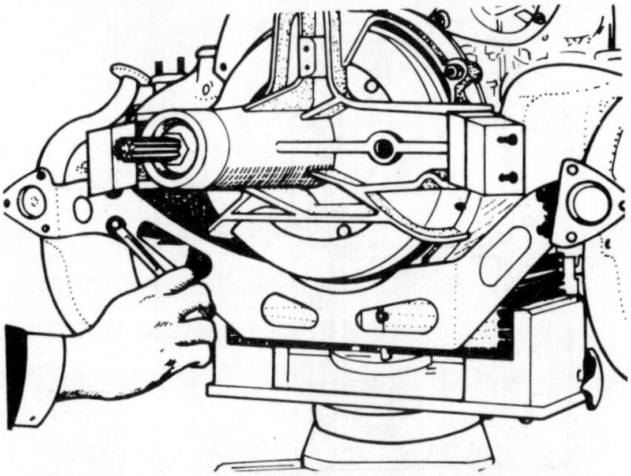

FIG 5:2 Removing the heat exchanger cross-brace

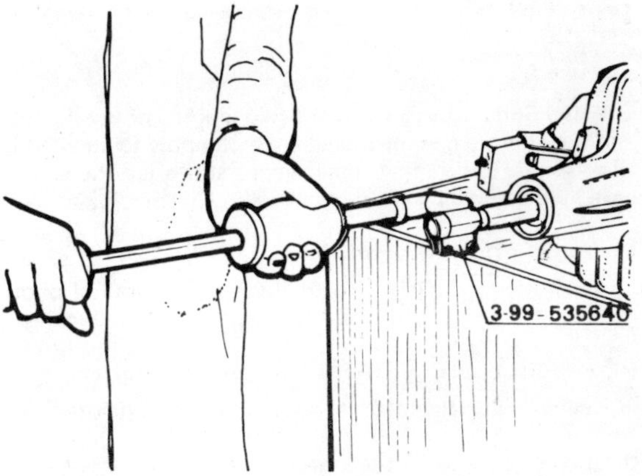

FIG 5:3 Using the special tool to remove the clutch housing

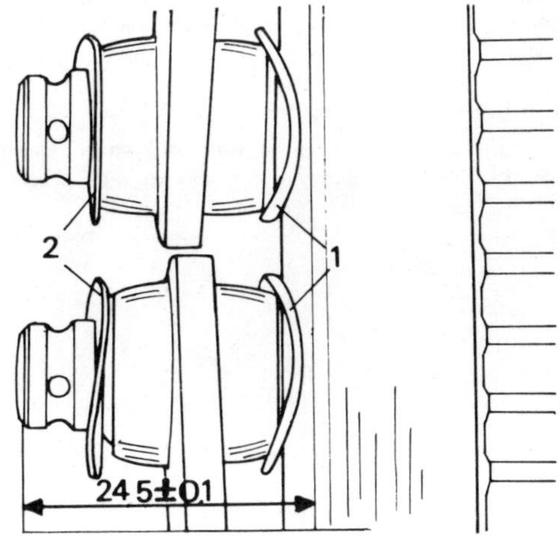

FIG 5:4 Pivot post for steel clutch shoe

Key to Fig 5:4 1 Thick spring washer 2 Thin spring washer

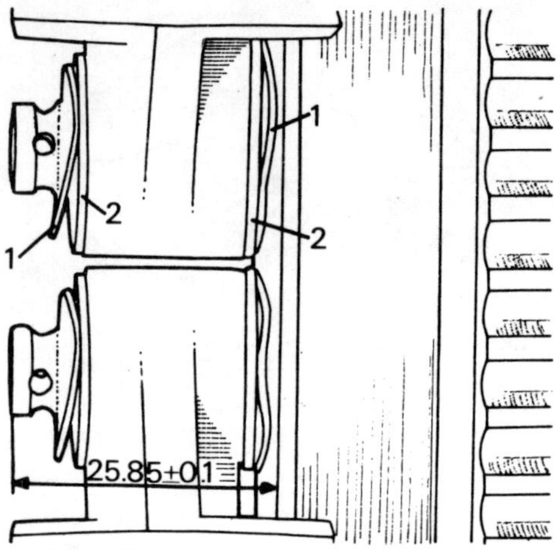

FIG 5:5 Pivot post for alloy clutch shoe

Key to Fig 5:5 1 Undulating spring washer 2 Plain washer

FIGS 5:4 and **5:5** show the two lengths of pivot post and the arrangement of washers which apply to steel and alloy shoes. Ensure that replacement shoes are the same type as those which were removed.

Clutch shaft pilot bearings:

As shown in **FIG 5:1** there are three variants of pilot bearing. Each type has a different renewal procedure.

Plain pilot bearing, DAF 31, 32 and 33 models:

Remove the flywheel as described in **Chapter 1, Section 1:13** and with a suitable extractor, withdraw the bearing. Press in the new bearing using a suitable mandrel.

Ballbearing

Refer to **Chapter 1, Section 1:13**. On this type, the ballbearing is removed as part of the flywheel removal procedure.

Clutch housing bearing:

Using a wooden block, drive the clutch shaft assembly out of the housing. Remove the circlip and press the bearing out of the housing. Use tool 3-99-535379 with extension 3-99-535387 to press in the new bearing.

Place the clutch housing in a press, support the end bearing with ring No. 3-99-535388 and press the clutch shaft into the bearing.

From chassis number 648910 the clutch shaft is fitted with a spacer and circlip which serves as a butt for the transmission shaft.

Lubricate the clutch shaft splines with Molykote BR2-S or on DAF 46 models High Taek Permatex.

5:4 Installing the clutch

This is, for each type, the reverse of the removal procedure. Fill the space behind the plain pilot bearing (C in **FIG 5:1**) with Retinax A grease.

Torque tighten the clutch housing attachment nuts and bolts to 13.5 to 15.2 lb ft (1.9 to 2.1 kg m).

5:5 Fault diagnosis

(a) Drag

1 Oil or grease on shoe linings
2 Broken lining(s)
3 Distorted drum
4 Broken or weak pull-off spring(s)
5 Idling speed too high

(b) Fierceness or snatch

1 Check 1 in (a)
2 Shoe(s) tight on pivot pins
3 Worn shoe linings

(c) Slip

1 Check 1 in (a); 2 and 3 in (b)
2 Shoe(s) seized on pivot post(s)

(d) Uneven lining wear

1 Check 4 in (a); 2 in (b); 2 in (c)
2 Excessive flywheel runout
3 Loose flywheel
4 Worn pilot bearing
5 Bent clutch shaft
6 Pull-off springs wrongly connected

(e) Rattle

1 Check 4 in (a); 4 and 5 in (d)

CHAPTER 6

THE DRIVE UNIT

6:1 Description

Since the Variomatic drive unit is not an independent 'gearbox' but operates with mating features in the rear axle, it will be found useful to read this description in conjunction with that of the rear axle given in **Chapter 7** in addition to **FIG 6:1** which shows a horizontal and vertical cross-section through a DAF 31A Variomatic drive unit and rear axle. Although earlier and later DAF 31 model transmissions and DAF 44 model transmissions differ dimensionally and in detail design, the cross-sections illustrated in **FIG 6:1** are representative of the transmissions fitted to twin belt models. The transmission fitted to the DAF 46 is a single belt system but the units used are similar to the units previously used on earlier models.

The Variomatic transmission is a variable ratio automatic belt drive in which the ratio of drive can vary between an approximate 2:1 reduction to a 1:2 step-up. Inclusive of the bevel gearing in the drive unit and the reduction gearing in the rear axle, the overall transmission ratio is variable between approximately 16:1 and 4:1 in the case of DAF 31, 32 and 33 models, or 12.3:1 and 3.1:1 in the case of later models.

The drive unit and the rear axle are each provided with two sets of conical pulley discs on all models except the DAF 46 and belts of trapezial cross-section (the flank angles match the conical angles of the pulley discs) are driven by the drive unit pulley discs and drive the rear axle pulley discs. In each set one of the pulley discs can move axially on its shaft in relation to the other pulley disc and, in consequence of this, the diameters at which the belt is driven by the drive unit and drives the rear axle can vary. The ratio of the drive and driven diameters is the 'gear' ratio of the belt drive at that point.

The DAF 46 single belt system is basically similar in operation to previous models.

The sliding pulley discs in the rear axle units are spring loaded towards its fixed counterpart. The diameter at which the belts drive the rear axle units is dictated by the position of the belts on the drive unit pulley discs. The greater the 'pull' on the belts, the smaller will the diameter be at which the rear axle units will operate since the 'pull' of the belts forces the pulley discs apart against the spring load. The position of each of the drive unit sliding pulley discs is dictated by a combination of the force exerted by centrifugal weights and the pressures across the diaphragm in the drive unit drums. The higher the engine speed, the greater will be the centrifugal load on the sliding pulley discs and the closer together (and therefore the larger the diameter of belt operation) they

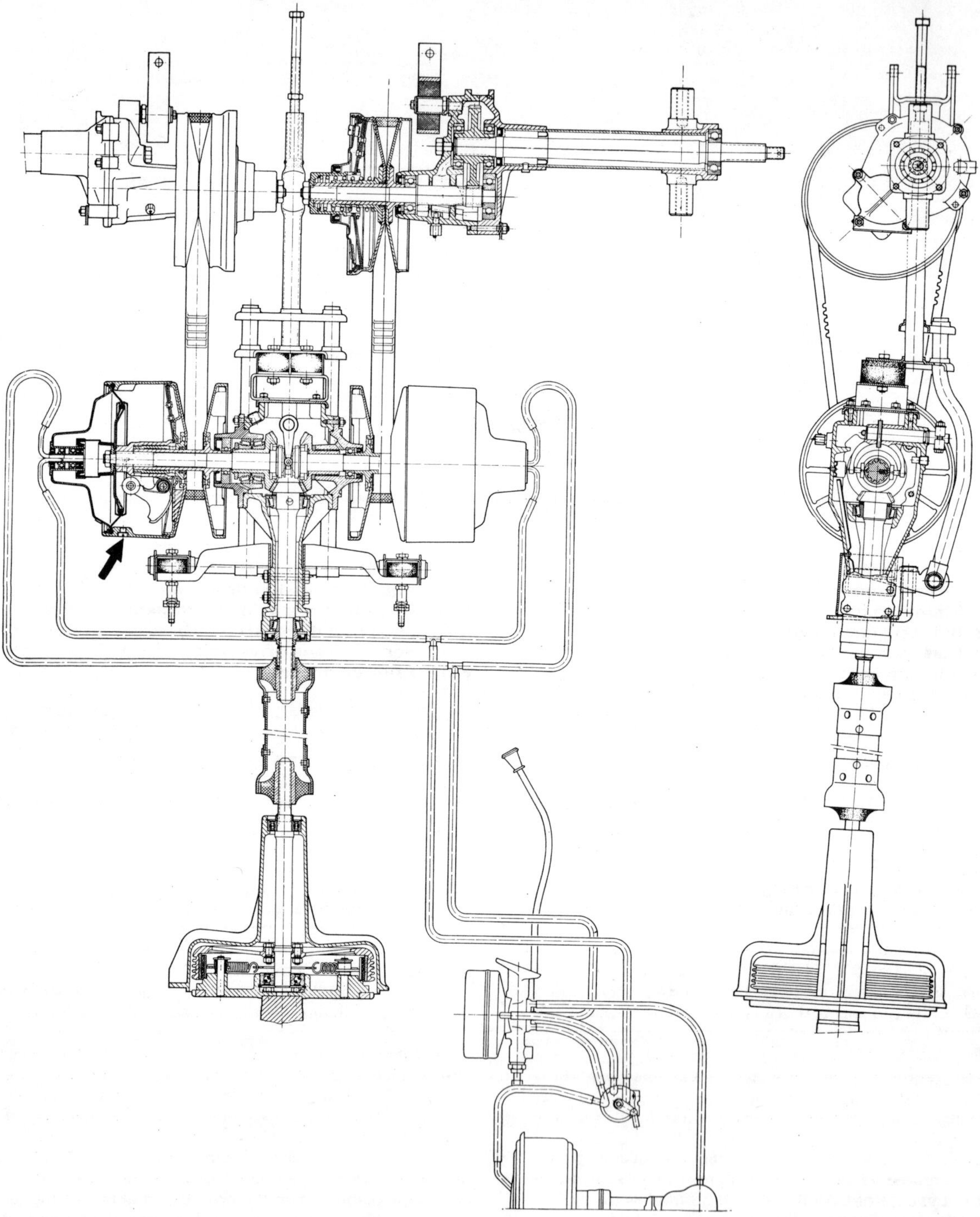

FIG 6:1 Cross-sections through a DAF type 31A Variomatic transmission. The arrow is referred to in the text

will come. The differential pressure across the diaphragm results in a load which may, depending upon available engine power and drive requirements, either act with or against the centrifugal load on the sliding discs. The vacuum control system units which admit vacuum or ambient pressure to either side of the diaphragm are described later.

As the drive unit pulley discs come closer together, the rear axle pulley discs are forced further apart and the drive ratio changes from reduction to step-up. As either a reduction in engine speed or the vacuum control system allows the drive unit pulley discs to separate, the rear axle pulley discs will, under spring load, come closer together and the drive ratio will change from step-up to reduction. When the vehicle is stationary, the drive unit drive diameter will be at a minimum (discs fully apart with neither centrifugal nor differential pressure load acting to bring them together) and the rear axle driven diameter will be at a maximum (pulley discs together under spring load and no 'pull' on the belts forcing them apart). **FIG 6:1** illustrates this condition.

Since each set of drive unit pulley discs on twin belt drives, and also each set of rear axle pulley discs operate independently, the Variomatic transmission normally provides differential action between the rear wheels but should one wheel encounter low adhesion conditions such as mud or ice, the other wheel will drive normally as would be the case with a limited slip differential drive. It should be noted however that at very low speeds (both drives at full reduction ratio) if the steering is put on full lock, only the drive to the outer wheel can change ratio and as the drive to the inner wheel cannot decrease ratio any further, there will be a tendency to skid and it will be necessary to increase engine speed to get the vehicle moving.

On DAF 46 models differential action is built into the secondary Variomatic unit.

The input shaft bevel gear engages with a bevel gear on each half of the drive unit. Neither of these driven bevels is itself splined to the cross shaft which drives the pulley discs. Between the bevels there is a sliding dog clutch which is splined to the cross shaft. This dog clutch can be engaged with either of the driven bevels to provide forward or reverse drive or neutral if not engaging either. The Variomatic selector lever has three positions which correspond with these three positions of the dog clutch.

Vacuum control:

The system which is applicable to all DAF 31, 32 and 33 models and to DAF 44 models up to chassis No. 565049 is shown in **FIG 6:2** and is also included in **FIG 6:1**. It comprises a rotary vacuum control valve which is connected by an adjustable rod with the throttle valve lever of the carburetter and a brake vacuum valve which is either operated by brake fluid pressure or mechanically from a manual control on the dashboard. **FIG 6:3** shows the later system. Here the brake vacuum valve is electrically operated either when the stop signal switch is closed (when the brakes are applied) or when the engine braking switch on the dashboard is manually operated.

Brake vacuum valve:

To preclude possible damage to the engine and transmission, the actuation of this valve by operation of the dashboard control must not occur **if the vehicle speed is over 30 mile/hr (50 km/hr)**. When the valve is actuated by the foot brake through the stop signal switch there is, of course, no question of a speed limitation since, when the brakes are applied, the speed of the vehicle is mainly decreased by the brakes and the engine braking effect is secondary and not severe.

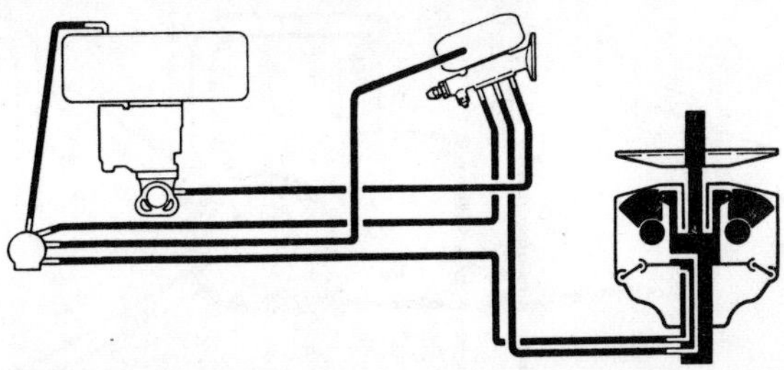

FIG 6:2 Vacuum control system, DAF 31, 32 and 33 models and 44 models up to chassis No. 565049

Variomatic drive ratio changes:

The following is a brief summary of the conditions which result in changes in the drive ratio.

The transmission changes up when:

1 A reduction in the tractive force required occurs. An example of this is when the vehicle reaches the level after climbing a gradient.
2 At an intermediate throttle range when a maximum differential pressure is 'assisting' the centrifugal weights. This may be termed an 'overdrive' condition.
3 The engine speed is increased and the road gradient conditions remain unchanged.

The transmission changes down when:

1 Acceleration increases the tractive effort required.
2 The throttle position is constant but the tractive effort required increases.
3 Full throttle is suddenly applied and differential pressure operates against the force of the centrifugal weights. This may be termed 'kick-down'.
4 The brakes are applied and the stop signal switch actuates the brake vacuum valve.
5 The brake vacuum valve is actuated by manual operation of the dashboard control. **This control must not be operated if the vehicle speed is higher than 30 mile/hr (50 km/hr).**
6 When the throttle is fully closed and engine speed decreases.

6:2 Maintenance

Drive belt tension:

Every 3000 miles (5000 km), check and adjust if necessary, the drive belt tension. The procedure is described in **Section 6:3**.

New belts stretch slightly until they are stabilized by use. After fitting new belts as described in **Section 6:4**, readjust the tension after 300 miles (500 km) and again after 1000 miles (1500 km). The tension may then be checked at 3000 mile (5000 km) intervals.

6:3 Belt tension adjustment

Belt tension is correct when the gap between the rear pulley disc hubs is a specified dimension. To allow for the fact that new belts will stretch slightly until they stabilize with use, the gap must be greater for a new belt

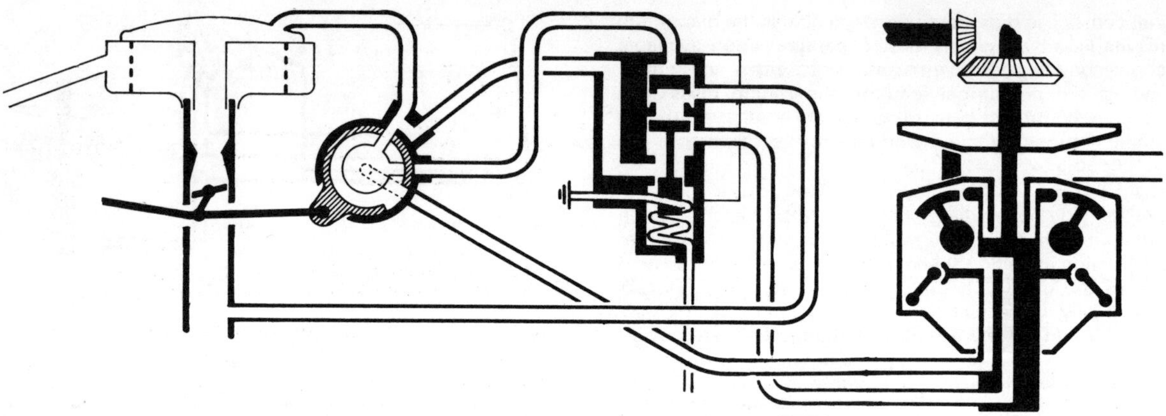

FIG 6:3 Vacuum control system, later models

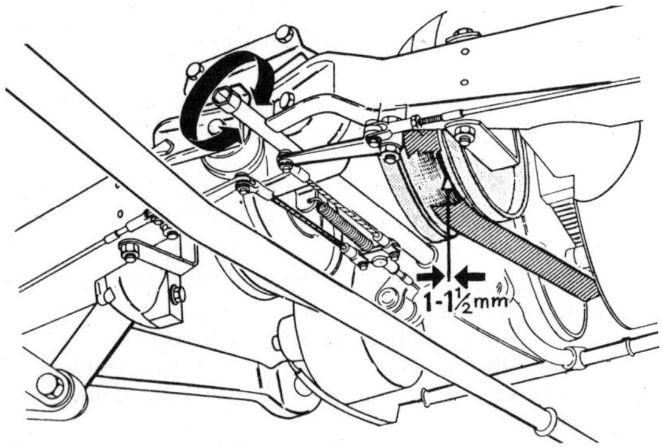

FIG 6:4 Belt tension adjustment, DAF 31, 32 and 33 models

FIG 6:6 A view of the guard pans on earlier models

FIG 6:5 Belt tension adjustment, DAF 44 models

Key to Fig 6:5 1 Handbrake cable casing locknut 2 and 3 Front mounting points 4 Rear mounting point 5 Adjustment screw and locknut LH arrow Filler plug RH arrow Drain plug

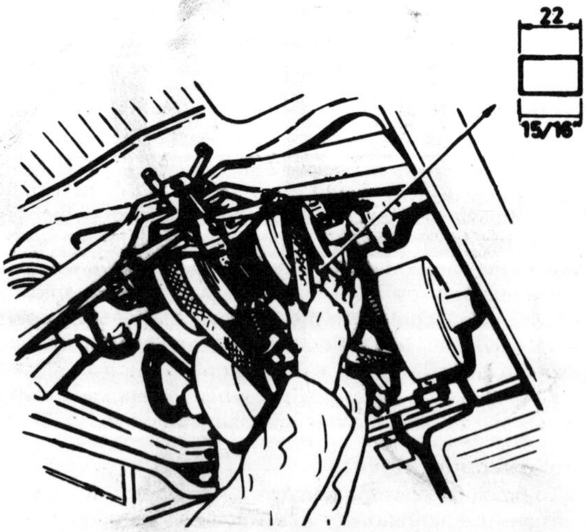

FIG 6:7 Separating the discs

than for one which has stabilized. The pulley disc gaps are increased by increased belt tension. Increase in belt tension is achieved by moving the complete Variomatic drive unit forwards (further from the rear pulley discs) and vice versa. The belt tensioning procedure is the same for all models although the gap and the method of adjustment are not identical for all models. When carrying out the procedure it is consequently necessary to refer to the information given later for different models.

Tensioning procedure:

1 Push the car by hand to and fro on level ground over a distance of about 6 or 7 ft (2 m) to settle the belts on the pulley discs. Remove the guard pans. Using feeler gauges, measure the pulley disc gap.

2 Release the drive unit locks. Release the adjusting screw locknut.

3 Adjust the gap to the dimension specified for the model which is being worked on. Repeat operation 1 and recheck the gap. **Operation 1 must be repeated after each adjustment**.

4 When the specified gap has been achieved, lock the adjusting screw locknut and tighten the drive unit locks.

DAF 31, 32 and 33 models:

Refer to **FIG 6:4**. Set the gap to 1.5 mm (.06 inch) for new belts or, for stabilized belts, to 1 mm (.04 inch). The drive unit is not provided with locks. The adjusting tube is not provided with a locknut.

DAF 44 models:

Refer to **FIG 6:5**. The minimum permissible gap is .5 mm (.02 inch). For new belts set the gap to 2 mm (.08 inch). The drive unit locks are 2, 3 and 4. The adjusting screw and its locknut is 5. Each time the belt-tensioner position is changed, the car must be moved back and forth some 7 ft (2 m) before rechecking the gap.

If during servicing the gap is found to be less than 1.5 mm (.06 inch) readjust to 2 mm (.08 inch).

DAF 46 models:

The adjustment is similar in procedure to the DAF 44 but is carried out on the secondary variomatic unit. The gap is 1.5 to 2 mm (.06 to .08 inch) and the minimum gap is .5 mm (.02 inch).

6:4 Belt removal and fitment:

Even if only one belt should break or cannot be adjusted satisfactorily, both belts must be renewed. The procedure is the same though the method of detensioning the belts is not identical for all models. Follow the procedure and refer to the illustrations and specific model information given later. The DAF 46 only has one belt but the procedure is similar.

Belt removal:

1 Position the car over a pit or on a hoist and remove the guard pans, also if necessary the exhaust pipe (see **FIG 6:6**).

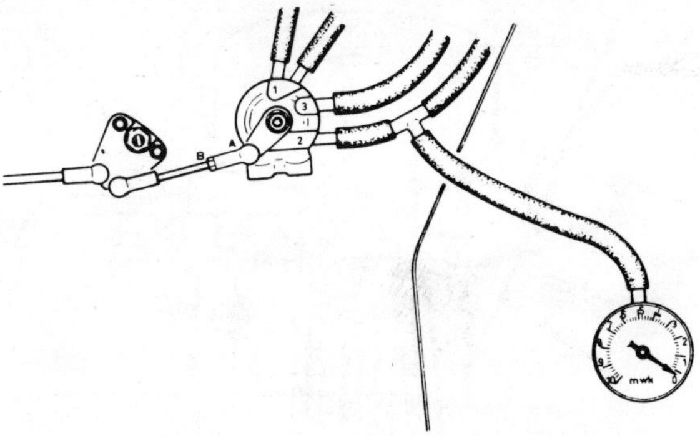

FIG 6:8 Method of adjusting the vacuum control valve, showing the ball joint A and the locknut B

2 Loosen the drive unit or secondary Variomatic locks. Loosen the locknut (if fitted) and turn the adjusting screw to fully release the tension in the belts. Disconnect the hoses from the pulley. Separate the rear pulley discs by pulling the belt down sharply (see **FIG 6:7**) or use special tool 3-99-535758 if available.

3 Insert a spacer of specified width between the hubs of the pulley discs. This prevents them from coming together again and avoids the possibility of injury to the operator.

4 Disengage the belts from the rear pulley discs. On DAF 46 models the four bolts securing the secondary Variomatic unit (see **FIG 7:46**) should be unscrewed about 1 cm (.4 inch) to give clearance for the belt to pass over the pulley, pull the belt as far as possible between the front pulley discs. Disengage the belts from the front discs.

5 Clean all pulley disc faces with a rag moistened with either petrol or acetone.

Belt fitment:

1 Engage the belts over the front pulley discs and reconnect the vacuum pipes.

2 Pull down on the belts to draw the front pulley discs apart. Engage the belts over the rear pulley discs.

3 Refit in the reverse order of removal. Tension the belts as described in **Section 6:3**. Refit the guard pans.

FIG 6:9 A view of the ball joint A and the locknut B on the vacuum control valve linkage

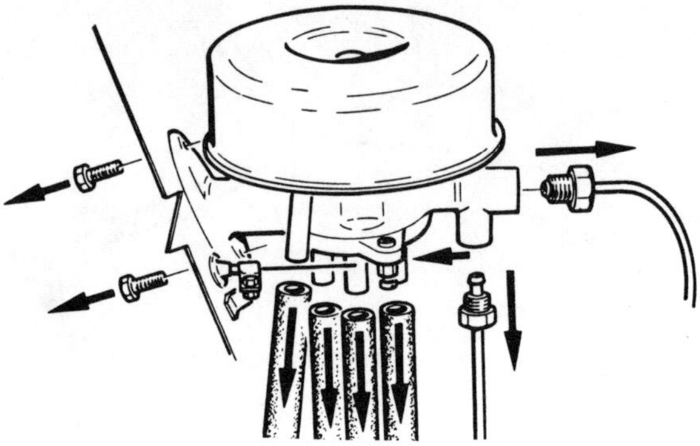

FIG 6:10 Removing the brake vacuum valve, DAF 31, 32, 33 and earlier DAF 44 models

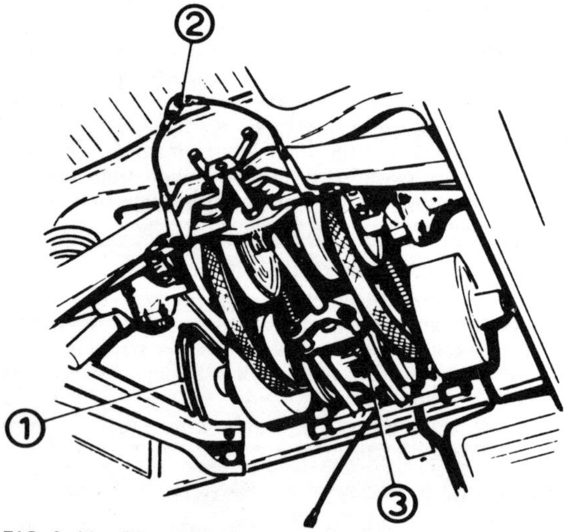

FIG 6:11 Disconnecting the vacuum pipes 1, the handbrake cable 2 and the selector rod 3

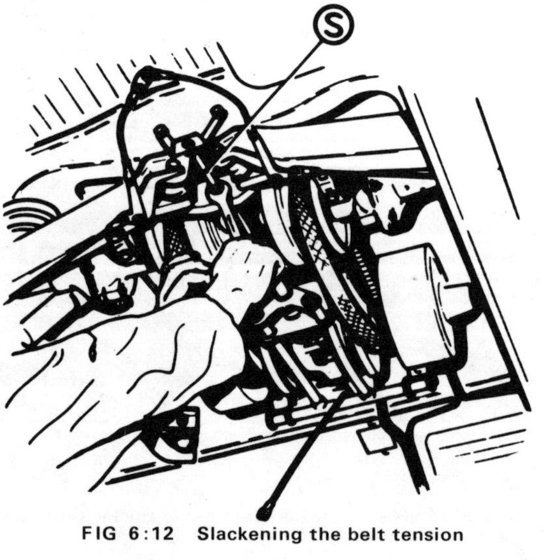

FIG 6:12 Slackening the belt tension

DAF 31, 32 and 33 models:

The drive unit is not provided with locks. The adjusting tube is not provided with a locknut. Refer to **FIG 6:4**. Use $\frac{5}{16}$ inch (22 mm) spacers between the pulley disc hubs.

DAF 44 models:

Refer to **FIG 6:5**. The drive unit locks are 2, 3 and 4. The adjusting screw and its locknut is 5. Use .08 inch (20 mm) spacers.

DAF 46 models:

Procedure is similar to DAF 44 models but is carried out on the secondary Variomatic unit.

6:5 Vacuum control valve

This section is relevant to DAF 31, 32, 33 and 44 models. The linkage between the vacuum control valve and the carburetter must always be adjusted as described later if the throttle linkage has been disconnected or adjusted or if the vacuum control valve has been removed and refitted.

Adjustment:

FIG 6:8 illustrates a DAF 31, 32 and 33 installation but the following procedure also applies to DAF 44 models.

Adjust the engine to the correct idling speed as described in **Chapter 2**, **Section 2:5** or **Section 2:6**. Connect a vacuum gauge as shown in **FIG 6:8** in the line between the control valve and the Variomatic transmission.

The valve setting is correct when, while maintaining a constant engine speed corresponding to 9 to 15 mile/hr (15 to 25 km/hr) with minimum throttle opening, the vacuum gauge just begins to register vacuum. Upon fully releasing or fully depressing the accelerator pedal, the gauge should not indicate any vacuum.

Adjustment, which should not be effected other than at this ball joint, is made by running the engine at 3000 ± 50 rev/min, loosening locknut B (see **FIG 6:9**) and turning the ball joint A after uncoupling it from the valve lever. **Do not remove the lever from the control valve.** Vacuum is applied earlier if the ball joint is unscrewed (lengthening the linkage) and vice versa. Tighten the locknut on completion.

A comparative road speed of 9 mile/hr (15 km/hr) should be taken as the lowest limit at which the gauge may indicate vacuum.

The vacuum control valve setting must always be checked with a vacuum gauge after any disturbance of the throttle linkage.

Removal:

Uncouple the ball joint A in **FIG 6:8** from the control valve lever. Identify and disconnect the pipes. Remove the attaching bolts and dismount the unit.

Refitment:

Refitment is the reverse of the removal sequence and must be followed by adjusting the linkage as described earlier.

6:6 Brake vacuum valve

This Section is only relevant to DAF 31, 32, 33 and earlier 44 models.

Adjustment:

With the dashboard control pushed fully in, the brake valve quadrant must be fully forward with slight slack in the cable. If necessary, loosen the cable attachment at the quadrant, adjust the cable and retighten the attachment.

Removal:

Refer to **FIG 6:10**. Loosen the control cable attachment at the quadrant and disconnect the cable. Identify and disconnect the four transmission pipes and the two brake lines. From the opposite side of the scuttle, remove two attaching bolts and dismount the unit.

Refitment:

This is the reverse of the removal sequence. Adjust the control cable as described earlier. Bleed the brakes hydraulic system as described in **Chapter 10, Section 10:7**.

6:7 Changing fluid in drive unit

Access to the unit requires removal of the relevant guard pans.

The power divider:

The drain and fluid level plugs on a DAF 44 model are shown arrowed in **FIG 6:5**. Other models have plugs which are similarly positioned.

Remove both plugs and allow the unit to drain. Refit the drain plug and use a syringe to inject the specified quantity of recommended fluid. Note that if the power divider is completely dry after an overhaul, the specified quantity of fluid required is slightly greater than for a refill after draining. Torque tighten the plugs to 30 lb ft (4.2 kg m).

Power divider fluid type and quantities:

Use 425 cc (.75 pint) of ATF type A/A in a 'dry' unit of DAF 31, 32 and 33 models and 400 cc (.7 pint) of the same fluid for a refill. In DAF 44 and 46 models use 475 cc (.84 pint) for initial filling and 430 cc (.76 pint) for a refill.

Pulley disc assemblies:

Use ATF type A/A in all models. Lubrication during overhaul is covered in **Section 6:10**. To refill after draining, 100 cc (.18 pint) is required for each side. The quantity is the same for all models.

The drain plug on DAF 31, 32 and 33 models is shown arrowed in **FIG 6:1**. It must be at the bottom for draining and, by moving the car, raised for filling.

6:8 Drive unit removal and fitment

DAF 31, 32 and 33 models, removal:

1 Position the vehicle on a hoist or over a pit. Remove the exhaust pipe and the guard pans (see **FIG 6:6**).

FIG 6:13 Removing the support bracket 1

FIG 6:14 Lowering the drive unit to rest in the belts

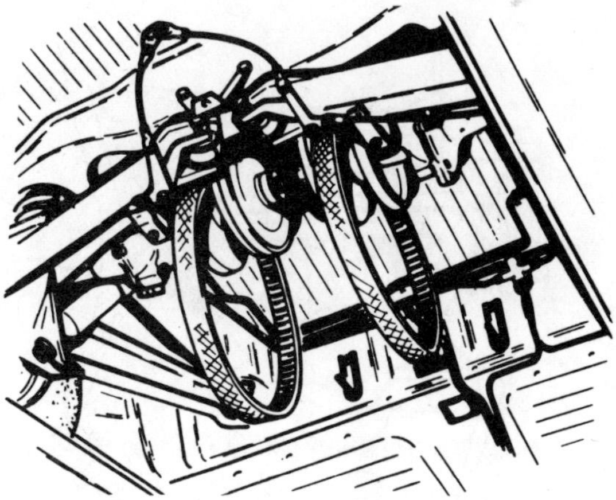

FIG 6:15 The drive unit removed

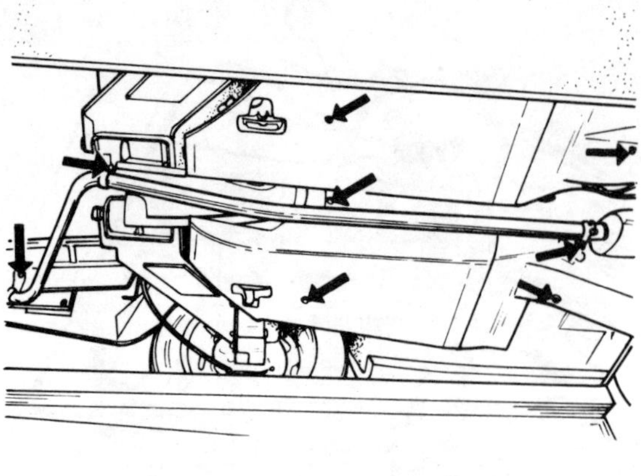

FIG 6:16 Removing the main guard pans early models

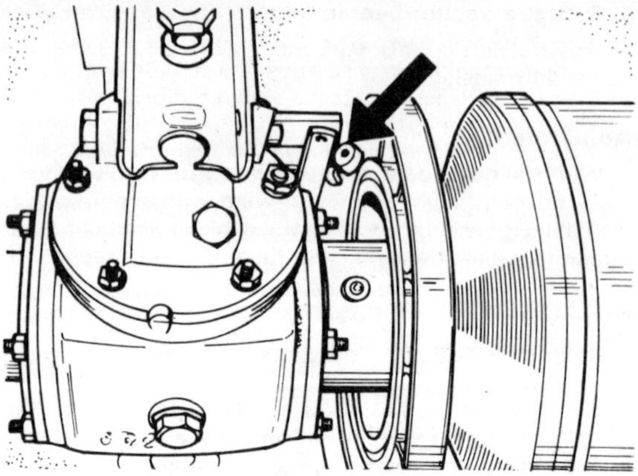

FIG 6:19 The selector rod at the drive unit lever

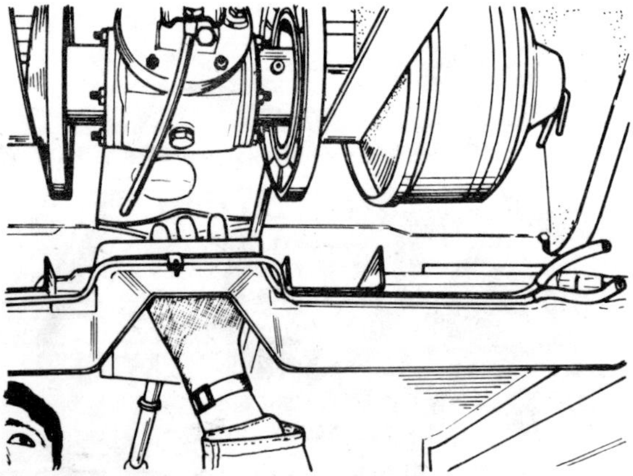

FIG 6:17 Removing the forward guard pan

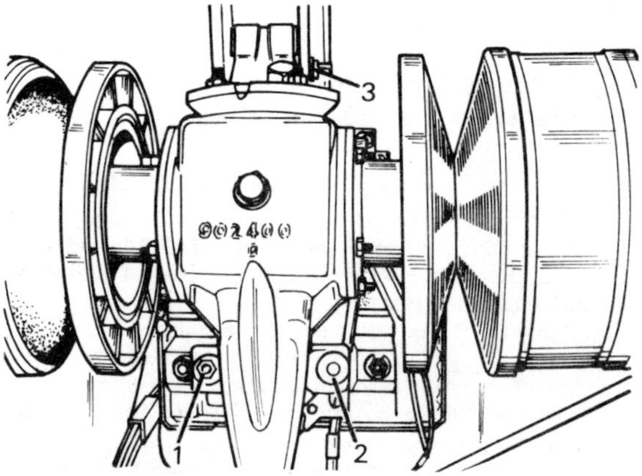

FIG 6:20 The drive unit retaining nuts 1, 2 and 3 early models

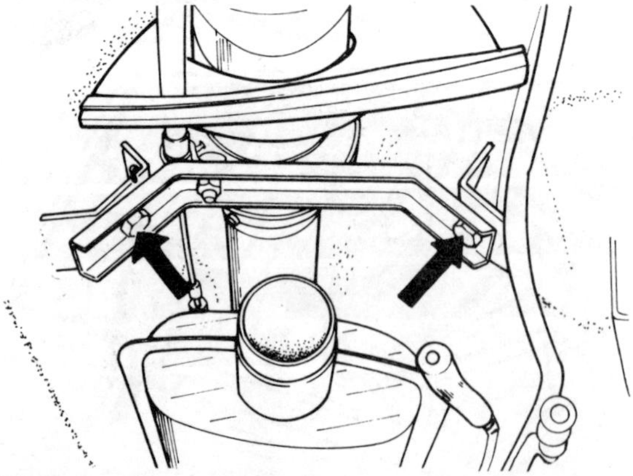

FIG 6:18 Tunnel brace retaining nuts shown arrowed

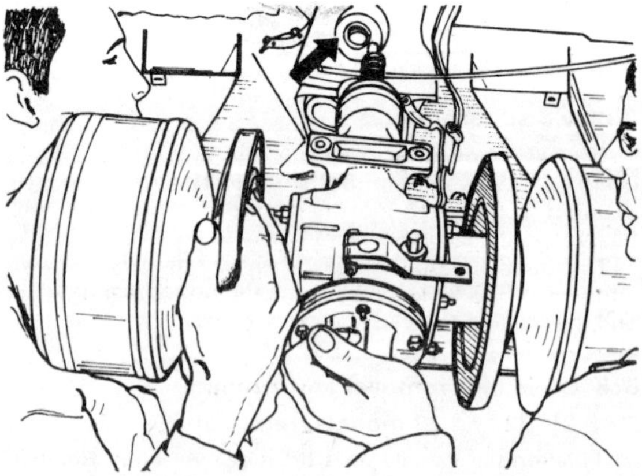

FIG 6:21 Lifting out the drive unit

2 Pull down on the belts to separate the rear pulley discs (see **FIG 6:7**) and insert $\frac{15}{16}$ inch (22 mm) spacers between the pulley disc hubs to keep them apart.
3 Identify and disconnect the vacuum pipes 1 (see **FIG 6:11**) from the drive unit. Disconnect the handbrake cable 2 at the equalizer and the Variomatic selector rod 3 at the drive unit lever.
4 Refer to **Section 6:3** and slacken off the belt tension (see **FIG 6:12**) by a few turns. Remove the nuts attaching the support bracket (see **FIG 6:13**), tap the bolts back and remove the support bracket and access plate.
5 Hold the propeller shaft while pulling the drive unit rearwards. Lower the drive unit and let it rest in the belts (see **FIG 6:14**). Lift the unit out of the belts (see **FIG 6:15**).

DAF 44 models, removal:

1 Position the car on a hoist or over a pit. Remove the exhaust pipe and the main guard pans (see **FIG 6:16**), later models have the centre three screws and two at each side.
2 Identify and disconnect the vacuum pipes from the drive unit and the connecting lines. Remove the forward guard pan (see **FIG 6:17**).
3 Disconnect the handbrake cable at the equaliser. remove the cable clamp and withdraw the cable from the bracket.
4 Remove the tunnel brace attaching nuts (see **FIG 6:18**). Disconnect the Variomatic selector rod at the drive unit lever (see **FIG 6:19**). Place a distance piece between the secondary discs.
5 Referring to **FIG 6:20**, remove the nuts 1, 2 and 3, on early units. Support the unit and tap out the rear mounting bolt. On later units slacken the two front and two rear bolts and the belt tensioner. Support the drive unit and remove the four nuts.
6 Lower the unit and draw it to the rear until the drive shaft is free. Remove the bolts and lift the unit from the support (see **FIG 6:21**).

DAF 46:

1 Position the car on a hoist or over a pit.
2 Remove the exhaust pipe attachment at the drum of the primary Variomatic.
3 Remove the guard pans.
4 Support the secondary variomatic with tool 3-99-535759, this is a girder between the lower suspension points with an adjustable support for the gear case.
5 Spread the discs of the secondary Variomatic and insert spacer 3-99-535334.
6 Disconnect the Variomatic hoses.
7 Disconnect the handbrake cable at the compensator.
8 Slacken the bolts and nuts securing the secondary Variomatic (see **Chapter 7, Section 7:9**).
9 Remove the front two nuts and bolts securing the interconnecting bracket to the unit. Disconnect the selector.
10 Support the unit, remove the bolts, and lower the unit moving it rearwards to clear the drive shaft. Note any spacer plates fitted.

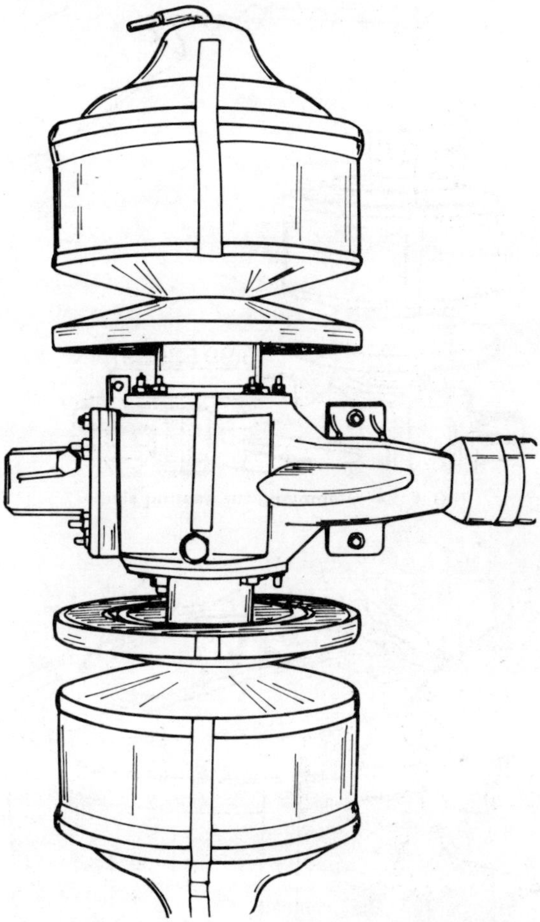

FIG 6:22 Method of marking the disc positions

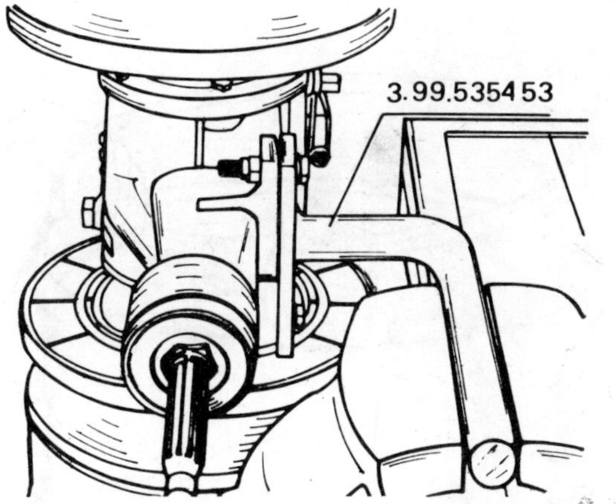

FIG 6:23 The unit attached to the special holding fixture. The holding fixture shown has been replaced by fixture 3-99-535374

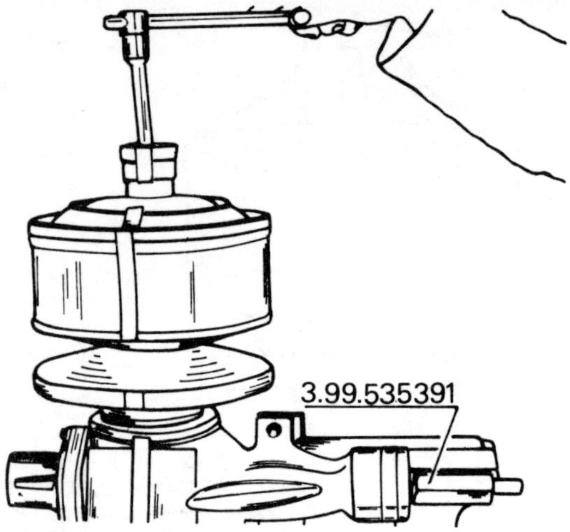

FIG 6:24 Removing the sealing sleeve

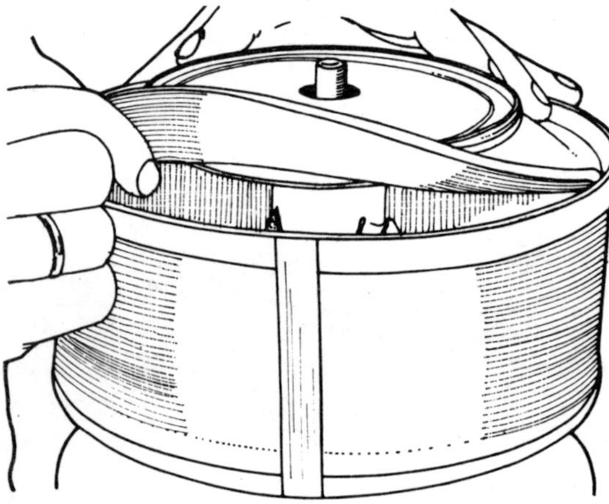

FIG 6:25 Removing a diaphragm

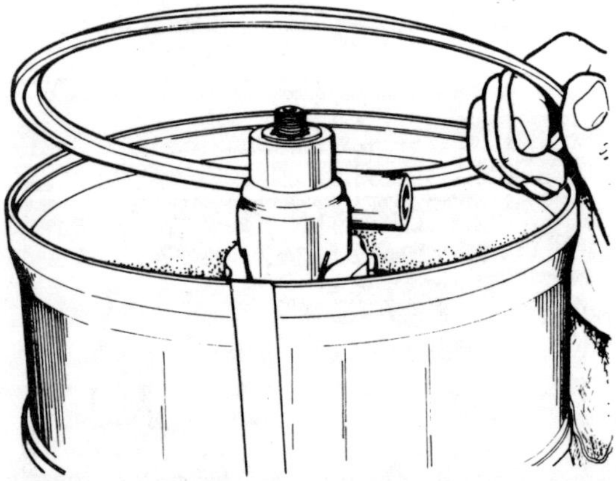

FIG 6:26 Removing the diaphragm support collar

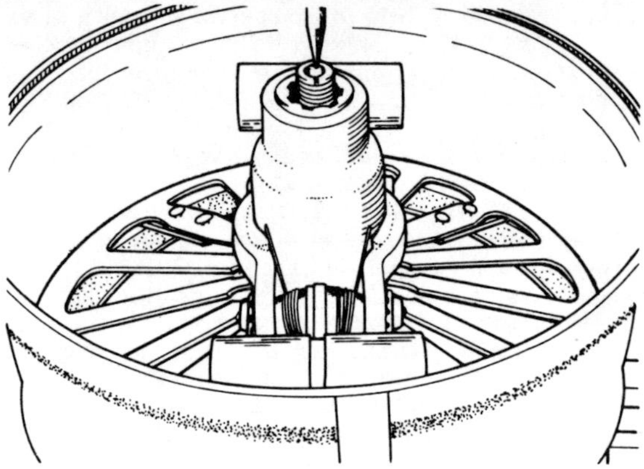

FIG 6:27 Marking the shaft in relation to the masking tape

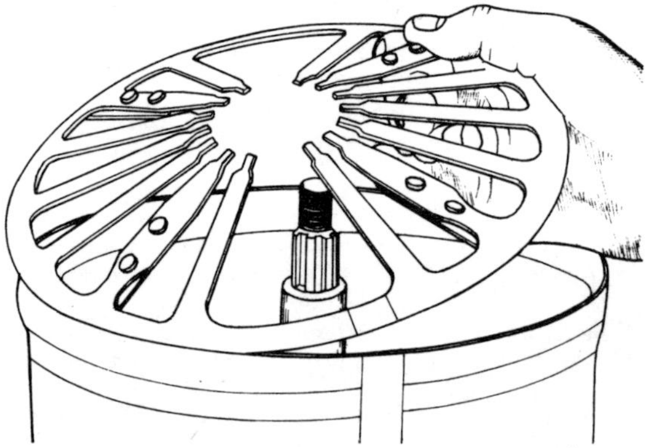

FIG 6:28 Removing the diaphragm spring

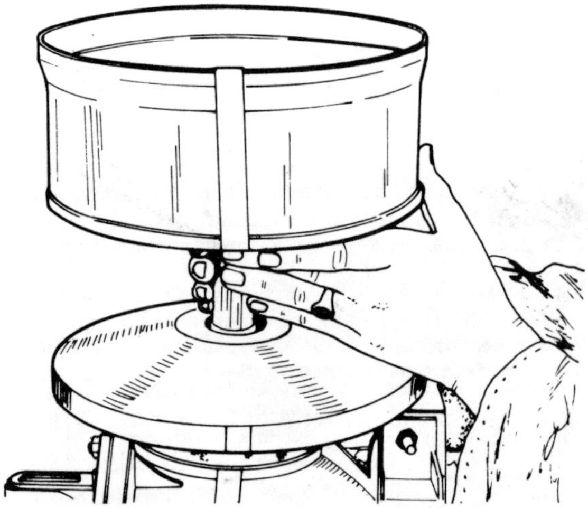

FIG 6:29 Removing the sliding disc

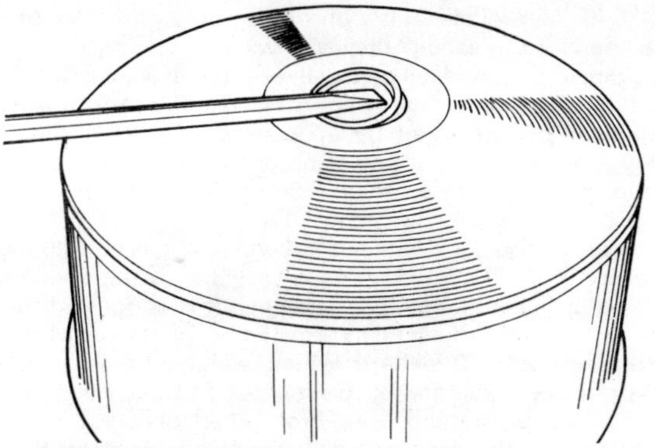

FIG 6:30 Removing the seal from the sliding disc bore

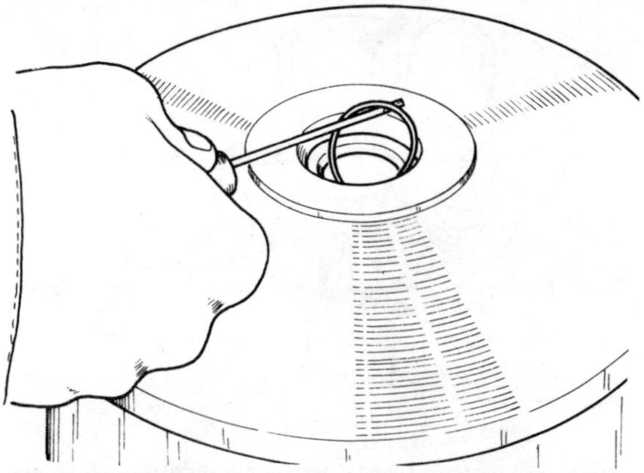

FIG 6:31 Removing the 'O' ring from the sliding disc bore

Refitment, all models:

In each case this is the reverse of the removal procedure. Use new belts if there is any doubt about the condition of those removed and fit them as described in **Section 6:4**. Belt tensioning is described in **Section 6:3**. Refer to **Chapter 10**, **Section 10:8** and ensure that the handbrake is correctly readjusted.

6:9 The propeller shaft

The propeller shaft is located between the clutch and the drive unit. A cross-section through a propeller shaft is included in **FIG 6:1**. To provide flexibility, the splined hubs are rubber bonded to tubular fittings; these are rivetted to the tubular shaft. The splined hubs engage with the splines of the clutch shaft and the input shaft of the drive unit. A spring is fitted between the rear hub of the propeller shaft and the drive unit.

Removal:

Following removal of the engine unit as described in **Chapter 1**, **Section 1:4**, the propeller shaft may be withdrawn forwards. Alternatively, following the removal of the Variomatic drive unit as described in **Section 6:8**, the shaft may be withdrawn rearwards. The buffer spring may then be removed from the drive unit input shaft.

If the shaft is bent or if the coupling hubs are defective, a new propeller shaft should be installed.

Fitting:

Check that the shaft and hub splines are clean. Apply Molykote BR2-S to the drive unit shaft splines and to the clutch shaft splines. Fit the buffer spring over the drive unit shaft and ensure that the recessed end of the propeller shaft (into which the spring spigots) is fitted towards the drive unit.

6:10 Servicing the drive unit

This Section covers the renewal of diaphragms, bearings in the side covers, seals and 'O' rings in the sliding discs. The drive units of all models are basically the same but are not identical dimensionally or in detail design. Modifications also introduce variations between earlier and later units of the same type models. It is advised that careful note should be kept of differences from the arrangements described in the following procedures.

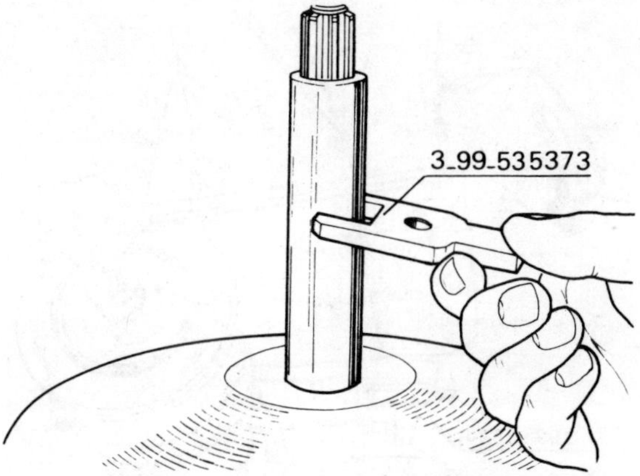

FIG 6:32 Checking the diameter of the fixed disc hub shaft

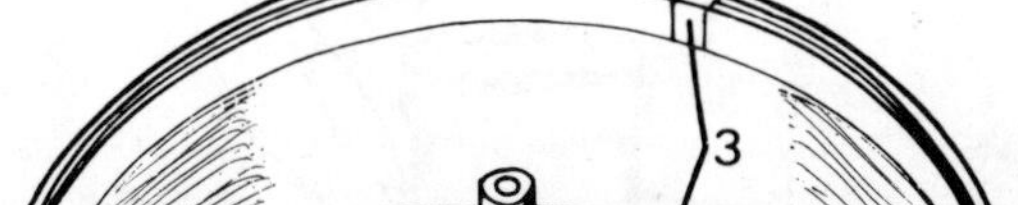

FIG 6:33 Assembling a diaphragm spring, showing the lug 1, the slot 2 and the aligning marks 3

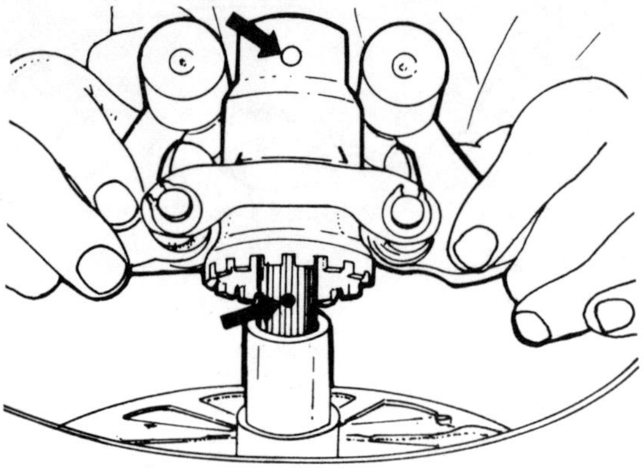

FIG 6:34 Fitting a centrifugal weight carrier assembly. The radial holes must be aligned

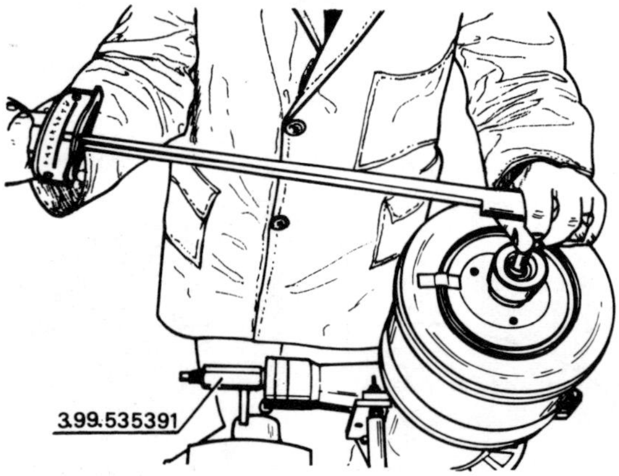

FIG 6:35 Fitting the sealing sleeve

FIG 6:36 Fitting the diaphragm sealing rim

DAF 46 models, although having only one drive unit are serviced in exactly the same way.

Since factory facilities will not be available to re-balance the drive unit, **certain critical components cannot be renewed by an owner** and an exchange replacement drive unit must be obtained if any of these critical components are found, on dismantling, to be unserviceable (see operation 10).

Special tools are required at certain stages and during reassembly, a vacuum pump is essential. If the operator is not a skilled automobile engineer, it is suggested that he will find much useful information in **Hints on Maintenance and Overhaul** which will be found in the **Appendix** at the end of this manual and that he should read it before starting work. Proceed as follows:

1 Remove the drive unit as described in **Section 6:8**. Use lengths of masking tape and mark the pulley discs and covers lefthand and righthand and in relation to each other as shown in **FIG 6:22**. Hold the unit right-hand side upwards in a vice using holding clamp 3-99-535374 or 3-99-535453 (see **FIG 6:23**).

Removing pulley discs:

2 Work firstly on the righthand side of the unit. Prise out the cover lock ring, tap the cover loose with a soft hammer and lift off the cover. Check that the diaphragm rim contact surface of the cover is not damaged or warped. If renewal is necessary the complete drive unit **must** be exchanged, as unbalance may otherwise result.

3 Use tool 3-99-535391 (see **FIG 6:42**) to hold the input shaft from turning (see **FIG 6:24**) and remove the nut in the sealing sleeve. Remove the sealing sleeve. Mark the diaphragm in relation to the masking tape so that, if it is serviceable, it can be reassembled in its original relative position. Refer to **FIG 6:25** and lift off the diaphragm assembly taking care that the centrifugal weight carrier assembly remains in position on the shaft.

4 Remove the diaphragm support collar (see **FIG 6:26**) and check it for possible damage. If necessary, obtain a new collar.

5 Refer to **FIG 6:27**. Mark the diaphragm spring and cross-shaft in relation to the masking tape. Remove the centrifugal weight carrier assembly (see **FIG 6:34**) and withdraw the diaphragm spring (see **FIG 6:28**).

6 Remove the sliding pulley disc (see **FIG 6:29**). Remove the fixed pulley disc using, if necessary, a suitable puller. **Do not attempt to remove the disc by using a hammer**.

7 Work now on the lefthand side of the unit and repeat operations 2 to 6 inclusive.

Inspecting the discs:

8 Remove the seal (see **FIG 6:30**), the 'O' ring (see **FIG 6:31**) and the grease from the bore of the sliding disc. Check the bore diameter using the blade end of gauge 3-99-535373. If the blade will enter the bore it is oversize and must be rejected. Refer to operation 10.

9 Using the caliper end of the same gauge, check the outer diameter of the fixed disc hub shaft (see **FIG 6:32**). If the jaws of the gauge pass over the

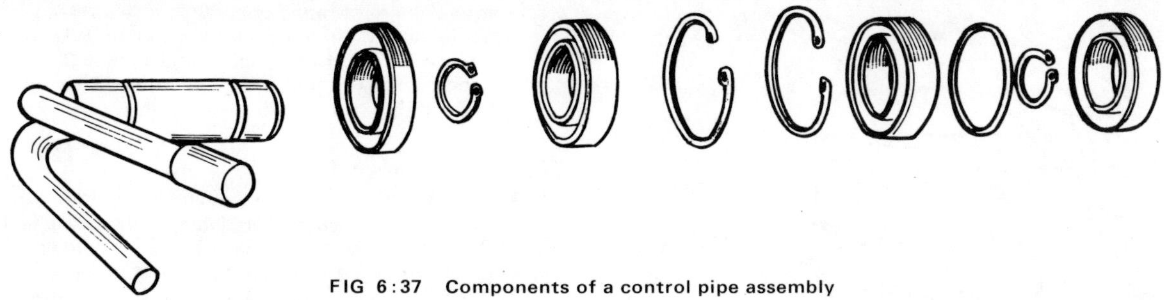

FIG 6:37 Components of a control pipe assembly

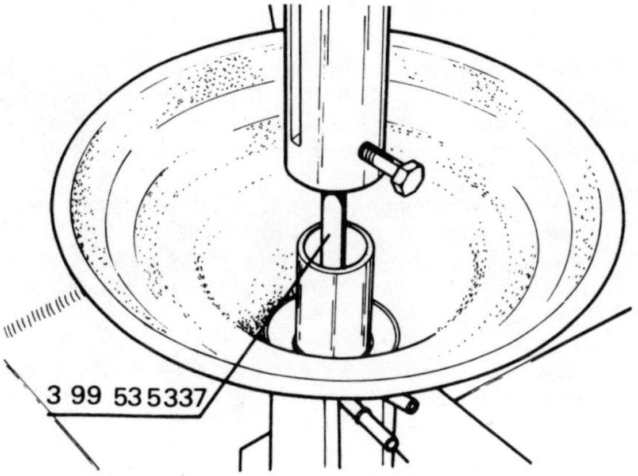

FIG 6:38 Pressing out the control pipe assembly

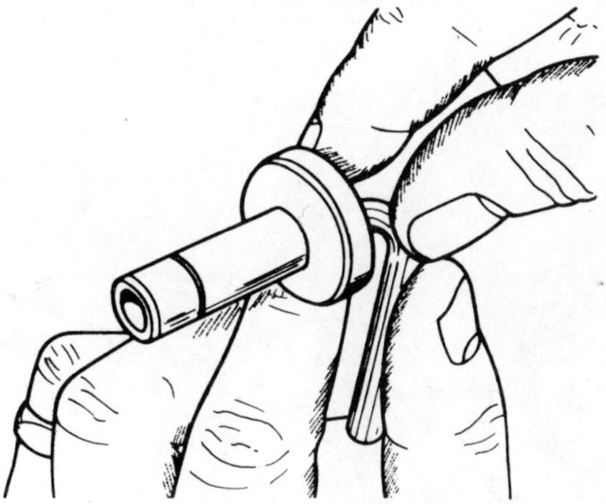

FIG 6:39 Removing the control pipe outer seal

diameter it is undersize and the fixed disc must be rejected. Refer to operation 10.

10 Note that if either of the discs, the cover, the diaphragm spring or the centrifugal weight carrier assembly is rejected, the complete drive unit should be replaced by an exchange unit. **Renewal of these parts is not practical without factory facilities to balance the assembly.**

Seal removal and fitment:

11 Remove the seals from both bearing housings. Support the case on ring 3-99-535388 and use adaptor ring 3-99-535378 and tube 3-99-535375 to press new seals into position.

Assembling the discs:

12 Fill the grease cavity of the sliding disc with 7 cc of Molykote BR2-S (DAF part No. 600090). Greaser tool 3-99-535682 may be used for this operation. Install two new 'O' rings and press a new seal into position using the mandrel part of greaser tool 3-99-535682.

13 Lightly grease the seals in the cover and sliding disc. Assemble the sliding disc to the fixed disc. Ensure that the marks on the discs and shaft are aligned. Refer to **FIG 6:33**. Fit the diaphragm spring with the lugs 1 engaging the slots 2 and the marks 3 aligned.

14 Refer to **FIG 6:34** and install the centrifugal weight carrier assembly with the radial holes in the carrier and shaft aligned and the fingers of the spring engaging the notches in the carrier. Pour 100 cc (.18 pint) of ATF type A/A fluid into the drum of the sliding disc.

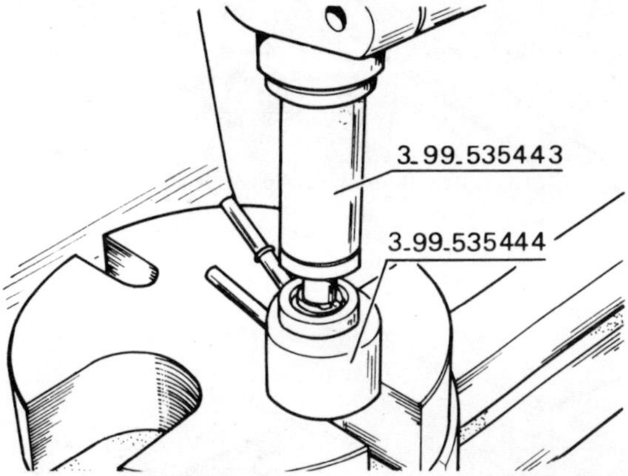

FIG 6:40 Pressing the control pipe into the cover

15 Fit the sealing sleeve into adaptor plate 3-99-535376 and support collar 3-99-535384. Remove the sealing ring and press a new ring into position. It should be flush with the upper side of the sealing sleeve.

16 Fit the diaphragm support collar and diaphragm and use tool 3-99-535389 to press down the diaphragm. Fit the sealing sleeve and nut and washer.

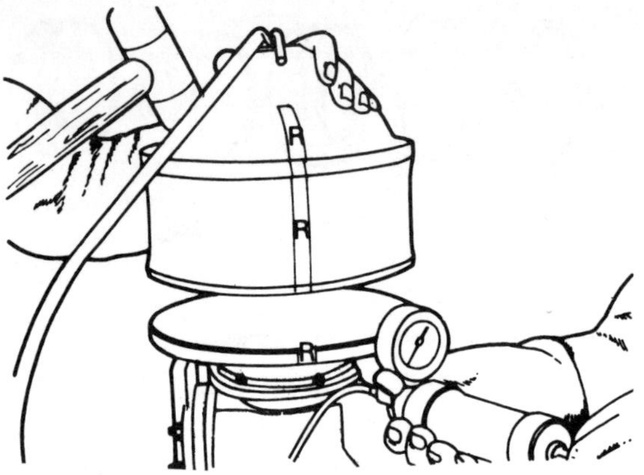

FIG 6:41 Fitting the cover with depression applied by a pump

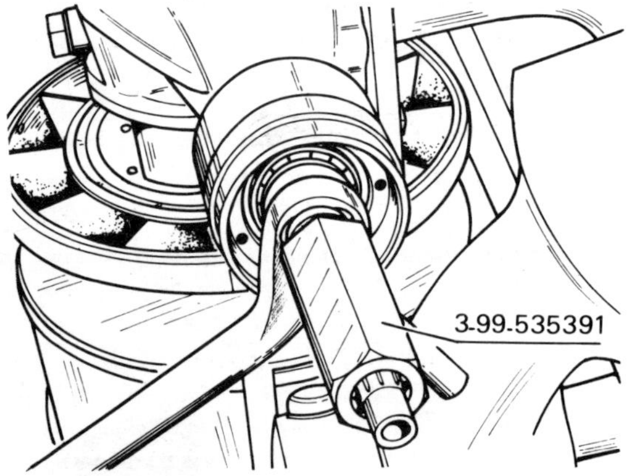

FIG 6:42 Removing the input shaft nut

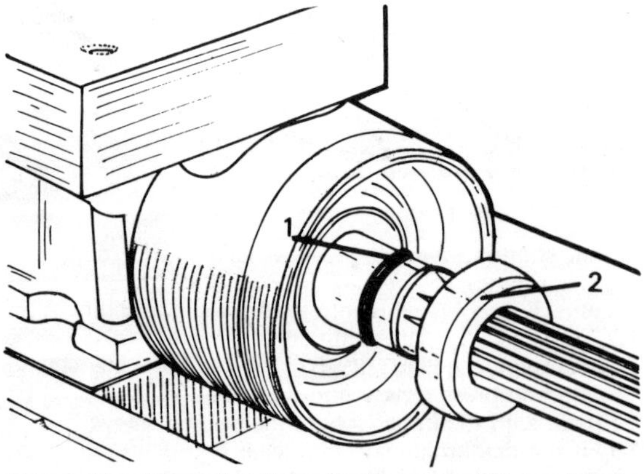

FIG 6:43 Removing the collar 2 and the 'O' ring 1 from the input shaft

17 Torque tighten the nut to 65 to 72 lb ft (9 to 10 kg m) while holding the input shaft from turning with tool 3-99-535391 (see **FIG 6:35**) as at operation 3. Press the sealing rim of the diaphragm into the drum (see **FIG 6:36**).

Control pipe assembly:

18 **FIG 6:37** shows the components of a later type assembly. The arrangement differs with earlier and other models. Take careful note of possible differences in the model being worked on.

19 Remove the sealing ring and circlip from the inside of the cover. Support the cover and press out the control pipe assembly (see **FIG 6:38**) with tool 3-99-535337. Withdraw both bearings from the cover.

20 Remove the circlip from the tube and slide off the outer seal. (see **FIG 6:39**). Check the control pipe for damage on the seal contact surfaces and if the condition is in any way doubtful, renew the component.

21 Coat two new bearings with Shell Alvania 3 and press them into the cover with tool 3-99-535443 while supporting the cover with plate 3-99-535377. Fit a new seal to the control pipe (lip facing outwards) and fit the circlip.

22 Support the inside of the cover with tool 3-99-535443 and using tool 3-99-535444 (see **FIG 6:40**), press the control pipe into the cover. Fit a circlip and a new seal on the inside.

Fitting the cover:

23 Lubricate the sealing sleeve sparingly with grease, align the marks and fit the cover assembly. Refer to **FIG 6:41**. Connect a vacuum pump to the short pipe of the control pipe assembly and, while centring the cover with a soft hammer, apply vacuum. Fit the cover lock ring.

Vacuum checks:

24 Rotate the pulley discs and confirm that vacuum is retained. Connect the vacuum pump to the long pipe and apply vacuum. The sliding disc should readily move upwards. Confirm that vacuum is retained within a loss rate of 1 inch (25 mm) of mercury column per minute.

25 Repeat operations 8 to 24 inclusive on the other side of the drive unit. On reassembly, ensure that the lefthand and righthand assemblies are aligned.

Input shaft seal:

26 Remove the oil seal. Hold the shaft from turning (see **FIG 6:42**) with tool 3-99-535391 and remove the nut. Refer to **FIG 6:43** and remove collar 2 and 'O' ring 1.

27 Fit a new 'O' ring and a new collar (bore chamfer towards the 'O' ring). Fit a new nut and torque tighten it to 29 to 43 lb ft (4 to 6 kg m). Use a centre punch to lock the nut by peening.

28 Use adaptor ring 3-99-535378 and tube 3-99-535375 to fit a new oil seal and, after installing the drive unit into the car, check the oil level as described in **Section 6:7**.

6:11 Fault diagnosis

(a) Broken drive belt(s)

1 Belts have seen long service
2 Belt tension incorrect
3 Damaged or defective belt
4 Improper use of brake vacuum control (manual)

(b) Slipping drive belt(s)

1 Check 1 in (a)
2 Belts require tensioning
3 Fluid or grease on pulley disc faces

(c) Dashboard brake vacuum control inoperative

1 Inner cable broken or detached from valve, DAF 31, 32, 33 and early 44 models
2 Outer cable not anchored, DAF 31, 32, 33 and early 44 models
3 Switch not making contact, DAF later 44 models
4 Electrical connection(s) defective, DAF later 44 models
5 Valve defective

(d) Absence of engine braking effect

1 Check 4 in (c), DAF later 44 models; 5 in (c), all models
2 Hydraulic pipe connection with valve blocked
3 Stop signal switch not making contact, DAF later 44

(e) Delayed ratio change operation

1 Control valve requires adjustment, DAF 31, 32, 33 and 44 models
2 Vacuum pipe partially blocked
3 Leaking vacuum pipe or loose joint

(f) 'Deranged' ratio changes

1 Check (a); (b); (e); 5 in (h) and (j)
2 Centrifugal weights seized
3 Sliding disc seized on splines
4 Diaphragm sealing defective
5 Diaphragm ruptured
6 Control pipe(s) disconnected or leaking
7 Electrical connection loose or disconnected
8 Control valve defective
9 Control valve linkage uncoupled, DAF 31, 32, 33 and 44 models

(g) No drive obtainable

1 Clutch inoperative
2 Selector dog clutch not engaged
3 Drive belts broken
4 Propeller shaft coupling sheared

(h) Fluid leaks

1 Input shaft seal defective
2 Drain or filler plug loose
3 Pulley disc seal(s) defective
4 Control pipe assembly seal(s) defective
5 Casing joint defective

(j) Driven pulley assembly defective (see **Chapter 7**)

NOTES

CHAPTER 7

THE REAR AXLES AND REAR SUSPENSION

7:1 Description

Two separate axle units, each of which incorporates a set of Variomatic transmission driven pulley discs and reduction gearing, are mounted independently of each other on individually sprung suspension arms on all models except the DAF 46.

The DAF 46 has a single Variomatic unit mounted on a reduction gearbox, incorporating a conventional differential unit connected to the wheels through drive shafts having constant velocity joints at each end.

The suspension layout of **DAF 31**, **32** and **33** models is shown in **FIG 7:1** together with the complete Variomatic transmission which consists of the drive unit (covered in **Chapter 6**) and two driven units. The L-shaped independent suspension arms are pivoted to the chassis at both ends. A wheel hub, coil suspension spring and a damper is located at the angle of each suspension arm. Each axle unit is flexibly mounted in the rear arm of each L. The design of the outboard mountings of the axle units to the suspension arms differs between earlier and later models. Earlier units are provided with sandwich type mounting blocks and the trunnions on the axle tubes have external threads to take retaining nuts. The trunnions of the later type axle tubes are internally threaded to take retaining bolts and this type of axle tube is shown on the axle assemblies which are illustrated in **FIG 6:1**. The further mounting trunnion on the reduction gear casing which is also shown in **FIG 6:1**, is the same design on earlier and later models. A coil spring is mounted between each suspension arm and the chassis. It is spigoted to the mountings at both ends. A rubber bump stop is attached to the spring mounting of each suspension arm and is located inside the coil spring. A double-acting telescopic hydraulic damper is angularly mounted between each suspension arm and the chassis.

The suspension layout of the **DAF 44** models is shown in **FIG 7:2** together with the complete Variomatic drive unit and the two driven units. Each axle tube is rigidly attached to a suspension arm which is pivoted at its inner end to a T-shaped subframe which is attached to the chassis at three points. A coil spring serves each suspension arm and each spring is provided with a rubber bump stop at its centre point. A vertically mounted double-acting telescopic hydraulic damper is mounted between each suspension arm and the chassis.

The suspension layout in DAF 46 models is shown in **FIG 7:3**. The main features of this arrangement are a strong transverse tube, curved to clear the differential, in conjunction with single leaf springs at each side of the vehicle. Each end of the tube is welded to a substantial bracket to which the centre of the spring is bolted. The bracket also provides a rigid attachment for the rear wheel hub and the lower end of the telescopic double acting damper.

A cross-section through the **DAF 31**, **32** and **33** driven pulley discs, reduction gears and axle tubes is shown in **FIG 6:1**. A corresponding cross-section through a **DAF**

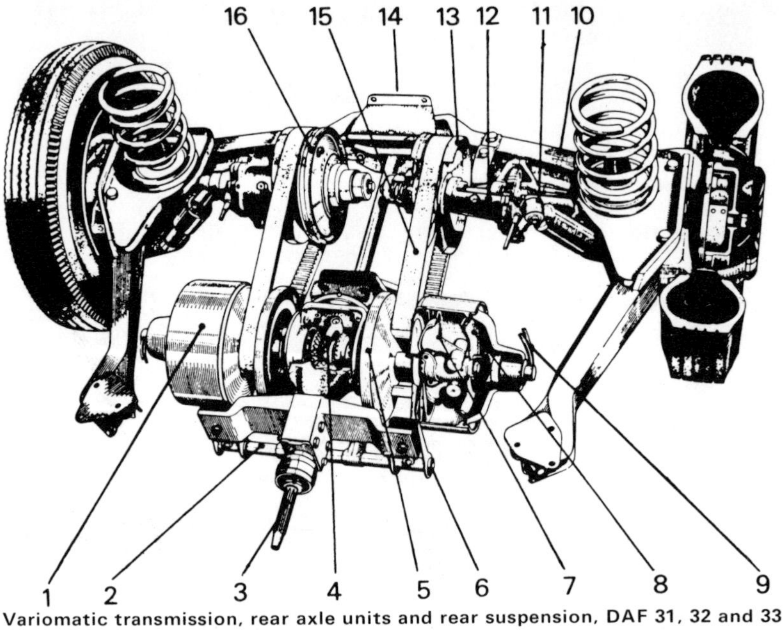

FIG 7:1 Variomatic transmission, rear axle units and rear suspension, DAF 31, 32 and 33 models

Key to Fig 7:1 1 Vacuum cylinder 2 Drive unit mounting 3 Input shaft 4 Forward/reverse dog clutch 5 Fixed driving pulley disc 6 Mounting 7 Centrifugal weights 8 Diaphragm 9 Control pipe assembly 10 Suspension arm 11 Damper 12 Reduction gearing 13 Driven fixed pulley disc 14 Belt tension adjusting screw 15 Drive belt (in low ratio position) 16 Driven sliding pulley disc

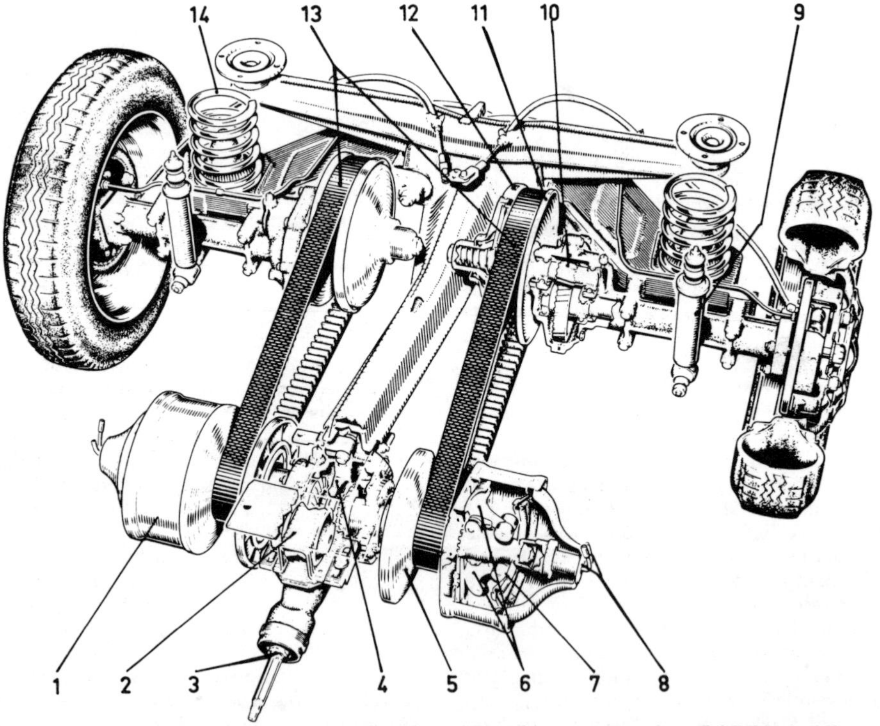

FIG 7:2 Variomatic transmission, rear axle units and rear suspension, DAF 44 models

Key to Fig 7:2 1 Vacuum cylinder 2 Drive unit mounting 3 Input shaft 4 Forward/reverse dog clutch 5 Fixed driving pulley disc 6 Centrifugal weights 7 Diaphragm 8 Control pipe assembly 9 Damper 10 Reduction gearing 11 Driven fixed pulley disc 12 Driven sliding pulley disc 13 Drive belt (in low ratio position) 14 Coil suspension spring

44 model rear drive assembly is shown in **FIG 7:5**. These differ in detail design but the principle of operation is the same.

Reference should be made to **Chapter 6** for a description of the operation of the Variomatic transmission of which the rear axle spring loaded driven pulley disc assemblies are an essential part. The shaft on which each pulley disc assembly is mounted, on all models except the DAF 46, carries a pinion gear which meshes with a larger gear carried on the axle shaft. The reduction ratio of these gears is not the same for all models. Gear ratios are quoted in **Technical Data** in the **Appendix**. The hub bearing for each rear wheel is carried in the outer end of each axle tube. Lubrication drain and filler/level plugs are provided in each reduction gear casing. Each of the gears in the reduction gear casings is supported on two bearings and an oil seal is located where each shaft passes through the gear casing. A further oil seal is incorporated in the hub/brake drum assembly.

Since the pivot axis of each suspension arm is close to the fore and aft line of each Variomatic transmission drive belt, the twist in the plane of the belt drive is small when a road wheel rises and falls within the operating range of the suspension arms and the small amount of twist is accommodated within the flexibility of the drive.

DAF 46 models are not affected by suspension movement.

7:2 Maintenance

Tyre pressures:

Rear tyres should, for general service, be inflated to the following pressures:

DAF 31, 32 and 33 models:

Tyre	*Passenger cars*	*Commercial vehicles*
Cross-ply	22 lb/sq inch (1.55 kg/sq cm)	28 lb/sq inch (2.0 kg/sq cm)
Radial-ply	24 lb/sq inch (1.7 kg/sq cm)	30 lb/sq inch (2.2 kg/sq cm)

DAF 44 models:

Tyre	*Pressure*
Semperit	31 lb/sq inch (2.2 kg/sq cm)
Michelin	28 lb/sq inch (2 kg/sq cm)
Kleber Colombes, Uniroyal	25 lb/sq inch (1.8 kg/sq cm)

DAF 46 models:

Tyre	*Pressure*
All recommended types	26 lb/sq inch (1.8 kg/sq cm)

Drive belt tension:

Every 3000 miles (5000 km), check and adjust the drive belt tension as described in **Chapter 6**, **Section 6:3**.

Lubrication:

The procedure for draining and refilling of the reduction gear casings is described (as part of the axle shaft removal and fitment procedure) in **Section 7:4**.

Lubrication and overhaul of the driven pulley disc assemblies is included in **Section 7:8** (operation 11). The quantity of fluid required to replenish after draining off is less than that required for a 'dry' assembly at overhaul. The replenishment quantity is 60 cc (.1 pint) of ATF type A/A for all models.

7:3 Dampers

A telescopic double-acting hydraulic damper is fitted between each suspension arm and the chassis. Their locations are shown at 11 in **FIG 7:1** (DAF 31, 32 and 33 models) and at 9 in **FIG 7:2** (DAF 44 models). Rear dampers require no routine maintenance; they cannot be reconditioned by an owner and a defective damper must be removed and a replacement fitted.

Removal, DAF 31, 32 and 33 models:

With the car on a hoist or over a pit, remove the locknut and the attachment nut from the lower end of the damper and collect the washer and lower rubber buffer. Remove the nut and bolt from the upper attachment point and collect the spring washer and two bushes. Withdraw the damper and collect the second rubber buffer from its lower end.

Removal, DAF 44 models:

Start with the upper attachment point which is accessible from inside the luggage compartment. Use two spanners and hold the piston rod from turning while the attachment nut is loosened. Remove the attachment nut. With the car on a hoist or over a pit, remove the nut and bolt from the lower end of the damper. Collect the washers and withdraw the damper. Renew the rubber bush at the upper attachment point if its condition is doubtful.

Removal DAF 46 models:

Remove the upper attachment in a similar manner to the DAF 44. The lower attachment is similar to the upper attachment and should be treated in the same way.

Fitment:

In each case, fitment of a damper is the reverse of the removal sequence.

7:4 Hubs and axle shafts DAF 31, 32, 33 and 44

DAF 31, 32 and 33 models:

A cross-section through a hub bearing and an axle shaft is included in **FIG 6:1**.

Hub bearing removal:

1 Jack up the car and remove the relevant road wheel. Remove the brake drum as described in **Chapter 10, Section 10:5**.
2 Pry out the old oil seal. Dismount the brake back plate as described in **Chapter 10**, **Section 10:5**.
3 Withdraw the shim(s) and bearing from the axle tube.

Hub bearing fitment:

1 Install the new bearing into the axle tube and fit the shim(s).
2 Install the brake back plate as described in **Chapter 10, Section 10:5**.

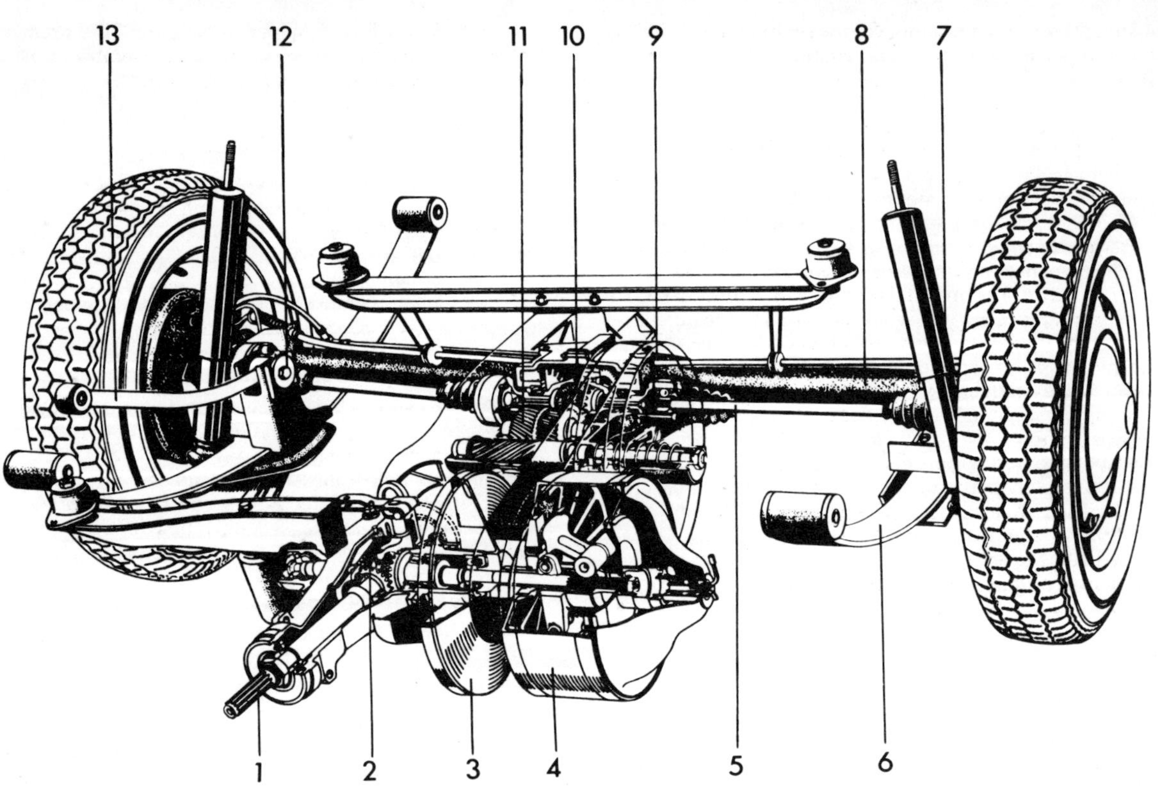

FIG 7:3 Variomatic transmission, rear axle and suspension, DAF 46 models

Key to Fig 7:3 1 Input shaft 2 Forward/reverse dog clutch 3 Fixed disc 4 Primary Variomatic unit 5 Drive shaft 6 Leaf spring 7 Damper 8 'De Dion' type rear axle 9 Secondary Variomatic unit 10 Differential 11 Reduction gears 12 Connecting rod 13 Torque rod

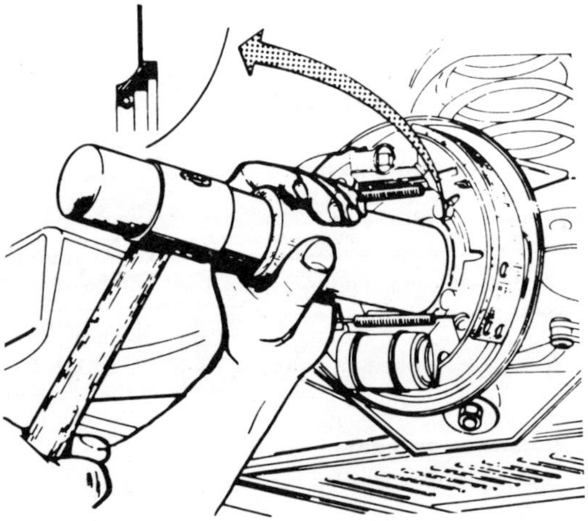

FIG 7:4 Fitting a rear hub seal, DAF 31, 32, 33

3 Refer to **FIG 7:4** and fit a new oil seal. Ensure that the seal is the correct way round with the lips inwards as shown in the inset to the illustration.

4 Fit the brake drum as described in **Chapter 10, Section 10:5**. Fit the road wheel and lower the car.

Axle shaft removal:

1 Jack up the car and remove the relevant road wheel. Remove the brake drum and dismount the back plate as described in **Chapter 10, Section 10:5**.

2 Remove the drain and filler plugs from the relevant reduction gear unit and drain off the lubricant. Access to the plugs requires the removal of the guard pans.

3 With a suitable puller, withdraw the axle shaft complete with the hub bearing. Collect the shim(s) and remove the bearing from the shaft.

Axle shaft fitment:

1 Take great care when fitting the axle shaft not to damage the seal which is immediately outboard of the axle shaft bearing.

2 Fit the hub bearing, the shim(s), the brake back plate, the oil seal, the brake drum and the road wheel as described earlier in this Section.

3 Fit the drain plug and, using a syringe, inject 140 cc (.23 pint) of ATF type A/A oil into the reduction gear casing filler orifice. Fit the filler plug. Fit the guard pans and lower the car.

DAF 44 models:

A cross-section through an axle assembly is shown in **FIG 7:5**.

Axle shaft and hub bearing removal:

1 Jack up the car and remove the relevant road wheel. Remove the brake drum as described in **Chapter 10, Section 10:5**.
2 Remove the drain and filler plugs (these are arrowed in **FIG 7:6**) and drain off the oil. Access to the plugs requires the removal of the guard pans.
3 Dismount the brake backing plate as described in **Chapter 10, Section 10:5**. Do not uncouple the brake hydraulic pipe but bend open the pipe clip to allow the back plate to be moved aside.
4 Remove the bearing retainer and, as shown in **FIG 7:7**, use tool 8-99-535538 to withdraw the axle shaft complete with the hub bearing. Press the bearing off the shaft.

Axle shaft and hub bearing fitment:

1 Press a new bearing onto the shaft. Smear the bearing outer diameter and the axle tube bore with Lubri-Kote type A-1040GR (DAF part No. 600131) and fit the shaft and bearing assembly using the tubular part of tool 8-99-535538 to drive it finally home.
2 Fit a new oil seal to the bearing retainer cover. The end clearance between the bearing and the retainer should be zero to .003 inch (zero to .076 mm). Restrict the clearance to within these limits by measuring the bearing protrusion and the depth of the retainer bore and fitting shims as required. Shims are available in thicknesses of .003, .005, .008, .010 and .020 inch (DAF part Nos. 891466 to 891470).
3 Fit the shim(s) and the bearing retainer. Fit the brake back plate and drum as described in **Chapter 10, Section 10:5**. Reclip the brake hydraulic pipe and **ensure that it does not foul the suspension spring**.
4 Fit the drain plug and, using a syringe, inject 230 cc (.41 pint) of SAE 80 oil into the reduction gear casing filler orifice. Fit the filler plug. Fit the guard pans. Fit the road wheel and lower the car.

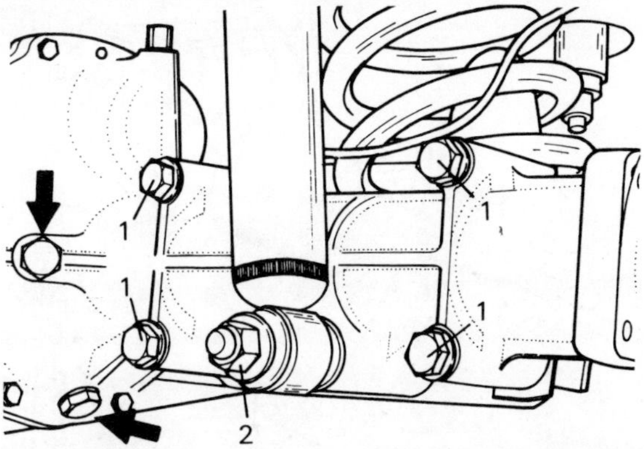

FIG 7:6 Reduction gear and damper attachment, DAF 44

Key to Fig 7:6 1 Bolts securing axle tube to suspension arm 2 Damper lower attachment. The arrows show the drain and filler plugs

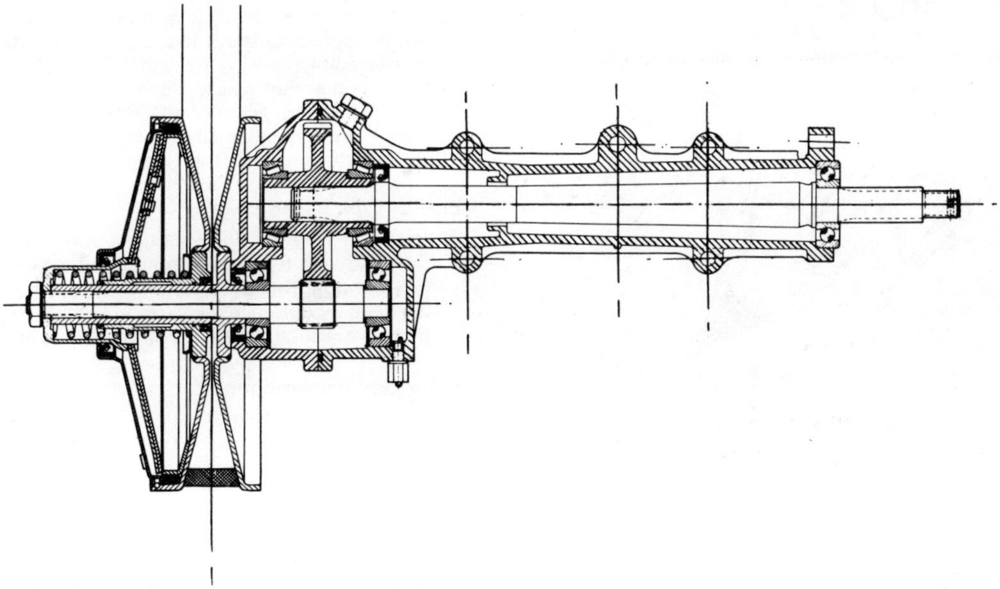

FIG 7:5 A sectional view of a rear axle unit, DAF 44

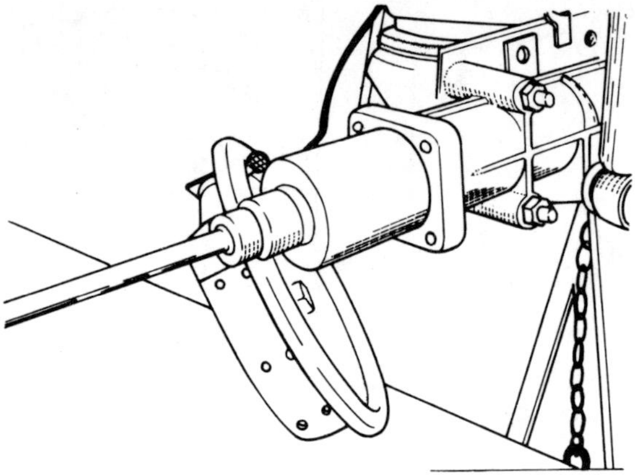

FIG 7:7 Removing axle shaft and hub bearing, DAF 44

FIG 7:8 Withdrawing a suspension spring

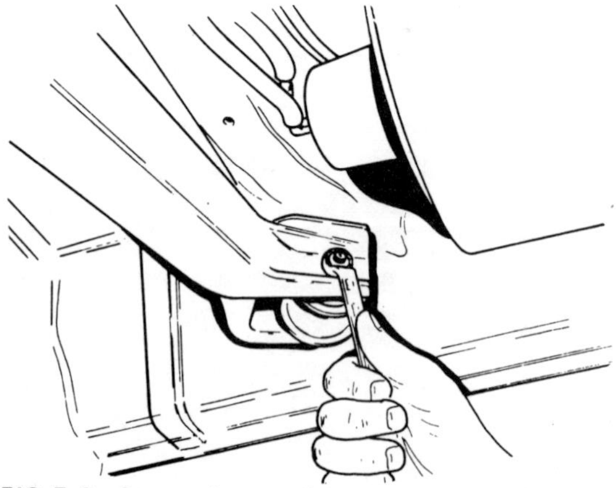

FIG 7:9 Suspension arm front mounting, DAF 31, 32, 33

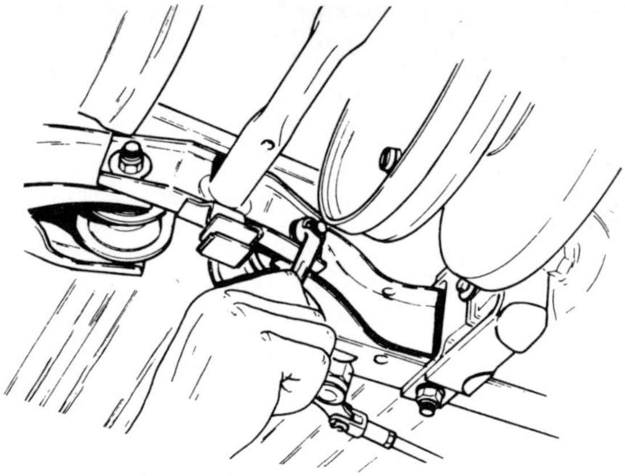

FIG 7:10 Suspension arm rear mounting, DAF 31, 32, 33

7:5 Reduction gear unit removal and fitment

Removal, DAF 31, 32 and 33 models:

1 With the car on a hoist or over a pit, remove the exhaust pipe. Disengage the drive belt from the relevant pulley disc assembly as described in **Chapter 6, Section 6:4**.

2 Refer to **Chapter 10, Section 10:8** and uncouple the handbrake cable. Disconnect the brake hydraulic pipe at the support bracket and fit caps to preclude dirt from entering the open pipe ends. Disconnect the lower end of the damper from the suspension arm as described in **Section 7:3**.

3 Raise the rear of the chassis and withdraw the suspension spring (see **FIG 7:8**).

4 Refer to **FIG 7:9** and remove the suspension arm front mounting nut. Refer to **FIG 7:10** and remove the suspension arm rear mounting nut.

5 Withdraw the suspension arm mounting bolts and lift out the complete reduction gear unit and suspension arm assembly.

6 Remove the road wheel. Remove the brake hydraulic pipe and uncouple the handbrake cable from the back plate lever. Remove the brake drum and the back plate as described in **Chapter 10, Section 10:5**.

Earlier type assemblies:

7 Refer to **FIG 7:11** and remove the bolts which attach the sandwich type outer mounting block to the suspension arm. Remove the nut and bolt which retains the inner mounting block to the suspension arm. Withdraw the reduction gear unit from the suspension arm.

Later type assemblies:

8 Refer to **FIG 7:12** and remove the bolts which retain the conical bushes to the trunnions on the axle tube. Withdraw the conical bushes and the washers (see **FIG 7:13**). Remove the nut and bolt which retains the inner mounting block to the suspension arm.

9 Drain off the oil from the reduction gear unit and remove the axle shaft (see **FIG 7:14**) as described in **Section 7:4**. Separate the reduction gear unit from the suspension arm as shown in **FIG 7:15**.

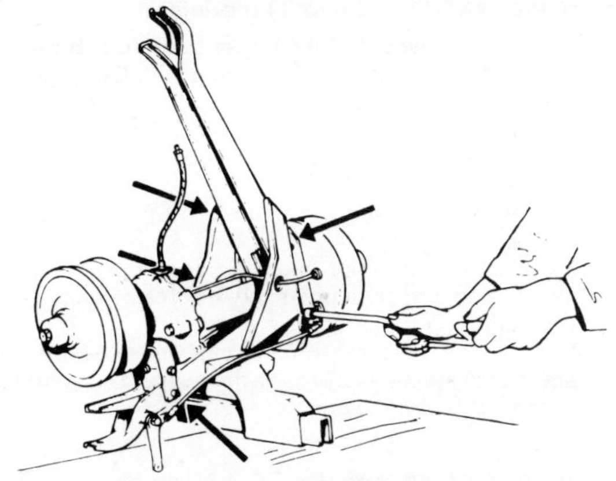

FIG 7:11 Removing a reduction gear unit from a suspension arm, DAF 31, 32, 33 earlier models

Fitment, DAF 31, 32 and 33 models:

Fitment of the reduction gear unit to the suspension arm and installation of the assembly to the car is the reverse of the removal sequence. Fit the inner washers for the conical bushes (later type assemblies) onto the trunnions with the chamfered edge of the hole facing the axle tube and tighten the retaining bolts evenly in succession. Ensure that the collar of the nylon spacer is properly centred in the hole in the bracket when assembling the suspension arm rear mounting. Bleed the brakes hydraulic system as described in **Chapter 10, Section 10:7**. Tension the drive belts as described in **Chapter 6, Section 6:3** and, on later assemblies, do not neglect to refill the reduction gear unit with approved lubricant (see **Section 7:4**).

Removal, DAF 44 models:

1 Raise the rear of the car until the wheels are clear of the ground and fit stands under the subframe.
2 Remove the exhaust pipe. Disengage the drive belt from the relevant pulley disc assembly as described in **Chapter 6, Section 6:4**.
3 Remove the relevant road wheel. Remove the brake drum and the brake back plate as described in **Chapter 10, Section 10:5**.
4 Refer to **FIG 7:6** and remove the axle tube mounting bolts 1 and the damper lower attachment bolt nut 2.
5 Support the reduction gear unit, tap out the damper attachment bolt and dismount the reduction gear unit.

Fitment, DAF 44 models:

Installation of a reduction gear unit is the reverse of the removal sequence. Tension the drive belts as described in **Chapter 6, Section 6:3**.

7:6 Road springs

Removal, DAF 31, 32 and 33 models:

Refer to **Section 7:5** and carry out operations 1 to 3 inclusive.

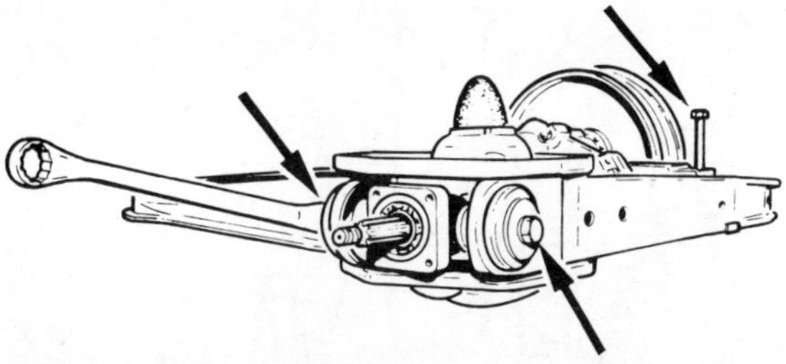

FIG 7:12 Removing a reduction gear unit from a suspension arm, DAF 31, 32, 33 later models

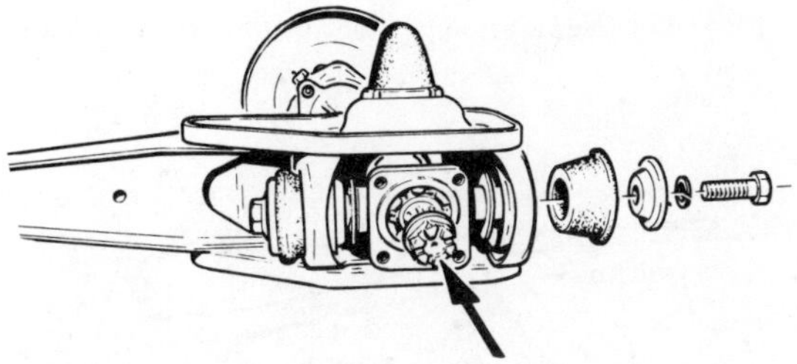

FIG 7:13 Suspension arm bushes and washers

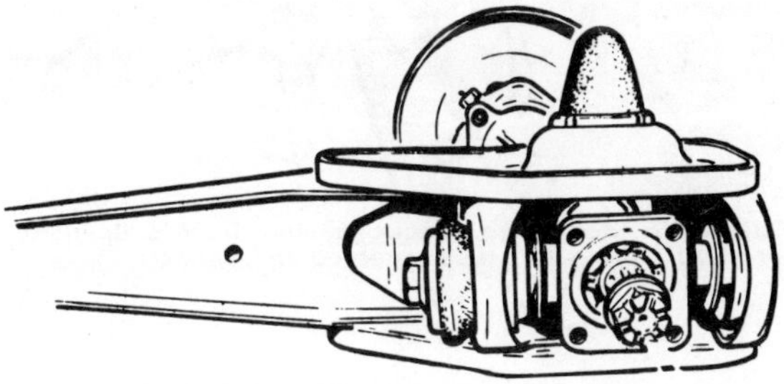

FIG 7:14 Withdrawing axle shaft

FIG 7:15 Withdrawing reduction gear unit from suspension arm, later DAF 31, 32, 33

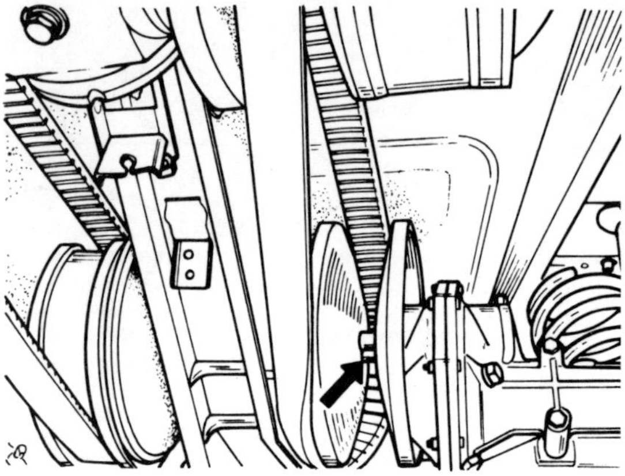

FIG 7:16 Separation of discs by spacer (arrowed)

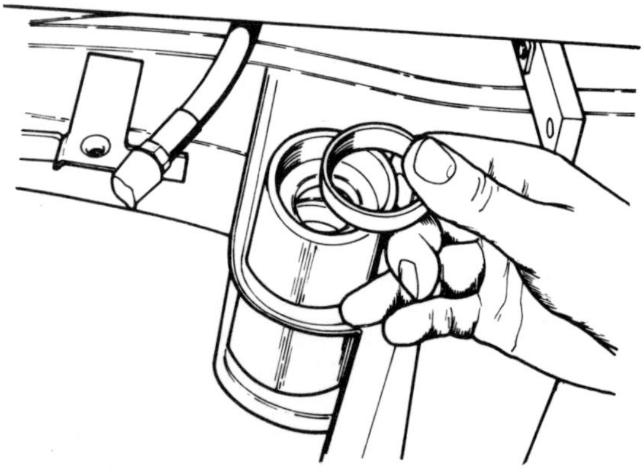

FIG 7:17 Removing spacer washer from suspension arm, with brake line disconnected and capped

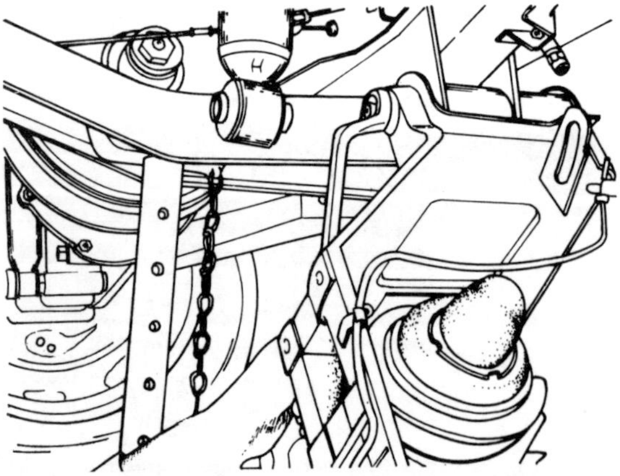

FIG 7:18 Lifting out the suspension arm assembly

Fitment, DAF 31, 32 and 33 models:

This is the reverse of the removal sequence. Bleed the brakes hydraulic system as described in **Chapter 10, Section 10:7**.

Removal, DAF 44 models:

1 Remove the relevant reduction gear unit as described in **Section 7:5**.
2 Disconnect the brake hydraulic line adjacent to the suspension arm pivot point and fit caps to preclude dirt from entering the open pipe ends.
3 Support the suspension arm, remove the suspension arm travel stop screw, lower the suspension arm and withdraw the road spring.

Fitment, DAF 44 models:

This is the removal sequence in reverse. Ensure that the spring is correctly seated before fitting the travel stop screw. Bleed the brakes hydraulic system as described in **Chapter 10, Section 10:7**.

7:7 Suspension arms

Removal, DAF 31, 32 and 33 models:

On these models, removal of a suspension arm entails removal of the reduction gear unit and the suspension arm assembly. Only after removal of the combined assembly can the arm be separated from the reduction gear unit. The procedure is described in **Section 7:5**.

Fitment, DAF 31, 32 and 33 models:

This is the reverse of the removal procedure.

Removal, DAF 44 models

1 Remove the exhaust pipe and lift off the main guard pan sections after removing the retaining screws. Disconnect the hoses at pulleys and lines and remove the front guard pan section.
2 Slacken the drive unit mounting bolts, back off the belt tensioner and slide the drive unit backwards.
3 Part the reduction gear pulley discs fully by pulling on the respective drive belt, place a 1 inch (25 mm) spacer between the discs (see **FIG 7:16**) and remove the belt.
4 Disconnect the brake line and close it off with a cap (see **FIG 7:17**). Remove the suspension arm travel stop screw and the wheel, supporting the suspension arm to avoid damage to the damper.
5 Remove the gearcase and damper mounting bolts (1 and 2 in **FIG 7:6**) and lift out the gear unit.
6 Lower the suspension arm and withdraw the coil spring. Remove the suspension arm mounting bolt nut, tap out the bolt and lift off the suspension arm assembly, as shown in **FIG 7:18**.
7 Remove the spacer washers (see **FIG 7:17**), bearing cones, spacer ring and spacer sleeve from the pivot tube. Extract the bearing cups with a suitable puller and remove the nylon grease seals. Check the bearing cups and cones for wear or damage. An exploded view of the suspension arm pivot parts is given in **FIG 7:19**.

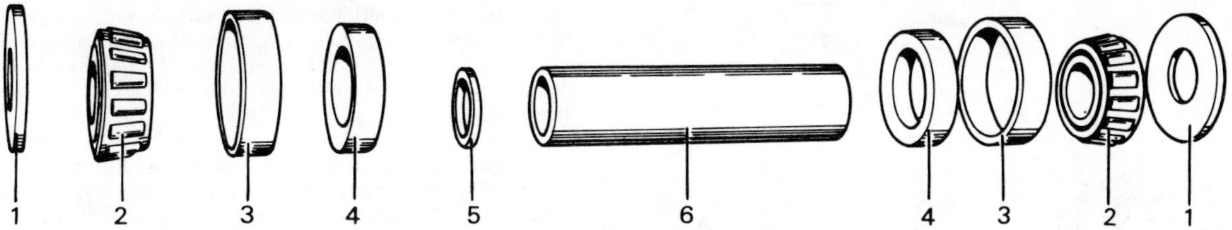

FIG 7:19 Suspension arm pivot components

Key to Fig 7:19 1 Spacer washer 2 Bearing cone 3 Bearing cup 4 Grease seal 5 Spacer ring 6 Spacer sleeve

Fitment, DAF 44 models:

Before fitment of the suspension arm can proceed, the pivot bearing preload must be adjusted by selection of a suitable thickness of spacer ring. Spacer rings are available in various thicknesses. Two dummy distance pieces (1.81 inch long (46 mm), 1.024 inch OD (26 mm) and .787 inch bore (20 mm)) are required for this adjustment. These dummy distance pieces represent the fork ends of the suspension arm.

Pivot bearing preload adjustment:

1 Install the nylon grease seals with their lips facing outwards. Lubricate the bearing cup locations and fit the cups.
2 Onto the pivot bolt, slide a dummy distance piece, a bearing cone, the spacer ring and the spacer tube. Pack the bearing cone with Molykote BR2S.
3 Introduce this assembly into the pivot housing and fit the second bearing cone (also packed with Molykote BR2S), the second dummy distance piece, washer and nut from the opposite end. Torque tighten the nut to 72 to 86 lb ft (10 to 12 kg m).
4 Use a low range torque meter as shown in **FIG 7:20** and measure the torque required to rotate the bolt. If this torque is less than 1 lb inch (1 kg cm), fit a thinner spacer ring. If the torque exceeds 8.5 lb inch (10 kg cm), fit a thicker spacer ring.

Reassembly:

5 When the preload has been adjusted to within these limits, remove the bolt and the dummy distance pieces leaving the other parts in position in the pivot housing.
6 Fit the spacer washers and slide the fork of the suspension arm over the pivot housing. Spacer washers are available in various thicknesses to enable the fork to be fitted without clearance. Torque tighten the pivot bolt nut to 72 to 86 lb ft (10 to 12 kg m).
7 The remaining operations are those of the removal sequence in reverse.

7:8 Servicing the reduction gear units

This Section covers the renewal of sliding disc assemblies and their oil seals, cover seals and pinion shaft seals of the DAF 44 model driven unit, a cross-section of which is shown in **FIG 7:5**. The driven units of all models are basically the same but they are not identical dimensionally nor in detail design. Modifications

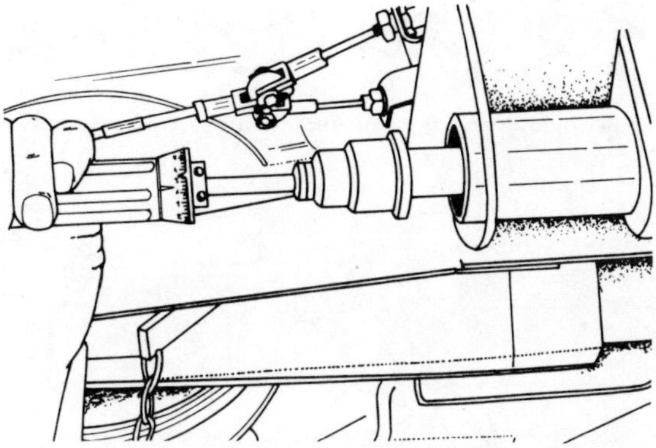

FIG 7:20 Measuring the pivot bearing preload, DAF 44

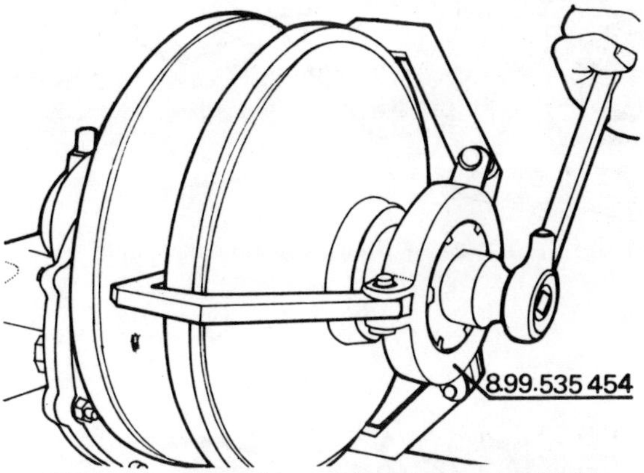

FIG 7:21 Removing a pinion shaft nut, DAF 44

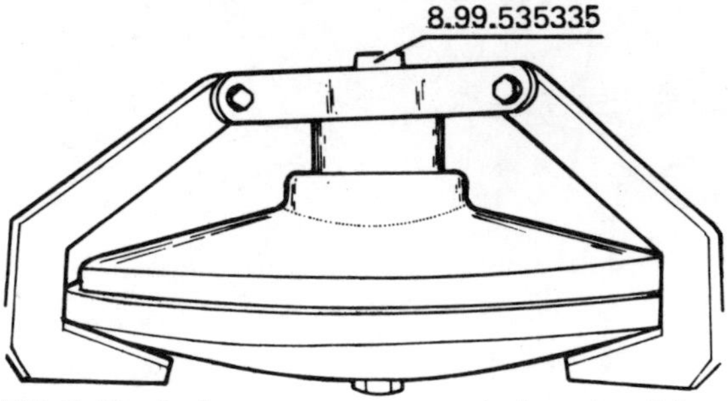

FIG 7:22 Spring compressor attached to the sliding pulley disc assembly

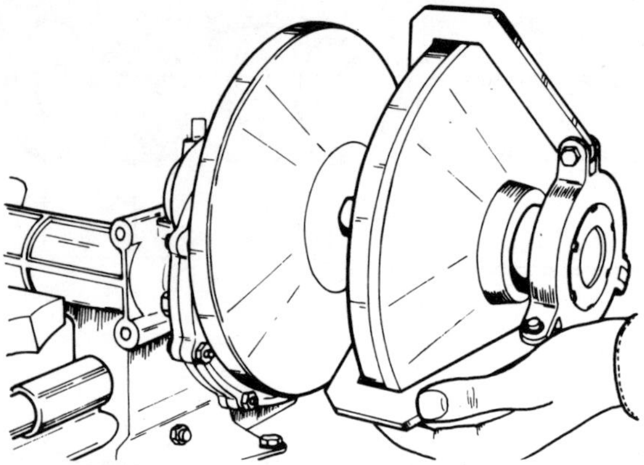
FIG 7:23 Fitting a new sliding pulley disc assembly

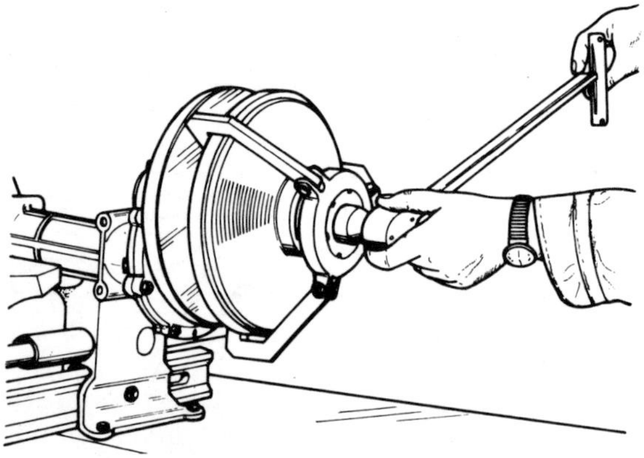
FIG 7:24 Fitting the pinion shaft nut

FIG 7:25 Removing the locking ring

also introduce variations between earlier and later units of the same type models. It is advised that careful note should be kept of differences from the arrangements described in the following procedures. Special tools are required.

If the operator is not a skilled automobile engineer, it is suggested that he will find much useful information in **Hints on Maintenance and Overhaul** which will be found in the **Appendix** at the end of this manual and that he should read it before starting work.

No overhaul procedures are prescribed for the reduction gearing and, should internal defects arise, a complete driven unit should be obtained on an exchange basis.

Sliding pulley disc renewal:

1 Remove the reduction gear unit as described in **Section 7:5**. Temporarily refit the brake drum (refer to **Chapter 10**, **Section 10:5**). Clamp the unit in a vice and fit clamping tool 8-99-535454 onto the sliding pulley disc assembly.

2 By means of the brake drum, keep the axle shaft from turning and remove the pinion shaft nut as shown in **FIG 7:21**.

3 Pull the sliding pulley disc assembly (complete with the clamping tool) off the hub of the fixed pulley disc. Position a spring compressing tool 8-99-535335 in the hub of the sliding pulley disc assembly and tighten the nut until the clamping tool can be removed (see **FIG 7:22**).

4 Fit the clamping tool onto the new sliding pulley disc assembly (see **FIG 7:23**) and remove the spring compressing tool which is provided with the new assembly.

5 Lubricate the oil seal in the hub sparingly with Shell Retinax G and slide the assembly onto the hub of the fixed pulley disc.

6 Fit the pinion shaft nut and tighten it to a torque of 65 to 72 lb ft (9 to 10 kg m) while keeping the shaft from turning by holding the brake drum (see **FIG 7:24**). The brake drum may now be removed.

Cover seal renewal:

7 Mark the cover in relation to the sliding pulley disc with masking tape so that it may be refitted in its original relative position. Remove the lock ring from the groove (see **FIG 7:25**).

8 With a soft hammer, carefully tap the cover loose (see **FIG 7:26**) and remove it. Examine the cover. If it is damaged or warped, a complete new sliding pulley disc assembly must be fitted as described earlier in this Section.

9 Remove the seal from the cover. Use mandrel 8-99-535331 to fit the new seal (see **FIG 7:27**) which should be lubricated sparingly with Shell Retinax G.

10 Pry the sealing ring from the sliding pulley disc. Lubricate a new sealing ring sparingly with Shell Retinax G. Refer to **FIG 7:28** and fit the new sealing ring. **The round edge must face inwards.**

11 Pour 75 cc of ATF type A/A fluid into the disc. Align the marks and fit the cover. Tap it carefully into position with a soft hammer. Fit the lock ring (see **FIG 7:29**).

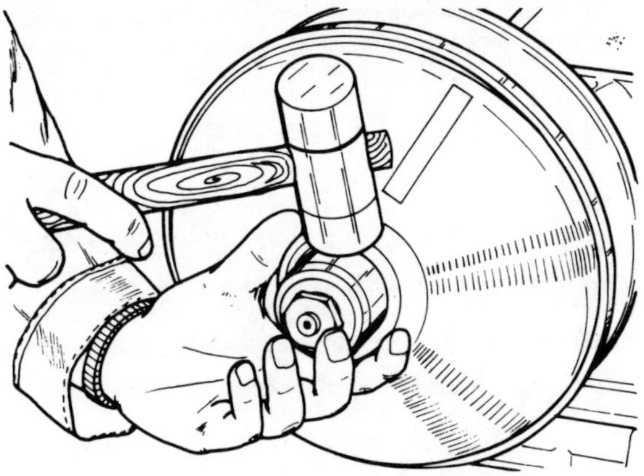

FIG 7:26 Removing the sliding pulley disc cover

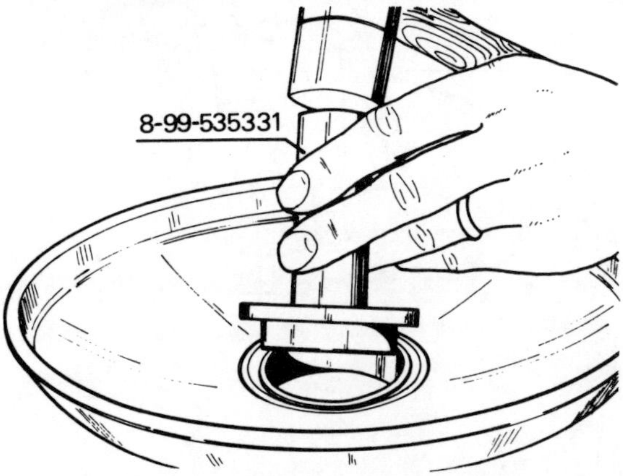

FIG 7:27 Fitting a new cover seal

Sliding pulley disc seal renewal:

12 Mark the sliding pulley disc in relation to the fixed pulley disc with masking tape so that it may be refitted in its original relative position. Fit clamping tool 8-99-535454 and, as shown in **FIG 7:21** and described in operation 2 of this Section, remove the sliding pulley disc assembly from the hub shaft of the fixed pulley disc.

13 Pry the oil seal (see **FIG 6:30**) from the counterbore in the hub of the sliding pulley disc. Remove the 'O' ring seals (see **FIG 6:31**) from the hub of the sliding pulley disc. Clean out the old grease from the hub cavity.

14 Check the bore diameter using the blade end of gauge 3-99-535373 (see **FIG 7:30**). If the blade enters, the complete sliding disc **must** be renewed.

15 Using the caliper end of the same gauge, check the outer diameter of the fixed disc hub shaft (see **FIG 6:32**). If the jaws of the gauge pass over the diameter, it is undersize and the fixed pulley disc must be renewed.

16 Fit new 'O' ring seals. Refer to **FIG 7:31** and, using tool 3-99-535398, fill the grease cavity of the sliding pulley disc with 7 cc of Molykote BR2-S (DAF part No. 600090).

17 Use tools 8-99535333 and 8-99-535387 (see **FIG 7:32**) to fit a new seal to the sliding pulley disc **with the lip facing inwards**. The remaining assembly operations are the reverse of the dismantling sequence.

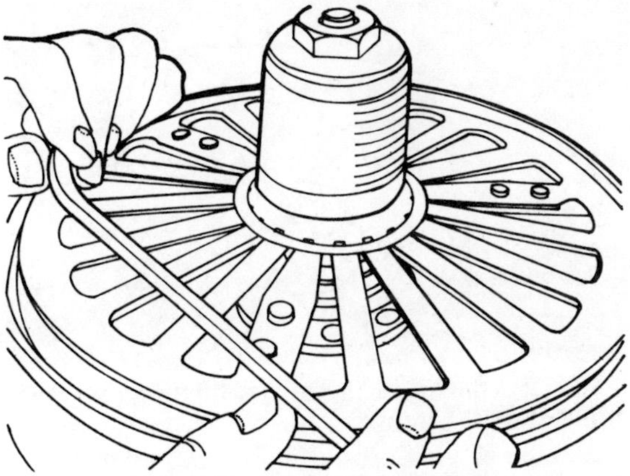

FIG 7:28 Fitting a sealing ring

Pinion shaft seal renewal:

18 Mark the sliding and fixed pulley discs and the end face of the pinion shaft in relation to each other as shown in **FIG 7:33**. Fit clamping tool 8-99-535454 and remove the sliding pulley disc (see operations 2 and 3).

19 Remove the fixed pulley disc. Check that it is in good condition and carry out operation 15. Renew the pulley disc if necessary.

20 Prise out the oil seal from the reduction gear casing and clean out the counterbore. Use mandrel 8-99-535326 and adaptor ring 8-99-535336 and install a new seal.

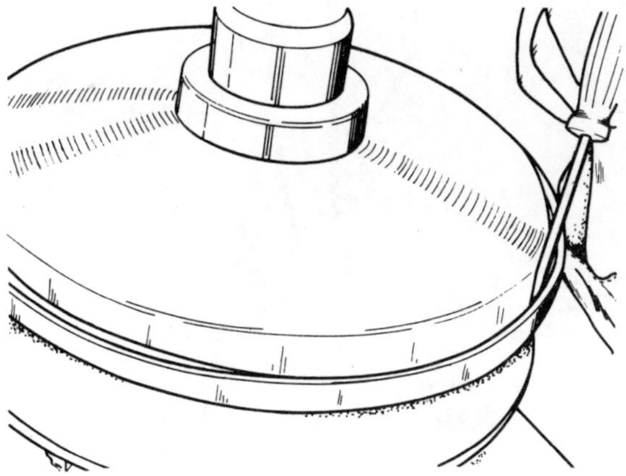

FIG 7:29 Method of fitting the locking ring

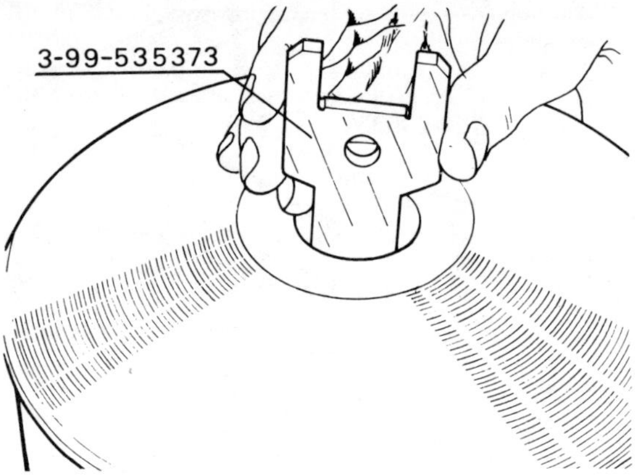

FIG 7:30 Gauging the disc bore diameter

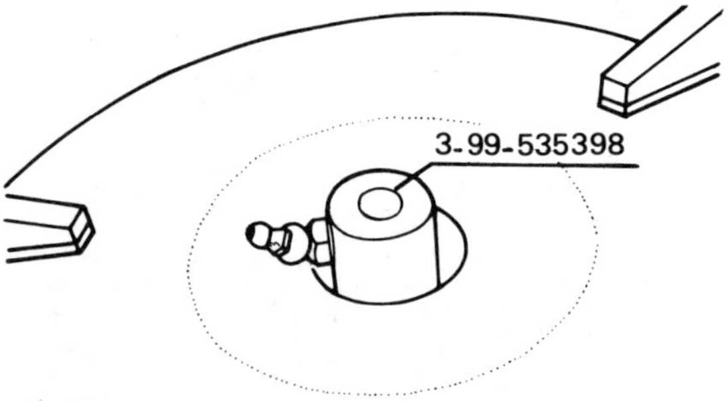

FIG 7:31 The special tool used to fill the grease cavity of the sliding pulley disc

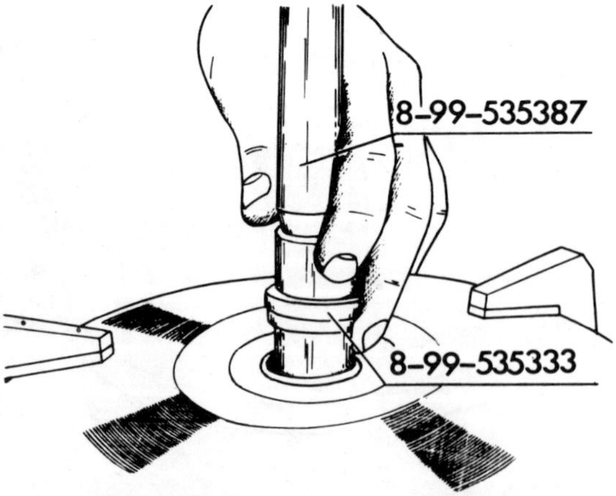

FIG 7:32 Fitting a pinion shaft seal

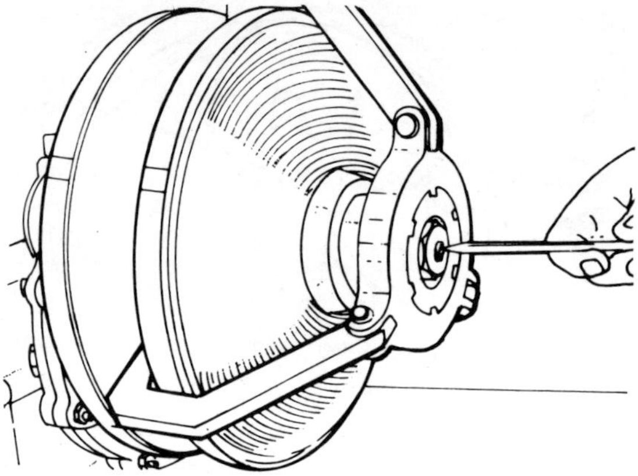

FIG 7:33 Marking the end of the pinion shaft in relation to the pulley discs

Lubricate the seal lip and the shaft splines sparingly with Shell Retinax G. Reassembly is now the reverse of the dismantling sequence. **Ensure that the alignment marks are observed.**

7:9 Axle shaft and hub bearing, DAF 46

1 Raise the rear of the car and fit firm supports. Remove the wheel and withdraw the brake drum with the aid of a soft-faced hammer. Disconnect the constant velocity joint at the wheel and suspend out of the way.

2 Using a 36 mm socket spanner, slacken the nut of the companion flange on the wheel side. For this operation, block the drive shaft with the hub puller No. 7-99-535017 (see **FIG 7:34**) and the spreading tool No. 8-99-535711. If required the hub puller may be adapted by welding a tube on the hub puller as shown in **FIG 7:35**.

3 Remove the companion flange on the wheel side with a puller (see **FIG 7:36**) and tap out the drive shaft, interposing a copper protection block.

4 Remove the four attaching bolts of the anchor plates and bearing housing. Slightly pull forward the anchor plate and remove the bearing housing. Heat the bearing housing on a heating element such as a boiling plate (see **FIG 7:37**) to facilitate the removal of the bearing.

5 Clean the bearing housing with special attention to the contact faces of the bearings. Smear new bearings with grease, either Dura-Lith EP2 or a corresponding quality. Again heat the bearing housing to install both bearings. Tap them into position with a suitable tool (see **FIG 7:38**) so that they fit tightly. Once the bearing housing has cooled down, the spacer bush between the two bearings should be fixed so that it can only just be moved. Fit new oil seals and install both with the same drift.

6 Reassembly of the bearing housing and axle shaft is undertaken in the reverse order of the removal operations. Tighten the attaching bolts of the bearing housing and anchor plates to a torque of 36.2 to 40 lb ft (5 to 5.5 kgm).

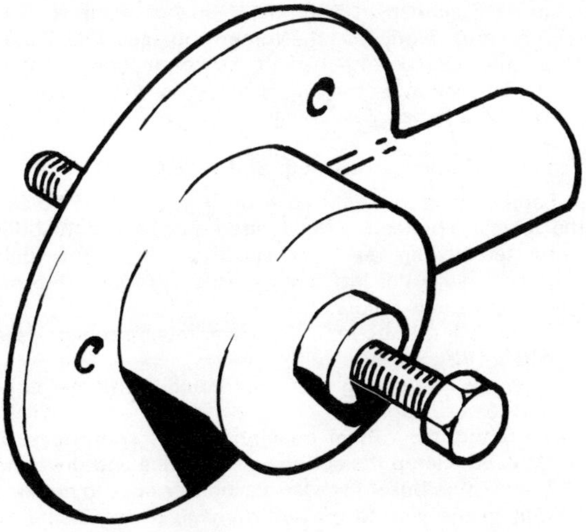

FIG 7:34 Hub puller 7-99-535017

FIG 7:35 Hub puller adapted to hold rear hub from turning

7 Clean the companion flange with petrol, removing any grease and old sealer from the screw threads of the attaching nut and from the axle shaft. Use Loctite 241 or corresponding locking fluid on the screw threads of the nut and the axle shaft, also on the splines of the companion flange. Turn the flange to distribute the fluid over the splines. Fit the components (see **FIG 7:39**) and tighten the axle shaft nut to a torque of 130 to 145 lb ft (18 to 20 kgm). Refit the brake components and the wheel and adjust the brake shoes of both rear wheels as described in **Chapter 10**.

7:10 Connecting rod, DAF 46

To remove and refit the connecting rod on DAF 46 vehicles, preliminary operations are to remove both rear wheels, brake drums, axle shafts and bearing housings as previously described. Proceed as follows:

1 Withdraw the bolt attaching the torque rod to the connecting rod.
2 Disconnect the handbrake cables on the anchor plate side and completely remove the brake lines from the connecting rod. Referring to **FIG 7:40** suspend the two anchor plates complete with brake lines on the upper attachment points of the dampers.
3 Remove the eight attachment nuts of the lower retaining plates and extract the bolts to withdraw the connecting rod.
4 Reassemble in the reverse order of removal. The attaching nuts of the lower spring retaining plates are

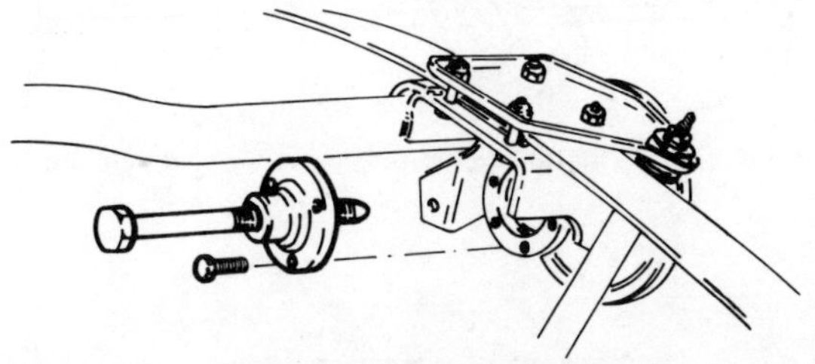

FIG 7:36 Puller 260517 for removing companion flange

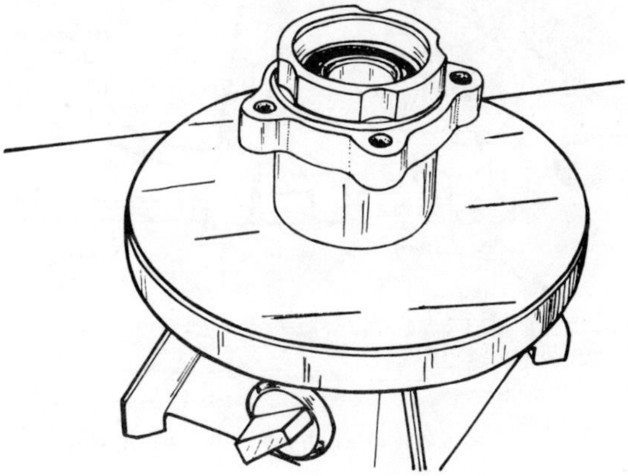

FIG 7:37 Heating bearing housing for removal of bearings

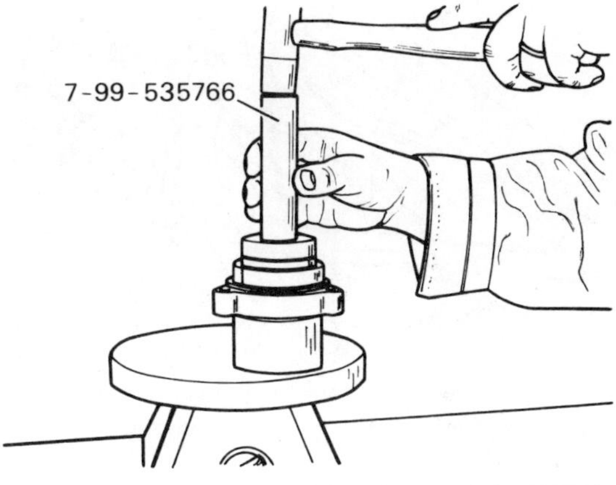

FIG 7:38 Installing bearings with tool 7-99-535766

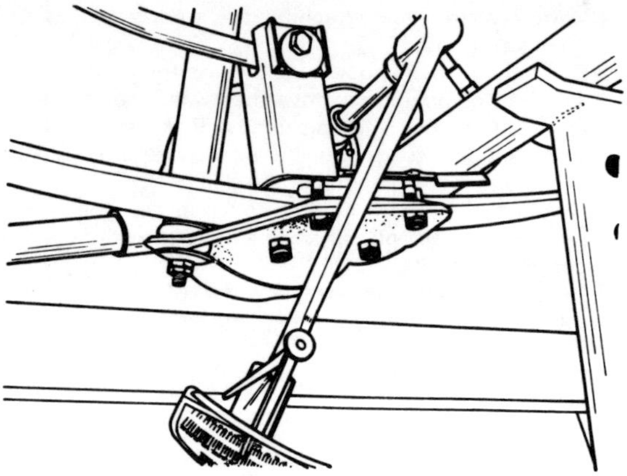

FIG 7:39 Installing bearing housing and axle shaft

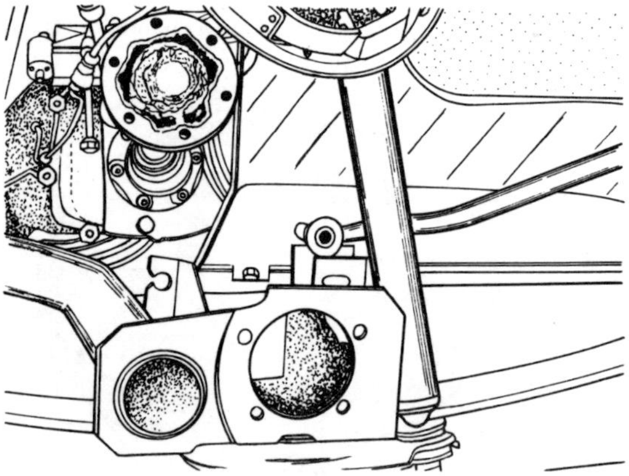

FIG 7:40 Withdrawing the connecting rod

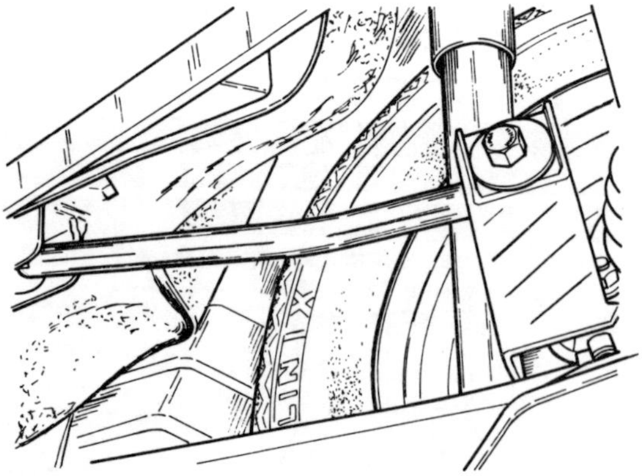

FIG 7:41 The torque and connecting rods

to be tightened to a torque of 36.2 to 40 lb ft (5 to 5.5 kgm). Note that the torque rod (see **FIG 7:41**) should only be attached to the connecting rod with the car resting on its wheels, otherwise the suspension will be affected.

7:11 Leaf spring removal and refitting DAF 46

For removing and refitting a leaf spring on DAF 46 cars the vehicle is preferably to be raised on a lift and the body supported at the rear jack supports. The lift is then lowered until the leaf spring is unstressed. Further operations are as follows:

1. Remove the bolts from the lower retaining plate (see **FIG 7:42**).
2. Unscrew the spring bolt nuts, remove the eye bolts and then the spring.
3. To renew the rubber bushings in the spring eyes if required, clamp the spring leaf in a vice and drive out the existing bushings. Use plastic vice jaws to hold the unit in the vice to prevent damage to the inside, or tension side of the spring leaf, which might cause it to rupture. The method of introducing the bushings into a spring leaf is shown in **FIG 7:43**. Tyre grease and soap

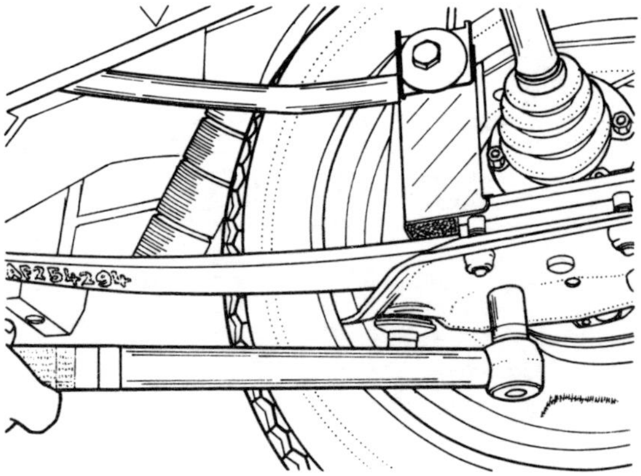

FIG 7:42 Spring retaining plate

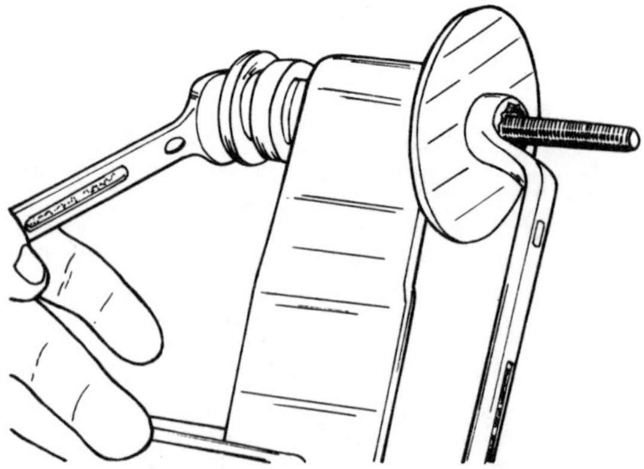

FIG 7:43 Renewing spring bushes

solution on the spring eye and spring bracket will help to facilitate operations.

4 Refitting the spring leaf is a reversal of the dismantling procedure. Note that the part of the spring leaf which bears the part number should point towards the front spring bracket in order to avoid misalignment of the connecting rod.

5 Tighten the spring leaf nuts and the nuts of the retaining plate uniformly to a torque of 36 to 40 lb ft (5 to 5.5 kgm). When tightening the spring leaf nuts the car should rest on the wheels with a load of 50 kg (110 lb) in the luggage compartment to ensure that the designed spring characteristics are maintained.

7:12 Drive shafts, DAF 46

Renewing bellows:

1 Remove the complete guard pan.
2 Remove the flange bolts and washers at each end and lift out the shaft.
3 Remove the circlips from the drive shaft (see **FIG 7:44**).
4 Tap off the steel protection caps (see **FIG 7:45**).
5 Remove the clamps from the bellows.
6 Using a press, press out the drive shaft from the joints and remove the cap, gasket and bellows.
7 Use a new gasket between the steel cap and the joint, and reassemble in the reverse order.
Do not dismantle the homokinetic joints.

7:13 Secondary Variomatic unit, DAF 46

Removing:

1 Jack-up the car and support on stands.
2 Release the exhaust pipe attachment at the front end of the lefthand spring leaf.
3 Remove the guard pan.
4 Disconnect the drive shafts from the gearcase and secure out of the way.
5 Slacken the locknut 5 (see **FIG 7:46**) and unscrew adjusting screw 6 fully.
6 Slacken nuts 3, 4, 7 and 8.
7 Remove nuts 3 and 4 and let the brackets hang from the two front bolts.
8 Replace nuts 3 and 4 until the bolt end and nut are flush.
9 Unscrew nuts 1 and 2 to a similar position.

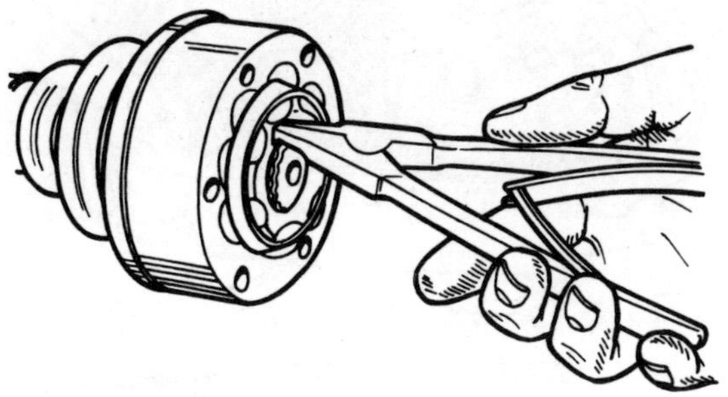

FIG 7:44 Removing circlip from drive shaft homokinetic joint

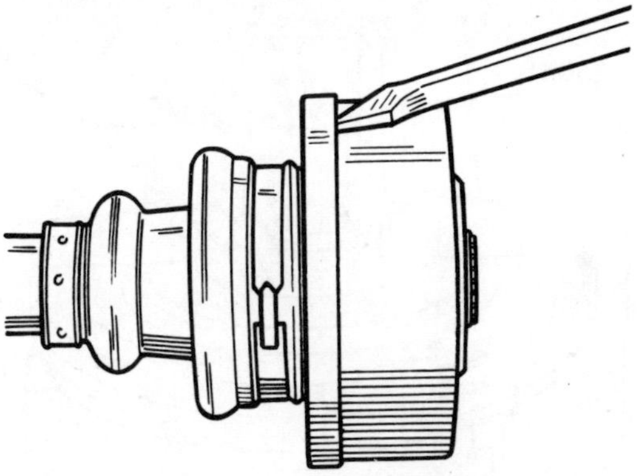

FIG 7:45 Tapping off steel protection cap with a suitable punch

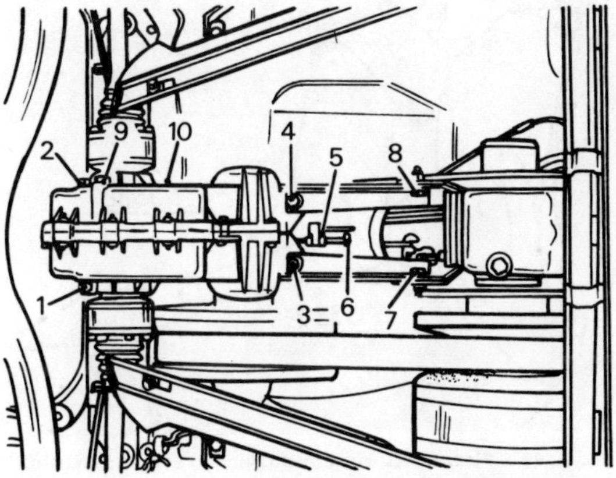

FIG 7:46 Secondary Variomatic unit

Key to Fig 7:46 1 to 4 Variomatic unit retaining nuts 5 Locknut 6 Adjusting screw 7 and 8 Bracket retaining bolts 9 Drain plug 10 Filler/level plug

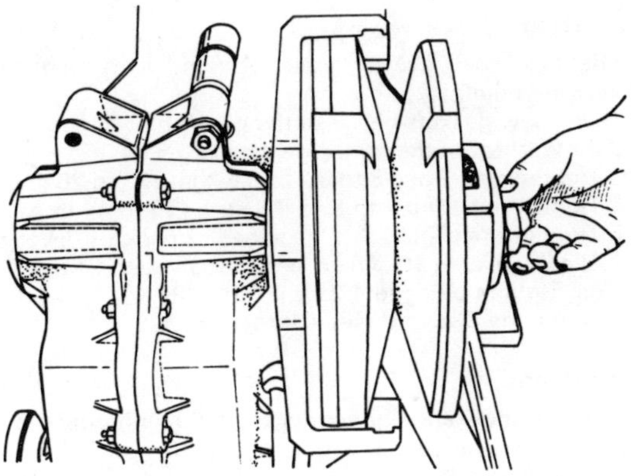

FIG 7:47 Sliding disc clamped together with tool 8-99-260509. Fixed disc held with tool 260508 to enable nut to be unscrewed

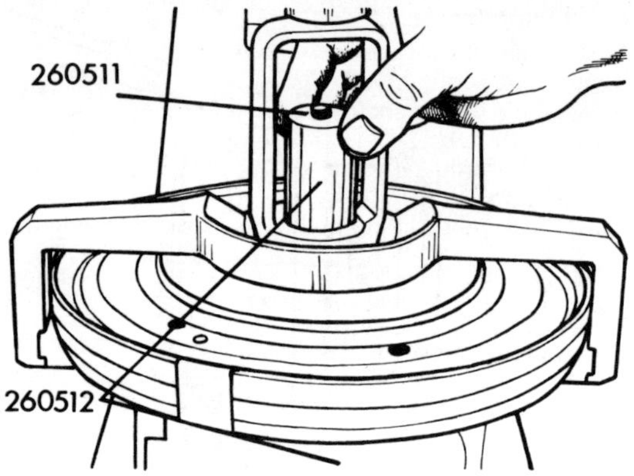

FIG 7:48 Dismantling sliding disc assembly

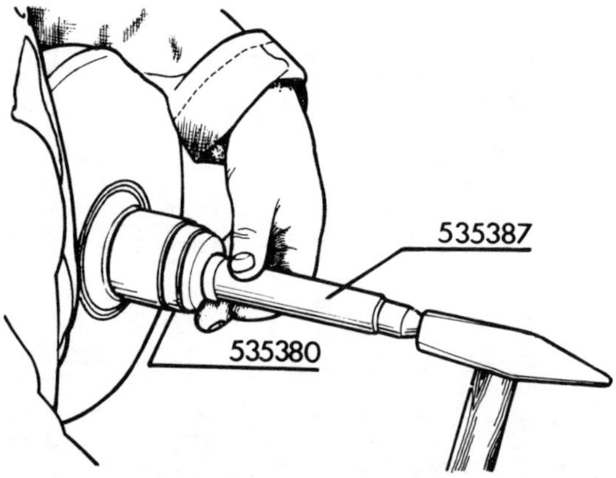

FIG 7:49 Fitting 'O' ring and grease retainer to sliding disc

10 Spread the secondary discs and insert a 23 mm (.906 inch) spacer, remove the belt.
11 Support the unit securely and remove the four nuts.
12 Lower and remove the unit.

Refitting:

Refit in the reverse order of removal noting the following points:
1 Use new gaskets between the drive shaft flanges.
2 Fit washers under the screw heads.
3 Tighten nuts 7 and 8 to 3.2 to 3.6 kgm (23 to 26 lb ft).
4 Tighten nuts 1 to 4 to 5 to 5.5 kgm (36 to 40 lb ft).
5 Tighten drain plug 9 if necessary, check oil level at filler/level plug 10 or refill as necessary with SAE.80EP oil. Tighten plugs to 4.2 kgm (30 lb ft).
6 Check the disc gap (see **Chapter 6**).

Servicing:

Special tools are required for the following operations and if not available the unit should be taken to an authorised agent.
1 Remove the secondary Variomatic unit as previously described.
2 Mark all parts in relation to each other and to the pinion shaft.
3 Clamp the sliding disc together with tool 8-99-260509 and hold the fixed disc with tool 260508, unscrew the shaft nut (see **FIG 7:47**).
4 Remove the fixed disc from the shaft with the aid of a puller.
5 Check the outer diameter of the fixed disc hub with 'NO-GO' gauge 260516.
6 Remove the sliding disc assembly from the shaft. Lay the disc with the diaphragm facing upwards to prevent loss of oil.
7 Remove the grease retainer, 'O' ring seals and grease from the grease chamber, and check the inner diameter of the hub with 'NO-GO' gauge 260516.
8 Place the hub of the disc with the diaphragm upwards on the longer part of the tool 260512 and place the shorter part on top (see **FIG 7:48**). Press down on the clamping plate with tool 260511 to overcome the diaphragm spring pressure, and screw on the shorter part of tool 260512 until it butts.
9 Remove the clamp 8-99-260509 from the disc, and take out the circlip, clamping plate, lock ring and diaphragm, marking for reassembly.
10 Install a new sealing rubber engaging the tabs in the disc recess, and top up with ATF type A/A oil if necessary.
11 Align marking and install diaphragm, press down using tool 260510 to overcome pressure of the sealing rubber, and fit the locking ring and clamping plate with the hole or recess in the clamping plate at 180 deg. to the hole in the spring collar and force it into its groove by using tool 260511 and a press.
12 Clamp the sliding disc with tool 8-99-260509 and remove tool 260512. Fill the grease chamber with Molykote grease (DAF part No. 600090).
Fit new 'O' rings and grease retainer using adapter 535380 and drift 535387 (see **FIG 7:49**).

The remainder of the operations are a reversal of the dismantling procedure. Use a hide faced hammer to tap the fixed disc onto the shaft splines. Use Loctite 241 on the threads of the shaft and nut and tighten the nut to a torque of 18 to 20 kgm (130 to 145 lb ft).

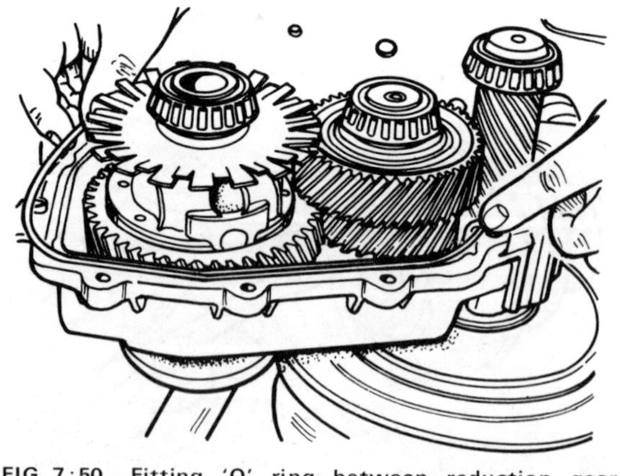
FIG 7:50 Fitting 'O' ring between reduction gear casing halves

Reduction gear oil seals:

All the oil seals can be renewed with the reduction gear in situ except the 'O' ring between the reduction gear half casings.

If the oil leak is from the drive shaft flange, disconnect the drive shaft at the reduction gear end and tie it up out of the way to the handbrake cables. Remove the flange from the gear case as already described. Prise out the old oil seal and drive in the new seal with the aid of tool 260515.

The discs will have to be removed as already described if the leak is from the discs end of the pinion shaft. Renew the oil seal in a similar manner.

A leak from the oil baffle at the other end of the pinion shaft can be dealt with by renewing the baffle in a similar manner.

To renew the 'O' ring between the halves of the reduction gear case, remove the Variomatic unit as already described and secure on the bench with the oil filler/level plug upwards. Remove the drive flange and unscrew the 12 casing bolts. Take off the top half of the casing and remove the 'O' ring, clean and dry out the groove and fit the new 'O' ring dry (see **FIG 7:50**).

Reassemble in the reverse order, installing the wave washers under the bolt heads and nuts. Tighten the nuts to 1.8 kgm (13 lb ft). The flange bolt to 2.3 to 2.6 kgm (16 to 19 lb ft).

After installation of the unit top up with oil and tighten the level plug to 4.2 kgm (30 lb ft).

7:14 Fault diagnosis

(a) Noisy rear axle unit(s)

1 Insufficient or incorrect lubrication
2 Worn bearings
3 Worn gears

(b) Excessive backlash

1 Check 2 and 3 in (a)
2 Worn shaft splines
3 Worn or broken wheel studs

(c) Fluid leaks

1 Defective cover seal
2 Defective sliding pulley disc seal
3 Defective pinion shaft seal
4 Defective hub seal
5 Defective reduction gear casing joint
6 Loose drain or refill plug
7 Sealing ring in sliding pulley disc assembly defective

(d) Vibration

1 Unbalance in Variomatic driven unit(s)
2 Driven unit loose in suspension arm

(e) Rattles

1 Suspension arm pivot(s) worn
2 Worn damper attachment(s)
3 Damper(s) loose
4 Broken road spring

(f) 'Settling'

1 Check 2, 3 and 4 in (e)
2 Weak road spring
3 Broken damper attachment bolt

(g) 'Bottoming' of suspension

1 Check 4 in (e); 2 in (f)
2 Worn or missing bump stop
3 Ineffective damper(s)

(h) Driven pulley disc assembly defective

1 Fluid or grease on pulley disc faces
2 Sliding pulley disc spring weak or broken
3 Sliding pulley disc seized

(j) Broken drive belt(s) (see **Chapter 6**)

(k) Slipping drive belt(s) (see **Chapter 6**)

(l) No drive obtainable (see **Chapter 6**)

(m) 'Deranged' ratio changes (see **Chapter 6**)

NOTES

CHAPTER 8

FRONT SUSPENSION AND HUBS

8 : 1 Description

FIG 8 : 1 gives a general view of the suspension at front and rear and **FIG 8 : 2** shows a section through a front hub and the transverse multileaf suspension spring arrangement which is basically the same for all models. The two hub bearings are carried in the brake drum. The stub axle on which they run is integral with a bracket which carries a ball joint and the double-acting telescopic hydraulic damper (see **FIG 8 : 3**). There is no kingpin as such and the angle of the axis of the damper (which passes through the ball joint) is, in effect, the kingpin inclination. Pivoting of each front wheel, for steering motion, is accommodated at the ball joint and between the damper body and the damper piston rod. A steering arm is integral with the top end of each damper body. The transverse multileaf spring is mounted to a chassis frame at two points. The socket of each 'kingpin' ball joint is attached to an end of the transverse spring. The rubber bump stops are carried on the chassis and operate against the transverse spring at points which are approximately midway between each spring extremity and each spring to frame attachment point. The speedometer drive cable, on all models, is driven from the lefthand front wheel hub.

8 : 2 Maintenance

Tyre pressures:

Front tyres should, for normal service, be inflated to the following pressures.

DAF 31, 32 and 33 models:

Tyre	*Passenger and commercial vehicles*
Cross-ply	17 lb/sq inch (1.2 kg/sq cm)
Radial-ply	20 lb/sq inch (1.4 kg/sq cm)

DAF 44 models:

Tyre	*Pressure*
Semperit	25 lb/sq inch (1.8 kg/sq cm)
Michelin, Uniroyal	22 lb/sq inch (1.6 kg/sq cm)
Kleber Colombes	20 lb/sq inch (1.4 kg/sq cm)

DAF 46 models:

All recommended types	23 lb/sq inch (1.6 kg/sq cm)

8 : 3 Hub bearings

DAF 31, 32 and 33 models, removal and fitment:

1 Remove the relevant brake drum as described in **Chapter 10, Section 10 : 4**. Working from the outer

FIG 8:1 A phantom view of a DAF 44 car

side, remove the outer circlip and, using a puller of the type shown in **FIG 8:4**, remove the outer hub bearing as shown in the illustration. Withdraw the spacer tube. Remove the inner circlip.

2 Turn the drum over and use a puller to withdraw the inner bearing. Clean off the bearing and circlip registers.

3 Working from the inner side and using a drift, tap the inner bearing into position. The dust shield must face outwards.

4 Turn the drum over and fit the inner circlip. Fit the spacer tube (collar outwards), tap the outer bearing into position and fit the outer circlip. Install the brake drum as described in **Chapter 10, Section 10:4**.

DAF 44 models, removal and fitment:

1 Remove the relevant brake drum as described in **Chapter 10, Section 10:4**. Working from the inner side, prise out the seal and remove the inner bearing cone (see **FIG 8:5**).

2 Use a drift as shown in **FIG 8:6** to tap out the inner and outer bearing cups. Clean off the bearing locations in the brake drum bore.

3 Working from the outer side, use a drift and tap new bearing cups into their respective positions (see **FIG 8:7**). Pack the inner bearing cone with grease, fit it and install a new seal. Fill the space between the bearings half full with grease (see **FIG 8:8**).

4 Slide the brake drum assembly on the wheel spindle, then pack the outer bearing cone with an approved grease and push it on the spindle and into the hub. Fit the locking ring and adjusting nut. Tighten the nut (see **FIG 8:9**) until the washer under the nut can just be moved radially by a screwdriver. Install the locking plate and locknut and tighten the latter. Secure both nuts by bending over the locking plate tabs (see **FIG 8:10**). Use new self-locking nuts and a new splitpin to secure the ball joint nut, which should be tightened to a torque of 40 to 47 lb ft (5.5 to 6.5 kgm). Fit a new ball joint if the end play of the ball pin exceeds .1 to .12 inch (2.5 to 3 mm). Complete reassembly as described in **Chapter 10**.

8:4 Dampers

Dampers (see **FIG 8:3**) may be overhauled with the aid of the service kit available without removing them completely from the car. Procedure is as follows:

1 Remove the nut from the top of the relevant damper piston rod. Use a soft drift to tap the rod fully downwards (see **FIG 8:11**). Remove two bolts and withdraw the damper mounting bush. Jack up the front of the car and fit firm stands.

2 Remove the dust cover from the top of the damper. Unscrew the gland nut with the special spanner shown in **FIG 8:12** and prise out the sealing washers with a pointed tool. Remove the piston rod guide nut with the spanner formerly employed, making sure that

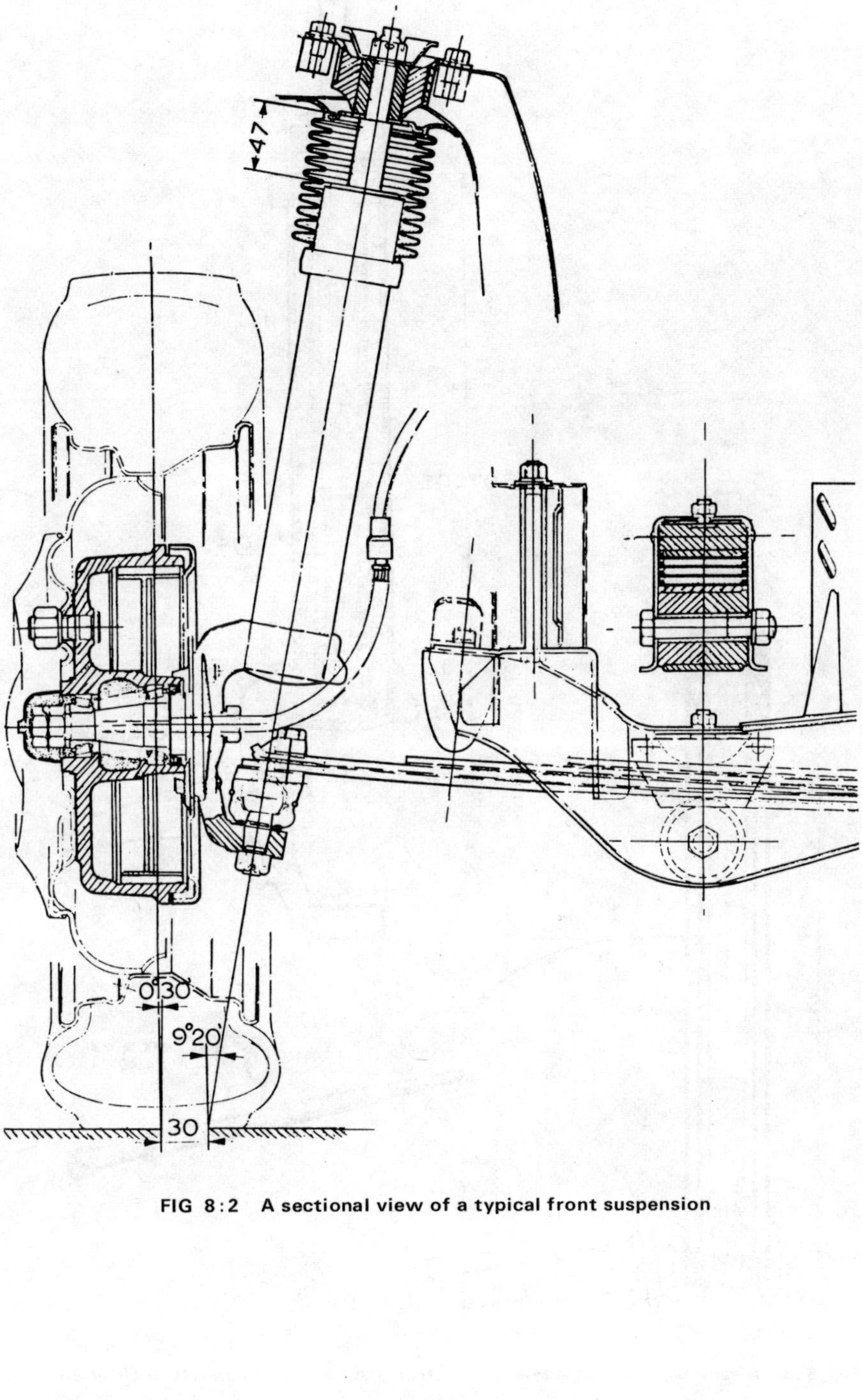

FIG 8:2 A sectional view of a typical front suspension

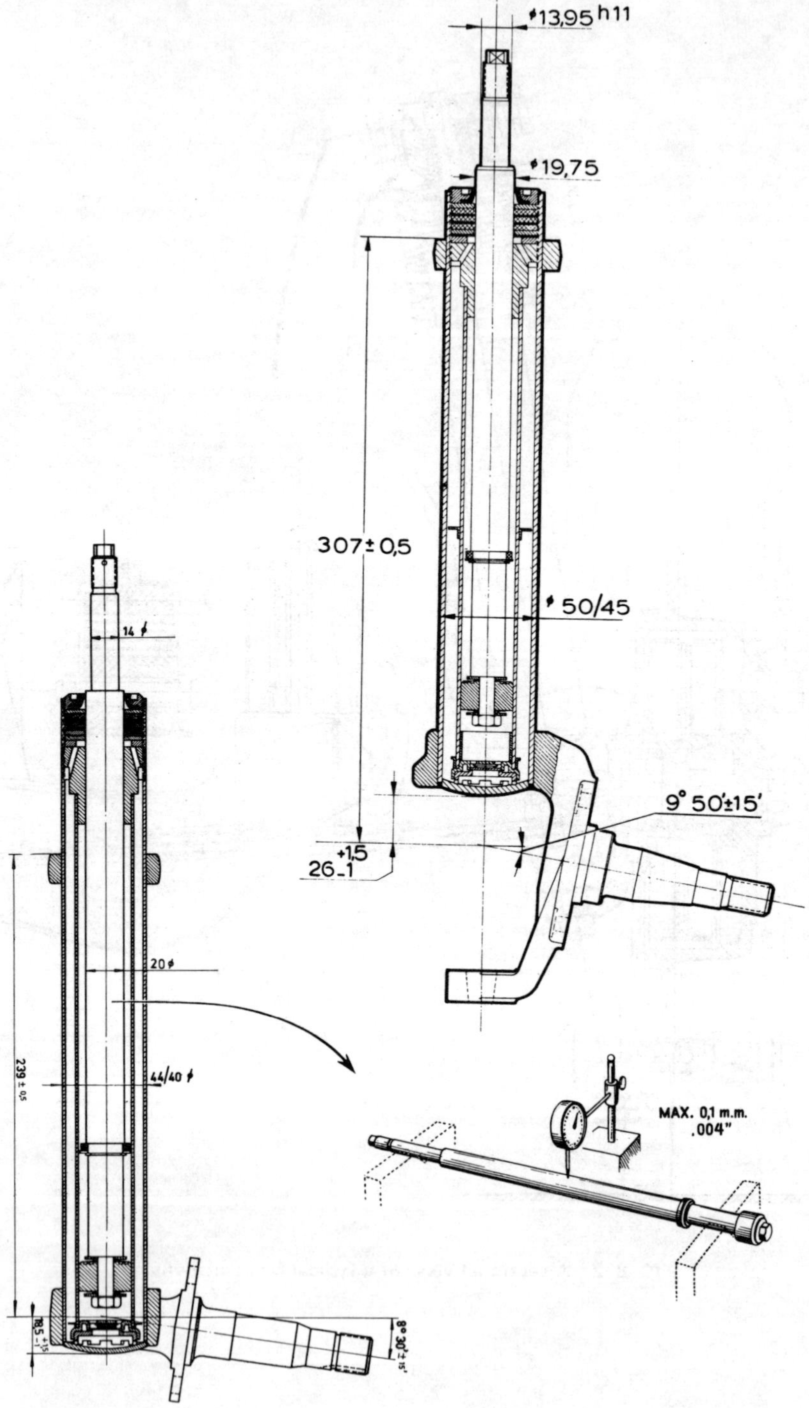

FIG 8:3 A sectional view of a telescopic strut, DAF 31, 32, 33 on left, DAF 44 on right

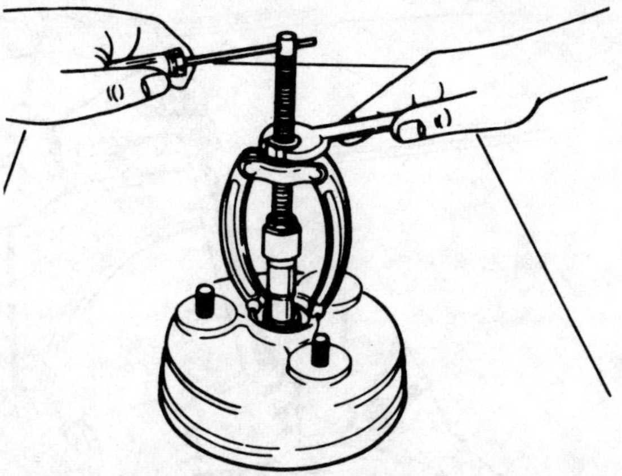

FIG 8:4 Removing an outer hub bearing, DAF 31, 32, 33

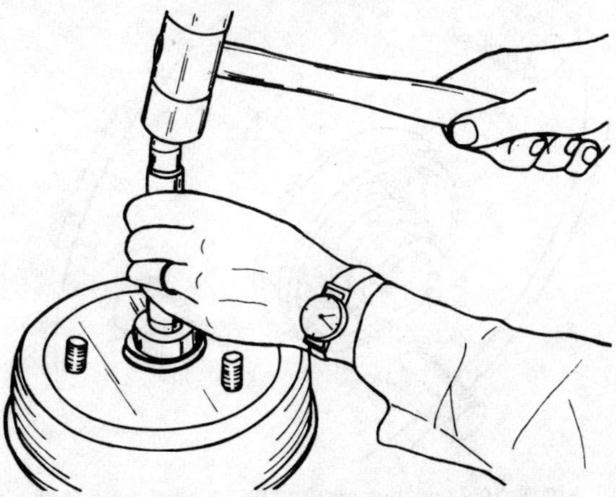

FIG 8:7 Fitting new bearing cups

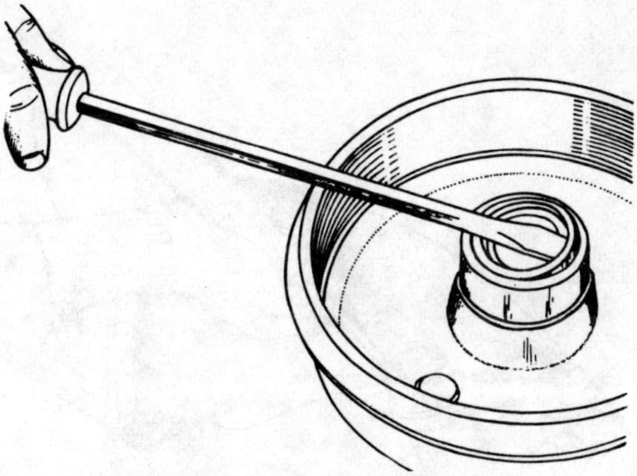

FIG 8:5 Extracting the grease seal

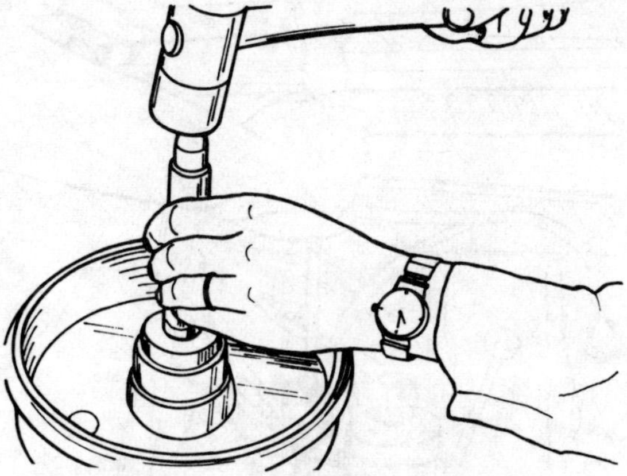

FIG 8:8 Installing new grease seal

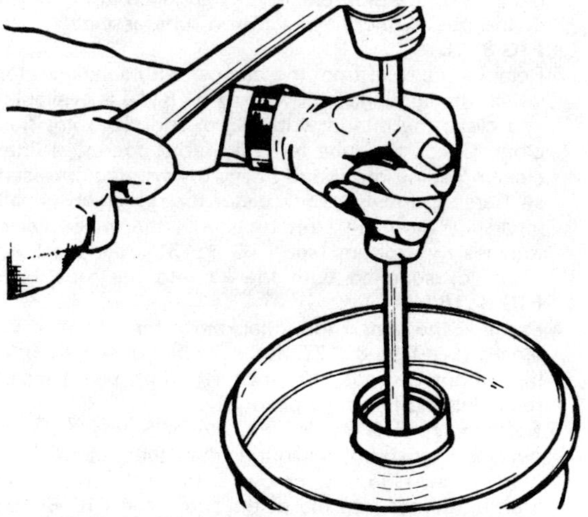

FIG 8:6 Removing hub bearing cups, DAF 44

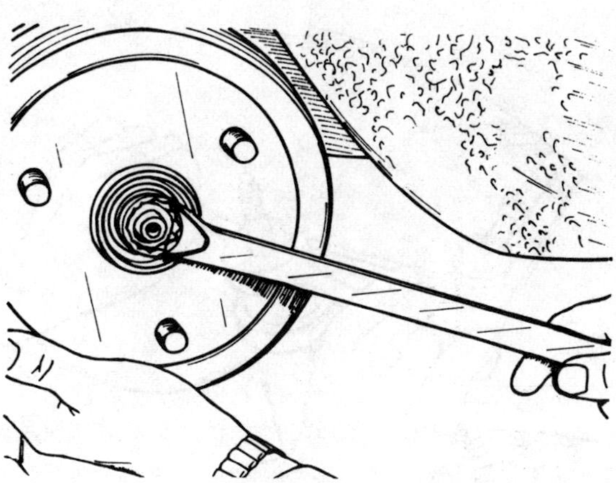

FIG 8:9 Adjustment of hub bearing

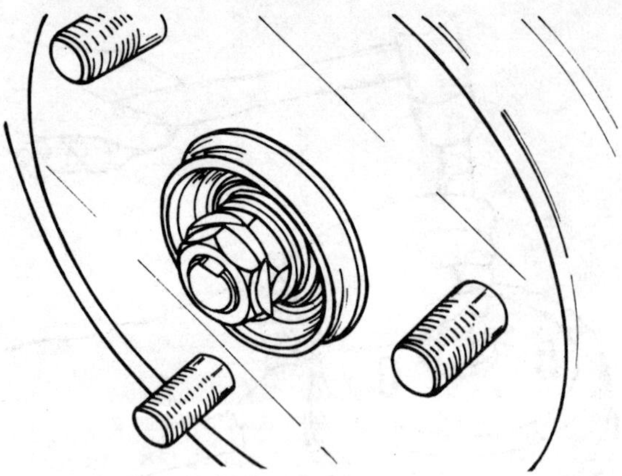

FIG 8:10 Locknut secured by locking plate tabs

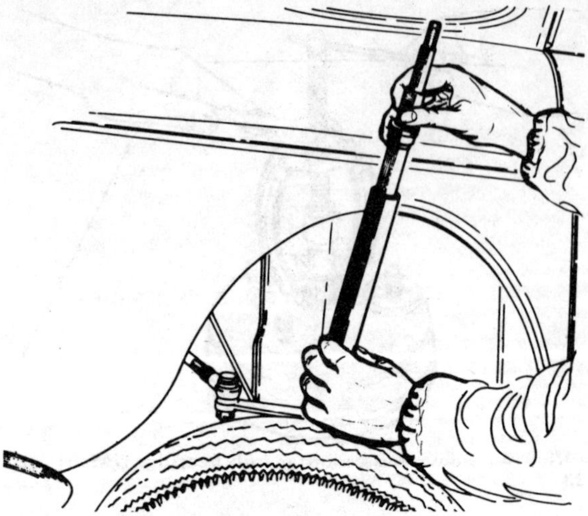

FIG 8:13 Withdrawing piston tube assembly

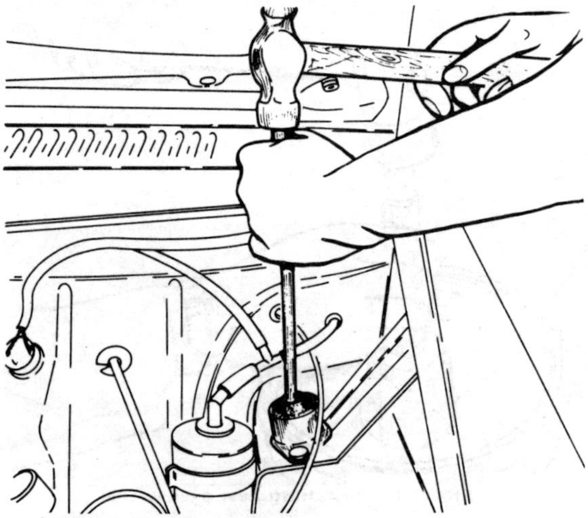

FIG 8:11 Tapping down the damper piston rod

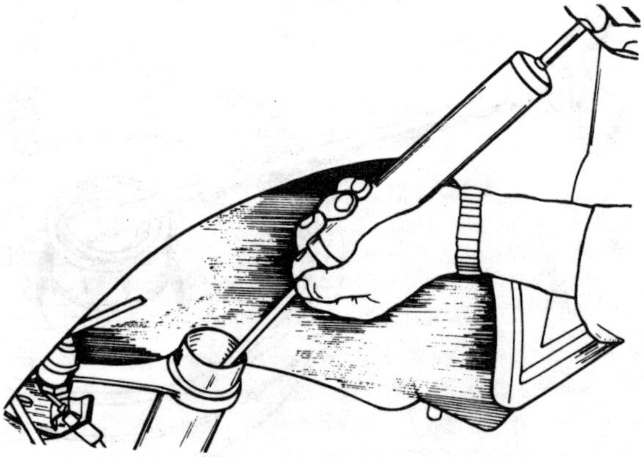

FIG 8:14 Extracting fluid from strut tube

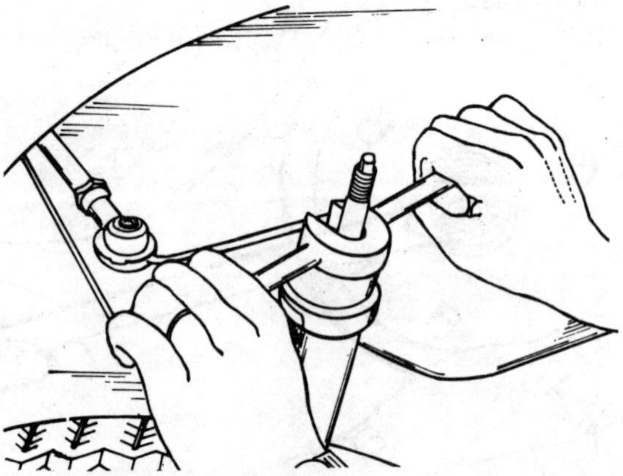

FIG 8:12 Unscrewing the gland nut

the pins of the tool remain fully engaged in the holes of the nut. Withdraw the piston tube assembly (see **FIG 8:13**).

3 Remove the fluid from the damper with a syringe, for which the appliance shown in **FIG 8:14** is available, and clean the interior with petrol and clean lint-free cloth. Check the tube for leakage by pouring a little cleaning spirit into it and finally dry with compressed air. Carefully lower the new piston tube assembly (small repair kit) into the strut tube until the check valve touches the bottom (see **FIG 8:15**). Pour the fluid (250 cc) supplied with the kit into the tube (see **FIG 8:16**).

4 Examine the piston rod, checking it for runout in V-blocks (see **FIG 8:17**). If it is scuffed or scored, or if the runout exceeds .004 inch (.1 mm), use a major repair kit and fit a new piston rod.

5 Referring to **FIG 8:18**, slide a new synthetic ring 1 over the pushrod, ensuring that the circlip 2 is correctly seated in the groove 3. Insert the piston rod with guide nut into the piston tube (see **FIG 8:19**) and secure the guide nut with the special spanner.

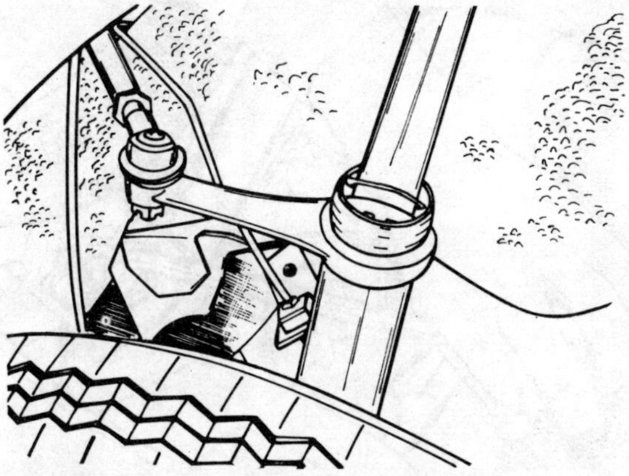

FIG 8:15 Inserting piston tube assembly into strut tube

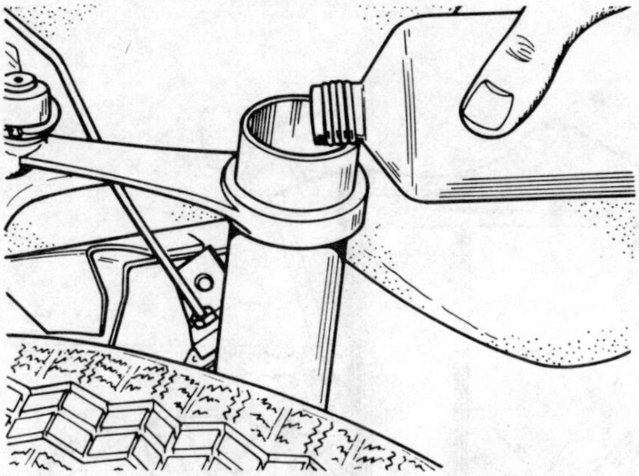

FIG 8:16 Refilling the tube

Check that the rod does not bind when rotated by hand. If it does, slacken off the nut and retighten.

6 Apply the graphite grease supplied in the kit to the rubber and fibre washers and fit the washers in the order shown in **FIG 8:20**.

7 Pump the piston rod up and down several times and then recheck the gland nut for tightness. The gland nut should be tightened to a torque of 87 to 100 lb ft (12 to 14 kgm). Fit the dust cover and pull the piston rod up through the mounting bush. Secure with a new self-locking nut, whilst keeping the piston rod from turning with an open-end spanner placed on the tang of the rod (see **FIG 8:21**). Note that this operation is more easily undertaken by first removing the mounting bush from the wheel arch and fitting it on the piston rod.

8:5 Removing and refitting a damper/stub axle unit

To remove and refit a telescopic strut assembly, operations are as follows:

1 Jack-up the car, remove the wheel and brake drum and disconnect the brake line (see **FIG 8:22**) and speedometer cable. Remove the brake backplate (see **FIG 8:23**).

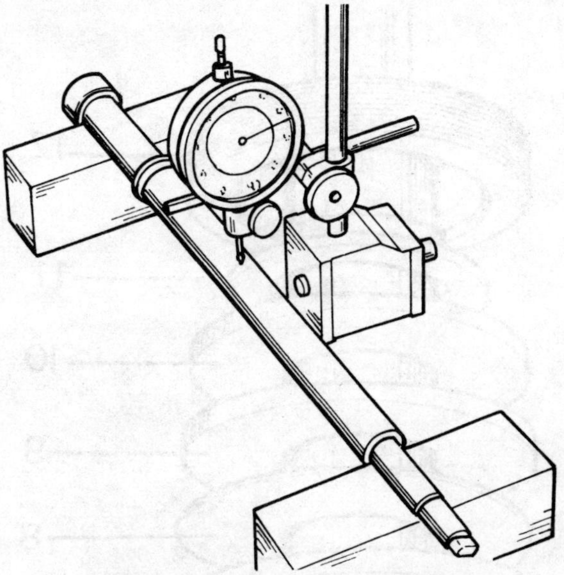

FIG 8:17 Checking piston rod runout

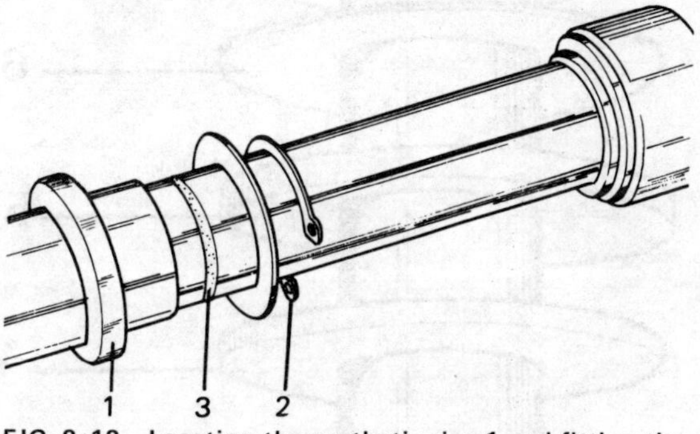

FIG 8:18 Locating the synthetic ring 1 and fitting the circlip 2 in the pushrod groove 3

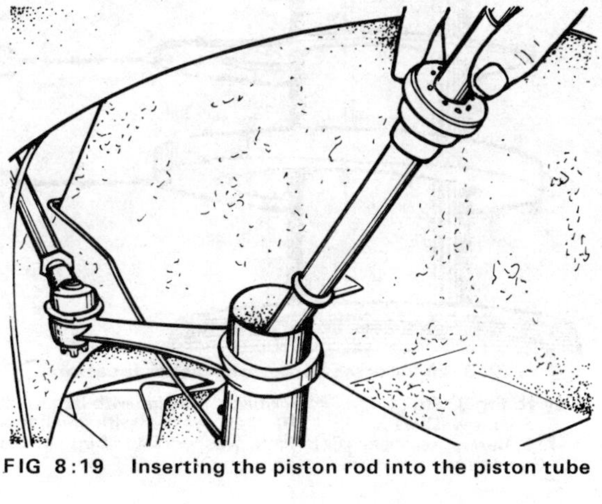

FIG 8:19 Inserting the piston rod into the piston tube

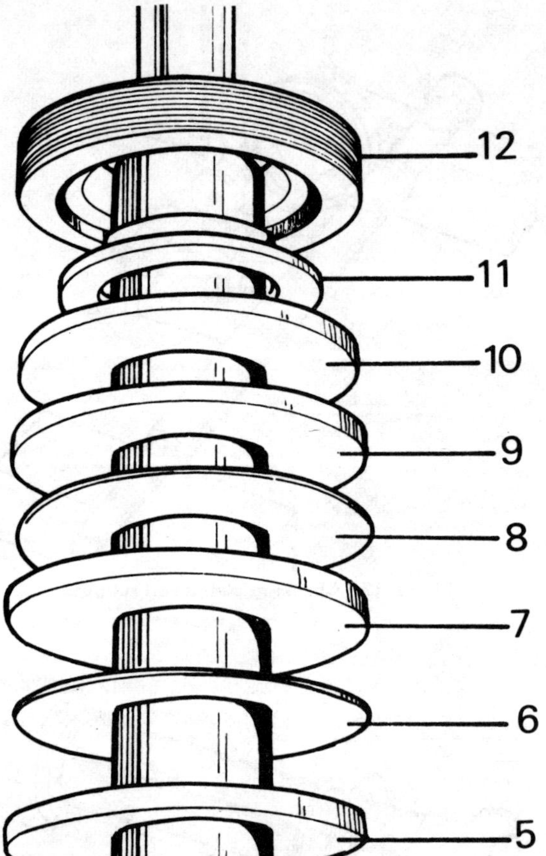

FIG 8:20 Correct order of washer location

Key to Fig 8:20 1 Spacer washer with large hole 2, 3 Spring washers 4, 10 Back washer with small hole 5, 7, 9 Rubber washers 6, 8 Fibre washers 11 Cupped seal 12 Gland nut

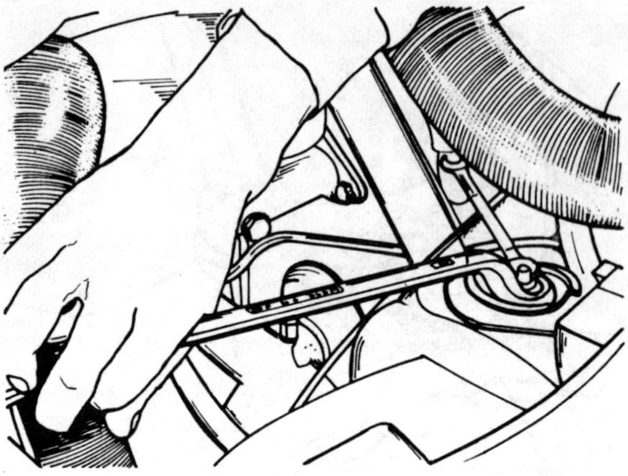

FIG 8:21 Securing a piston rod

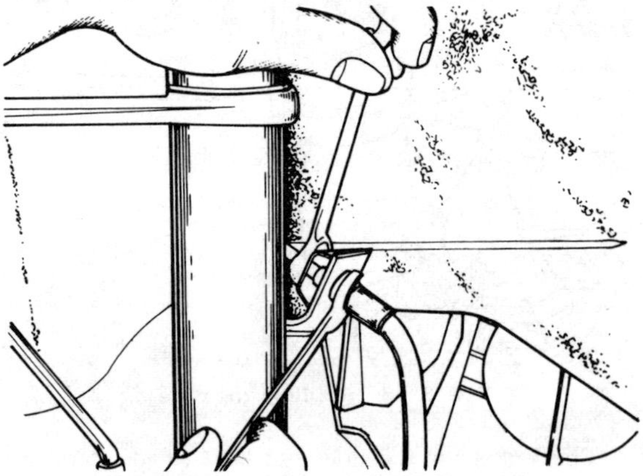

FIG 8:22 Disconnecting brake line

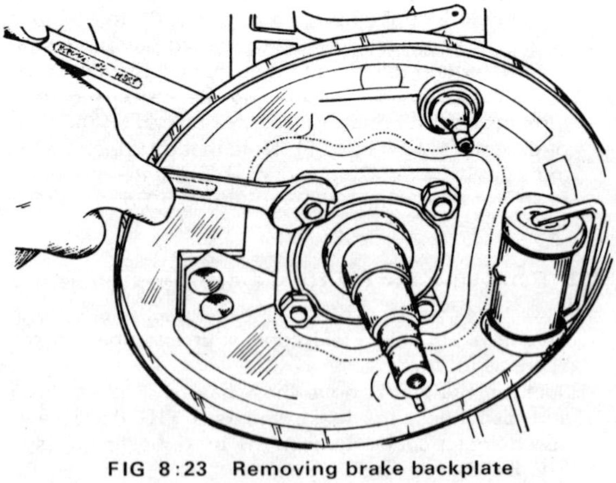

FIG 8:23 Removing brake backplate

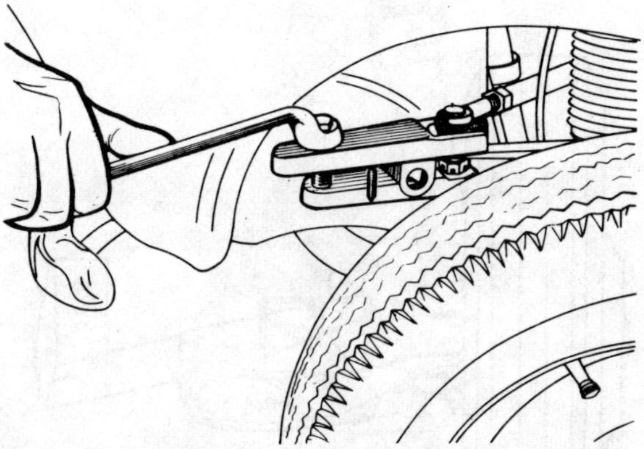

FIG 8:24 Removing track rod ball joint from steering arm

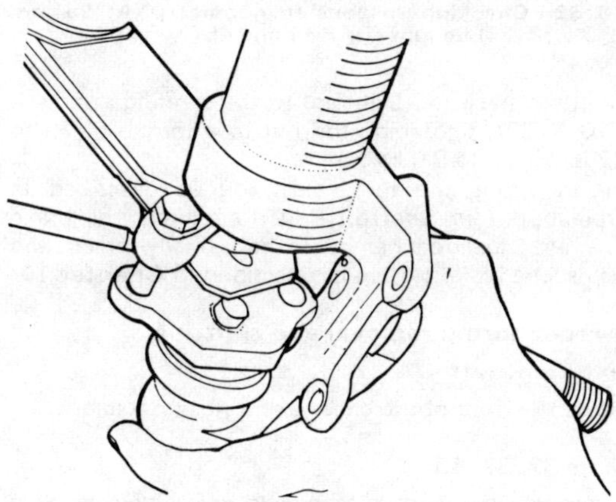

FIG 8:25 Removing strut assembly

2 Press the track rod ball joint from the steering arm with a suitable extractor, as shown in **FIG 8:24**.
3 Remove the piston rod attaching nut, tap the rod down and raise the front of the car, fitting firm stands. Do not trap the Variomatic vent tube. Remove the spring securing bolts and lift out the strut assembly as shown in **FIG 8:25**.
4 Press the ball joint out of the steering knuckle (see **FIG 8:26**) and check the joint for wear (see **FIG 8:27**). Renew the joint if the end play of the ball pin exceeds .1 to .12 inch (2.5 to 3 mm).
5 Refit the ball joint to the steering knuckle (see **FIG 8:28**), using a new splitpin and tightening the nut to a torque of 40.2 to 47.5 lb ft (5.5 to 6.5 kg m).
6 Install the strut assembly (see **FIG 8:29**), ensuring that the ball joint locating pin 1 engages in the hole 2 in the spring end.

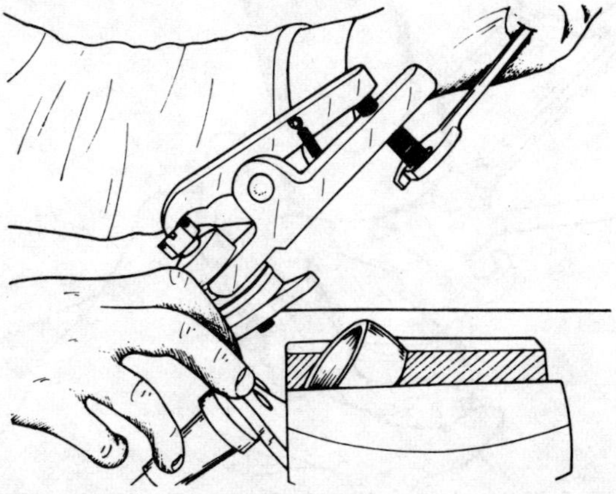

FIG 8:26 Removing ball joint from steering knuckle

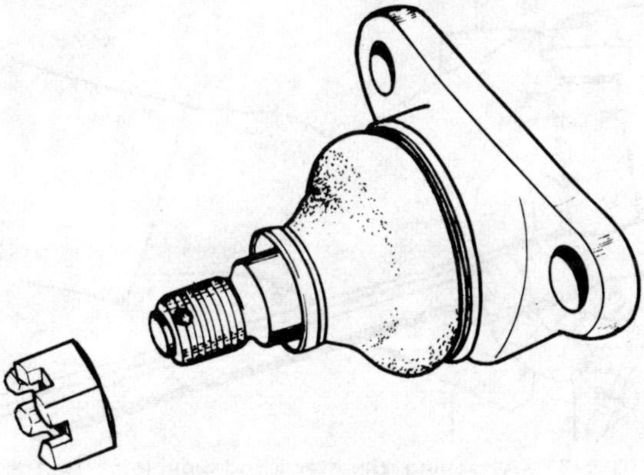

FIG 8:27 Ball joint

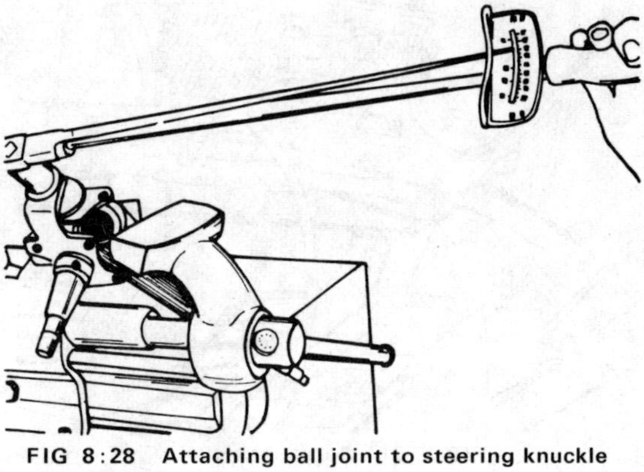

FIG 8:28 Attaching ball joint to steering knuckle

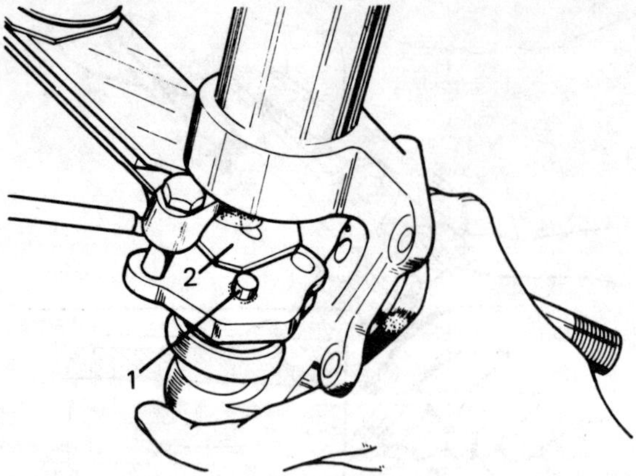

FIG 8:29 Installing the strut assembly, locating the pin 1 in the hole 2 in the end of the spring

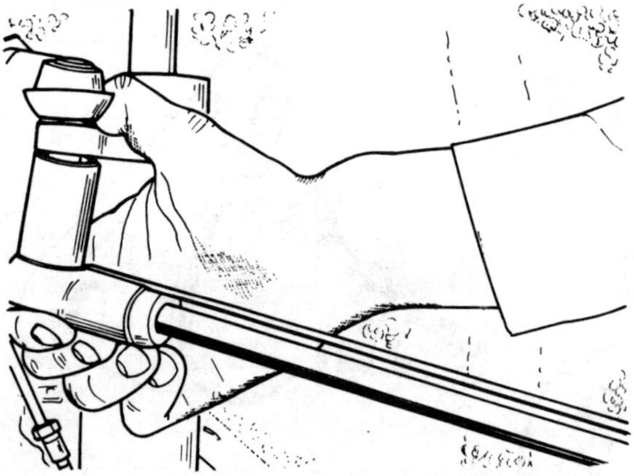
FIG 8:30 Attaching the track rod ball joint to the steering arm

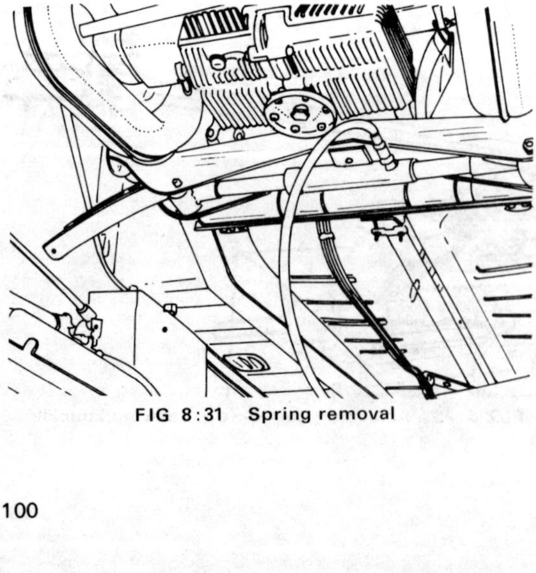
FIG 8:31 Spring removal

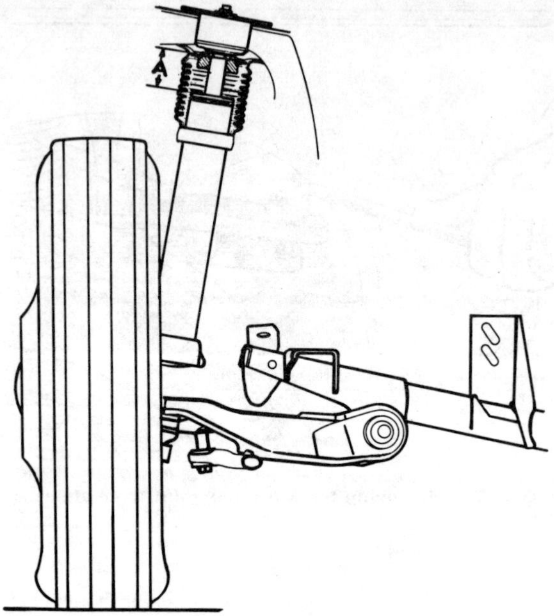

FIG 8:32 Checking suspension geometry. A: 90 mm (DAF 31, 32, 33) 85 mm (DAF 44 and 46)

7 Refit the track rod ball joint to the steering arm (see **FIG 8:30**), tightening the nut to a torque of 20 to 22 lb ft (2.7 to 3.0 kg m).

8 Fit the boot and the piston rod as described in Operation 7 in **Section 8:4**. Reconnect the brake line and speedometer cable and finally bleed and adjust the brake system as described in **Chapter 10**.

8:6 Front spring removal and refitting

Spring removal:

1 Raise the front of the chassis and position stands.

Models 31, 32, 33:

2 Remove both damper/stub axle assemblies as described in **Section 8:5**. Remove the silencer and hot spot pipe as described in **Chapter 2**. Remove the U-bolt nuts and dismount the spring.

Models 44 and 46:

3 Remove the bolts from the spring eyes, disconnect the radius rods from the strut, use a hydraulic or mechanical spreader (see **FIG 8:31**) to stretch the spring assembly sufficiently. Detach the spring assembly from the struts. Push the wheels outwards and remove the spreader, take out the spring assembly.

4 Press the spacer tubes from the eye bushes of the spring and withdraw the bushes.

Spring fitment:

This is the reverse of the removal sequence in each case.

A special tool 7-99-535568 is available to draw the ends of the spring assembly upwards for fitting to the ball joint.

Install the clamping plates and radius rods and tighten new self-locking bolts to 35 to 38 lb ft (4.8 to 5.3 kgm).

8:7 Suspension geometry

Suspension geometry includes the castor, camber and swivel pin or kingpin inclination angles. The castor angle, obtained by inclining the steering pivot, gives a self-centring action to the steering effort. Camber is an outward inclination of the top of the front wheels to facilitate cornering. Swivel pin inclination indicates that the swivel pins are inclined in the opposite direction, so that the line of the pin, if continued downwards, would meet the ground near the point of contact of the tyre.

The inclination angles are given in the **Technical Data** section of the **Appendix**. All are set during manufacture, but after renewing ball joints or fitting track rods to their ball joints it is advised that the alignments should be checked for accuracy. Place a piece of pipe, split lengthwise, of the dimension given in **FIG 8:32** around the piston rod of each damper. Load the front of the vehicle until the piece of pipe is just held tight, and weighing down the rear of the vehicle until the rear wheels are at right angles to the floor. The angles are adjusted if necessary by moving the damper attachment point, either inwards or outwards for the camber angle or forwards or backwards for the castor angle. In both cases the attachment bolts holes have to be elongated and washers have to be fitted and welded in position on completion of any adjustment. For checking the angles, however, special turntables and optical equipment of a proprietary nature are required, of which there are several different types, and it will be necessary to obtain the assistance of a service agent with the appropriate equipment.

8:8 Fault diagnosis

(a) Wheel wobble

1 Worn hub bearings
2 Broken front spring
3 Weak front spring
4 Uneven tyre wear
5 Worn ball joint(s)
6 Loose wheel fixings
7 Incorrect tracking

(b) 'Bottoming' of suspension

1 Check 2 and 3 in (a)
2 Bump stop rubbers worn or missing
3 Damper(s) defective
4 Vehicle excessively overloaded

(c) Heavy steering

1 Check 5 in (a) and 3 in (b)
2 Tyres underinflated

(d) Excessive tyre wear

1 Check 7 in (a) (**Chapter 9**)
2 Check camber and castor angles

(e) Rattles

1 Check 2 in (a)
2 Worn bushes
3 Damper top attachment worn or loose
4 Loose bump stop

(f) Excessive rolling

1 Check 2 and 3 in (a); 3 in (b); 3 in (e)

NOTES

CHAPTER 9

THE STEERING GEAR

9:1 Description

The steering unit is of the rack and pinion type and is mounted directly forward of the lower end of the steering column shaft in the engine compartment. The steering column shaft is coupled directly to the pinion shaft; there is no intermediate steering shaft. Both track rods are actuated from the same end of the rack, an extension of which projects from the steering unit. Two holes in the rack extension take the ball joint connections for the two track rods. Each track rod connects at its outer end with a steering arm which is integral with the damper/stub axle unit which is covered in **Chapter 8**. Each track rod tube is internally threaded at both ends and they are consequently adjustable for length.

Although the steering gear units fitted to different models are similar in operation, they are not identical due to design differences and modification standards. A sectional view of the steering gear is given in **FIG 9:1**.

9:2 Maintenance

Ball joints require no routine maintenance but, should steering backlash become excessive, check and, if necessary, renew the track rod ball joints as described in **Section 9:4**. If backlash is still excessive, check that play between the steering pinion and the rack is correctly adjusted or, if the vehicle has seen considerable service, dismantle the steering unit as described in **Section 9:3** and check the rack and the pinion for wear.

9:3 The steering unit

Removal:

1 Disconnect both track rod ball joints from the steering arms as described in **Section 9:4**. On DAF 31 models, disconnect the steering column shaft at the steering unit and pull up the shaft. On all other models, except later DAF 44 and DAF 46, refer to **FIGS 9:2** (lower arrow) and **9:3** and disconnect the shaft from the flexible coupling.

DAF 31, 32 and 33 models:

2 Remove the steering unit attachment bolts and withdraw the steering unit and the track rods through the opening in the wheel arch (see **FIG 9:4**). Press the track rods out of the rack with a suitable puller as shown in **FIG 9:5**.

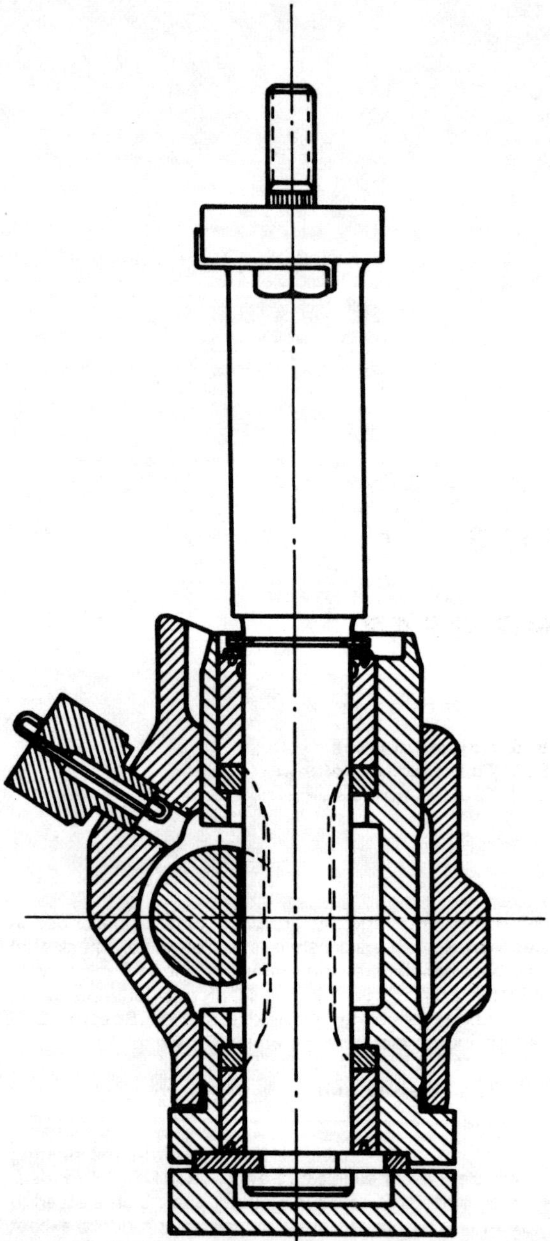

FIG 9:1 A typical sectional view of the steering gear

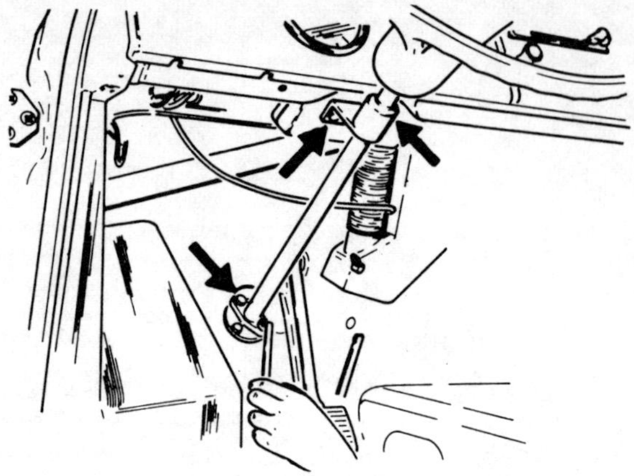

FIG 9:2 Disconnecting steering shaft, DAF 32 and 33

FIG 9:3 A view of the flexible coupling and securing bolts, DAF 44 early models

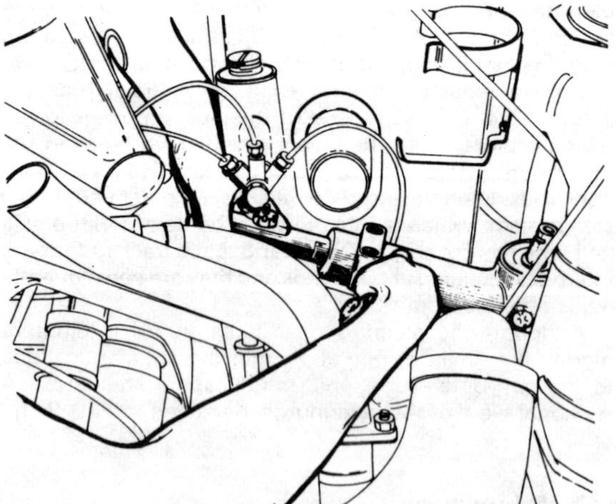

FIG 9:4 Removing the steering assembly through the wheel arch, DAF 31, 32, 33

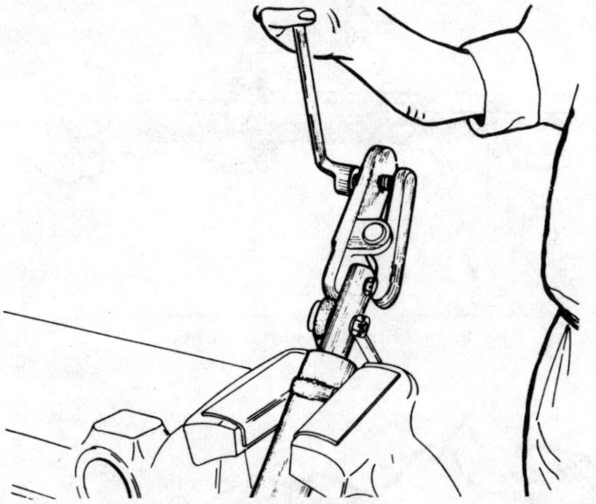

FIG 9:5 Pressing a track rod ball joint out of the steering rack

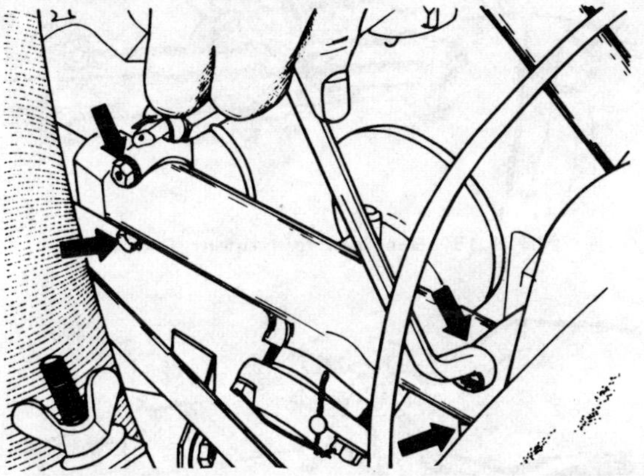

FIG 9:6 Removing the steering gear retaining bolts, DAF 44

DAF 44 early models:

3 Unscrew the track rods from the rack ball joints. Refer to **Chapter 1**, **Section 1:18** and remove the intake manifold. Remove the stop light switch. Remove the attachment bolts (see **FIG 9:6**), unscrew the track rods from the ball joints in the rack and lift out the steering gear assembly (see **FIG 9:7**).

Fitting, DAF 31, 32, 33 and early 44 models:

The procedure for refitting the steering unit is the reverse of the removal sequence in each case. Refer to **Section 9:4** when fitting the track rods and set the front wheel alignment as described in **Chapter 8** and **Section 9:5**.

DAF 31 models, dismantling and assembling:

The unit's fitted to these models have an adjusting screw in the pinion shaft end plate.

Remove the locking wire and the two retaining bolts and lift off the end plate (see **FIG 9:8**) and withdraw the

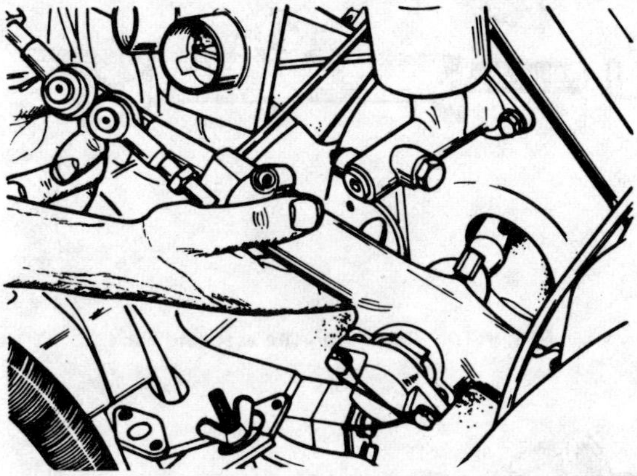

FIG 9:7 Lifting out the steering gear, DAF 44

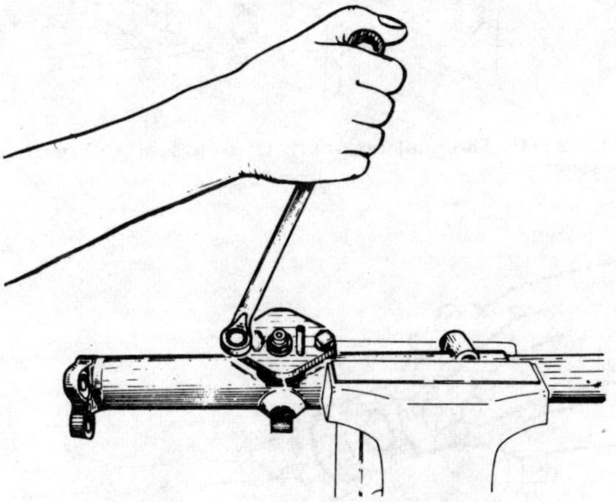

FIG 9:8 Removing the end plate

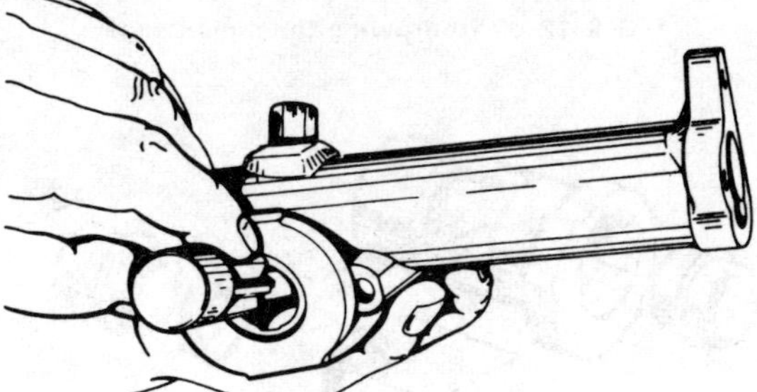

FIG 9:9 Withdrawing the steering pinion

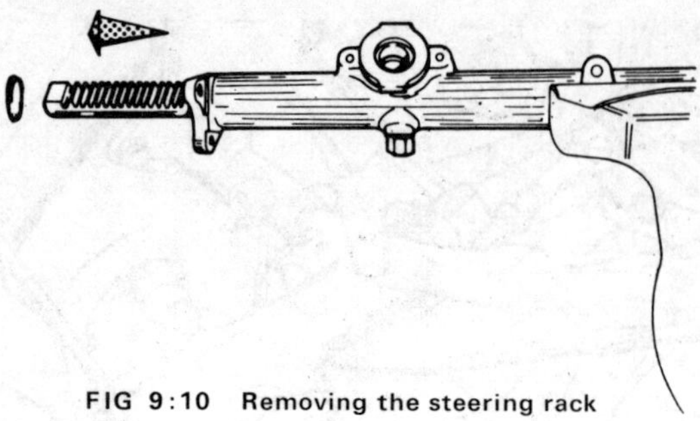

FIG 9:10 Removing the steering rack

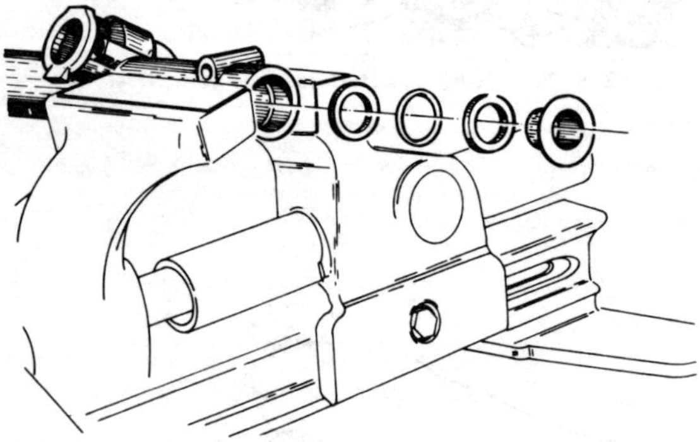

FIG 9:11 The seal retainer, 'O' ring seal and leather washers

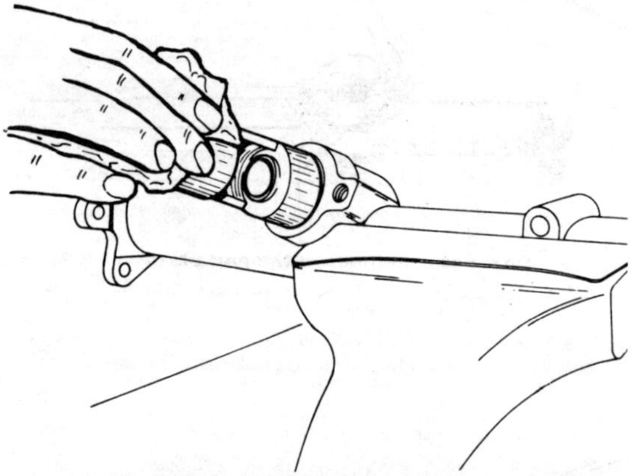

FIG 9:12 Withdrawing the pinion cage

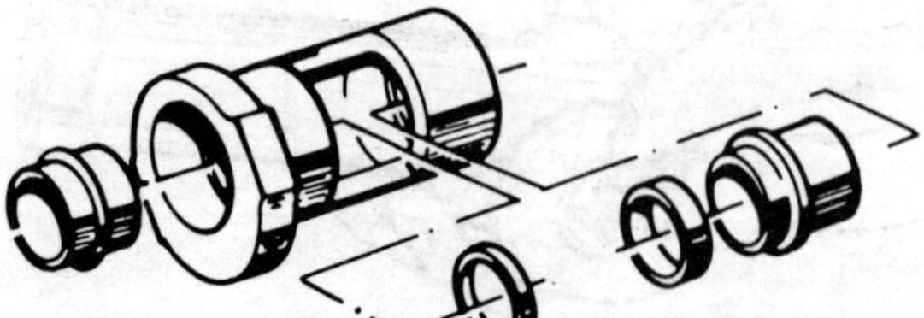

FIG 9:13 Pinion cage components, DAF 31

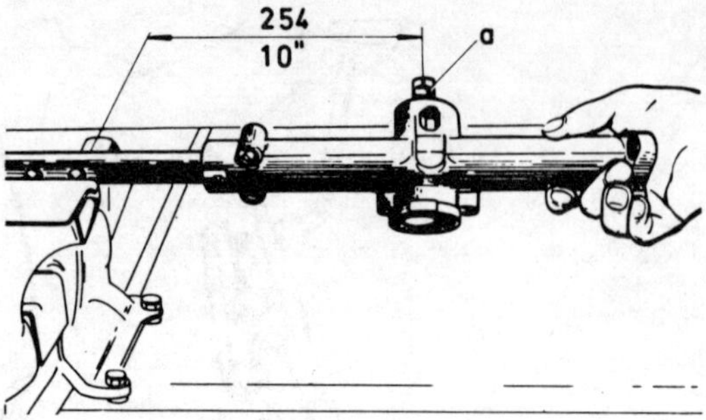

FIG 9:14 Steering unit assembly, DAF 31

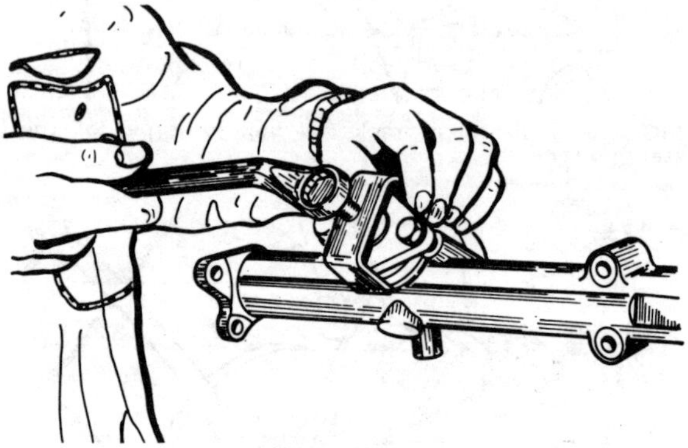

FIG 9:15 Backlash adjustment, DAF 31

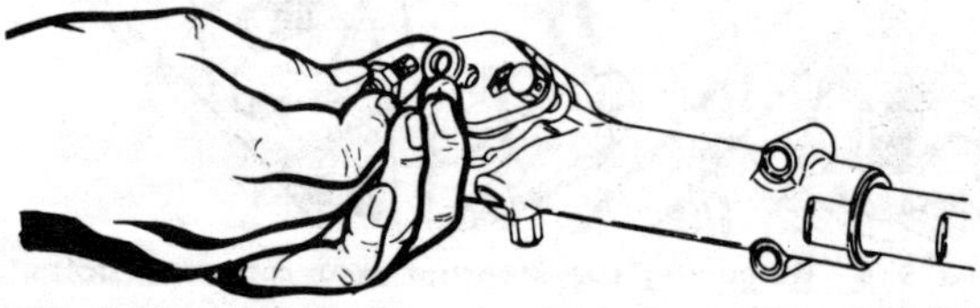

FIG 9:16 Fitting new nylon lock ring to the adjusting screw

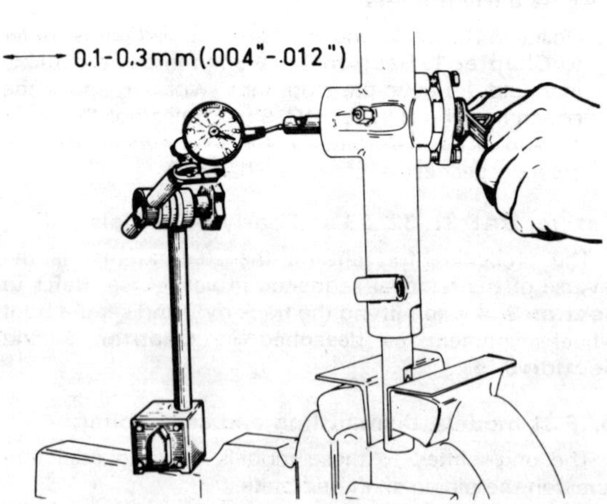

FIG 9:17 Checking pinion end play with dial indicator and adjusting to the specified limits

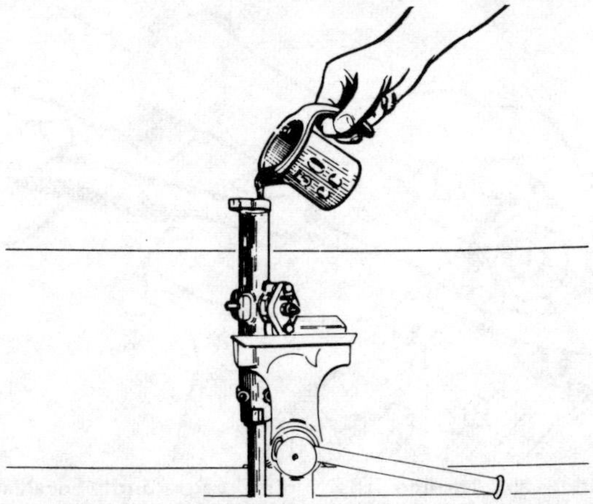

FIG 9:18 Filling steering gear housing with the specified lubricant

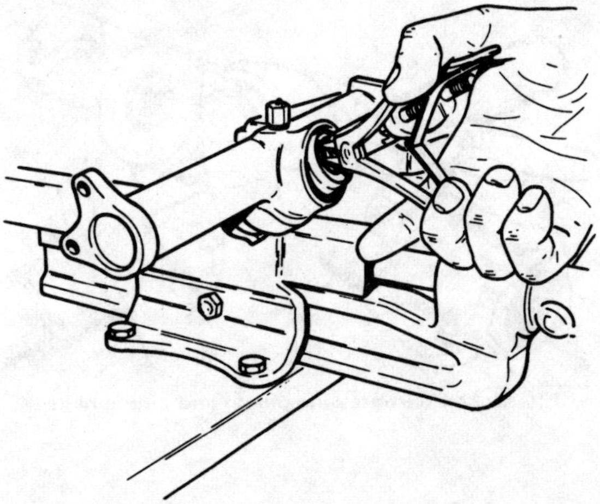

FIG 9:19 Removing the circlip from the pinion shaft

pinion (see **FIG 9:9**). Tap out the rack from the expansion plug end of the housing taking the expansion plug with it (see **FIG 9:10**). Remove the seal retainer, 'O' ring and leather washers (see **FIG 9:11**). Withdraw the pinion cage (see **FIG 9:12**) and remove the bushes, washer and ring from the cage as shown in **FIG 9:13**.

Assembly is the reverse of the dismantling sequence. Soak the new washers in oil for 30 minutes prior to fitting. Insert the rack (coated with Retinax G) from the expansion plug end of the housing and push it through until it projects at the other end by 254 mm (10 inch) as shown in **FIG 9:14**. Insert the pinion with the notch **a** parallel to the housing. Fit the end plate with its retaining bolts finger tight. Adjust the backlash as shown in **FIG 9:15** until a little play between the rack and the pinion is just perceptible. Torque tighten the end plate bolts to 20 to 25 lb ft (2.8 to 3.4 kg m) and fit a **new nylon lock ring** to the adjusting screw (see **FIG 9:16**). Adjust the pinion shaft end play to between .04 and .12 inch (.1 to .3 mm) by means of the adjusting screw (see **FIG 9:17**). Introduce 50 cc of Retinax G into the housing (see **FIG 9:18**) and fit a **new expansion plug**. Fit the ball joints to the rack extension as described in **Section 9:4**.

DAF 32, 33 and early 44 models, dismantling and assembling:

The steering unit fitted to DAF 32 and 33 models and those fitted to DAF 44 models are very similar but they are not identical. Note that, in the following procedure, certain operations are not the same for the two variants.

Remove the locking wire and the two retaining bolts and lift off the end plate as in **FIG 9:8**. Remove the circlip from the pinion shaft (see **FIG 9:19**) in the case of DAF 32 and 33 units. On all units, push the pinion shaft into its cage and remove the shaft locating plate (see **FIG 9:20**) and the gasket. Extend the rack fully by pulling on the rack extension (see **FIG 9:21**) and rotate the pinion cage until the rack can be withdrawn. Withdraw the pinion and then the cage (see **FIG 9:22**). Withdraw the seal retainer, the 'O' ring and the leather washers shown in **FIG 9:11**. Remove the nylon bushes from the pinion cage (see **FIG 9:23**) and, from DAF 32 and 33 units, also remove the washer and rings.

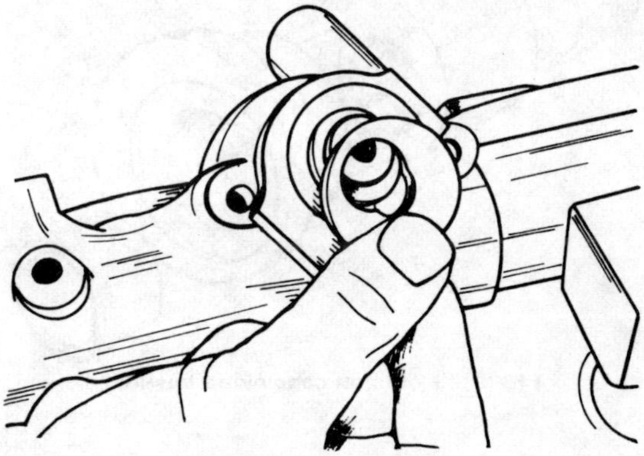

FIG 9:20 Removing the shaft locating plate

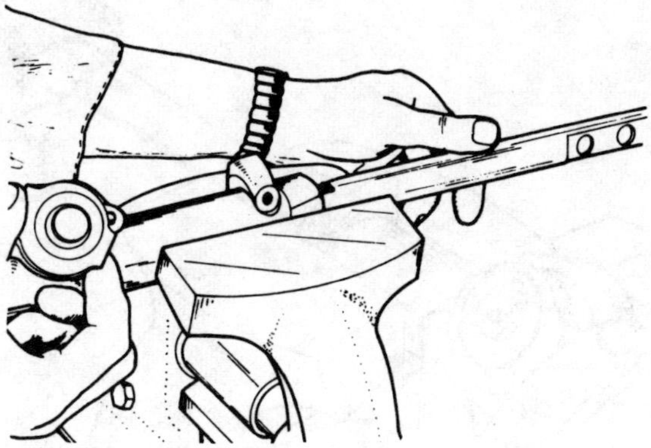

FIG 9:21 Pulling on rack extension and turning pinion cage to remove the rack

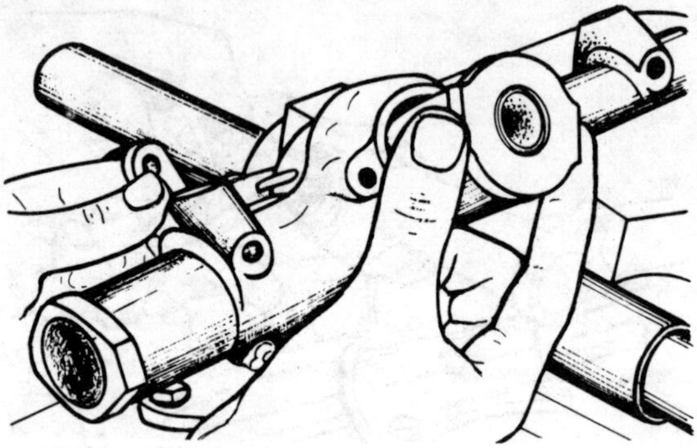

FIG 9:22 Withdrawing pinion and pinion cage

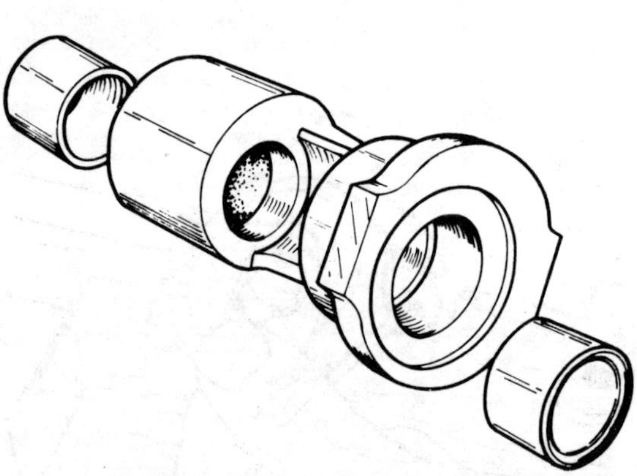

FIG 9:23 Pinion cage nylon bushes

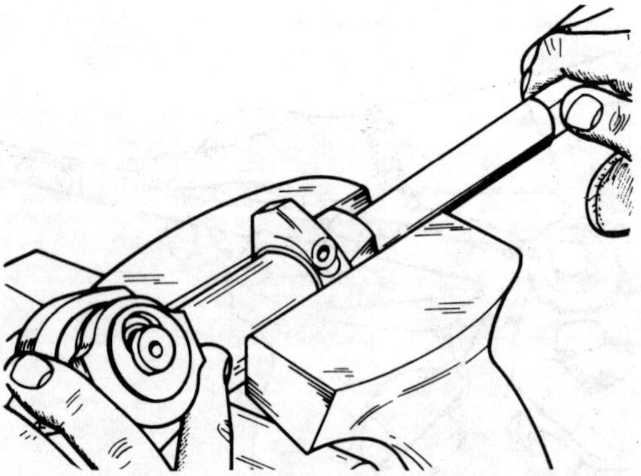

FIG 9:24 Fitting the rack in the steering gear housing with the pinion cage positioned as shown

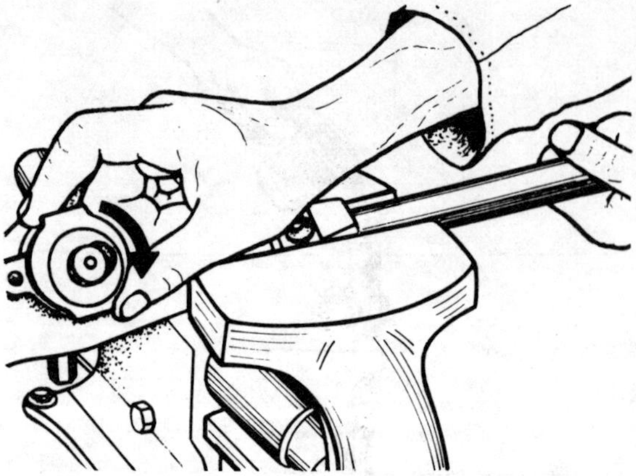

FIG 9:25 Turning the pinion cage until backlash between pinion and first tooth of rack is just perceptible

Assembly is the reverse of the dismantling sequence in each case. Soak the new leather washers in oil for 30 minutes prior to installation and fit them with their rough sides towards the 'O' ring. Lubricate all internal parts liberally with Retinax G and introduce 40 cc of this grease into the housing before fitting the pinion cage and the pinion. The pinion cage must be turned to the maximum clearance position (see **FIG 9:24**) before introducing the rack until it abuts against the cage. Turn the cage back until it clears the rack, push it approximately 5 mm (.2 inch) further in, turn the cage in the opposite direction (see **FIG 9:25**) until the backlash between the pinion and the first tooth of the rack is just perceptible. Push the rack into the housing until, as shown in **FIG 9:26**, it projects 252 mm (9.92 inch). Note that, in this position, the pinion shaft flange must be parallel to the housing. The finally adjusted backlash should be just perceptible ($1\frac{1}{2}$ deg. angular motion of the pinion). The end plate retaining bolts should be torque tightened to 20 to 25 lb ft (2.8 to 3.4 kg m) and wire locked. Fit the ball joints to the rack extension as described in **Section 9:4**.

DAF 44 later models and DAF 46:

1 Remove both castellated nuts from the track rod ball joints at the steering rack side, then remove both the ball joints from the rack with the aid of a suitable puller.
2 Disconnect the steering shaft from the flexible coupling.
3 Remove the pinion shaft end cover after detaching the two screws and removing the locking wire.
4 Turn the eccentric bush as shown in **FIG 9:27** so that the steering rack can be withdrawn.
5 Remove the four fixing bolts and withdraw the steering gear from the car (see **FIG 9:6**). Push down the eccentric bush to avoid the rubber boot coming away with the gear.
6 Press the pinion and the eccentric bush together to enable the locking disc (see **FIG 9:28**) to be removed, together with the joint behind it if fitted.
7 Remove the pinion and withdraw the eccentric bush from the steering gear housing. Remove the locating bush and washers.

8 Withdraw both nylon bearing bushes (see **FIG 9:23**) from the eccentric bush and fit new ones. Ensure that the grooves in the nylon bushes face outwards.

9 Soak both leather sealing rings (see **FIG 9:11**) from the steering gear housing in oil for 30 minutes and then fit them into the housing together with the locating bush. The rough sides of the rings must face the 'O' ring.

10 For refitting, coat the eccentric bush and the steering pinion liberally with Alvania R1 grease and then fit them into the housing (see **FIG 9:11**).

11 Clamp the pinion and the eccentric bush in a vice to compress them so that the locking disc (see **FIG 9:28**) can be fitted. Refill the steering gear with approximately 40 cc of Alvania R1 grease.

12 Locate the steering gear in the engine compartment. The eccentric bush together with the steering pinion should be pushed outwards, to make way for the connecting flange of the steering pinion to be guided through the rubber boot.

13 Tighten the four steering gear attaching bolts and reconnect the steering shaft to the pinion mounting flange.

14 Fit the steering rack into the housing, which involves turning the eccentric bush (see **FIG 9:27**) to its fully released position and turning the steering wheel approximately 20 deg. clockwise off the straight-ahead position.

15 Push the steering rack into the housing until it protrudes 165 mm (6.5 inch) as shown in **FIG 9:29**. With the eccentric bush turned to obtain the minimum running clearance between the pinion and the rack and with the steering wheel in the straight-ahead position, the rack must protrude a distance of 162 mm (6.38 inch).

16 Fit the cover and tighten the two bolts by hand. Turn the eccentric bush so that the minimum rack clearances at extreme right and left are obtained. Gradually tighten the cover bolts to a torque of 13 to 14.4 lb ft (1.8 to 2.0 kgm) and lock them crosswise with wire.

17 Refit the track rod ball joints to the two holes in the steering rack. Renew the dust boots and nylon washers, tighten the nuts to a torque of 20 to 22 lb ft (2.7 to 3.0 kgm) and fit new splitpins.

9:4 The steering linkage

A track rod connects each steering arm with the rack of the steering unit. The connection of each steering arm to its track rod and of each track rod to the rack is by ball joint. The track rod tubes are threaded internally at both ends for attachment of the ball joints and, after loosening the lock nuts, rotation of the tube will lengthen or shorten the assembly.

Ball joint removal:

Remove and discard the splitpin which locks the castellated nut. Remove the nut. Use an extractor to press the joint from the steering arm or the rack. A Matra VW-266-F extractor is shown in use on a steering arm joint in **FIG 9:30**. Examine and, if necessary, renew the rubber dust boot.

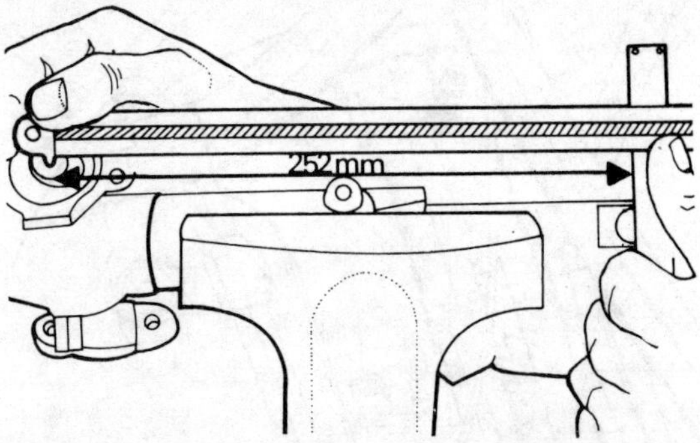

FIG 9:26 Locating the rack in the housing to the dimension shown, when the pinion shaft flange must run parallel to housing

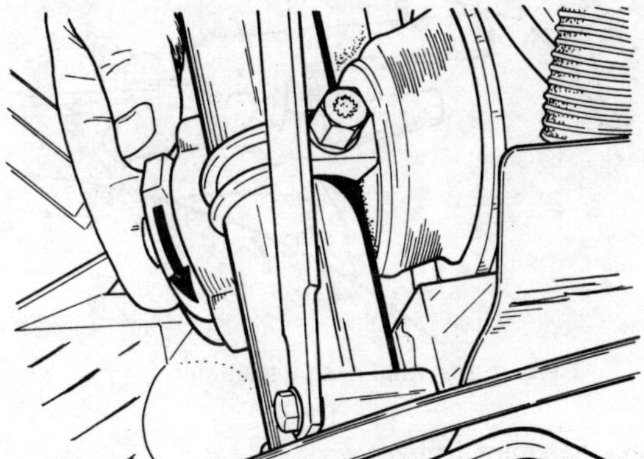

FIG 9:27 Turning the eccentric bush

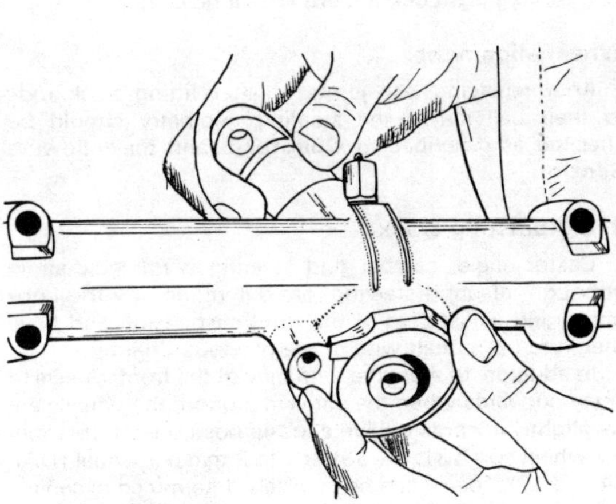

FIG 9:28 Removing the locking disc

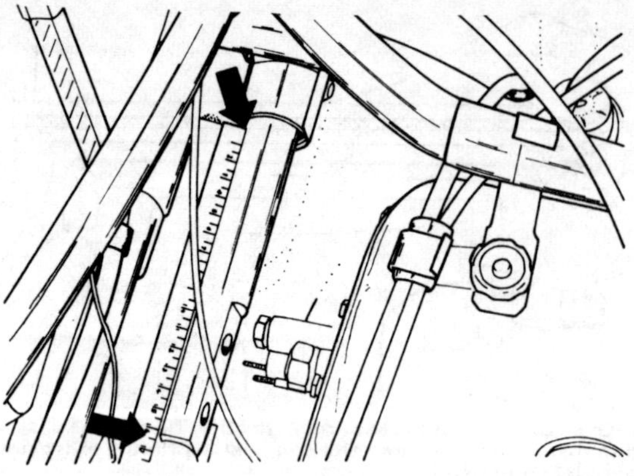

FIG 9:29 Measuring the rack protrusion on reassembly

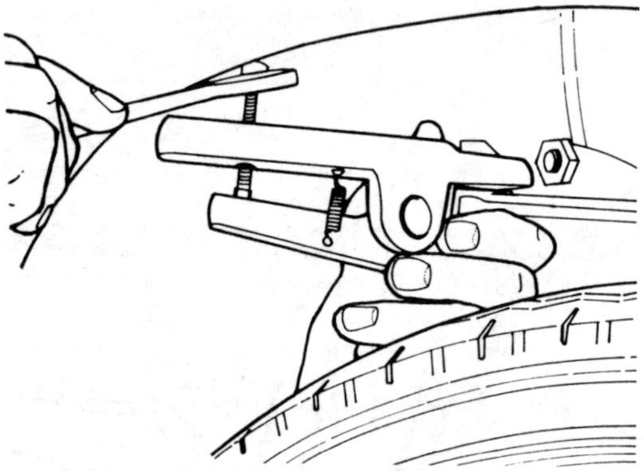

FIG 9:30 Removing a ball joint

Rack ball joint fitment:

Torque tighten the castellated nut to 20 to 22 lb ft (2.7 to 3 kg m). Lock the nut with a new splitpin.

Steering arm ball joint fitment:

Torque tighten the castellated nut to 25 to 29 lb ft (3.5 to 4 kg m). Lock the nut with a new splitpin

Wheel alignment:

After renewing ball joints or after fitting track rods to their ball joints, the steering geometry should be checked as described in **Chapter 8** and the following **Section**.

9:5 Adjusting track

Castor angle, camber and steering pivot inclination, although affecting steering, are determined by the condition and adjustment of the front suspension and have therefore been dealt with in the previous Chapter.

In addition, to meet the tendency of the front wheels to splay outwards when the car is in motion, the wheels are set slightly inwards to give a toe-in position of 0 to 1 mm per wheel (DAF 31, 32, 33) or 1 to 2 mm per wheel (DAF 44 and 46). Toe-in can be precisely determined in service workshops with the car wheels on turntables and using special proprietary equipment, or somewhat less accurately by ordinary measurement. For the latter, both front tyres are inflated to the same pressure with the car on level ground. With the wheels in the straight-ahead position, measure the distance between the rims at wheel centre height at the front. Mark these two points of measurement and then roll the car forward for exactly half a revolution of the wheels, so that the marks finish up at the rear. Measure again between the marked points. The difference between the measurements is the amount of toe-in or toe-out

With the steering wheel spoke position correctly centred, adjustment is made by simultaneously lengthening or shortening the left and right track rods, ensuring that the locknuts are correctly tightened on completion. The rods must be adjusted by equal amounts.

The specified rear wheel toe-in is 0 to .5 mm per wheel on DAF 31, 32 and 33 cars and 0 ± .5 mm per wheel on DAF 44 and 46 cars. In the former instance, adjustment is made by moving the suspension arm float attachment point as may be required and in DAF 44 cars by fitting or removing shims on the bolts retaining the axle housing to the suspension arm, shown at 1 in **FIG 7:6** in **Chapter 7**. No adjustment is provided on the DAF 46.

9:6 The steering column

Steering wheel removal and fitment:

Set the front wheels in the straight-ahead position. Prise off the ornamental button from the centre of the wheel (see **FIG 9:31**) and remove the retaining nut and the washer from beneath it. Use a suitable puller to remove the steering wheel (the official tool is No. 7-99-535702).

Fitment is this sequence in reverse. Torque tighten the retaining nut to 33 lb ft (4.5 kg m).

Steering column removal and fitment:

DAF 31, 32 and 33 models:

Uncouple the steering column shaft from the steering unit as described in **Section 9:3**. Refer to **FIG 9:2** and remove the bracket attachment bolts (upper arrows). Lift the column assembly out of the car.

Fitment is the reverse of this sequence.

FIG 9:31 Removing the steering wheel emblem

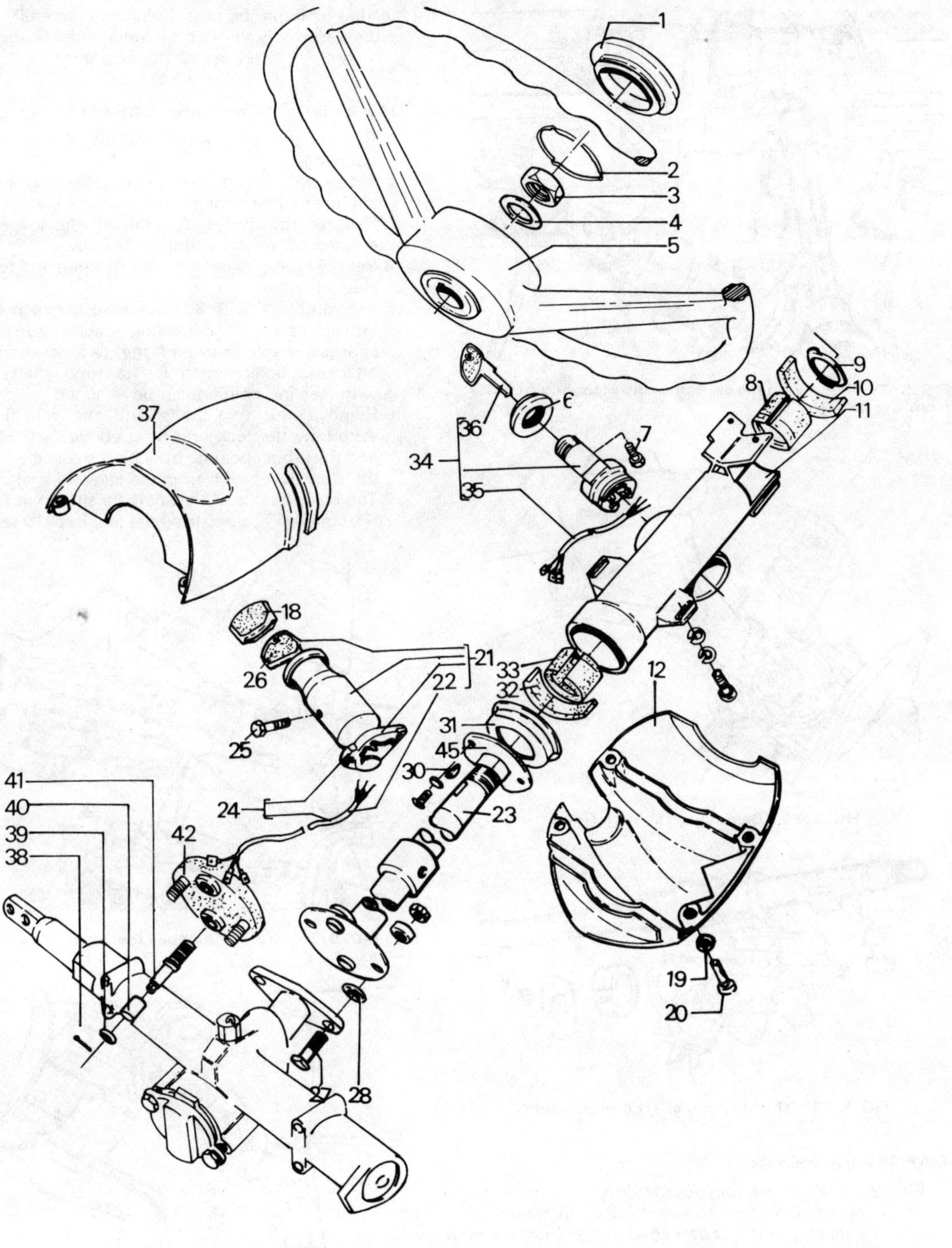

FIG 9:32 A typical exploded view of a steering column

Key to Fig 9:32 1 Ornamental button 2 Washer 3 Nut 4 Washer 5 Steering wheel 6 Switch bezel 7 Bolt 8 Bush 9 Locating ring 10 Felt strip 11 Steering column tube 12 Cover (lower) 18 Cover 19 Washer 20 Bolt 21 Ignition switch assembly (steering lock type) 22 Switch wiring 23 Shaft 24 Wiring connector 25 Bolt 26 Key 27 Bolt 28 Washer 30 Key 31 Cover 32 Felt strip 33 Bush 34 Ignition switch assembly (standard type) 35 Switch wiring 36 Key 37 Cover (upper) 38 Split pin 39 Nut 40 Distance tube 41 Stud 42 Coupling disc

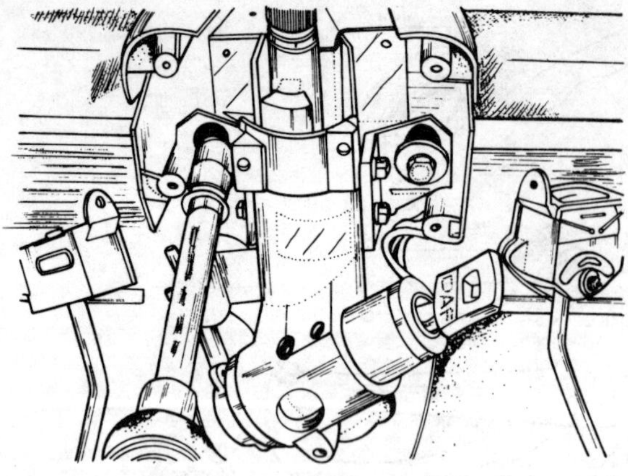

FIG 9:33 Removing the switches and attachment bolts from the column

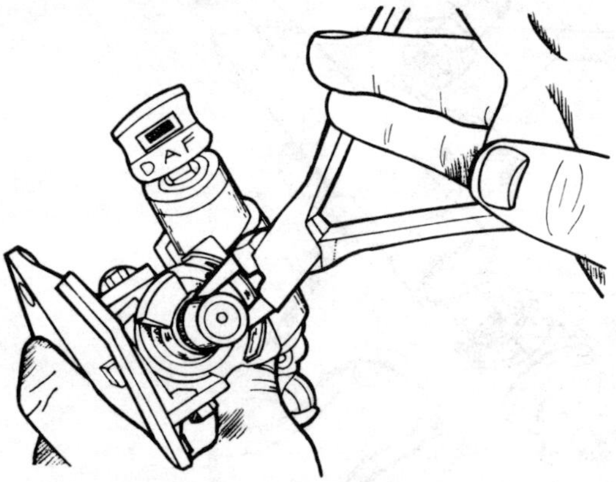

FIG 9:34 Removing the lock ring

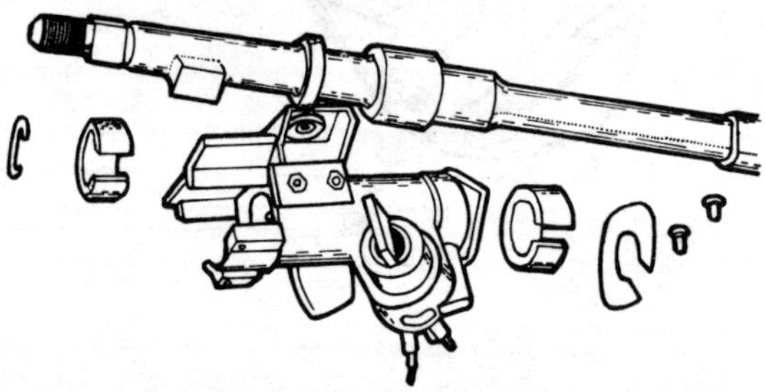

FIG 9:35 The steering shaft components

DAF 44 early models:

FIG 9:32 illustrates the general construction of the steering column. Disconnect the battery earth cable and remove the steering wheel as described earlier. Disconnect the shaft from the flexible coupling. Remove the steering column lower and upper covers 12 and 37 in **FIG 9:32**. Disconnect the ignition switch wiring. Remove the screws which attach the combined light and direction indicator switch and leave the switch hanging from the wiring. Remove the driver's seat. Remove the two steering column bracket bolts and carefully pull the column assembly through the hole in the dashboard.

Fitment is the reverse of this sequence.

DAF 44 later models and DAF 46:

1 Remove the driver's seat and disconnect the flexible coupling.
2 Disconnect the battery earth cable and detach the strangler cable control.
3 Remove the five bolts retaining the lower steering column cover and withdraw the cover.
4 Set the ignition key in the off position and remove the steering wheel.
5 Referring to **FIG 9:33** detach both switches and the ignition switch connecting cables. Unscrew the strangler cable nut and the two steering column attaching bolts, when the steering shaft complete with steering column can be removed.
6 Remove the two bolts and the retaining plate. Withdraw the lock ring from above (see **FIG 9:34**) and the rubber bearing from both sides, then withdraw the steering column from the steering shaft.
7 The components of the shaft are shown in **FIG 9:35**. If a collision has occurred the telescopic steering shaft

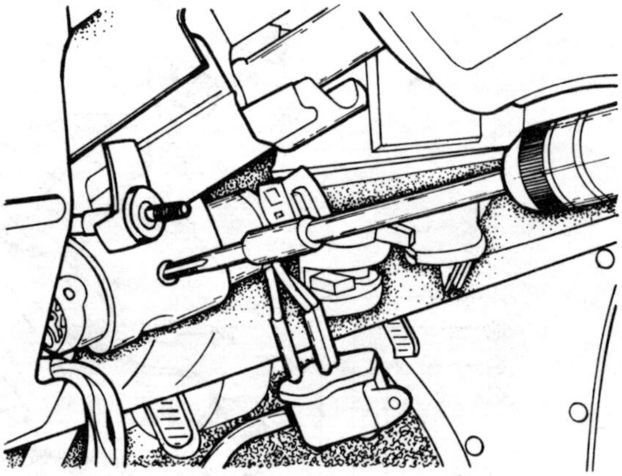

FIG 9:36 Removing the steering lock safety bolt

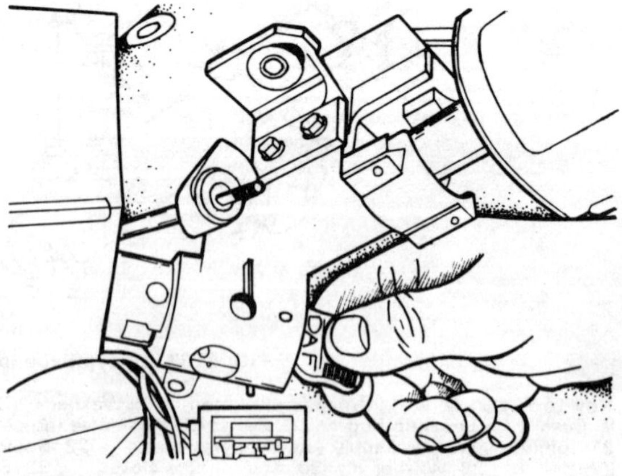

FIG 9:37 Removing steering lock with ignition switch

must be checked for the correct total length, which should be 568 ± 1 mm (22.36 ± .04 inch). If these limits are exceeded the shaft must be renewed. The shaft telescopes under a force of 120 to 160 kg (265 to 353 lb) and it is not permissible to reset the shaft to its original length

8 After greasing the shaft with Shell TS.WL.Z240, or an equivalent lubricant, reassembly is undertaken by following the dismantling operations in reverse.

Steering lock renewal is performed as follows:

1 Carry out the previous operations Nos. 1, 2 and 3 and detach both switches. Set the steering lock to 'O'.

2 Drill a 3 mm (.12 inch) hole (see **FIG 9:36**) in the steering lock safety bolt and use a lefthanded tap to remove the bolt.

3 Disconnect the ignition switch holder and take out the two attaching bolts from the steering column.

4 Withdraw the upper steering column cover and turn the column a little clockwise. Referring to **FIG 9:37** remove the steering lock with the ignition switch moving it upwards.

5 For renewing the ignition switch holder only, the same operations are carried out with the exception of the safety bolt removal. After turning the steering column slightly clockwise the ignition holder can be removed.

6 Install the new steering lock with the ignition switch and screw in a new safety bolt until the head breaks off.

7 Turn the ignition key fully anticlockwise and withdraw the key. Tighten the steering column bolts finger tight only and centre the steering column sufficiently to allow the lockpin to slide in and out without obstruction. Fully tighten both steering column bolts, then refit and reconnect the components and wiring removed for access in the reverse order of their dismantling.

9:7 Fault diagnosis

(a) Wheel wobble

1 Unbalanced wheels and tyres
2 Loose ball joint connections
3 Excessive wear in steering linkage
4 Defective front suspension (see **Chapter 8**)
5 Worn hub bearings

(b) Wander

1 Check 2 and 3 in (a)
2 Wheel alignment incorrect
3 Castor angle incorrect
4 Uneven tyre pressures
5 Uneven tyre wear
6 Ineffective dampers

(c) Heavy steering

1 Check 2 and 3 in (b)
2 Very low tyre pressures
3 Seized pinion or rack
4 Steering column bearing(s) tight

(d) Rattles

1 Check 2, 3, 4 and 5 in (a)
2 Loose damper top attachment

(e) Excessive backlash

1 Check 2 and 3 in (a)
2 Pinion/rack clearance requires adjustment
3 Column shaft to pinion shaft coupling worn or loose

NOTES

CHAPTER 10

THE BRAKING SYSTEM

10:1 Description

The brakes on all models are operated hydraulically by the foot pedal. DAF 31, 32, 33 and early 44 models have a single line hydraulic system. Later DAF 44 and all DAF 46 models have a dual line system.

The handbrake on all models operates mechanically on the rear brake assemblies only.

DAF 31, 32 and 33 models:

These models have drum brakes of 178 mm (7 inch) internal diameter on both front and rear wheels. Each brake assembly has two friction lined shoes. Each wheel hydraulic cylinder has two pistons which expand the two shoes against the drum. Wear of the friction linings is accommodated by routine adjustment of the anchor point against which one end of each shoe is located. Both shoes are adjusted concurrently and the procedure is given in **Section 10:2**.

The layout of the hydraulic system differs between earlier and later models and, where relevant, the modified system (introduced at chassis No. 118908) is referred to in the text. Wheel cylinder diameters are: $\frac{7}{8}$ inch (22.2 mm) front and $\frac{3}{4}$ inch (19.05 mm) rear. In addition to this dimensional bias, the hydraulic pipeline to the rear brakes incorporates a pressure limiting valve the purpose of which is, by limiting pressure to the rear wheel cylinders, to ensure differential braking load in favour of the front wheels when the brakes are applied with force.

DAF 44 models:

Drum brakes of 200 mm ($7\frac{7}{8}$ inch) internal diameter are fitted to both front and rear wheels. Routine adjustment is required to compensate for wear of the shoe friction linings. Each of the two shoes fitted to a brake assembly is adjusted separately as described in **Section 10:2**. Wheel cylinder diameters are: $\frac{7}{8}$ inch (22.2 mm) front and $\frac{11}{16}$ inch (17.46 mm) rear on single line systems. On dual line systems the front wheel cylinder diameter is the same but the rear is $\frac{5}{8}$ inch (15.87 mm). No pressure limiting valve is fitted.

DAF 46:

Drum brakes of 203 mm (8 inch) are fitted front and rear, but otherwise similar to the DAF 44 dual line system.

10:2 Maintenance

Brake fluid:

Use only approved fluid to maintain the level in the master cylinder reservoir(s). Brake fluid is hydroscopic and gradually absorbs moisture. For this reason and also because dust and wear particles contaminate the fluid in time, the fluid should be completely changed every year.

FIG 10:1 Front brake adjustment, DAF 31, 32, 33

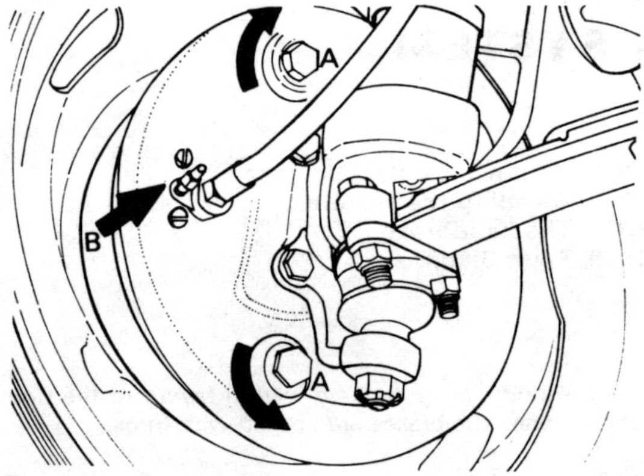

FIG 10:2 Front brake adjustment, DAF 44, showing the adjusting screws A and the bleed nipple B

FIG 10:3 Rear brake adjustment, DAF 31, 32, 33

Use SAE J-1703 in all models. Never mix different brands of fluid even though they conform to the same approved specification.

Front brake adjustment:

Routine adjustment of the front brakes is required to compensate for wear of the friction linings.

DAF 31, 32 and 33 models:

Raise the front of the car. Refer to **FIG 10:1** and turn the adjuster inwards to its full extent using tool 6-99-535309. Back the adjuster off again by three distinct clicks and check that the wheel rotates freely. Repeat this sequence on the other wheel.

DAF 44 models:

Raise the front of the car. The adjusters are marked A in **FIG 10:2**. Turn both adjusters until the wheel can just be rotated freely. Turning the adjusters away from the bleed nipple (arrowed B) moves the brake shoes inwards and increases their clearance with the drum. Turning the adjusters towards the bleed nipple decreases their clearance.

DAF 46 models:

Raise the front of the car. Turn both adjusters with special tool 267066 until the wheel can just be rotated freely. Turning the adjusters clockwise decreases brake shoe clearance and anti-clockwise increases clearance.

Rear brake adjustment:

Routine adjustment for wear of the friction linings is required on all models.

DAF 31, 32 and 33 models:

Refer to **Chapter 6, Section 6:4** and carry out operations 1 to 3 inclusive of the drive belt removal procedure. Now disengage the belts from the rear pulley discs. Adjust the brakes as shown in **FIG 10:3** and described earlier for the front brakes noting that the adjuster is located above the axle tube level.

Refit and tension the belts as described in **Chapter 6**.

DAF 44 models:

Raise the rear of the car. The adjusters are marked A in **FIG 10:4**. Turn both adjusters until the backlash in the reduction gearing is just perceptible. Turning the adjusters away from the bleed nipple (arrowed B) reduces the clearance between the shoes and the drum and vice versa.

DAF 46 models:

Turn the adjuster with special tool 267066 until the wheel is locked then slacken off 2 to 3 notches until the wheel is free to turn.

Handbrake adjustment:

This is described in **Section 10:8**.

10:3 The hydraulic system

If, when servicing the hydraulic system, the brake fluid appears to be thoroughly contaminated, the complete system should be dismantled and cleaned. Use only methylated spirits or clean brake fluid for cleaning internal components. Repair kits are available for all assemblies and all the parts in them should be used to avoid premature wear of new parts. If rubber seals are worn out, it is more than probable that the pistons will also be excessively worn or scored and they should be renewed at the same time. If a wheel or master cylinder bore is scored or corroded, obtain a replacement assembly and **do not attempt a salvage operation**.

Observe scrupulous cleanliness when working on all parts of the hydraulic system and refill the system only with new approved brake fluid as specified in **Section 10:2**.

Wheel cylinders:

1 Remove the wheel cylinders as described in the relevant part of **Section 10:4** (front drum brakes) or **Section 10:5** (rear drum brakes).

2 Remove the dust boots from both ends of the cylinder body. Extract the pistons (and, in the case of DAF 44 models, the spring which is fitted between the pistons). The rear wheels on DAF 46 models each have two wheel cylinders and each piston is fitted with a spring.
Remove the seal from each piston.

DAF 31, 32 and 33 models:

3 A dismantled wheel cylinder assembly is shown in **FIG 10:5** and, although the piston diameters are different, this illustration is relevant to both front and rear assemblies.

DAF 44 models:

4 A dismantled cylinder assembly is shown in **FIG 10:6**. Although piston diameters differ between front and rear cylinders, this illustration is relevant to both the front and rear units of DAF 44 models.

DAF 46 models:

5 The front wheel cylinders can be dealt with in a similar manner to the DAF 44, the rear wheel cylinders each have one piston and spring.

Assembly, all models:

6 Clean the components in new brake fluid. Check that the bleed and inlet orifices are clear. Fit new seals to the pistons and assemble with the internal parts wetted with brake fluid. In the case of DAF 44, insert the narrower end of the spring into a piston, install the piston and spring assembly into the cylinder and then fit the second piston.

7 Install the wheel cylinders as described in **Section 10:4** (front brakes) or **Section 10:5** (rear brakes).

Master cylinder removal, single line system:

Disconnect the battery earth cable. Drain off the brake fluid. Remove the master cylinder pushrod pivot pin from

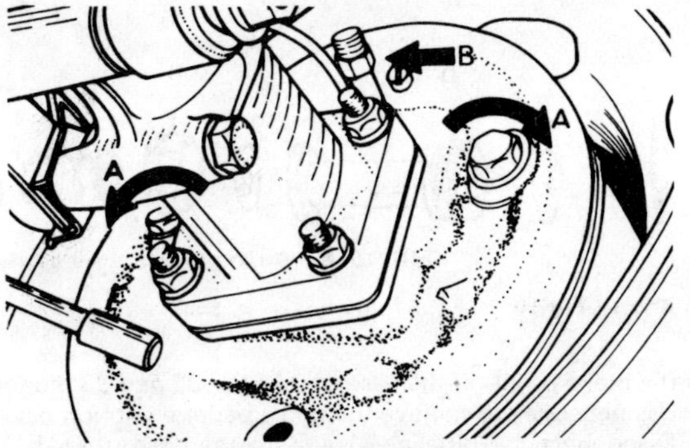

FIG 10:4 Rear brake adjustment, DAF 44, showing the adjusting screws A and the bleed nipple B

FIG 10:5 An exploded view of a wheel cylinder, DAF 31, 32, 33

FIG 10:6 An exploded view of a wheel cylinder, DAF 44

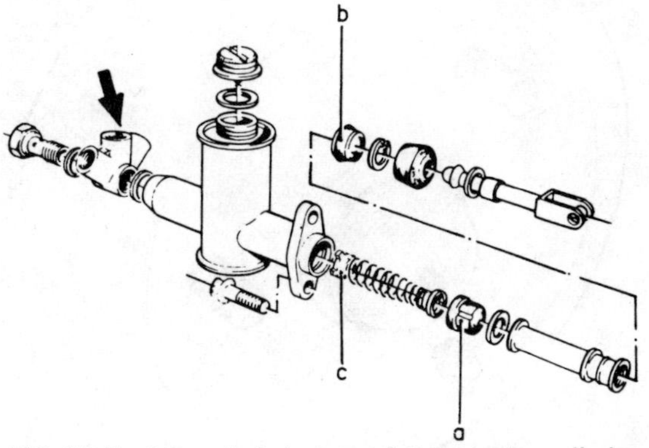

FIG 10:7 An exploded view of the master cylinder, DAF 31, 32, 33

Key to Fig 10:7 a Primary seal b Secondary seal c Check valve

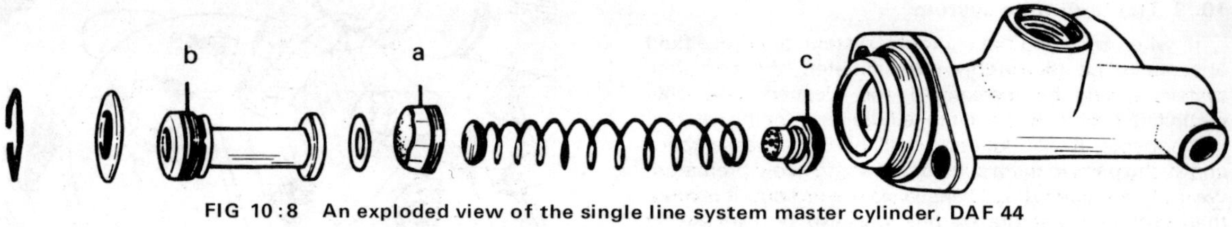

FIG 10:8 An exploded view of the single line system master cylinder, DAF 44

Key to Fig 10:8 a Cup seal b Seal c Check valve

the brake pedal (in the case of DAF 31, 32 and 33 models it is necessary to remove the brake pedal pivot bolt also). Disconnect the pipeline(s) and, in the case of DAF 44 models, the stop light switch connections. Remove the two attaching bolts and dismount the master cylinder.

Master cylinder fitment, single line system:

Fitment is the reverse of the removal sequence in each case. Refill the fluid reservoir(s) with new fluid and bleed the system as described in **Section 10:7**.

Master cylinder servicing, DAF 31, 32 and 33 models:

FIG 10:7 shows the components of a master cylinder. Note that the three-way branch piece (arrowed) is fitted only to earlier models. From chassis No. 118908, a single outlet pipe is fitted and a separately mounted distribution block takes the place of the branch piece. Removal of the circlip which engages a groove in the cylinder body bore allows the internal components to be withdrawn.

Use new brake fluid to clean the internal parts and assemble the unit with the internal components wetted with brake fluid. Make sure that the check valve c is installed the right way round, that the seals a and b are properly seated and that the circlip is correctly fitted in its groove.

Master cylinder servicing, DAF 44 single line system models:

The reservoir of this unit is not integral with the cylinder body and **FIG 10:8** shows the body (with the reservoir dismounted) and the internal parts. Although externally, the units are not identical, follow the servicing procedure given earlier for DAF 31, 32 and 33 models.

Pressure limiting valve, DAF 31, 32 and 33 models:

Only DAF 31, 32 and 33 models are provided with this valve. It is installed in the pipeline to the rear brakes and its purpose is to ensure differential braking load in favour of the front wheels when the brakes are applied with force. The components of a valve are shown in **FIG 10:9**.

Master cylinder, dual brake system DAF 44:

1 Detach the battery earth cable and remove the stop-light switch leads. Carefully clean the master cylinder and pipes and place a container under the outlet pipes to catch brake fluid spillage.
2 Disconnect the brake lines from the master cylinder and plug the open ends. Remove the retaining bolts and withdraw the master cylinder from the car. Clamp the assembly in a vice and remove the fluid reservoir with a tilting movement.
3 Hold the cylinder in the vice so that the cylinder section is not crushed, use a drift to press the main piston in the cylinder housing to the stop and remove the stop bolt with seal. Take out the circlip and allow the piston to rise.
4 Remove the main stop ring, both secondary cups and seals, noting the sequence of removal.
5 Remove the secondary piston by tapping the cylinder on a block of wood. Clean all parts in methylated spirit and blow dry with compressed air. Check the cylinder bore for grooves and rust which if present, necessitate the renewal of the complete unit.
6 Compress the spring and withdraw the retaining bolt from the main piston. Renewal of both pistons and all rubber cups is advised.

FIG 10:9 An exploded view of the pressure limiting valve, DAF 31, 32, 33

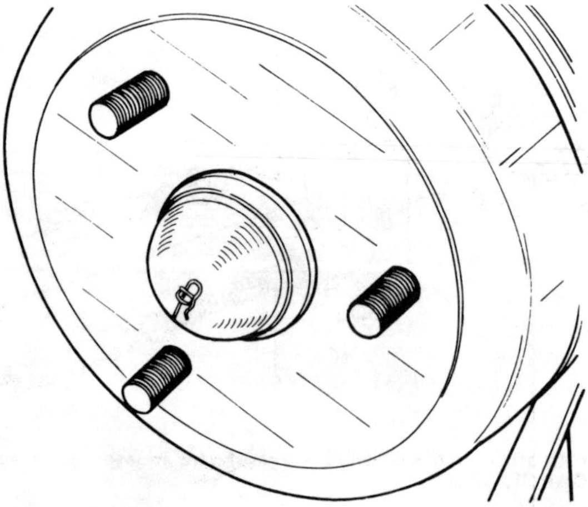

FIG 10:10 The speedometer cable clip on the lefthand front wheel

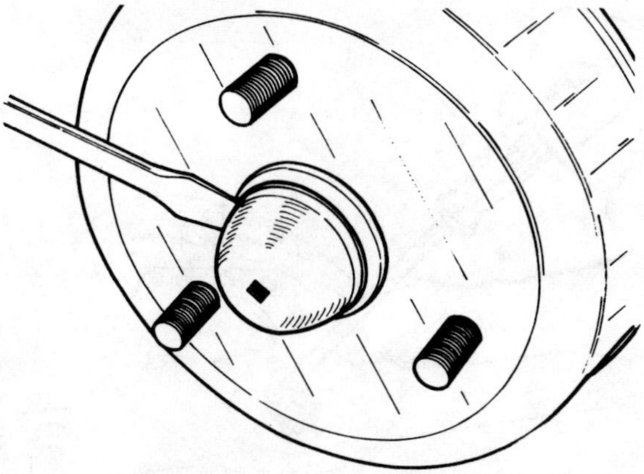

FIG 10:11 Removing a dust cap

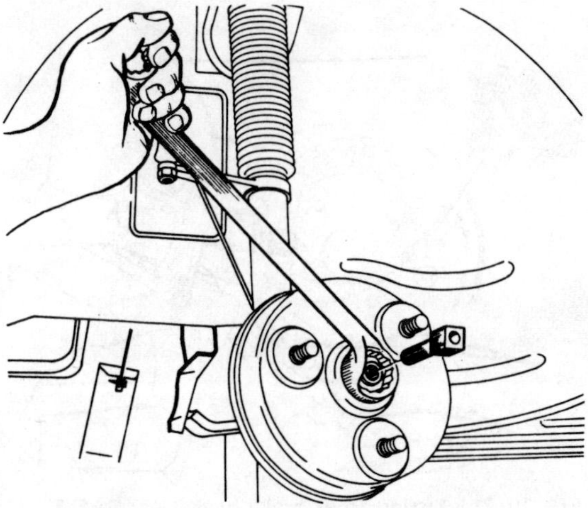

FIG 10:12 Unscrewing the spindle nut

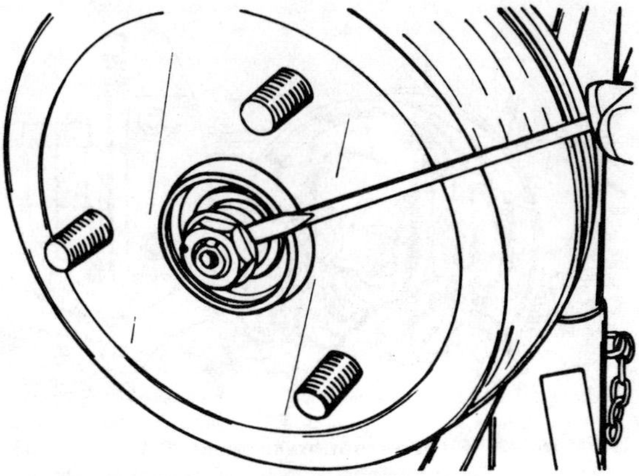

FIG 10:13 Removing the lockplate, adjusting nut and lock ring

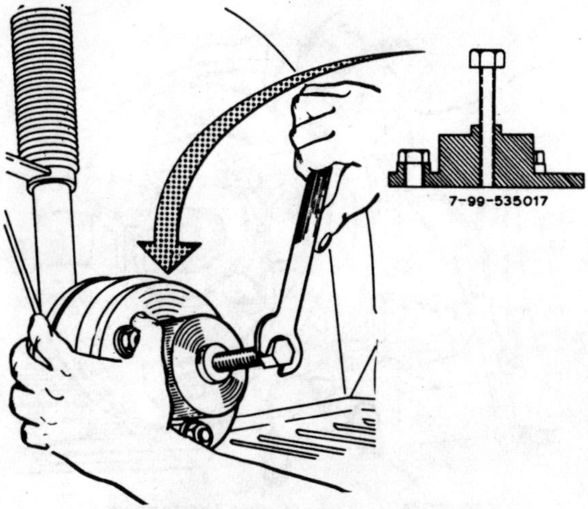

FIG 10:14 Removing a brake drum

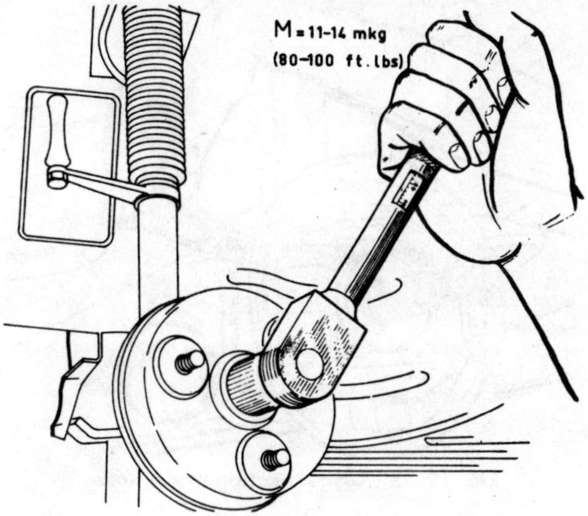

FIG 10:15 Tightening the spindle nut

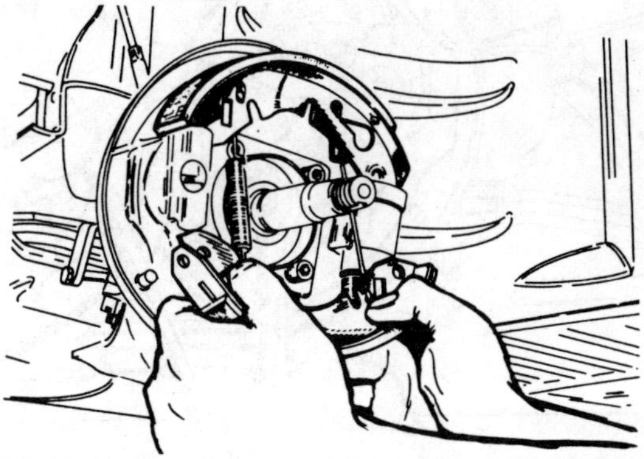

FIG 10:16 Removing the front brake shoes, DAF 31, 32, 33

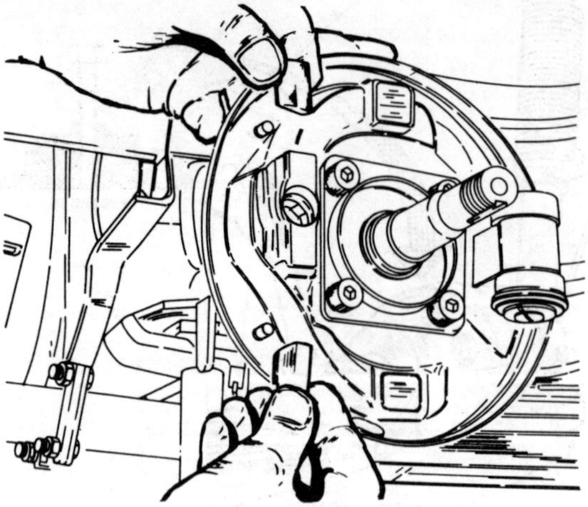

FIG 10:17 Withdrawing the tappets

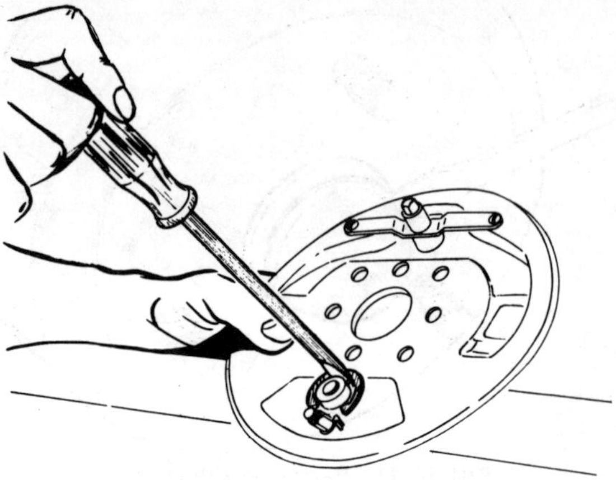

FIG 10:20 Removing circlip and wheel cylinder

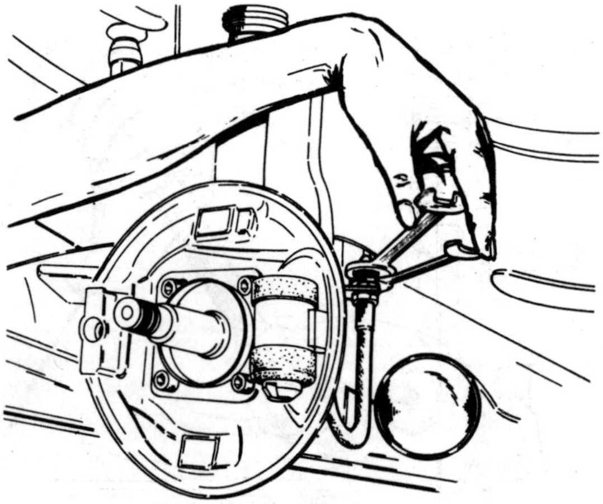

FIG 10:18 Disconnecting brake hose

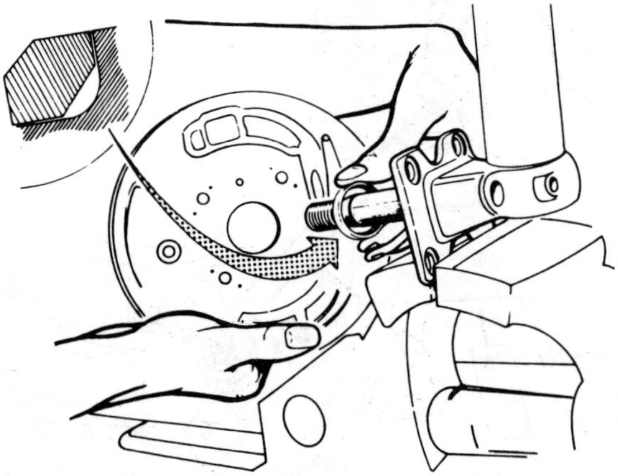

FIG 10:21 Fitting front brake backplate, DAF 31, 32, 33

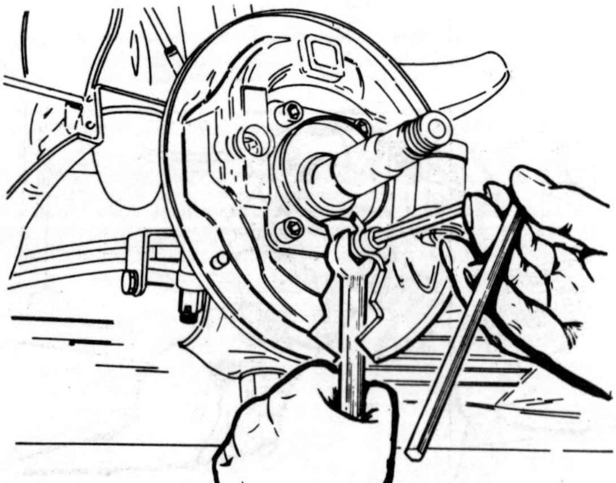

FIG 10:19 Removing backplate retaining bolts

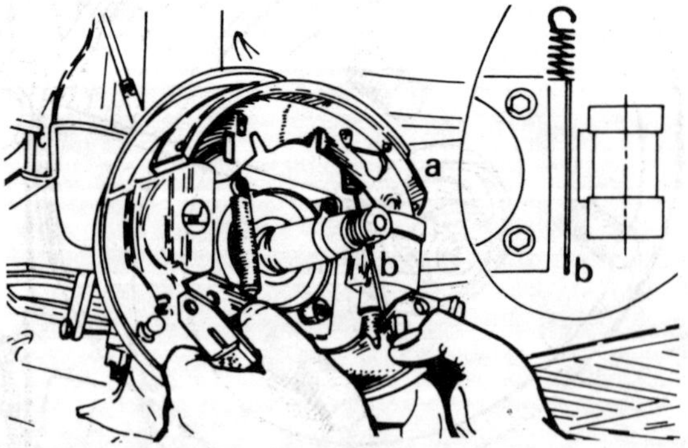

FIG 10:22 Fitting front brake shoes, DAF 31, 32, 33

Key to Fig 10:22 a Shoe locations b Pull-off spring at wheel cylinder side

7 Dip all components in clean approved hydraulic fluid, install the spacer ring and rubber cup on the primary piston. Clamp the pushrod in a vice and assemble the piston, spring, spring retainers and retaining bolt. Compress the spring and tighten the screw.
8 Install the cups in the grooves of the secondary piston, for which a special sleeve No. 6-99-535764 is available. Fit the spacer ring and the foremost rubber cup on the piston.
9 Clamp the master cylinder slanting downwards in a vice. Treat the cylinder bore, cups and secondary piston sparingly with ATE cylinder paste. Install the secondary piston with spring and spring retainer.
10 With the master cylinder held vertically, smear the cups and main piston sparingly with the ATE paste. Install the main piston complete with spring and spring retainer, press down the pistons as far as possible and screw in the stop bolt with seal. Coat the main piston rod sparingly with silicone grease and fill the cup grooves with the same grease.
11 Fit the stop ring and the circlip.
12 Refit in the reverse order to removal. Adjust pedal free travel to 3 to 5 mm if necessary. Bleed the system as described in **Section 10:7**.

Master cylinder, dual brake system, DAF 46:

Remove in a similar manner to the DAF 44 except that the pushrod is disconnected from the brake pedal. Remove the clips and pins and detach the reservoir. Remove the pin from the front piston, take off the dust cover, and remove the circlip. Take out the connecting rod and rear piston assembly.

Remove the front piston assembly by tapping the body against a block of wood.

Clean and inspect all parts for scores and corrosion and renew all cups.

Reassemble in the reverse order fitting new cups by hand and lubricating all parts with clean brake fluid.

10:4 Drum brakes, front

Routine adjustment to compensate for wear of the shoe linings is required on drum brakes. The procedure is described in **Section 10:2**. Servicing of wheel cylinders is described in **Section 10:3**. Removal and fitment of hub bearings is covered in **Chapter 8, Section 8:3**. Fitment of new linings to shoes is described in **Section 10:5**. Before removing brake drums mark for reassembly in the same position to maintain wheel balance.

Drum removal, DAF 31, 32, 33 and 44 models:

The following procedure is for the lefthand front wheel which drives the speedometer drive cable. In the case of the opposite wheel, the procedure is the same but operations which refer to the speedometer drive are not relevant.

Jack up and remove the road wheel. Push out the speedometer cable adaptor spring clip (see **FIG 10:10**) and prise off the dust cap (see **FIG 10:11**). Remove the speedometer cable adaptor.

In the case of DAF 31, 32 and 33 models, bend back the lockwasher, remove the stub axle nut (see **FIG 10:12**), the lockwasher and the lockring. In the case of DAF 44 models, bend back the lockwasher, remove the locknut, the lockwasher, the adjusting nut and the lockring (see

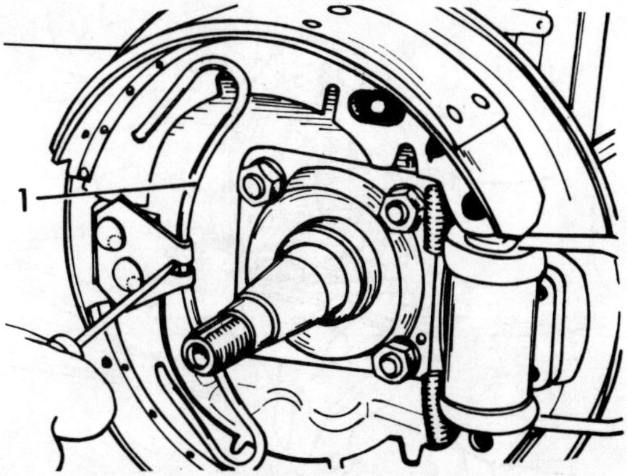

FIG 10:23 Removing the spring 1 in the front brake assembly, DAF 44

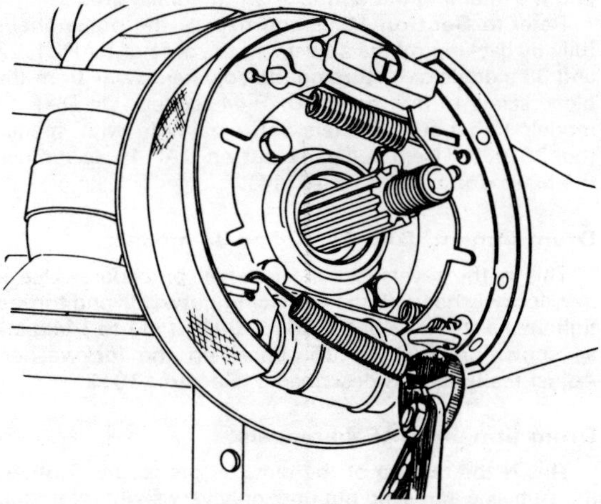
FIG 10:24 Unhooking the outer (red) spring

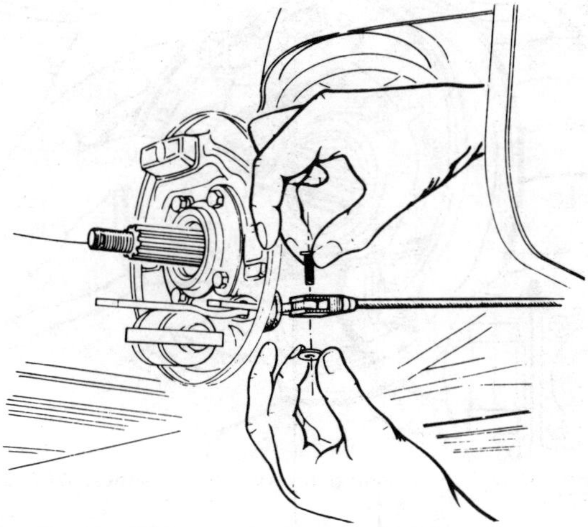
FIG 10:25 Disconnecting the handbrake cable at the lever, DAF 31, 32, 33

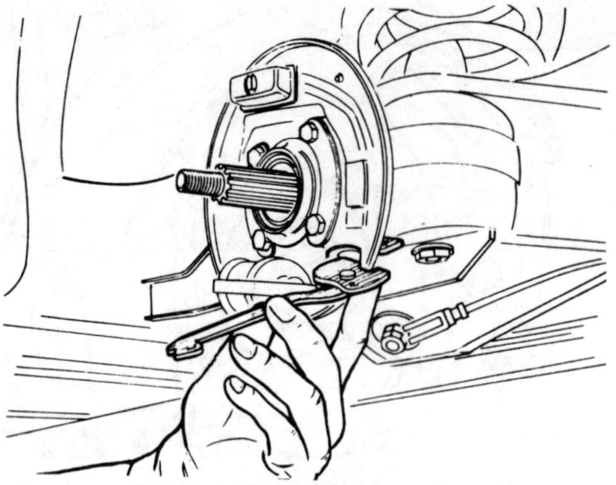

FIG 10:26 Removing the handbrake lever

FIG 10:13). On DAF 46 models remove the dust cover and the retaining nut and take off the brake drum.

Refer to **Section 10:2** and release the brake shoes fully by backing off the adjuster in the case of DAF 31, 32 and 33 models or by turning the adjusters away from the bleed screw in the case of DAF 44 models. On DAF 46 models turn both adjusters anti-clockwise with special tool 267066. Use a puller, except on DAF 46, to remove the brake drum (see **FIG 10:14**).

Drum fitment, DAF 31, 32 and 33 models:

This is the reverse of the removal procedure. Use a new lockwasher with the tab facing outwards and torque tighten the stub axle nut to 80 to 100 lb ft (11 to 14 kg m) as shown in **FIG 10:15**. Bend up the lockwasher. Adjust the brakes as described in **Section 10:2**.

Drum fitment, DAF 44 models:

This is the reverse of the removal procedure. Tighten the stub axle adjusting nut until only very slight rotational

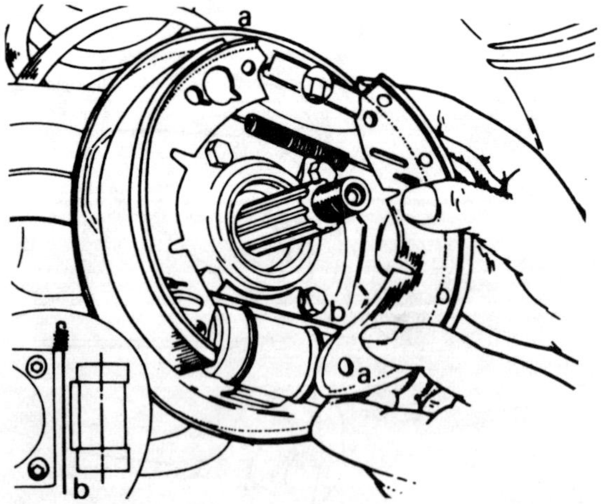

FIG 10:27 Positioning the rear brake shoes, DAF 31, 32, 33

Key to Fig 10:27 a Shoe locations b Pull-off spring at wheel cylinder side

movement of the lockring is possible. Use a new lockwasher. Fit and tighten the locknut, bend up the lockwasher and adjust the brakes as described in **Section 10:2**.

Drum fitment, DAF 46 models:

This is the reverse of the removal procedure. Turn the retaining nut until the washer can just be moved. Lock the nut and fit the dust cover.

Fit the wheel and adjust the brakes as described in **Section 10:2**.

Dismantling a front brake, DAF 31, 32 and 33 models:

1 Remove the brake drum as described earlier. Pull downwards and outwards on the lower shoe as shown in **FIG 10:16** and disengage the shoe from the adjuster and from the wheel cylinder.
2 Wrap wire round the wheel cylinder to prevent parts from sliding out. Disengage the pull-off springs and remove the upper shoe. Withdraw the tappets (see **FIG 10:17**) from the adjuster.
3 Disconnect the brake hose at the union as described in **Section 10:6** (see **FIG 10:18**) and blank off the pipeline. Remove the four bolts which attach the backplate to the stub axle flange (see **FIG 10:19**), remove the backplate and collect the pilot ring from the stub axle.
4 Disconnect the brake hose from the wheel cylinder, remove the circlip which retains the cylinder in the backplate (see **FIG 10:20**) and withdraw the cylinder.

Assembling a front brake, DAF 31, 32 and 33 models:

This is the dismantling sequence in reverse. Ensure that the pilot ring is fitted the correct way round as shown in **FIG 10:21**. Make sure that the shoes are correctly positioned as shown at a in **FIG 10:22** and that the centre part of the spring b is located as close as possible to the cylinder. Fit the brake drum as described earlier. Bleed the system as described in **Section 10:7** and adjust the brakes as described in **Section 10:2**.

Dismantling a front brake, DAF 44 models:

Remove the brake drum as described earlier. Take out the spring 1 (see **FIG 10:23**) and remove the brake shoes, ensuring that no parts drop from the wheel cylinder. Disconnect the brake hose at the union as described in **Section 10:6** and blank off the pipeline. Remove the four bolts (see **FIG 8:23** in **Chapter 8**) which attach the backplate to the stub axle flange and dismount the backplate. Disconnect the brake hose from the wheel cylinder, remove the two retaining screws and withdraw the wheel cylinder.

Assembling a front brake, DAF 44 models:

This is the dismantling sequence in reverse. After installing the wheel cylinder and fitting the backplate to the stub axle flange, connect the brake hose. The lower pull-off spring is fitted so that the centre part is located as close as possible to the wheel cylinder as shown in

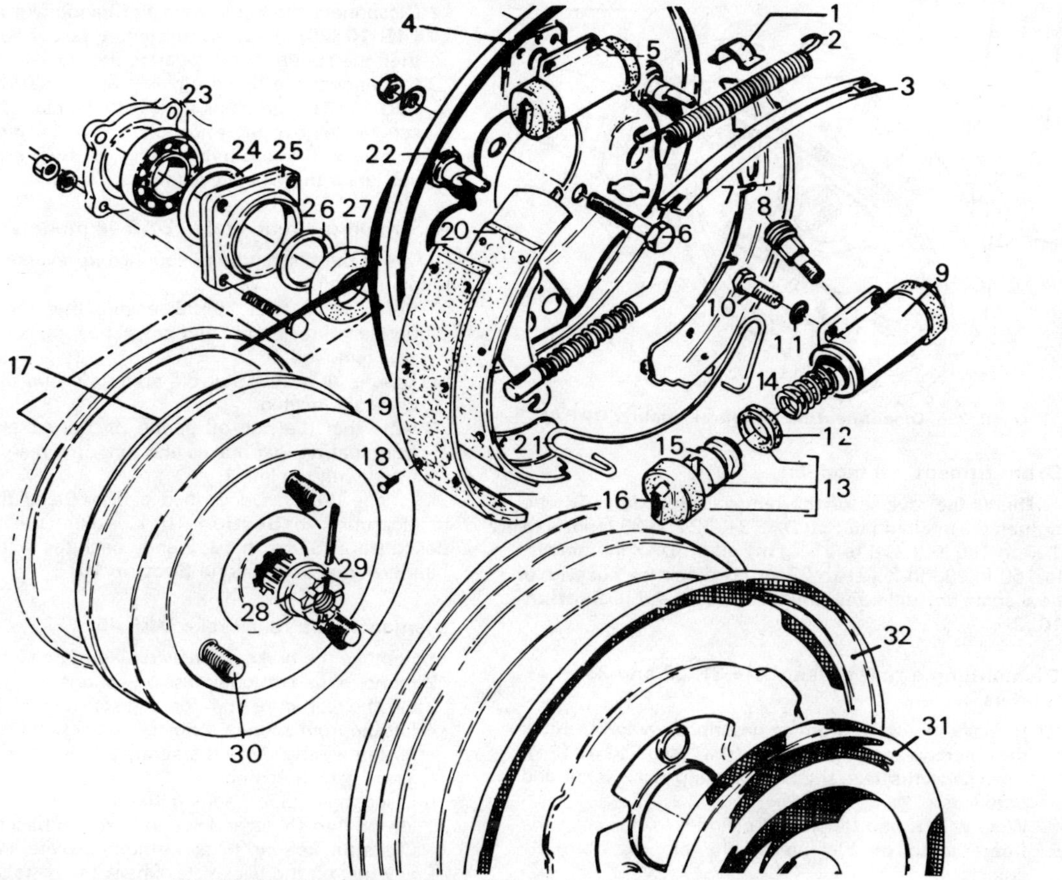

FIG 10:28 An exploded view of a rear brake and hub, DAF 44

Key to Fig 10:28 1 Clip 2 Pull-off spring 3 Link 4 Backplate 5 Wheel cylinder (assembled) 6 Bolt 7 Shoe 8 Bleed nipple 9 Wheel cylinder 10 Bolt 11 Washer 12 Seal 13 Piston assembly 14 Spring 15 Piston 16 Dust boot 17 Brake drum 18 Rivet 19 Lining 20 Shoe 21 Spring 22 Adjuster 23 Axle shaft bearing 24 Shim 25 Bearing retainer 26 Spacer ring 27 Seal 28 Castellated nut 29 Split pin 30 Road wheel retaining stud 31 Trim plate 32 Road wheel

FIG 10:23. Note point 3 of the assembly procedure described in **Section 10:5** for DAF 44 rear brakes. Fit the brake drum as described earlier. Bleed the system as described in **Section 10:7** and adjust the brakes as described in **Section 10:2**.

Dismantling a front brake, DAF 46 models:

Remove the brake drum as described earlier. Remove the spring clips from the shoe retaining pins. Using tool 267065 or similar remove the brake shoes. Clean the backplate and bearing pads.

Reassemble in the reverse order of dismantling, noting the procedure already described for fitment of the brake drum on this model.

10:5 Drum brakes, rear

Routine adjustment to compensate for wear of shoe linings is required on drum brakes. The procedure is described in **Section 10:2**. Servicing of wheel cylinders is described in **Section 10:3**. Fitment of new bearings and oil seals is covered in **Chapter 7, Section 7:4**. Fitment of new linings to shoes is described at the end of this Section.

Drum removal, all models:

Jack up and remove the relevant road wheel. Extract the split pin, remove the retaining nut and, in the case of DAF 31, 32 and 33 models, collect the washer. Refer to **Section 10:2** and release the brake shoes fully by backing off the adjuster in the case of DAF 31, 32 and 33 models or by turning the adjusters away from the bleed nipple in the case of DAF 44 models. Turn the adjuster anti-clockwise on DAF 46 models. Use a suitable puller to remove the brake drum as in **FIG 10:14**. On DAF 46 models the drum can be tapped off with a soft faced hammer.

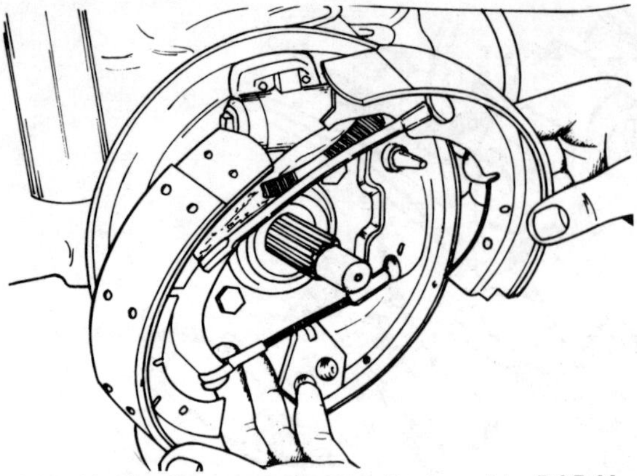

FIG 10:29 Disconnecting handbrake cable, DAF 44

Drum fitment, all models:

This is the reverse of the removal procedure. Torque tighten the retaining nut on DAF 31, 32 and 33 models to 130 to 150 lb ft (18 to 21 kg m) or, on DAF 44 models, to 150 to 208 lb ft (21 to 29 kg m). Lock the nut with a new splitpin. Adjust the brakes as described in **Section 10:2**.

Dismantling a rear brake, DAF 31, 32 and 33 models:

1 Remove the brake drum as described earlier. Unhook the outer lower pull-off spring (red) (see **FIG 10:24**). Disengage the rear shoes by pulling backwards and outwards.
2 Wrap wire round the wheel cylinder to prevent parts from sliding out. Withdraw the tappets from the adjuster.
3 Disconnect the handbrake cable at the backplate lever (see **FIG 10:25**) and withdraw the complete lever (see **FIG 10:26**). Remove the dust boot.
4 Disconnect the brake pipeline at the backplate. Bend back the tabs, remove the four bolts and dismount the backplate.
5 Remove the circlip which retains the wheel cylinder in the backplate and withdraw the cylinder.

Assembling a rear brake, DAF 31, 32 and 33 models:

This is the dismantling procedure in reverse. Use new lockplates and torque tighten the backplate retaining bolts to 20 lb ft (2.7 kg m). Make sure that the shoes are correctly positioned as shown at a in **FIG 10:27** and that the centre part of the lower inner spring b is located as close as possible to the wheel cylinder. Do not omit the lower outer (red) pull-off spring. Use a new splitpin to lock the handbrake lever cotter pin. Fit the drum as described earlier. Bleed the system as described in **Section 10:7**. Adjust the brakes as described in **Section 10:2** and check the handbrake setting as described in **Section 10:8**.

Dismantling a rear brake, DAF 44 models:

1 Remove the brake drum as described earlier. Refer to **FIG 10:28**, remove spring 21 and withdraw the brake shoes. Wrap wire round the wheel cylinder to prevent parts from sliding out.
2 Disconnect the cable from the handbrake lever (see **FIG 10:29**). Remove the link 1 (see **FIG 10:30**), then the spring 2 and separate the shoes.
3 Disconnect the brake pipeline at the backplate (see **FIG 10:31**) and blank it off with the cap of the bleed screw. Remove the four nuts and bolts arrowed and dismount the backplate. Remove two screws and withdraw the wheel cylinder.

Assembling a rear brake, DAF 44 models:

This is the dismantling sequence in reverse. Note the following points.

1 Referring to **FIG 10:32**, ensure that the spacer 3 between brake drum and wheel bearing is refitted if it was removed.
2 Ensure that the pull-off spring 2 and link 1 are correctly located.
3 Note that the pull-off spring on front brakes differs from that on rear brakes and that only rear brakes are fitted with the link 1.

Fit the drum as described earlier. Bleed the system as described in **Section 10:7**. Adjust the brakes as described in **Section 10:2** and check the setting of the handbrake as described in **Section 10:8**.

Dismantling a rear brake DAF 46:

1 Remove the brake drum as previously described
2 Remove the two compression springs and pins
3 Lift the rear shoe from the adjuster (see **FIG 10:33**).
4 Lift the front shoe in a similar manner and remove the bottom spring, note the springs fitted for reassembly in the same positions.
5 Disengage the rear shoe from the handbrake lever and lift the two shoes and spring from the backplate.

Clean the bearing pads on the backplate and remove any rust on the backplate. Check the handbrake parts for free movement. Check the adjuster assembly for ease of movement.

Assembling a rear brake DAF 46:

Reassemble in the reverse order of dismantling noting the following points:

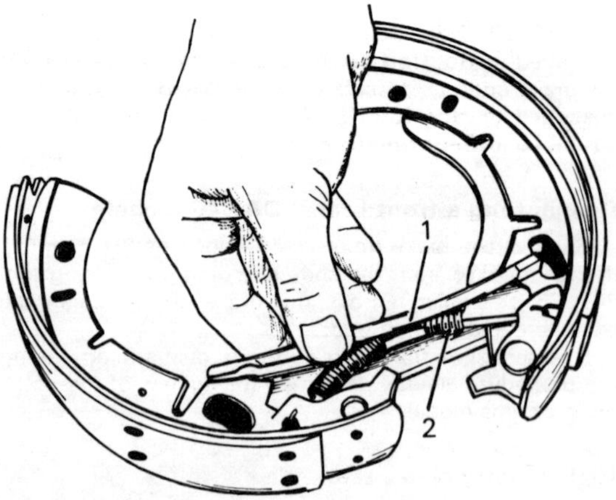

FIG 10:30 Unhooking the link 1 from the brake shoe (DAF 44) and removing the spring 2

1 The springs must be fitted in their original position.
2 Do not press the pistons too far into the wheel cylinders or the cups may be damaged.
3 Fit the wheels and adjust the brakes.

Fitting new linings to brake shoes:

Drill out the rivets or, as shown in **FIG 10:34**, use a suitable punch. Thoroughly clean the brake shoe surface before rivetting on the new linings. Commence rivetting at the middle of the shoe and work outwards to the ends. Stretch the linings to achieve good contact with the shoes. There must be no gap between the linings and the shoes.

10:6 Removing a flexible hose

Never attempt to remove a flexible hose by turning either end until it is disconnected from the connecting metal pipeline and from the retaining bracket. Start by unscrewing the metal pipeline then hold the flexible hose hexagon with a spanner and remove the locknut which secures the hose to the bracket. Still holding the hexagon of the hose, remove the union body. The other end of the flexible hose may now be unscrewed from the wheel cylinder or from the caliper without twisting the hose itself. Fitting a flexible hose is the reverse of this sequence.

10:7 Bleeding the system

This procedure is normally only necessary if air has entered the system because the level of the fluid in the reservoir has dropped so low that air has been drawn into the system or because part of the system has been dismantled and reassembled. It is important to keep the reservoir topped up during the bleeding operation to preclude air from being drawn into the system. Do not use fluid which has been bled through the system to replenish the reservoir as it will be aerated. Use fresh fluid straight from the supply tin.

Check that all connections are tight and all bleed screws closed. The procedure (which requires two

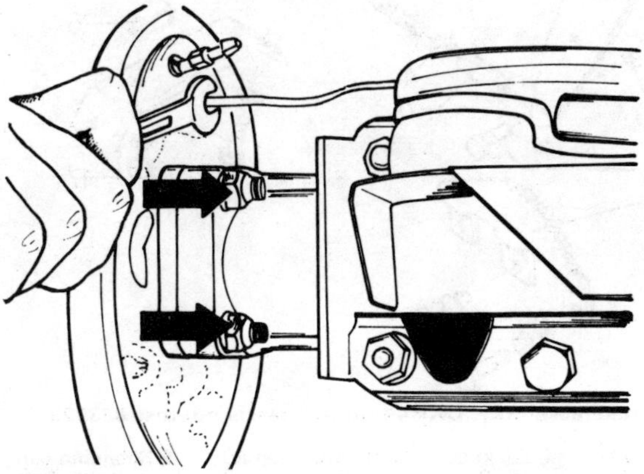

FIG 10:31 Disconnecting brake line at backplate, DAF 44, and showing the backplate retaining bolts arrowed

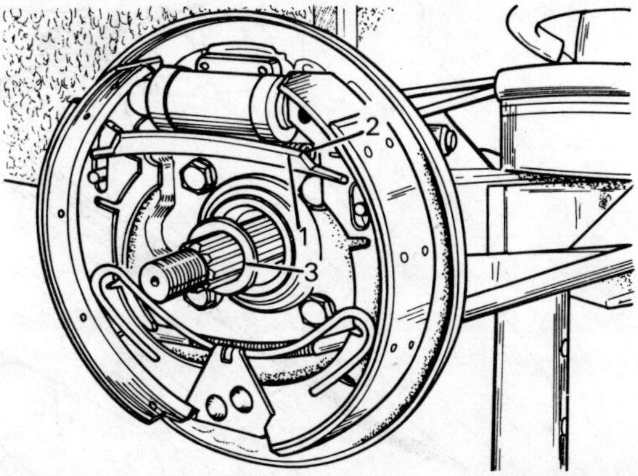

FIG 10:32 Rear brake assembly, DAF 44, showing the correct locations of the link 1 and the spring 2, also the spacer 3 between the brake drum and wheel bearing

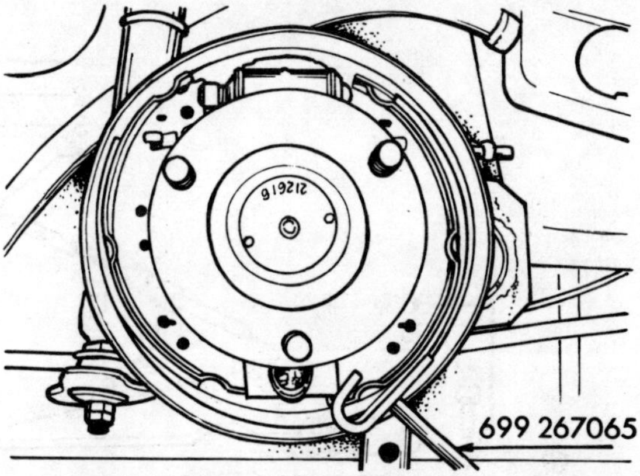

FIG 10:33 Tool 6-99-267065 being used to lift the rear shoe, on DAF 46 models, from the adjuster

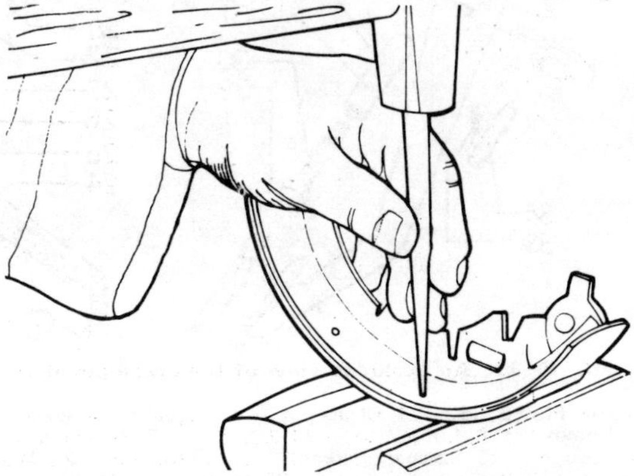

FIG 10:34 Removing a rivet from a shoe lining

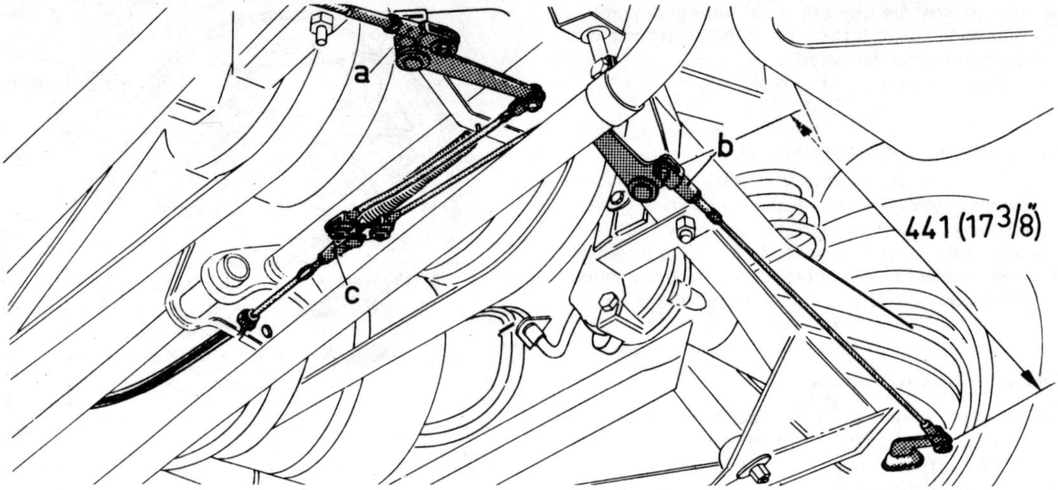

FIG 10:35 Handbrake linkage

Key to Fig 10:35 a Clevis and pin b Clevis and pin c Clevis

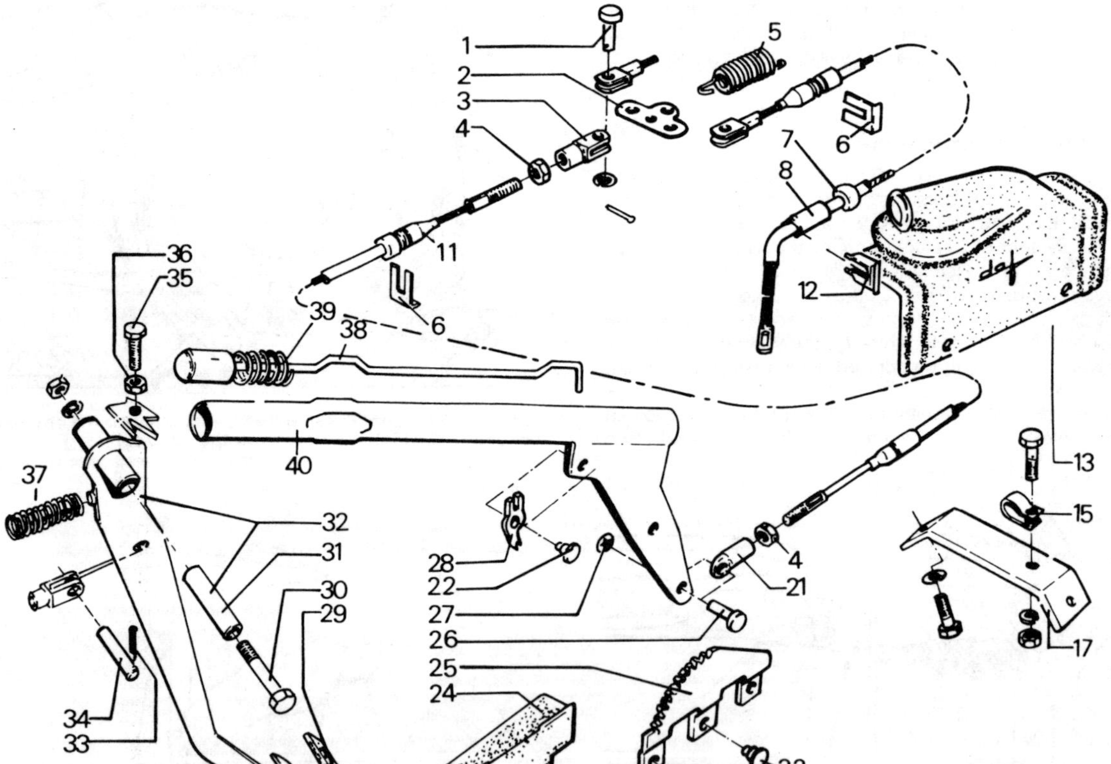

FIG 10:36 An exploded view of the brake pedal and handbrake assembly, DAF 44 up to chassis number 633999

Key to Fig 10:36 1 Clevis pin 2 Equalisation lever 3 Clevis 4 Locknut 5 Pull-off spring 6 Retaining clip 7 Grommet 8 Connector 11 Cable 12 Retaining clip 13 Cover 15 P-clip 17 Bracket 21 Clevis 22 Bolt 24 Trough 25 Ratchet quadrant 26 Clevis pin 27 Washer 28 Ratchet lever 29 Pedal cover 30 Bolt 31 Bearing bush 32 Brake pedal pivot 33 Splitpin 34 Clevis pin 35 Bolt 36 Locknut 37 Spring 38 Ratchet release 39 Ratchet release spring 40 Handbrake lever operators) is the same for all models but the order in which each of the four brakes should be bled varies. **It is important that the sequence given later for each model is followed** if possible damage to master cylinder components is to be avoided.

1 Attach a bleeder tube to the first bleed screw and immerse its free end in a small quantity of brake fluid in a clean glass jar. Loosen the first bleed screw.

2 Depress the brake pedal and keep it depressed. Brake fluid mixed with air will issue from the bleed tube as the pedal is operated. Close the bleed screw and release the brake pedal.

3 Repeat this operation until no further air bubbles are seen coming through the fluid in the glass jar and finally tighten the bleed nipple firmly.

4 Repeat this operation on each brake in the order given.

Sequence for DAF 31, 32 and 33 models:

Commence with either rear brake. Follow with the other rear brake. Carry out the procedure on either front brake and finally bleed the remaining front brake.

Sequence for DAF 44 and 46 models:

Commence with the lefthand rear brake. Proceed then to the righthand rear brake. Follow with either front brake and complete the sequence with the remaining front brake.

Draining and refilling the system:

To drain the system, open each bleed nipple in turn and operate the brake pedal until no further fluid is pumped out of each brake.

To refill the system, replenish the reservoir and carry out the bleeding procedure described earlier.

10:8 The handbrake

The handbrake operates mechanically on the rear brakes. Routine adjustment to compensate for wear of the friction linings of the rear shoes is required on all models. The handbrake lever tensions the inner element of a Bowden type flexible cable. The actuation divides at an equalization yoke and two cables operate the rear brakes from that point.

DAF 31, 32 and 33 models:

The layout of the rear part of the system is shown in **FIG 10:35**. The setting procedure is as follows:

1 Raise both rear wheels. Adjust the rear brakes as described in **Section 10:2**.

2 Remove clevis pins a and b and, by turning the adjustable clevises, set the centre to centre dimension between the adjustable and the fixed clevises to 441 mm (17.362 inch). Refit clevises a and b.

3 Set the handbrake lever to the third notch of the ratchet and adjust clevis c until both rear wheels are locked.

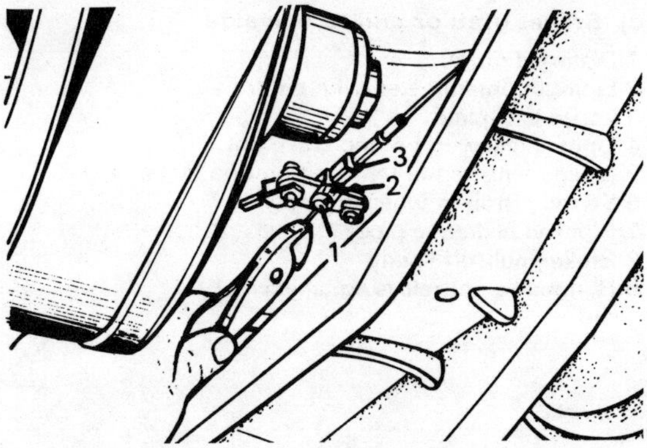

FIG 10:37 Handbrake adjustment DAF 44, showing the clevis pin 1, the clevis 2 and the locknut 3

4 Release the handbrake lever and check that both rear wheels can be roted freely. If necessary, further adjustment of clevis c may be made.

DAF 44 models up to chassis number 633999:

Adjust the rear brakes as described in **Section 10:2** before setting the handbrake.

The components of the system are shown in **FIGS 10:36** and **10:37**. Referring to the former illustration, handbrake adjustment is carried out at the yoke by loosening locknut 4, turning clevis 3 and retightening the locknut. The setting should be such that the handbrake lever has three notches of free travel before the rear wheels lock. Further adjustment, if required, may be effected at clevis 21.

DAF 44 from chassis number 634000 and DAF 46:

A modified handbrake lever is fitted with an adjuster incorporated.

Slide back the dust cap and hold the slotted head of the threaded cable with a screwdriver while loosening the locknut. Jack-up the rear of the car and set the handbrake lever in the fifth notch. Adjust the adjusting nut on the lever until the wheel cannot be turned manually.

10:9 Fault diagnosis

(a) 'Spongy' pedal

1 Leak in hydraulic system
2 Worn master cylinder
3 Defective master cylinder seals
4 Defective wheel seals
5 Air in hydraulic system

(b) Excessive pedal movement

1 Check 1 and 5 in (a)
2 Excessive shoe lining wear
3 Very low fluid level

(c) Brakes grab or pull to one side

1 Distorted drum
2 Linings contaminated with oil or fluid
3 Loose backplate
4 Linings renewed on one brake only
5 Drum refinished or renewed on one brake only
6 Seized piston in wheel cylinder
7 Blocked hydraulic pipe
8 Broken pull-off spring
9 Handbrake not releasing, check (e)

(d) Brakes do not operate on all wheels

1 Check 6 and 7 in (c)
2 Pressure limiting valve blocked or seized (DAF 31, 32 and 33 models)

(e) Handbrake not releasing

1 Broken spring
2 Seized cable
3 Seized pivot
4 Adjustment incorrect

CHAPTER 11

THE ELECTRICAL EQUIPMENT

11:1 Description

The various cars covered in this manual may be fitted with 6- or 12-volt electrical systems. On all models the negative battery terminal is earthed and **under no circumstances should the terminal connections be reversed.** The battery is located in the engine compartment.

Earlier models have a DC generator (dynamo), the output of which is controlled by a regulator located in the engine compartment. Type 46 models have an alternator, the AC output of which is rectified by an integral diode rectifier. Either type is belt driven from a pulley on the crankshaft.

Instructions are given in this chapter for the servicing of the main items of electrical equipment. It must be accepted that it is not sensible to try to repair units which are seriously defective, electrically or mechanically. Such equipment should be replaced by new units obtained on an exchange basis. It must be stressed that accurate meters are essential when checking or altering control settings.

The main circuits are protected by fuses the location and identity of which are given in **Section 11:6**. Wiring diagrams are included in the **Appendix**.

11:2 The battery

The capacity of the storage battery, as well as its voltage, varies according to the car model. In all cases the negative terminal is earthed and it is most important that this polarity should not be reversed.

Maintenance:

Keep the top and surrounding parts of the battery dry and clean. Dampness can cause current leakage. Keep metal parts free of corrosion and clean, if necessary, with diluted ammonia. Paint the battery mounting with anti-sulphuric and smear the terminal posts, after removing the cables and cleaning them, with petroleum jelly. Remake the connections firmly. By topping up the electrolyte level with distilled water, keep the level to just above the separators.

Testing:

If the condition of a battery is suspect, test the state of the cells with a hydrometer. The indications from the reading of the specific gravity are as follows.

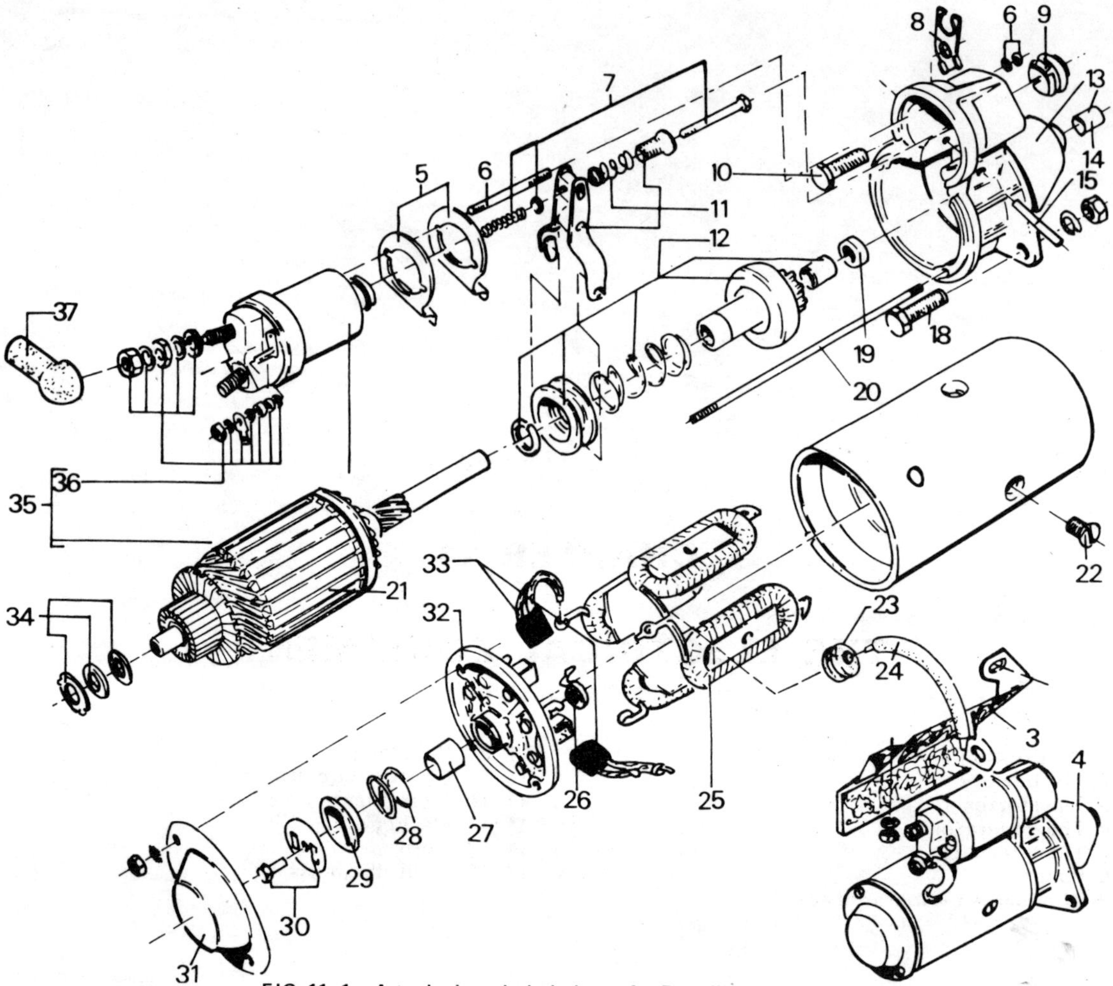

FIG 11:1 A typical exploded view of a Ducellier starter motor

Key to Fig 11:1 3 Guard 4 Starter motor (assembled) 5 Shims 6 Washer, stud, nut 7 Pinion engagement fork assembly 8 Clip 9 End cap 10 Attachment bolt 11 Pinion engagement fork assembly spring 12 Pinion assembly 13 Housing 14 Bearing bush 15 Pivot pin 18 Attachment bolt 19 Stop 20 Assembly stud 21 Armature 22 Pole-piece retaining screw 23 Grommet 24 Cable 25 Field coils 26 Brush spring 27 Bearing bush 28 Spring 29 Sleeve 30 End washer and retaining screw 31 Cover 32 Brush carrier plate 33 Brushes 34 Thrust washers 36 Terminal assembly parts 37 Rubber terminal cover

For climates below 80°F or 27°C:

Cell fully charged	Specific gravity 1.270 to 1.290
Cell half-discharged	Specific gravity 1.190 to 1.210
Cell discharged	Specific gravity 1.110 to 1.130

For climates above 80°F or 27°C:

Cell fully charged	Specific gravity 1.210 to 1.230
Cell half-discharged	Specific gravity 1.130 to 1.150
Cell discharged	Specific gravity 1.050 to 1.070

These indicative figures assume an electrolyte temperature of 60°F or 16°C. If the electrolyte temperature exceeds this, add .002 to the reading for each 5°F or 3°C rise. Subtract .002 for any corresponding drop below 60°F or 16°C.

If it is necessary to prepare new electrolyte due to loss of spillage, **add sulphuric acid to distilled water. It is highly dangerous to add water to acid. Never add neat acid to the battery cells.**

Recharging:

If the state of the battery is low, take the vehicle for a long daylight run or put the battery on charge at 4 amps. If the battery is to stand unused for a long period, give it a monthly freshening up charge. It will be ruined if left discharged.

11:3 The starter

Operationally, the different starters fitted to DAF models covered by this manual are identical. They differ in make and type and particulars are given in **Technical Data** in the **Appendix**. The starters are straightforward in design and conventional dismantling, servicing and assembly procedures apply. Positive engagement of the drive pinion is incorporated. The solenoid has two coils, an engagement coil and a secondary coil which, when engagement has been effected, holds the pinion in the

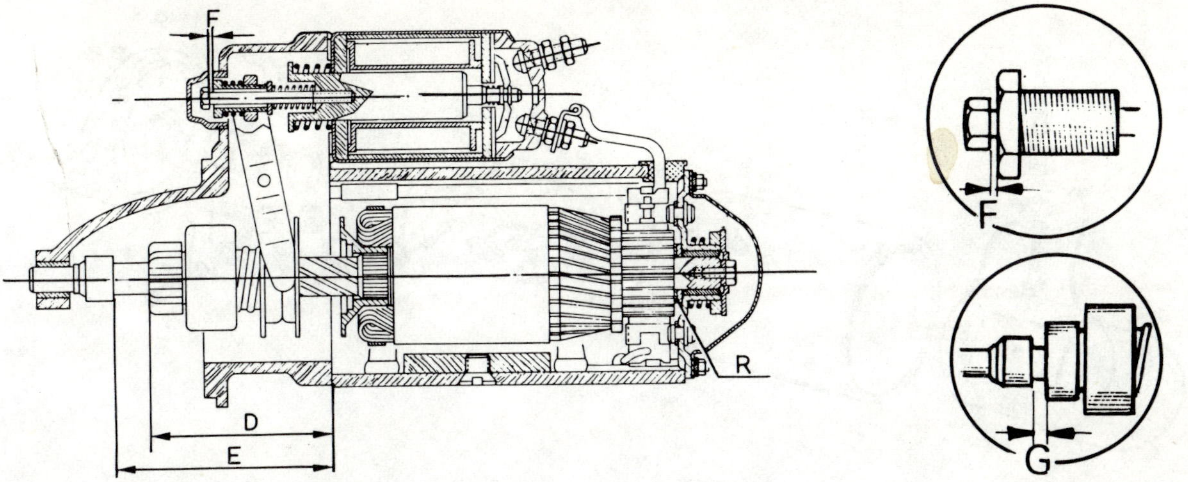

FIG 11 : 2 A sectional view of a solenoid and starter motor

Key to Fig 11 : 2 D, E, F, G Dimensions given in text R Shims

drive position and the contacts of the main switch closed. **FIG 11 : 1** shows the components of a typical Ducellier starter motor.

Tests for a starter which does not operate:

Check the condition of the battery and its connections. If it is charged, switch on the lights and operate the starter switch. Current is reaching the starter if the lights go dim. If they do not, check the solenoid and all cable connections through to the switch and to the battery. The solenoid has two windings, the engagement coil and the holding coil. If the pinion does not engage, suspect the former coil. If the hold coil is defective, the pinion will engage and disengage repeatedly. If these checks show that the wiring, the switch and the solenoid are in good order, remove the starter for examination of the brushes, the commutator and the motor windings.

Removal and refitting a starter:

Disconnect the battery earth cable. Identify and disconnect the cables from the starter motor unit. Remove two retaining nuts, bolts and washers and dismount the unit. Refit as removed.

Starter motor servicing:

Dismantling is straightforward, using **FIG 11 : 1** as a general guide.

Brushes and brush springs:

The minimum serviceable brush length is .275 inch (7 mm) in the case of Ducellier motors and .630 inch (16 mm) in the case of the Bosch unit fitted to DAF 33 and 44 models with 6-volt systems, 12-volt systems .512 inch (13 mm). Ensure that new brushes move freely in their holders. Relieve any sluggishness by polishing the sides of the brushes on a smooth file. Brush spring load should be approximately 3 lb (1.35 kg) with new brushes.

Commutator:

A commutator in good condition will be smooth and free from pitting and burned segments. Clean with a cloth and petrol and, if necessary, polish with fine glasspaper while rotating the armature. **Do not use emerycloth.** Skim a badly worn commutator in a lathe. Use a high speed and take a light cut with a sharp tool. Remove the minimum amount to clean up and finally polish with fine glasspaper. Undercut the insulation between the segments. The refinished commutator diameter must not be less than 1.200 inch (30.5 mm) on DAF 31 and 32 models or 1.320 inch (33.5 mm) on DAF 33 and 44 models.

Assembly settings:

Refer to **FIG 11 : 2** for details. Dimension D should be 2.323 ± .024 inch (59 ± .6 mm) for Ducellier motors or 2.343 ± .024 inch (59.5 ± .6 mm) for Bosch motors and is adjusted by means of shims R. Position the stop sleeve so that dimension E is 2.776 ± .04 inch (70.05 ± 1 mm) for Ducellier motors and 2.780 ± .035 inch (70.6 ± .035 mm) for Bosch motors. Depress the pinion lever bolt manually and adjust the sleeve so that dimension G is .002 to .060 inch (.05 to 1.5 mm). The clearance between the faces of the sleeve and the bolt (dimension F) must be .004 to .020 inch (.1 to .5 mm).

11 : 4 The generator

An exploded view of the Bosch type generator fitted in DAF 33 and 44 cars is given in **FIG 11 : 3**, which except for individual details of design is also representative of the general construction of the Ducellier unit fitted in DAF 31 and 32 models. A matching voltage regulator (see **Section 11 : 5**) is provided in each case. On all models, the generator is belt driven from a pulley on the crankshaft. Before removing a generator which is suspectedly defective, check that the connections both at the generator and at the voltage regulator are in good order and that, as described later, the drive belt tension is correct.

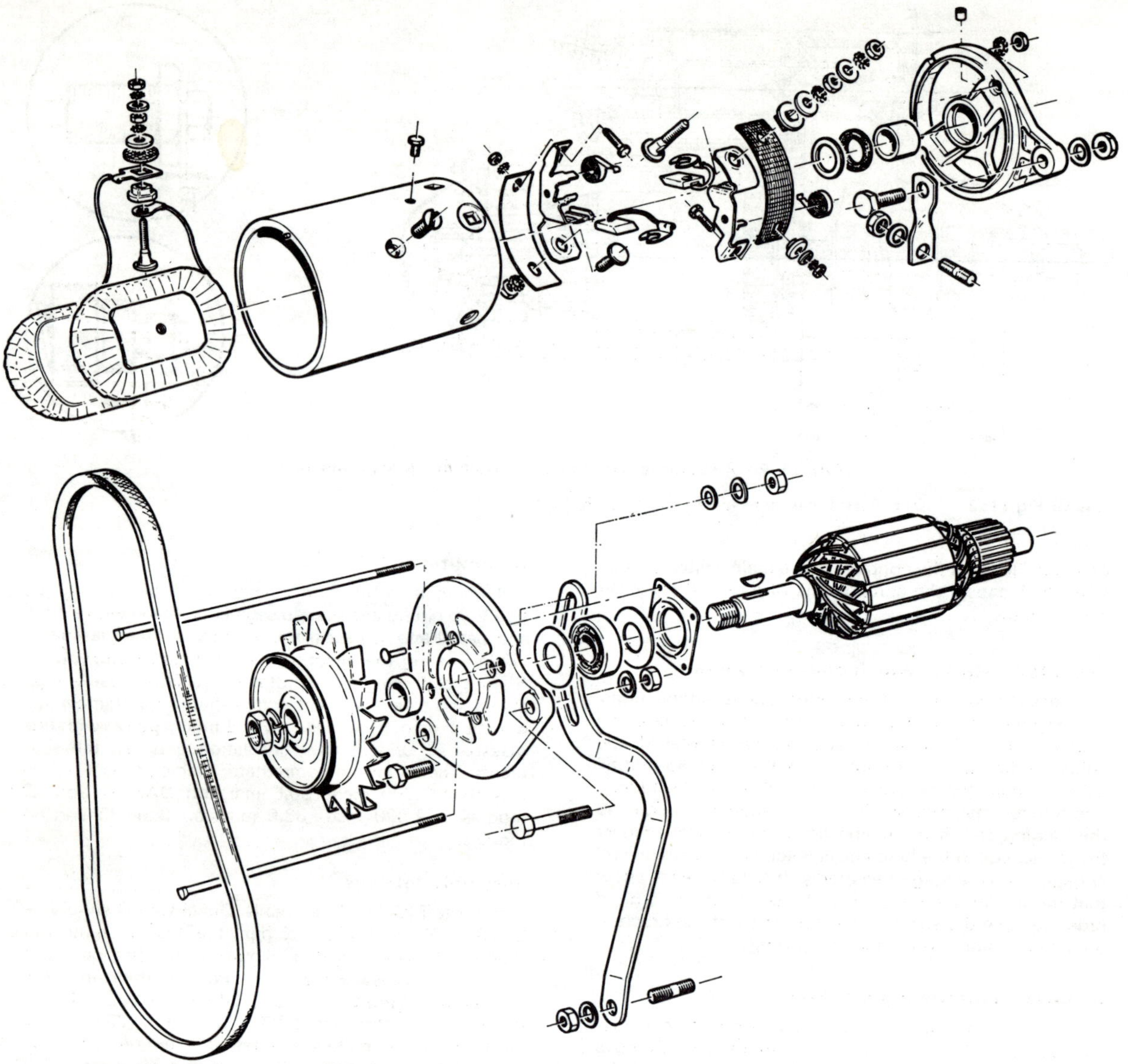

FIG 11 : 3 An exploded view of a Bosch generator

Removing and refitting a generator:

Disconnect the battery earth cable. Identify and disconnect the cables from the generator. Disengage the drive belt from the generator pulley as described later in operation 1 of the belt removal procedure. Remove the mounting and clamp bolts and dismount the generator.

Refitting is the reverse of this sequence and must be followed by tensioning the belt as described later.

Servicing a generator:

Dismantling is straightforward and follows normal procedures. Use **FIG 11 : 3** as a specific guide in the case of DAF 44 models and as a general guide in the case of other models.

Brushes and brush springs:

The minimum serviceable brush length is .433 inch (11 mm) in the Ducellier generator, and .551 inch (14 mm) in the Bosch generator. Ensure that new brushes move freely in their holders. Relieve any sluggishness by polishing the sides of the brushes on a smooth file. Brush spring load (with new brushes) should be 1.2 to 1.75 lb (.55 to .8 kg) for Ducellier units and 1 to 1.3 lb (.45 to .6 kg) for Bosch units.

Commutator:

A commutator in serviceable condition will be smooth and free from pitting and burned segments. If refinishing is not required, clean it with a cloth and petrol and, if necessary, polish with fine glasspaper while rotating the armature. **Do not use emerycloth**. If refinishing is required, use a high speed and take a light cut with a sharp tool in a lathe. Remove the minimum amount of metal to clean up and finally polish with fine glasspaper. Undercut the insulation between the segments with a hacksaw blade which has been ground down to the required width.

Tensioning a drive belt:

Refer to **FIG 11:4** and loosen the generator mounting and brace bolts A and B slightly. Swing the generator away from the engine and retighten the bolts. When correctly tensioned, it should be possible to depress the belt by finger approximately $\frac{1}{2}$ inch (1 to 1.5 cm) as shown in **FIG 11:5**.

Drive belt removal:

1 Loosen the generator mounting and clamp bolts A and B in **FIG 11:4**, swing the generator towards the engine and disengage the drive belt from the generator pulley.
2 Remove the bumper and grill as described in **Chapter 12, Sections 12:3** and **12:4**. In the case of DAF 44 models this necessitates dismounting the bonnet as described in **Chapter 12, Section 12:2**.
3 Remove the impeller shroud screen and the impeller as described in **Chapter 4, Section 4:3**. Disengage the drive belt from the crankshaft pulley and impeller hub and withdraw it as shown in **FIG 11:4**.

Drive belt fitment:

Fitting a new drive belt is, in each case, the reverse of the removal sequence and must be followed by tensioning the belt as described earlier.

The voltage regulator:

The voltage regulator fitted to each model matches the generator and details are given in **Technical Data** in the **Appendix**.

Removal and fitment:

The voltage regulator is located in the engine compartment. Disconnect the battery earth cable. Identify and disconnect the cables from the regulator (see **FIG 11:8**). Remove the attachment screws and dismount the unit.

Fitment is the reverse of this sequence.

11:5 The alternator

In place of the earlier DC generator, type 46 models are fitted with an alternator. Advantages include a higher output at low engine speeds, enabling high-current accessories such as a heated rear window to be used without discharging the battery.

Dismantling and overhaul operations on the alternator call for special experience and test equipment, especially for electronic details, and it is advised that such work should be undertaken by a qualified service agent.

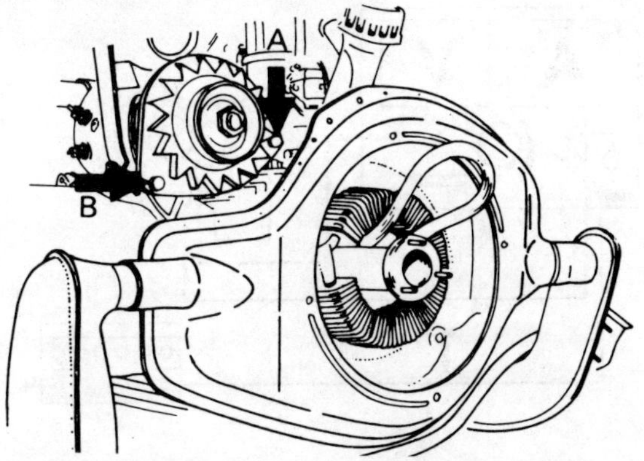

FIG 11:4 Generator mounting, showing the pivot bolt A and the clamp bolt B

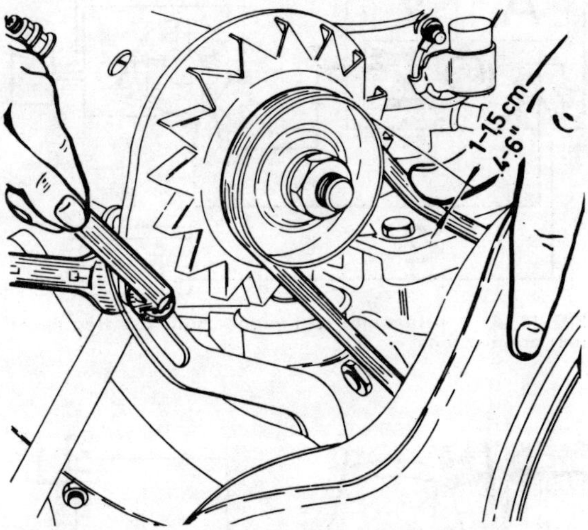

FIG 11:5 Adjusting the generator belt tension

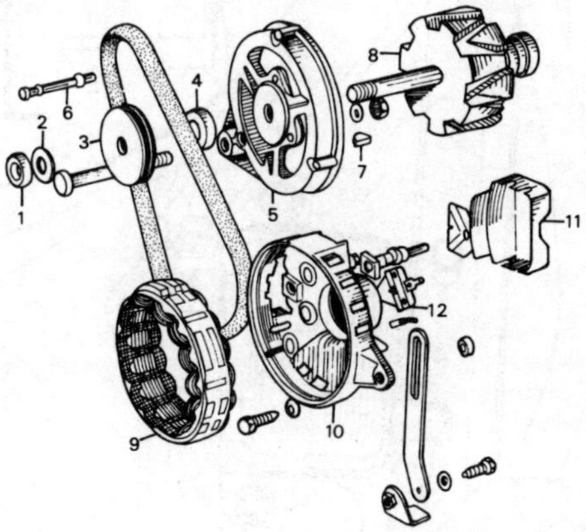

FIG 11:6 An exploded view of a Ducellier alternator

Key to Fig 11:6 1 Nut 2 Washer 3 Pulley 4 Spacer 5 Drive end shield and bearing assembly 6 Retaining screws 7 Woodruff key 8 Rotor 9 Stator 10 Slip ring end shield and bearing assembly 11 End cover 12 Brush carrier

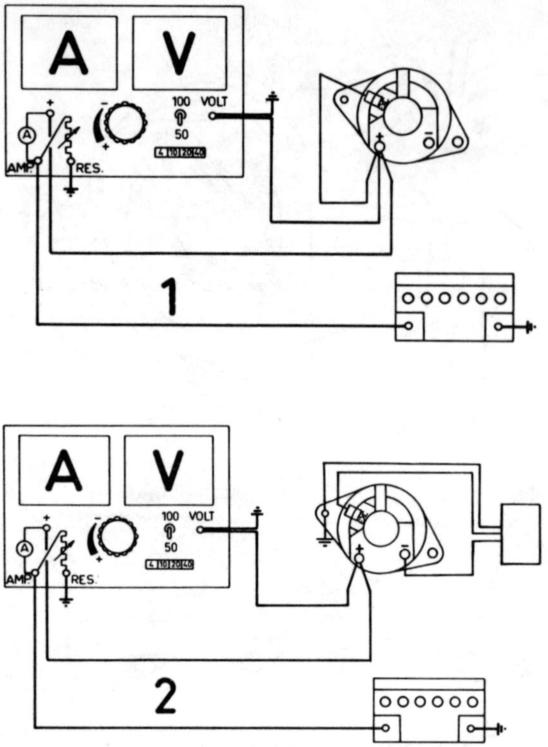

FIG 11:7 1 Alternator test connections 2 Regulator test connections

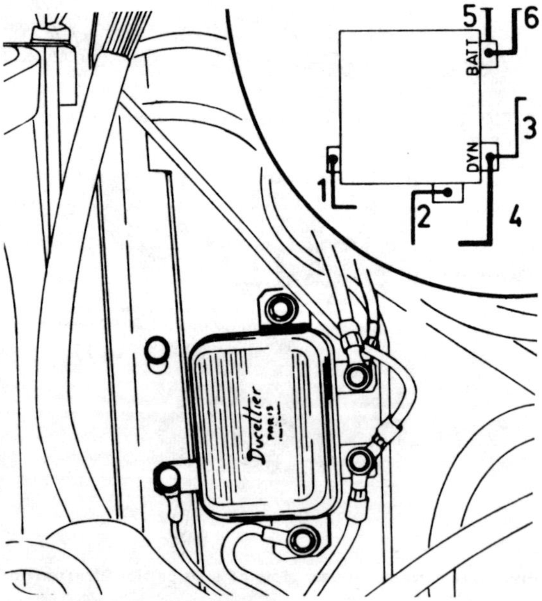

FIG 11:8 Regulator connections

Key to Fig 11:8 1 Green 2 Black 3 White 4, 5, 6 Black

Typical details of a Ducellier alternator, however, are shown in **FIG 11:6**.

The unit illustrated consists mainly of a rotor, a stator, a slip ring end shield with two rectifying diodes and a safety fuse in series with each diode, a drive end shield, a pulley and a fan. The current is generated with a stationary armature and a revolving field system. The stator and rotor are housed between the drive end slip ring end shields, the whole assembly being secured by bolts. Two brushes are mounted on the slip ring end shield and bear on the two smooth slip rings on the end of the rotor shaft. The slip rings replace the commutator on DC generators and because there is no interruption of current to cause sparking the alternator can run at higher speeds. The alternating current generated is rectified, or changed to direct current, by means of the silicon diodes also contained within the slip ring end shield. These diodes do not allow the return of current from the battery to the alternator windings and hence the normal cut-out on DC generators is not required. A fuse element in series with each diode is provided to interrupt the circuit in the event of the diode becoming short-circuited. The rotor, mounted on ballbearings, carries the excitation winding which receives the feed through the collector rings and the brushes. The regulator keeps the output voltage of the alternator within defined limits by varying the excitation current of the alternator.

Caution:

Whenever work is undertaken on an alternator charging system care must be taken as follows to avoid serious damage to the diodes:

1 All alternator systems have negative earth and the leads of the battery must never be reversed, otherwise the diodes will be burned out and the wiring possibly damaged.
2 Battery leads, or any wires in the charging system, must not be disconnected whilst the engine is running. The peak voltages under such conditions will damage the diodes in the alternator.
3 Disconnect the battery leads if charging the battery from an outside source.
4 The alternator must never be run with the output disconnected.
5 Never check the operation of the unit by short-circuiting either the positive terminal and earth or the excitation terminal and earth.
6 The regulator should never operate without being earthed, otherwise the regulator windings will be destroyed.
7 If electric welding is undertaken on the vehicle, disconnect the battery earth lead to protect the alternator diodes against welding currents.

Testing:

Faults in the charging system are first to be sought in the condition of the battery, defective wiring connections or the loose adjustment of the driving belt. If the alternator is then suspect an output test with the unit on the vehicle can be made as follows with apparatus such as that shown in **FIG 11:7**.

1 Connect an electronic rev counter to the engine and connect the voltmeter and ammeter as shown in the diagram. Disconnect the battery earth cable to avoid

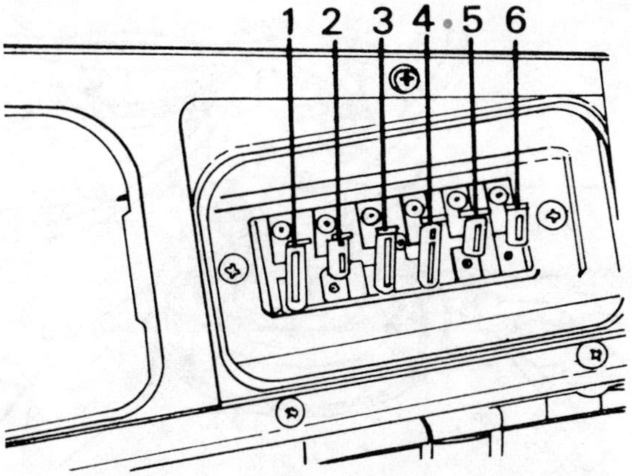

FIG 11:9 Fuses, DAF 31, 32, 33

Key to Fig 11:9 1 Horn and interior light 2 Direction indicators, windscreen wiper motor and stop lights 3 Righthand parking light and righthand rear light 4 Lefthand parking light, lefthand rear light, number plate light and instrument panel illumination 5 Dipped beams 6 Headlamp main beams

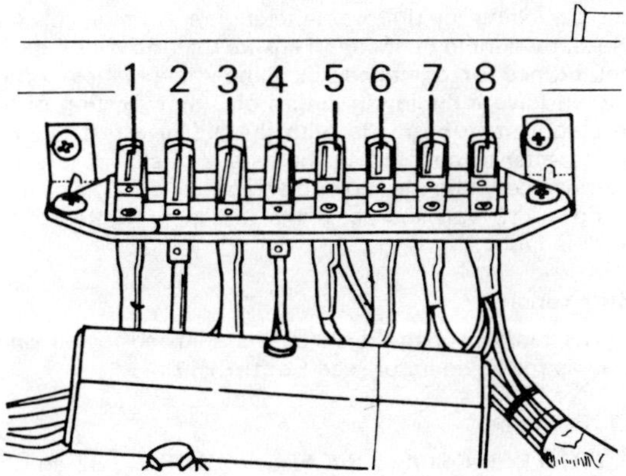

FIG 11:10 Fuses, DAF 44

Key to Fig 11:10 1 Spare 2 Horn and interior light 3 Lefthand parking light, lefthand rear light and instrument panel illumination 4 Righthand parking light and righthand rear light 5 Direction indicators and stop lights 6 Windscreen wiper motor 7 Dipped beams 8 Headlamp main beam

short-circuiting on the positive side of the alternator whilst connecting the ammeter.

2 Set the control knob of the load resistance to zero, with the alternator at 'no load'.

3 Start the engine and turn the resistance control to put the alternator under load, then gradually run up to about 4000 rev/min (2100 rev/min engine speed). When the alternator feels warm, check the readings on the meters, when the output should be at least 30 amp at approximately 14.4 volt. The test should take as little time as possible.

4 Disconnect the battery earth before disconnecting the test circuit.

The regulating voltage may be tested by connecting the test instruments as shown in **FIG 11:7**. After starting

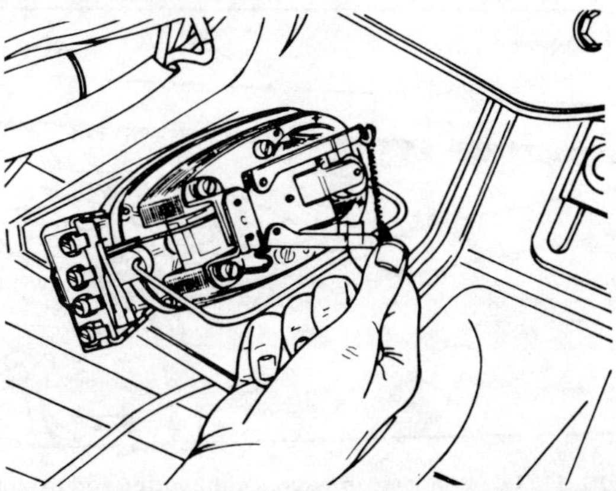

FIG 11:11 Windscreen wiper motor brushes, DAF 31, 32, 33

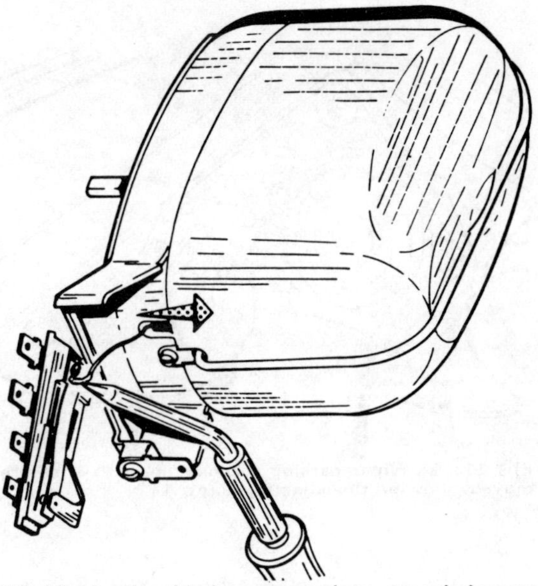

FIG 11:12 Unsoldering connections on windscreen wiper motor parking switch

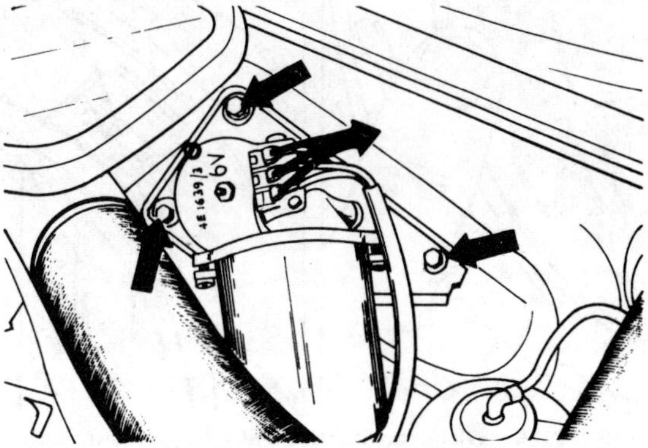

FIG 11:13 Wiper motor securing bolts (arrowed)

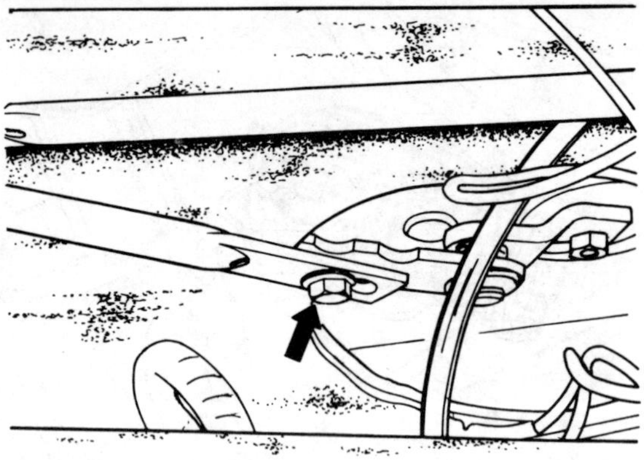

FIG 11:14 Windscreen wipers connecting rod attachment

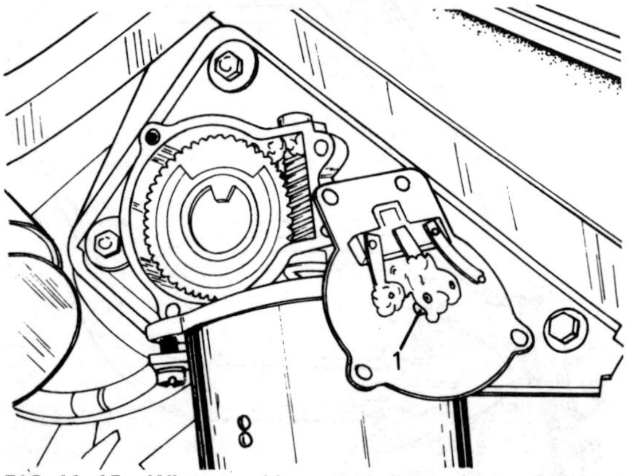

FIG 11:15 Wiper parking mechanism with cover removed, showing the adjusting screw 1

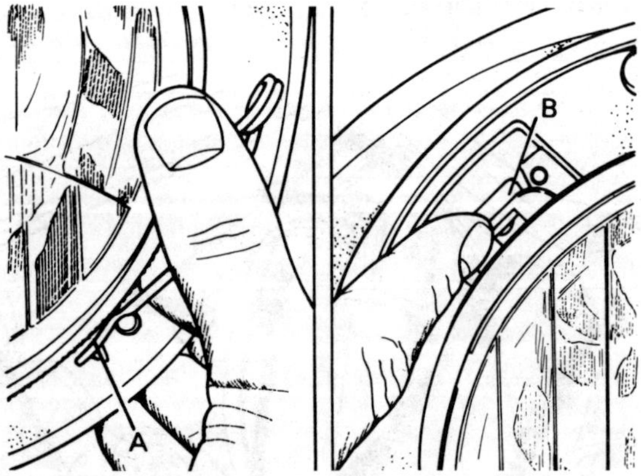

FIG 11:16 Withdrawing the headlight assembly, showing the spring A and the attachment at B

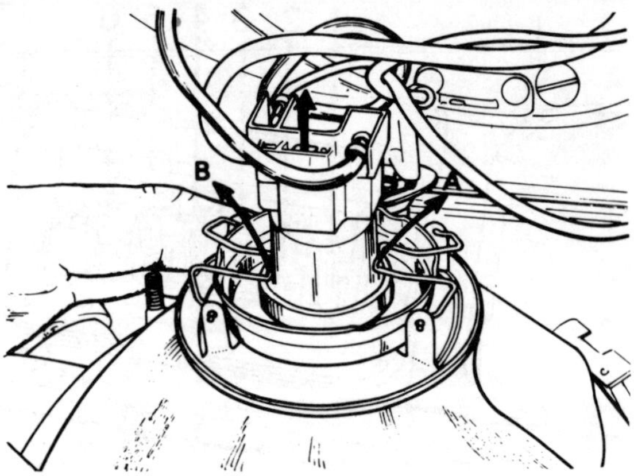

FIG 11:17 Clips A and B securing headlight bulb

the engine the voltmeter reading should be between 13.4 and 14.4 volt at a load of approximately 30 amp.

Removal of the alternator is attained by disconnecting the leads from the terminals, slackening the driving belt and unbolting the unit from the engine. A visual check of the stator should be made to ensure that the windings are not burned or damaged. Examine the brushes, which should have a minimum length of 3 mm. Testing of the insulation may be made with the aid of a test lamp in series, after disconnecting the diodes. A similar test may be made between the slip ring and one of the pole clamps, using a 110-volt source. If the test lamp lights up, the rotor is faulty.

Belt tension:

The tension of the drive belt is adjusted in the same way as for a generator (see **Section 11:4**).

11:6 Fuses

FIG 11:9 identifies the fuses in DAF 31, 32 and 33 models. The fuse box is located behind the lid of the glove compartment. **FIG 11:10** identifies the fuses in DAF 44 6-volt models. The fuse box, in this case, is located in the engine compartment. For later models see the wiring diagrams in **Technical Data**.

Never fit a replacement fuse of greater capacity than that specified for the position in the fuse box as, by doing so, circuit protection may be jeopardized. If a fuse blows repeatedly, trace the cause of it doing so without delay. The fuses are included in the main wiring diagrams in the **Appendix**.

11:7 Windscreen wiper motor

DAF 31, 32 and 33 models:

Although the position of the motor is not identical in DAF 31 models, the geometry of the adjustable linkage rods is the same for all models. When correctly adjusted, the wiper arms describe arcs of 100 deg. The length of the rod which links the cranks of the wiper arms should be 16.024 inch (407 mm) between centres and that of the actuating rod from the motor should be 5.847 inch (148.5 mm).

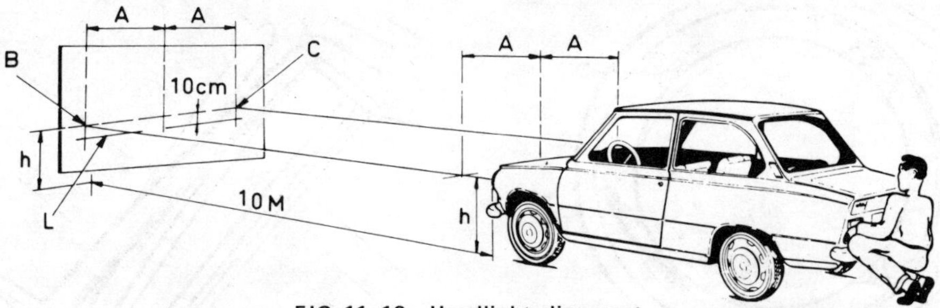

FIG 11:18 **Headlight alignment**

Key to Fig 11:18 A Half distance between headlamps B and C Projected positions of headlamps h Headlamp height above ground L Line 4 inch (10 cm) below BC

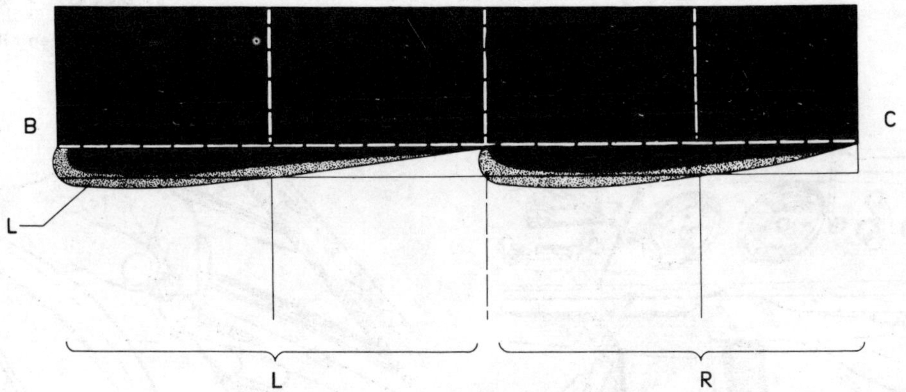

FIG 11:19 **Headlight aligning pattern**

Note: Lefthand drive shown, reverse for RHD cars

Brush renewal:

Disengage the retaining clip and remove the cover to give access to the brushes. Brush renewal is effected as shown in **FIG 11:11**.

Removing and fitting the motor:

To dismount the motor, remove the crankarm clamping screw and slide the arm off the shaft of the motor. Identify and disconnect the wiring, remove the attaching screws and withdraw the motor.

Installation is the reverse of this sequence.

Parking switch renewal:

A defective parking switch may be renewed. Dismount the motor, withdraw the switch and unsolder the connection (see **FIG 11:12**). Solder the connection to the new switch and reassemble. If necessary, adjust the contact points to give gaps of .02 inch (.5 mm) by bending the outer spring contact point arms. **Never bend the centre spring arm on which the centre contact points are mounted**.

DAF 44 models:

The wiper arms describe arcs of 95 deg. The length of the rod which links the cranks of the wiper arms should be 17.618 inch (447.5 mm) between centres and that of the actuating rod from the motor should be 8.189 ± .295 inch (208 ± 7.5 mm) between centres.

Removing and fitting the motor:

To remove the motor from either model, identify and disconnect the wiring, remove three attaching screws (see **FIG 11:13**) detach the connecting rod (see **FIG 11:14**) and withdraw the motor assembly. Installation of the unit is this sequence of operations in reverse.

Parking mechanism renewal:

To renew the parking mechanism, dismount the motor, remove four screws, remove the cover and contacts (see **FIG 11:15**) and disconnect the wiring. Slacken the adjusting screw 1, fit the new cover, tighten the adjusting screw fully and then slacken it by $\frac{1}{4}$ turn. Secure the adjusting screw with the locknut.

Brushes and brush plate:

Access to the brushes requires the motor body to be separated from the gearbox and motor end plate. To renew the complete brush plate, unsolder the wiring, remove the three rubber mounting pins and withdraw the brush plate. Fitting the new plate and assembling the unit is the reverse of this sequence.

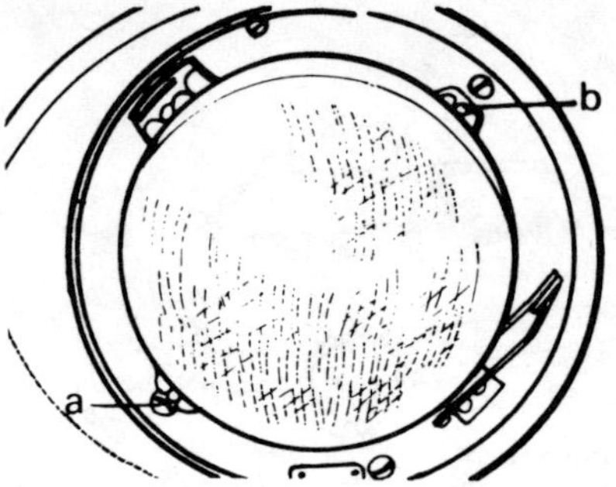

FIG 11:20 Headlight aligning screws a and b

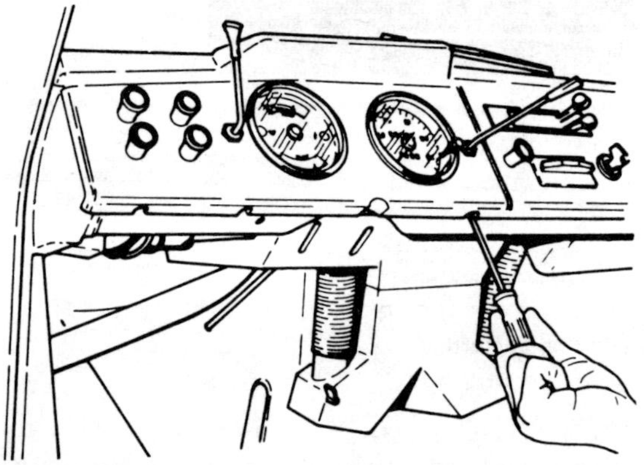
FIG 11:21 Releasing the instrument panel, DAF 31, 32, 33

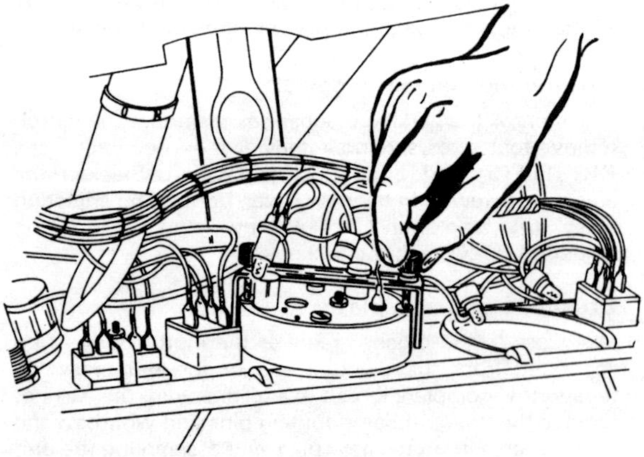
FIG 11:22 Removing instruments

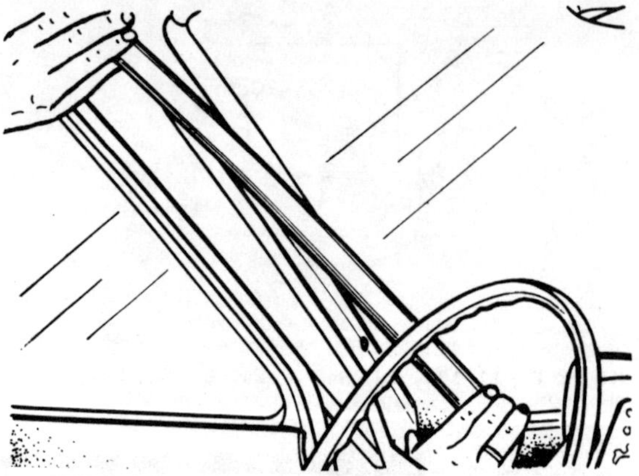
FIG 11:23 Removing windscreen pillar trim

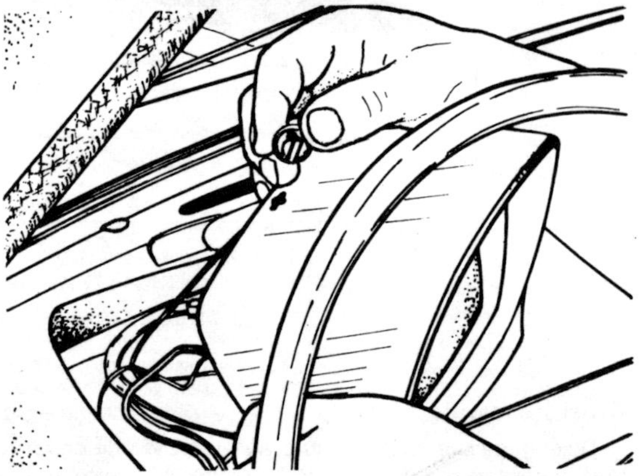
FIG 11:24 Speedometer head fastener

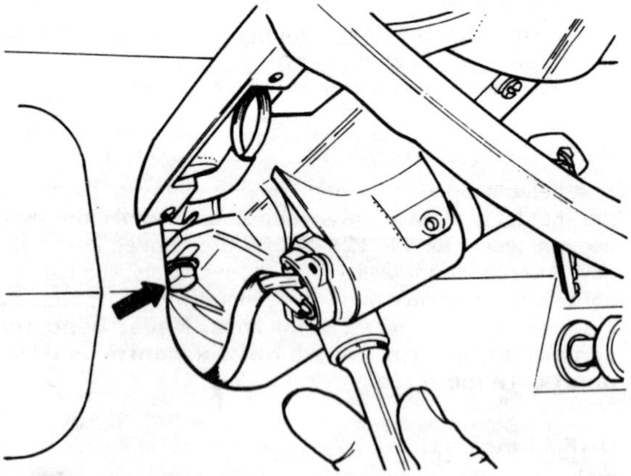
FIG 11:25 Steering shaft support bracket retaining screws

FIG 11:26 Steering shaft switch connections

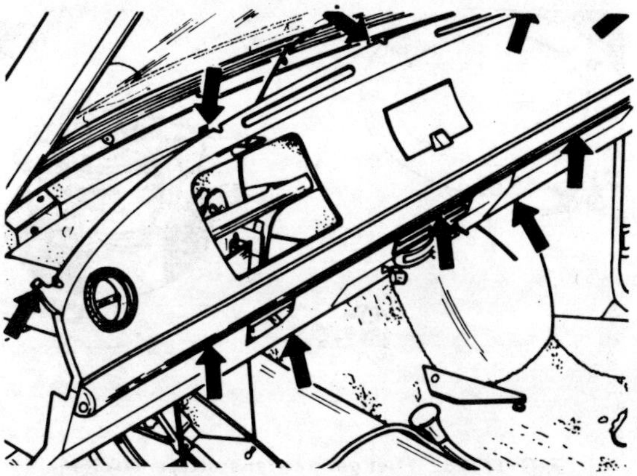

FIG 11:27 Locations of dashboard attaching screws

11:8 Headlamps

Each headlamp is fitted with a dual filament bulb and is provided with adjusting screws which allow the headlamp beam to be aligned by adjusting it upwards and downwards and from side to side.

Bulb renewal:

Remove the chromium rim from the headlamp. In the case of DAF 31, 32 and 33 models, use a screwdriver (wrap rag round it to avoid possible damage to the paintwork) inserted at the bottom of the rim and prise it off. In the case of DAF 44 and 46 models, removal of the rim is effected by inserting two fingers into the openings at the bottom of the rim and pulling it forward.

Release the spring A (see **FIG 11:16**), carefully slide the reflector from its upper attachment point B and remove the assembly.

Pull the contact block off the base of the lamp. Pull back the two clips A and B in **FIG 11:17** and withdraw the bulb. In the case of a defective parking light bulb, the holder must be pulled out from the reflector.

Fitment of the new bulb is the reverse of this sequence in each case but ensure that, when fitting the dual filament bulb, the projections on the bulb fitting engage with the corresponding locations in the edge of the reflector.

Aligning the headlamps:

The procedure for aligning the headlamps is the same for all models.

On level ground, face the car squarely in front of a wall or vertical screen with the front of the headlamps 33 ft (10 m) from it as shown in **FIG 11:18**. Set out points B and C the same distance apart (2A) as the headlamps and the same distance (h) as the headlamps from the ground. Draw a line L 4 inch (10 cm) below the line joining B and C and parallel to it.

Turn on the headlamps and switch to the dipped beam position. The headlamps are correctly aligned when they are adjusted so that the boundaries between light and darkness are as shown in **FIG 11:19**. It will be found useful to shield one headlamp while the other is being adjusted.

The adjusting screws are shown in **FIG 11:20**. Access to them requires the removal of the chromium rims as described earlier. When adjuster a is screwed inwards (clockwise), the beam is raised and vice versa. When adjuster b is screwed inwards (clockwise) the beam is moved to the right and vice versa.

11:9 Lighting circuits

Fitting new bulbs:

With the exception of the interior light lens which clips into position and the headlamps which are covered in **Section 11:8**, all other lenses are retained by screws. If a new bulb is being fitted, clean the contacts and, before discarding the old bulb or refitting the lens, check that the new bulb lights up. If it does not, check the relevant fuse which may be identified from **FIG 11:9** (DAF 31, 32 and 33 models) or from **FIG 11:10** (DAF 44 6-volt models). For later 12-volt systems refer to the wiring diagrams in the **Appendix**. If the fuse is in order, check the relevant switch and the continuity of the wiring.

Refer to **Section 11:2** and check the condition of the battery. Recharge if necessary. Check the condition of the reflectors. Renew any bulbs which have darkened with age.

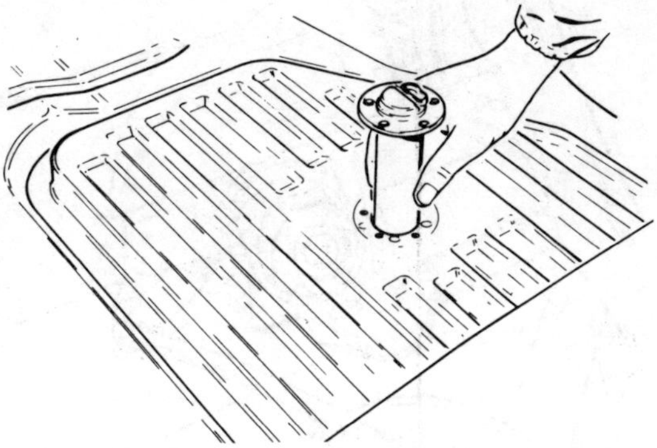

FIG 11:28 Fuel gauge transmitter, DAF 31, 32, 33

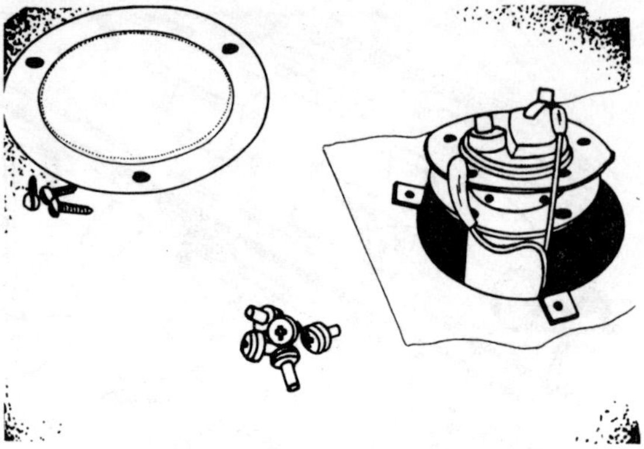

FIG 11:29 Fuel gauge transmitter, DAF 44

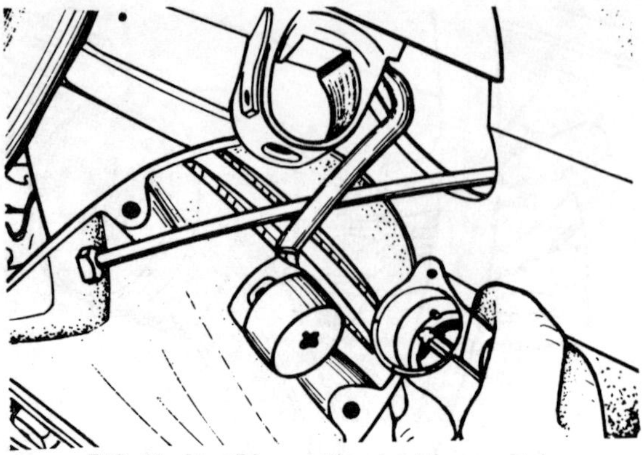

FIG 11:31 Dismantling ignition switch

Bulbs burn out frequently:

Suspect that the voltage regulator is defective.

Lamps light but gradually fade:

Refer to **Section 11:2** and check the condition of the battery as it is not capable of supplying current for any length of time.

Brilliance of lights varies with car speed:

Check the condition of the battery and its connections. Clean the battery terminal posts, renew defective cables, make sure that they fit tightly to the terminal posts and check that the battery earth connection is making good contact.

11:10 Instruments

Access to the instruments, warning lights and panel illumination bulbs requires that the instrument panel be released from the dashboard.

DAF 31, 32 and 33 models, access to instruments:

Disconnect the battery earth cable. Refer to **Chapter 9, Section 9:6** and lift out the steering column assembly. Remove the screws from the bottom edge of the instrument panel as shown in **FIG 11:21** and tip the instrument panel forwards. While doing so, ensure that nothing fouls the choke cable. Remove the clamps and withdraw the instruments as necessary (see **FIG 11:22**). Refitment is the reverse of this procedure.

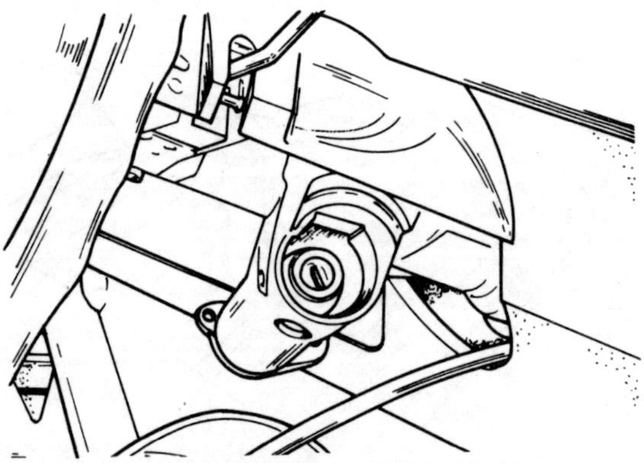

FIG 11:30 Ignition switch and holder

DAF 44 and 46 models, access to instruments:

Access to instruments on DAF 44 and 46 models is obtained in a similar manner.

1. Remove the windscreen pillar trim to prevent it being damaged (see **FIG 11:23**). Disconnect the battery.
2. Release the speedometer head fastener (see **FIG 11:24**), lift out the head assembly, disconnect the speedometer cable and electric wiring and remove the unit.
3. Disconnect the choke wire and cable casing at the carburetter and remove the lower half of the steering column jacket. Remove the steering shaft support bracket screws and the upper jacket half (see **FIG 11:25**).
4. Disconnect the ignition switch wiring and remove the light switch and direction indicator light switch screws (see **FIG 11:26**). Leave the switches hanging from the wires.
5. Disconnect the steering shaft from the steering gear pinion and carefully pull the shaft and wheel assembly through the hole in the dashboard.
6. Disconnect the control cable wires and cable casings at the brake vacuum valve and heater valves, then remove the light switch, wiper motor switch and screen washer pump from the dashboard. Remove the dashboard attaching screws (see **FIG 11:27**) and withdraw the dashboard assembly.
7. Remove the retaining nuts on the inside of the dashboard to remove the crash roll and ornamental strip. Remove the dashboard frame if required. Installation of frame, dashboard and controls is in the reverse order of the dismantling operations.

Speedometer:

The speedometer is driven from one of the front wheels by a flexible cable drive. To renew the drive cable, gain access to the back of the instrument panel as described earlier and uncouple the drive from the speedometer.

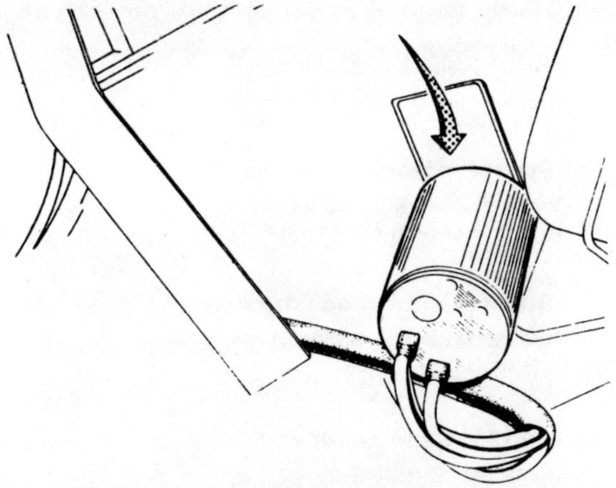

FIG 11:32 Flasher unit

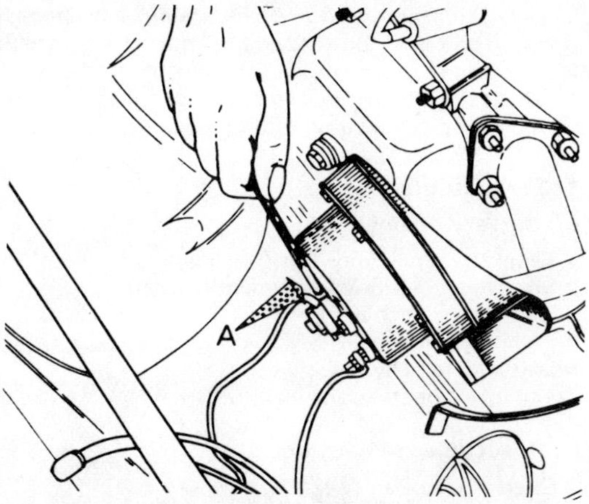

FIG 11:33 Horn adjustment A, DAF 31, 32, 33

Uncouple the other end from the joint adjacent to the front wheel, unclip and withdraw the cable. Follow the same route and clipping when installing the new drive.

To remove the speedometer, uncouple the drive cable, remove the retaining screws and the bulbs and withdraw the speedometer. Repair of the speedometer or adjustment of it or the integral odometer should be entrusted to a specialist.

Oil pressure warning light:

With the engine stationary but with the ignition switched on, the oil pressure warning light should be illuminated. If, under these conditions, it does not light up, suspect that the bulb is defective. Gain access to the back of the instrument panel as described earlier and check the bulb. If the bulb is not defective, the pressure switch or the continuity of the wiring must be suspect. At zero and low oil pressure the switch contacts are closed and, as oil pressure builds up, the contacts open (at approximately 6 lb/sq inch) and the warning light goes out. A defective warning light switch cannot be serviced by an owner and, if defective, should be replaced by a new switch.

Ignition warning light:

With the engine stationary but with the ignition switched on, the ignition warning light should be illuminated. If, under these conditions, it does not light up, gain access to the back of the instrument panel as described earlier and check the bulb. If, when the engine is running fairly fast, the warning light does not go out, it indicates that the generator is not charging. Refer to **Section 11:4** and check that the generator drive belt is in order.

Fuel gauge:

The fuel gauge is actuated by a transmitter which is installed in the fuel tank. To remove the gauge, gain access to the back of the instrument panel, disconnect the wiring, withdraw the panel lighting bulb(s), remove the retaining screws and withdraw the gauge.

Fuel transmitter:

To remove the transmitter, pull back the floor covering in the luggage compartment. In the case of DAF 31, 32 and 33 models, disconnect the electrical lead, remove five retaining screws and, as shown in **FIG 11:28**, withdraw the unit. In the case of DAF 44, refer to **FIG 11:29**, remove three screws which retain the cover plate, disconnect the wiring, remove five retaining screws and withdraw the transmitter. For DAF 46 models refer to **Chapter 2, Section 2:3**.

When installing a new transmitter to DAF 31, 32 and 33 models, remove the float locating pin in the standpipe before fitting the unit to the tank. In the case of DAF 44 ensure that the new transmitter is installed with its flange in the same relative position, rotationally as that of the unit removed.

Ignition switch:

To remove the ignition switch, remove the lower steering column casing and press the ignition switch out of the holder as shown in **FIG 11:30**. Separate the two parts (see **FIG 11:31**) by removing the screw which holds them together. Follow the reverse procedure for reassembly and installation.

11:11 Flasher unit

Before condemning a suspectedly defective flasher unit, confirm that the bulbs and indicator light are in order and, by using a jump wire, confirm that the wiring and the direction indicator switch are not at fault. A defective flasher unit cannot be serviced by an owner and, after identifying the connections, it should be removed (see **FIG 11:32**) and replaced by a new unit. On installation of the replacement unit, ensure that it is effectively earthed.

11:12 Horn

FIG 11:33 shows the adjustment of the tone pitch of a DAF 31, 32 and 33 model horn by turning the adjuster A inwards or outwards.

If the horn becomes inoperative, refer to **Section 11:6** and check the relevant fuse. If this is in order, disconnect the wiring from the horn and use a jump wire from the battery. If the horn now operates, the fault is in either the horn button switch or in the wiring. A defective horn cannot be serviced by an owner and should be removed and a new replacement unit fitted.

11:13 Fault diagnosis

(a) Battery discharged

1 Terminal connections loose or dirty
2 Shorts in lighting or instrument circuit(s)
3 Generator not charging
4 Regulator defective
5 Battery internally defective
6 Lights accidentally left on

(b) Insufficient charging rate

1 Check 1 and 4 in (a)
2 Generator drive belt slipping

(c) Battery will not hold charge

1 Low electrolyte level
2 Battery plates sulphated
3 Electrolyte leakage from cracked case
4 Battery plate separators defective

(d) Generator output low or nil

1 Drive belt broken or slipping
2 Regulator out of adjustment
3 Worn bearings, loose polepieces
4 Commutator worn, burned or shorted
5 Armature shaft bent or worn
6 Insulation proud between commutator segments
7 Brushes sticking
8 Brush springs weak or broken
9 Coils shorted or burned

(e) Starter motor lacks power or will not operate:

1 Battery discharged, loose cable connection(s)
2 Starter switch faulty
3 Starter solenoid defective
4 Brushes worn or sticking
5 Brush springs weak or broken
6 Connections loose or detached
7 Commutator worn, burned or shorted
8 Motor shaft bent
9 Engine abnormally stiff, perhaps after rebore

(f) Starter motor runs but does not turn engine

1 Pinion engagement lever pin broken or missing
2 Broken teeth on pinion
3 Broken teeth on flywheel ring gear

(g) Starter motor inoperative

1 Check 1, 2, 3, 4, 5 and 6 in (e)
2 Armature or field coils faulty

(h) Starter motor rough or noisy

1 Damaged teeth on pinion or ring gear
2 Retaining bolts loose

(j) Lights inoperative or erratic

1 Check (a)
2 Bulbs burned out
3 Faulty earthing of lamps or battery
4 Switch faulty
5 Connection(s) loose or adrift
6 Fuse blown

(k) Windscreen motor sluggish

1 Faulty armature
2 Commutator dirty or shorting
3 Brushes worn or sticking
4 Brush springs weak or broken
5 Motor drive binding
6 Linkage or arm pivot binding

(l) Windscreen wiper motor runs but does not drive

1 Motor drive slipping
2 Linkage pin broken or missing

(m) Instruments do not work

1 Speedometer drive broken or uncoupled
2 Gauge defective
3 Transmitter defective
4 Bulb burned out (warning lights)
5 Check wiring for continuity
6 Faulty earthing

CHAPTER 12

THE BODYWORK

12:1 Bodywork finish

Large-scale repairs to body and wing panels are best left to expert panel beaters. Even small dents can be tricky, as too much hammering will stretch the metal and make things worse instead of better. Filling minor dents and scratches is probably the best method of restoring the surface. The touching-up of paintwork is well within the powers of most owners, particularly as self-spraying cans of paint in the correct colours are readily available. A paint may change colour with age and it is better to spray a whole wing, door or panel rather than touch up a small area.

Before spraying, remove all traces of polish with white spirit. More drastic treatment is required if silicone polishes have been applied. Use a primer surfacer or paste stopper according to the amount of filling which is required and, when it is dry, rub it down with 400 grade 'Wet or Dry' paper until the surface is smooth and flush with the surrounding area. Spend time in getting the best finish as this will control the final effect. Apply the retouching paint, keeping it wet in the centre and light and dry round the edges. After a few hours of drying, use a cutting compound to remove the dry spray and finish with a liquid polish.

12:2 Bonnet

DAF 31, 32 and 33 models, bonnet removal and fitment:

To remove the bonnet, remove the two nuts which attach each bonnet hinge to the bonnet (see **FIG 12:1**). Collect the washers. With the help of an assistant, lift off the bonnet as in **FIG 12:2**.

Fitment is the reverse of this sequence.

DAF 31, 32 and 33 models, bonnet latch:

To remove the latch, remove the retaining screws (see **FIG 12:3**) and dismount the latch. On DAF 31 models, a turning motion is required to withdraw the latch lever.

Fitment is the reverse of this sequence.

DAF 31, 32 and 33 models, safety catch:

This is in two parts. The hook (see **FIG 12:4**), which is attached to the grill assembly, may be removed by undoing the attaching nut. The catch is attached to the bonnet by two screws.

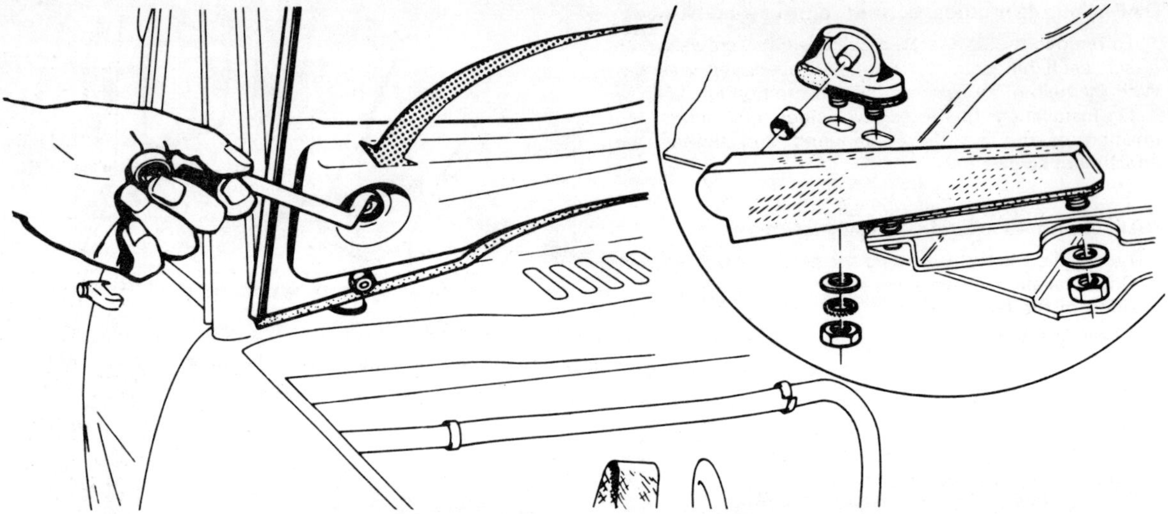

FIG 12:1 Removing a bonnet hinge

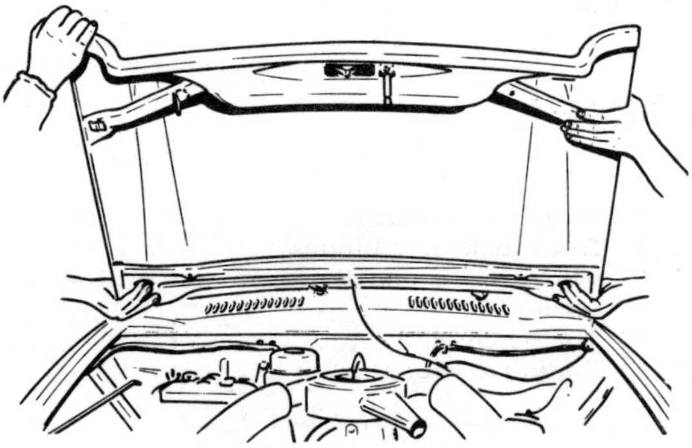

FIG 12:2 Lifting off the bonnet

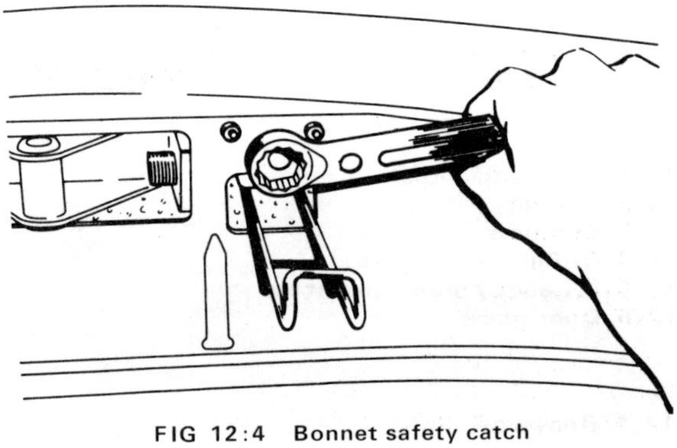

FIG 12:4 Bonnet safety catch

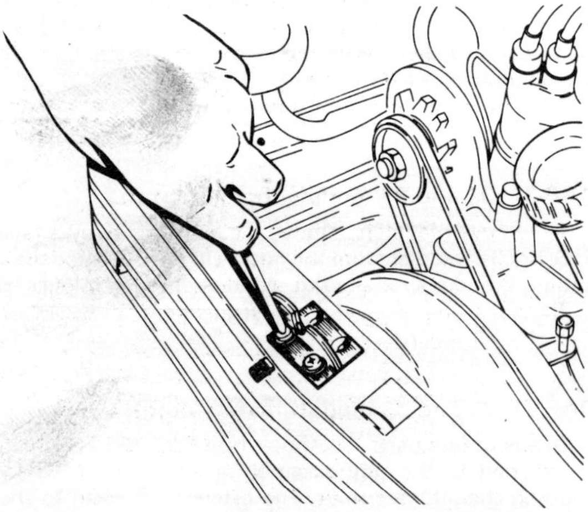

FIG 12:3 Removing the bonnet latch screws

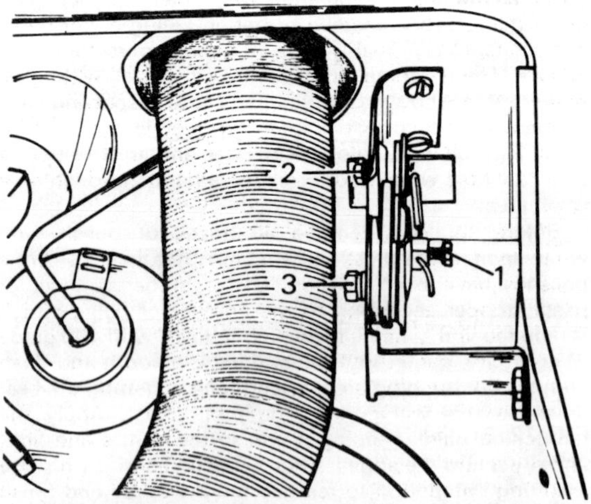

FIG 12:5 Bonnet cable attachment, DAF 44

DAF 44 and 46 models, bonnet removal and fitment:

To remove the bonnet, remove the two screws which attach each hinge to the bonnet. Collect the washers. With the help of an assistant, lift off the bonnet.

On installation, fit the screws finger tight, adjust the position of the bonnet as required and tighten the attachment screws fully.

DAF 44 and 46 models, bonnet latch:

To remove the latch, remove the two retaining screws.

On installation, fit the screws finger tight, adjust the position of the latch as required and tighten the attachment screws fully.

DAF 44 and 46 models, bonnet catch:

Slacken the cable retaining screw and withdraw the cable from the catch swivel. Remove the two attaching screws and dismount the catch.

On installation, fit the screws finger tight, connect the cable to the swivel, position the catch as required and tighten the attachment screws fully.

DAF 44 and 46 models, bonnet cable release:

To remove the assembly, release the cable from the bonnet catch swivel by loosening the clamp screw 1 (see **FIG 12:5**), remove the two nuts 2 and 3 which retain the assembly and, from inside the car, withdraw the unit.

Fitment is the reverse of this sequence.

12:3 Bumpers

Front and rear bumper removal and fitment, all models:

Remove the two nuts and bolts which attach each bumper bracket to the chassis at each side.(see **FIG 12:6**). Dismount the bumper by pulling on it.

Fitment is the reverse of this sequence in each case.

12:4 Grille

DAF 31, 32 and 33 models, grille removal and fitment:

Dismount the front bumper as described in **Section 12:3**.

Disconnect the wiring to the direction indicator lamps. In the case of DAF 31 models, unhook springs. Remove three attaching screws from each side (see **FIG 12:7**) and dismount the grille assembly (see **FIG 12:8**).

Fitment is the reverse of this sequence.

DAF 44 and 46 models, grille removal and fitment:

Dismount the bonnet as described in **Section 12:2**. Remove the front bumper as described in **Section 12:3**.

Remove the cross-brace and grille attaching nuts (see **FIG 12:9**) and bolts (grille attaching nuts on cold air deflection shield channels are accessible from outside the car) and dismount the grille assembly.

Fitment is this sequence in reverse.

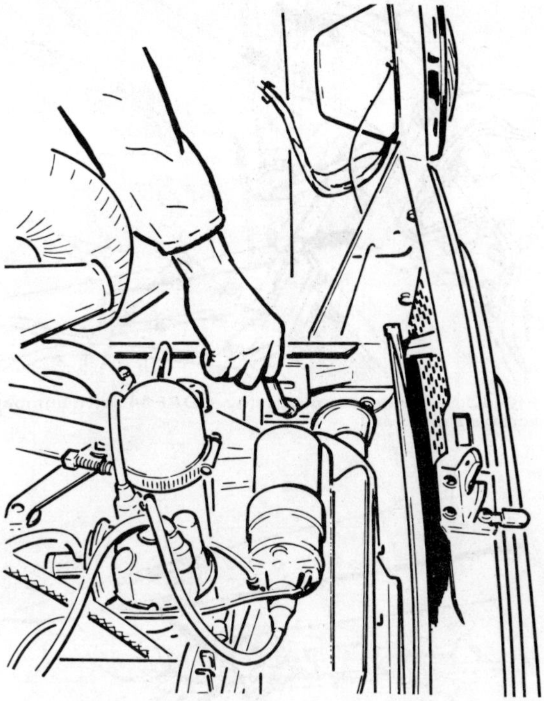

FIG 12:6 Removing bumper, DAF 31, 32, 33

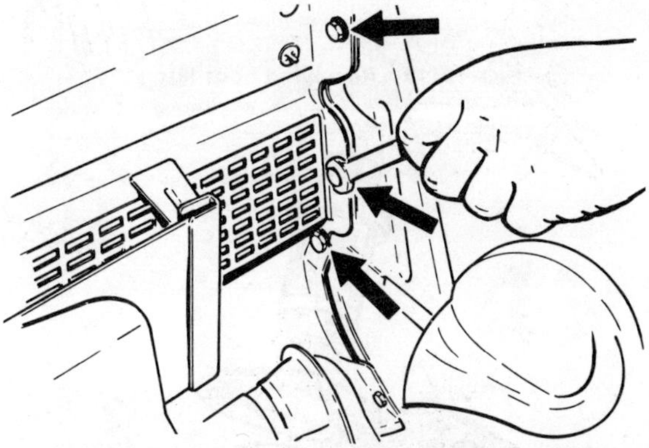

FIG 12:7 Grill retaining screws, DAF 31, 32, 33

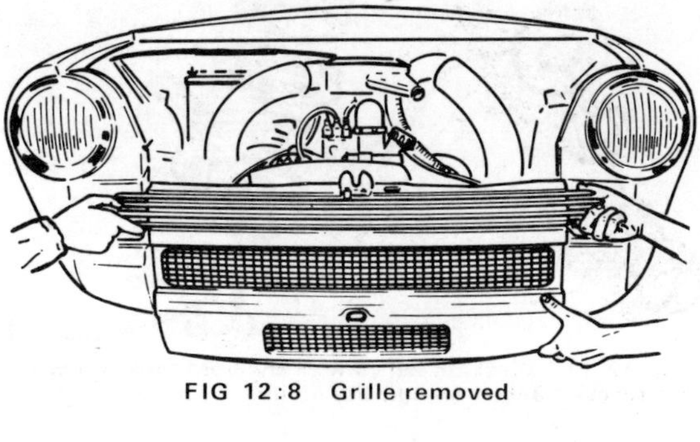

FIG 12:8 Grille removed

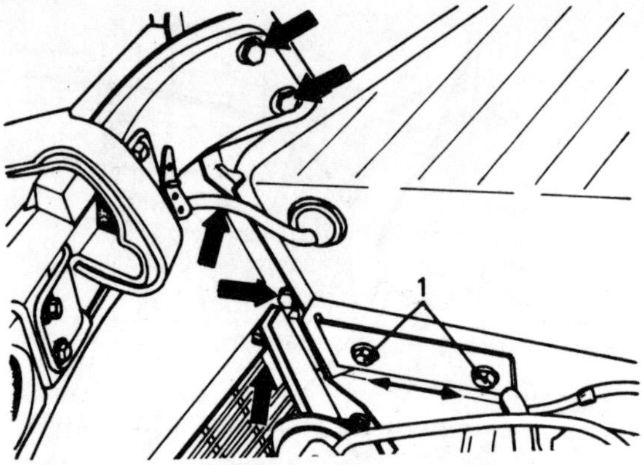

FIG 12:9 Grille retaining screws, DAF 44, with bumper screws shown at 1

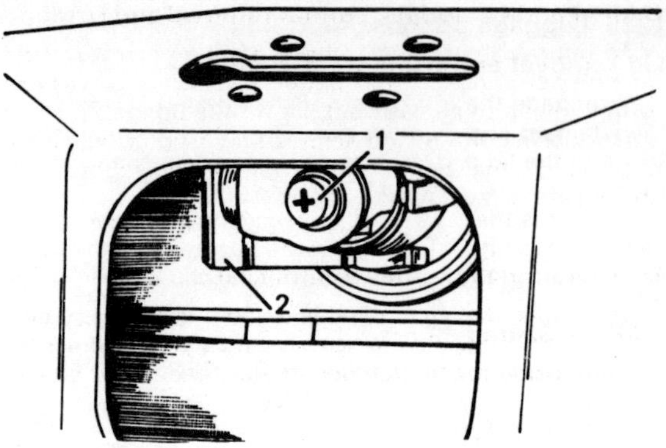

FIG 12:12 Boot lock on DAF 44 cars, showing the locking lever retaining screw 1 and the lock retainer 2

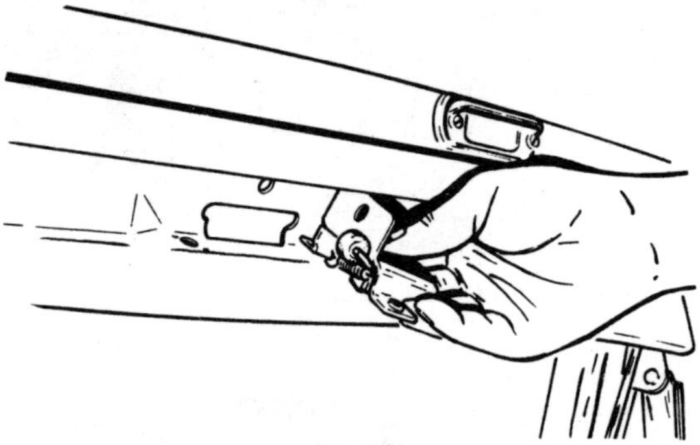

FIG 12:10 Removing boot latch

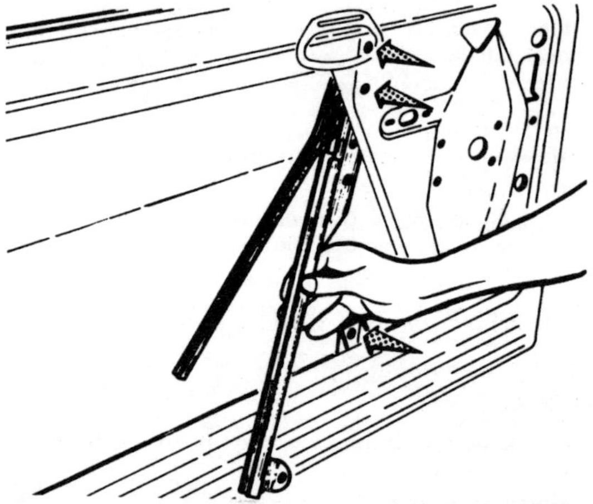

FIG 12:13 Removing the window glass channel, DAF 31, 32, 33

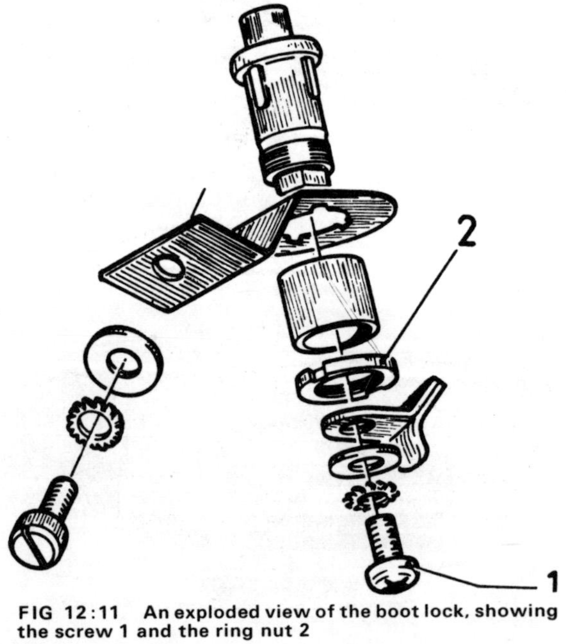

FIG 12:11 An exploded view of the boot lock, showing the screw 1 and the ring nut 2

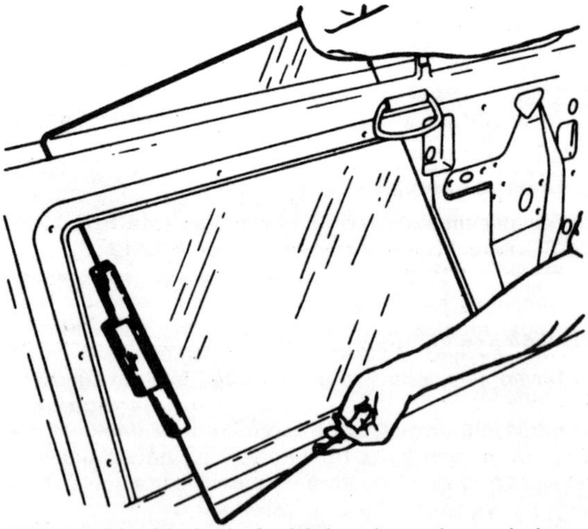

FIG 12:14 Method of withdrawing a door window

12:5 Luggage compartment lid

Lid removal and fitment, all models:

Disengage the lower end of the lid stay by removing the retaining clip. Remove two screws which retain each hinge to the lid and, with the help of an assistant, lift off the lid.

Fitment is the reverse of this sequence. Fit the attachment screws finger tight, adjust the position of the lid as necessary and tighten the screws fully.

DAF 31, 32 and 33 models, lid lock removal:

From inside the lid, remove the latch retaining screws and withdraw the latch (see **FIG 12:10**). Remove the screw from the centre of the lock cylinder and collect the washers and lever. Remove the ring nut and distance piece. From outside, withdraw the lock cylinder shown in **FIG 12:11**. If necessary, the lock cylinder bracket may be dismounted by removing the single screw which retains it. Collect the two washers.

From inside the luggage compartment, remove the screws, collect the nuts and washers and lift out the lock catch.

DAF 31, 32 and 33 models, lid lock fitment:

This is the reverse of the removal procedure. Fit the catch attachment screws finger tight until its position is finally adjusted and then tighten them fully.

DAF 44 and 46 models, lid lock removal:

From inside the lid, remove the four screws which attach the catch. Remove the catch and collect the washers. Remove the screw from the centre of the lock cylinder, collect the washers and the lever. Slide out the lock retaining plate and (see **FIG 12:12**), from outside, withdraw the lock cylinder.

From inside the luggage compartment, remove the two retaining screws and dismount the lock latch. Collect the washers.

DAF 44 and 46 models, lid lock fitment:

This is the reverse of the removal procedure. Note that the lock latch may be adjusted upwards and downwards and that the lock catch can be adjusted from side to side. After adjustment, ensure that all attachment screws are tightened fully.

12:6 Door glass

DAF 31, 32 and 33 models, door glass removal:

Remove the window regulator mechanism as described in **Section 12:7**. Remove the three screws which are arrowed in **FIG 12:13** and withdraw the window glass run channel. Turn the lower edge of the glass away from the door hinges and withdraw the glass downwards as shown in **FIG 12:14**. If the weatherstrip is to be removed, prise one end loose and, by pulling, remove it.

DAF 31, 32 and 33 models, door glass fitment:

Fit the weatherstrip if it was removed. This requires a draw cord to be inserted in the lower lip as shown in **FIG 12:15**. Press the upper edge of the strip over the top edge of the door (see **FIG 12:16**), pull the lower edge

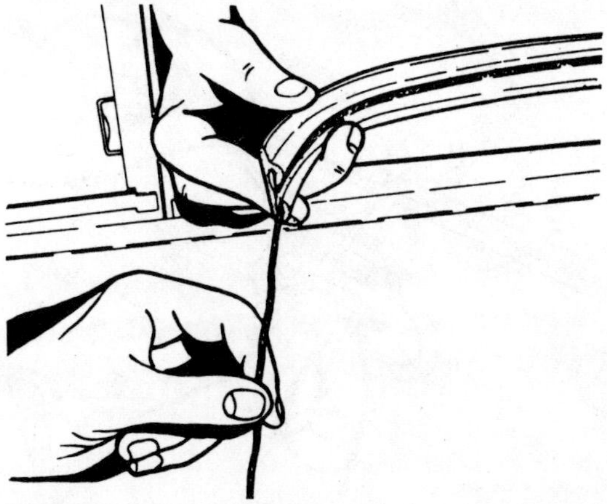

FIG 12:15 Fitting the door window weatherstrip, DAF 31, 32, 33

FIG 12:16 Fitting the weatherstrip over the top edge in the door

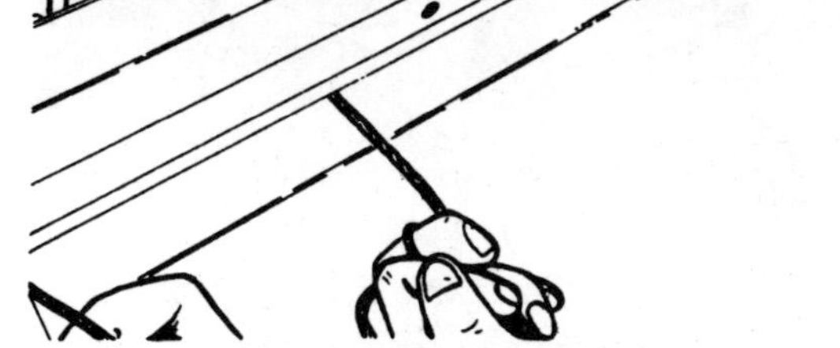

FIG 12:17 Using a draw cord to fit the lower edge of the weatherstrip over the inside edge in the door

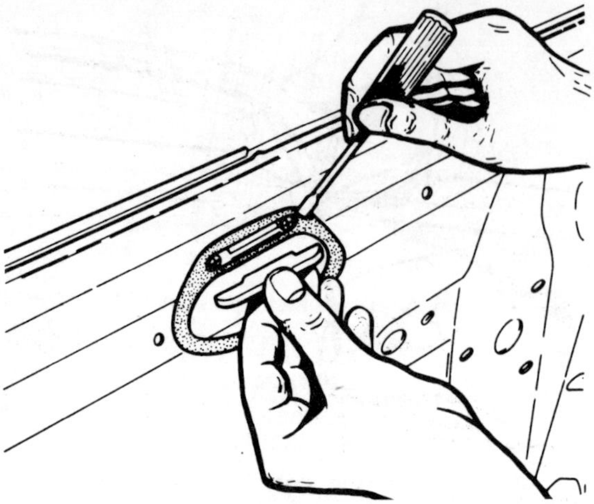

FIG 12:18 Fitting the handgrip

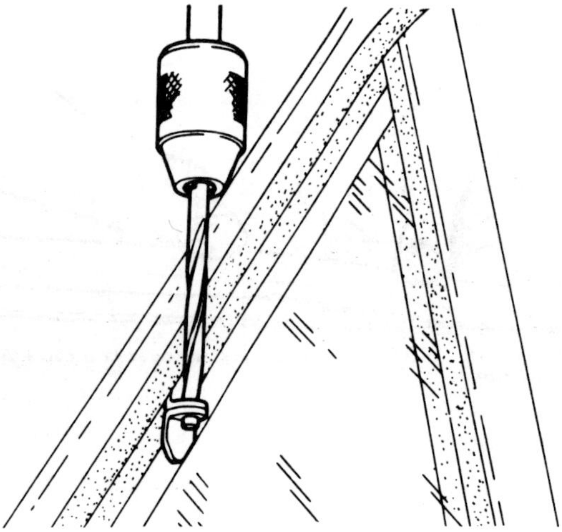

FIG 12:19 Drilling out vent window rivet

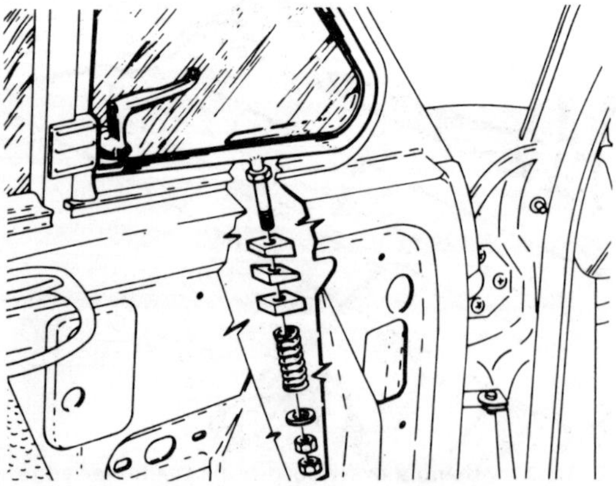

FIG 12:20 Removing vent window, DAF 31, 32, 33

over the inside edge of the door with the draw cord (see **FIG 12:17**) and press the inside of the strip into position on the door edge.

Introduce the glass into the door with its lower edge facing away from the door hinges. Turn the glass into its correct position and enter it into the runs (see **FIG 12:14**). Wedge the glass in the raised position, fit the glass run channel and secure it by the three screws which are arrowed in **FIG 12:13**. Check that the glass can be lowered and raised smoothly after refitting the window regulator mechanism but before installing the door trim. Refit the handgrip (see **FIG 12:18**) if removed.

DAF 31, 32 and 33 models, ventilation windows:

To remove the window, drill out the hinge rivet as shown in **FIG 12:19**, dismount the door trim, refer to **FIG 12:20** and remove the locknut, adjusting nut, washer, spring and packing pieces. Withdraw the window and, if necessary, the weatherstrip (see **FIG 12:21**).

Installation is this sequence in reverse. A suitable rivet must be fitted to the hinge. Tighten the adjusting nut until the pivot is appropriately stiff, fit and tighten the locknut to secure the assembly.

DAF 31, 32 and 33 models, rear side windows:

To remove a side window, drill out the blind rivets which secure the aluminium trim moulding (see **FIG 12:22**) and remove the moulding. Drill out the hinge rivets as in **FIG 12:23**. Remove the nut, bolt and washers from the window stay and dismount the window glass (see **FIG 12:24**).

Installation is the reverse of this procedure. A suitable blind riveting tool is required.

DAF 44 and 46 models, door glass removal:

Remove the door trim as described in **Section 12:7**. Referring to **FIG 12:25**, remove the Phillips screws and dismount the access panel 9 to which the inner weatherstrip 8 is attached. Raise the glass fully, remove the two attaching screws (see **FIG 12:26**) and lift out the glass with a turning motion. The weatherstrip may, if necessary, be withdrawn from the access panel after bending back the tabs slightly.

DAF 44 and 46 models, door glass fitment:

Fitment of a window glass is the removal sequence in reverse. If necessary, fit a new weatherstrip to the access panel and bend in the tabs to their original position to secure it. Check that the glass can be raised and lowered smoothly before refitting the door trim.

DAF 44 and 46 models, door glass weatherstrip:

Renewal of the weatherstrip along the lower inside edge of the glass is covered earlier under door glass removal and fitment. To renew the other section of weatherstrip, lower the window glass, pull out the ornamental surround part way, bend back the tabs slightly and withdraw the strip.

Installation of new weatherstrip is the reverse of this sequence.

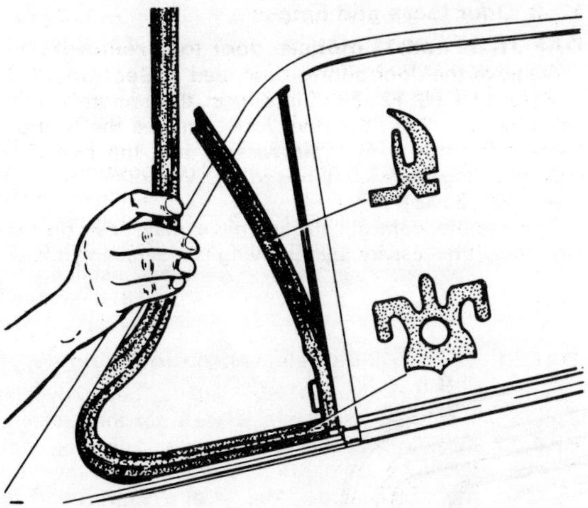

FIG 12:21 Vent window weatherstrip

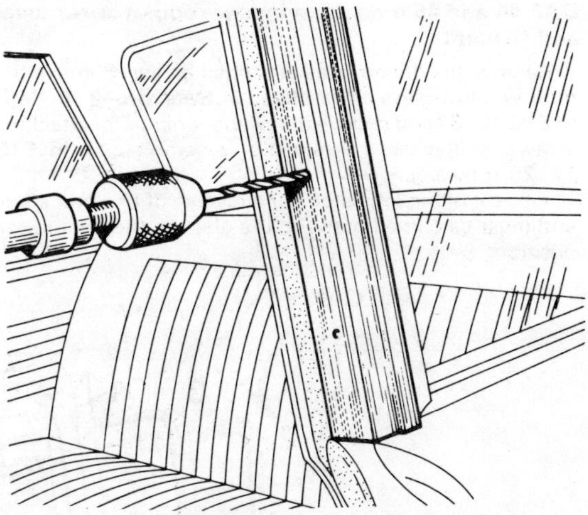

FIG 12:22 Drilling out blind rivets securing aluminium garnish moulding of rear opening window

12:7 Window regulator

DAF 31, 32 and 33 models, door trim removal and fitment:

Raise the window glass fully. Refer to **FIG 12:27**, insert a screwdriver between the regulator winding handle and the spring-loaded bush. Press inwards and tap out the retaining pin. Pull off the winding handle. Similarly remove the door handle (see **FIG 12:28**). In the case of DAF 32 and 33 models, remove the attaching screws and dismount the armrest. Use a screwdriver to prise off the door trim panel which is retained by spring clips (see **FIG 12:29**). Carefully release the plastic foil which is stuck to the top and sides of the door frame.

Fitment is the reverse of this procedure. Stick the plastic foil to the top and sides of the door frame. Its bottom edge hangs down **inside** the frame opening.

DAF 44 and 46 models, door trim removal and fitment:

Remove the attaching screws and dismount the armrest. Remove the retaining screws (see **FIG 12:30**) and pull off the regulator and door handles. In the case of DAF 44 models, collect the ornamental strips (15 in **FIG 12:25**). Release the spring clips at the sides of the door trim panel, lift up the panel and dismount it. Remove the door access cover as shown in **FIG 12:31**.

Quarter trim panels may be removed in a similar manner after dismounting the door pillar trim.

Refitting the door trim is the reverse of this procedure.

DAF 31, 32 and 33 models, window regulator removal and fitment:

Remove the door trim as described earlier. Refer to **FIG 12:32**. With the window glass raised, remove the window regulator retaining screws and withdraw the regulator (see **FIG 12:33**).

Fitment of the regulator, which is the reverse of this sequence, must be effected with the glass in the fully raised position.

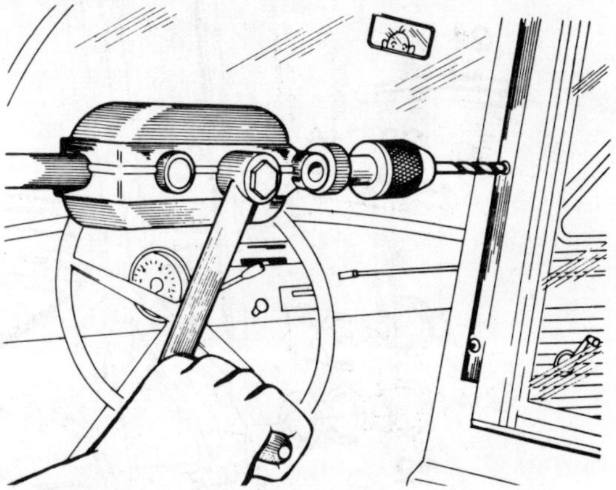

FIG 12:23 Drilling out window hinge rivets

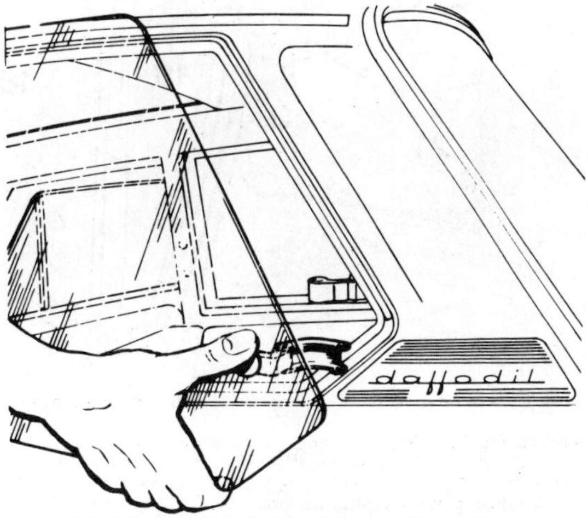

FIG 12:24 Removing side window glass

DAF 44 and 46 models, window regulator removal and fitment:

Remove the door trim as described earlier. Remove the door window glass as described in **Section 12:6**. Refer to **FIG 12:34** and remove the window regulator attaching screws. Withdraw the regulator assembly (17 in **FIG 12:25**) upwards.

Fitment of the regulator is the reverse of this procedure and must be carried out with the glass in the fully raised position.

12:8 Door locks and hinges

DAF 31, 32 and 33 models, door lock removal:

Remove the door trim as described in **Section 12:7**.

Refer to **FIG 12:35**. Disconnect the remote control link (arrowed 3) at the door lock. Remove the window frame attaching screw (arrowed 1) and the two door lock retaining screws (arrowed 2). Withdraw the lock (see **FIG 12:36**).

The remote control link assembly may now be dismounted, if necessary, by removing two retaining screws

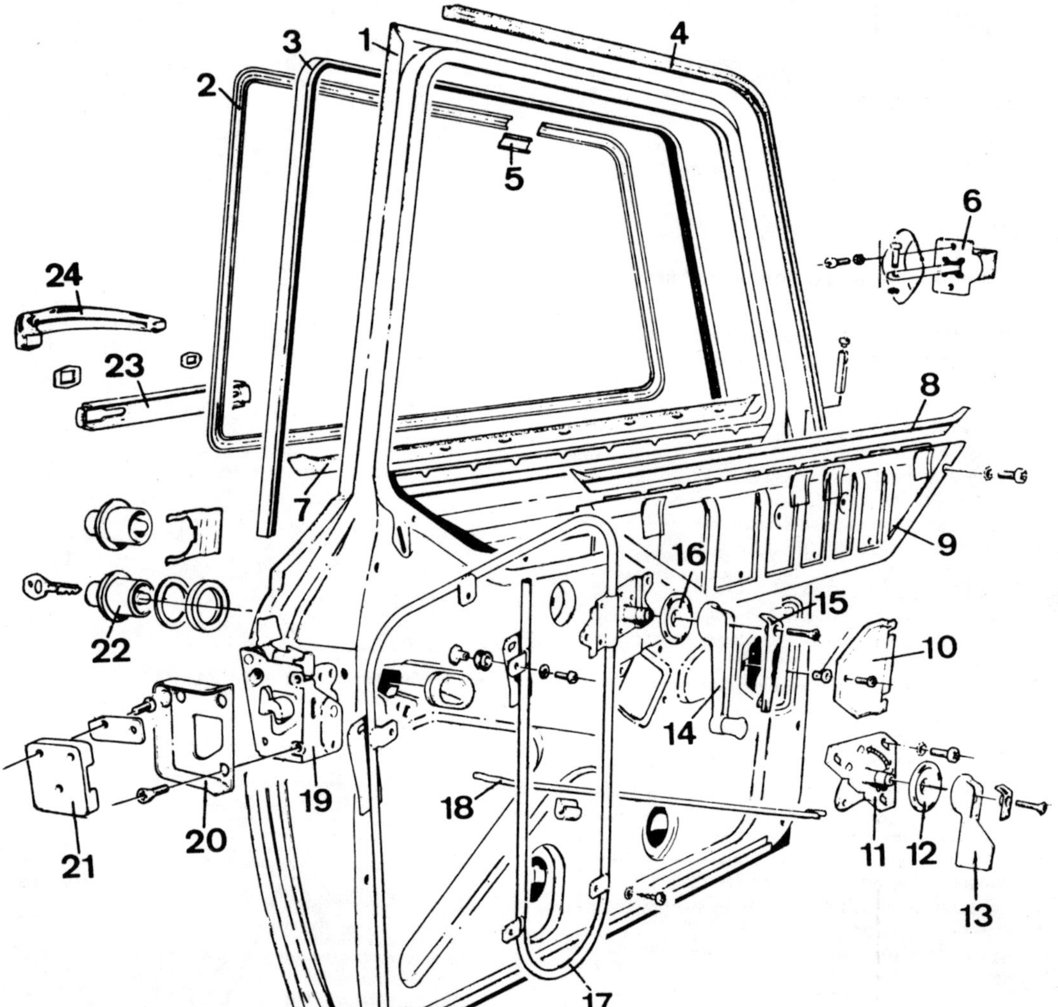

FIG 12:25 An exploded view of the door assembly, DAF 44

Key to Fig 12:25 1 Door 2 Ornamental surround 3 Guide channel 4 Rubber sealing strip 5 Surround joint cover 6 Door stay 7 Outer weatherstrip 8 Inner weatherstrip 9 Access panel 10 Access plate 11 Lock operating unit (remote) 12 Escutcheon 13 Door handle (inner) 14 Window regulating handle 15 Ornamental strip 16 Escutcheon 17 Window glass regulator assembly 18 Remote control link 19 Door lock 20 Guide plate 21 Striker plate 22 Lock cylinder 23 Retainer plate (outer door handle) 24 Door handle (outer)

FIG 12:26 Removing door glass, DAF 44

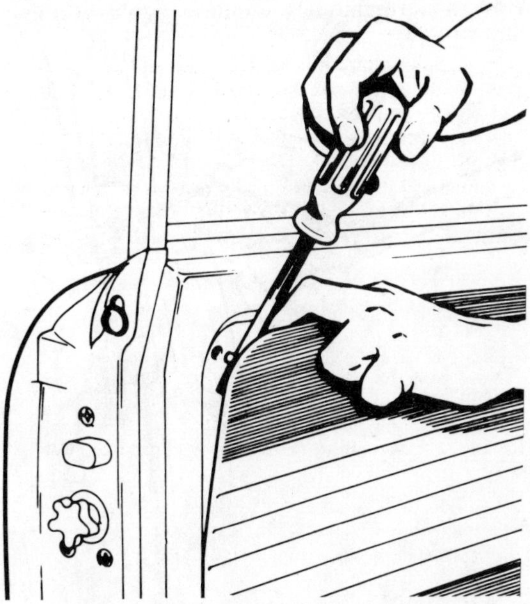

FIG 12:29 Removing the door trim panel

FIG 12:27 Removing door inner handles, DAF 31, 32, 33

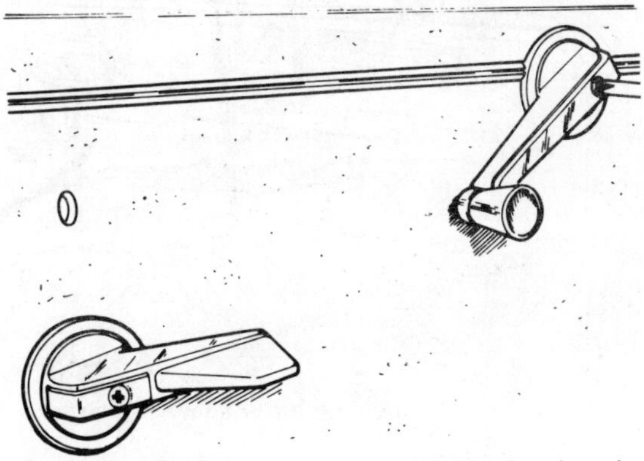

FIG 12:30 Door inner handles DAF 44, showing the retaining screws

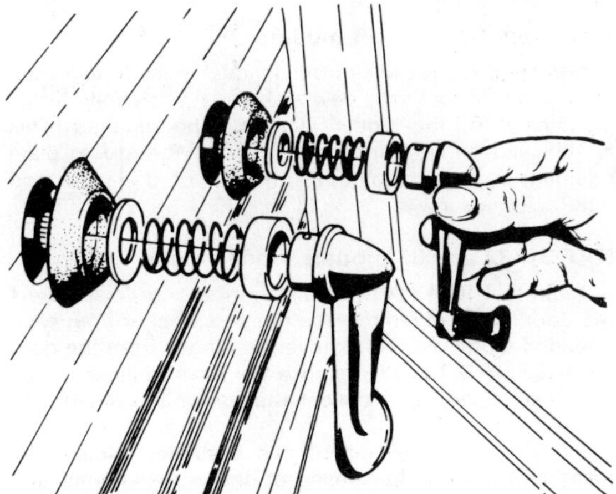

FIG 12:28 Door handle components, DAF 31, 32, 33

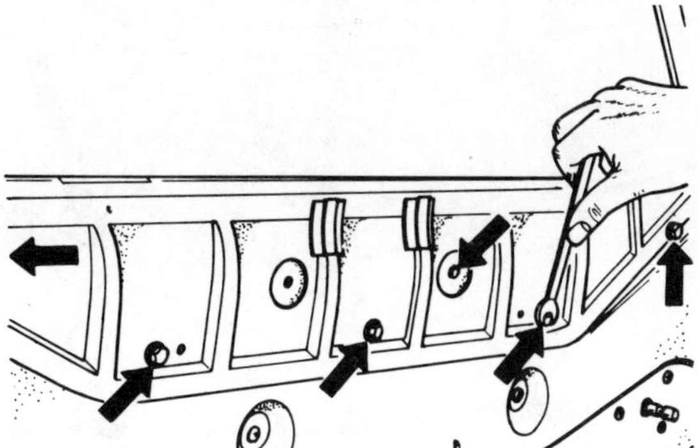

FIG 12:31 Door access cover, DAF 44

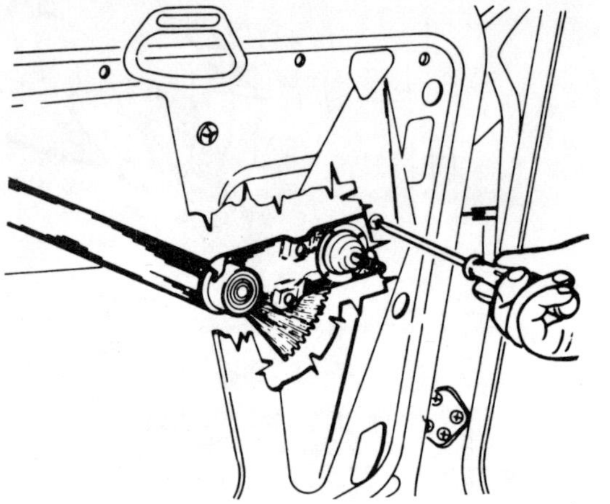

FIG 12:32 Detaching the window regulator, DAF 31, 32, 33

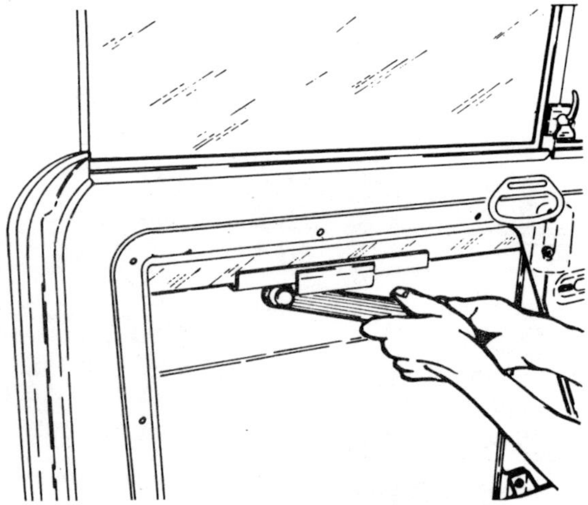

FIG 12:33 Withdrawing the window regulator

FIG 12:34 Window regulator retaining screws, DAF 44

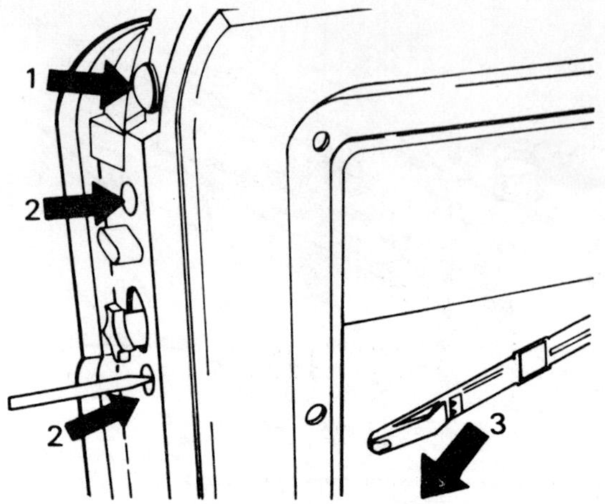

FIG 12:35 Removing a door lock, DAF 31, 32, 33, showing the window frame screw 1, the door lock screws 2 and the remote control link 3

(see **FIG 12:37**), one from each side of the inside door handle spindle. The striker plate may also, if necessary, be dismounted from the door pillar by removing the Phillips retaining screws shown in **FIG 12:38**.

DAF 44 and 46 models, door lock removal:

Remove the door trim as described in **Section 12:7**. Disconnect the remote control link (18 in **FIG 12:25**) at the door lock. Remove the door lock and guide plate retaining screws (see **FIG 12:39**). Dismount the guide plate and withdraw the lock assembly. If necessary, the outside door handle may be dismounted by removing the retainer plate 4 in **FIG 12:40**. Remove the retainer 1 and the nylon washer 2, then withdraw the lock cylinder 3.

The remote control assembly may be withdrawn after removing the screws which retain the inside handle spindle unit.

The striker plate may, if necessary, be dismounted from the door pillar by removing the three Phillips retaining screws.

Door lock fitment, all models:

Fitment is the reverse of the removal procedure in each case. If a new lock or a new striker plate has been fitted, adjustment of the striker plate will be required. This is achieved by trial and error. Loosen the striker plate retaining screws, adjust the position of the plate and retighten the screws.

DAF 31, 32 and 33 models, door hinges:

Refer to **FIG 12:41**. To dismount a door, disconnect the door stay and remove the nut and washer from each threaded hinge pin. To remove the hinges from the door pillar (see **FIG 12:42**), remove the three Phillips screws from each hinge and collect the packing washers and adjuster nuts.

Fitment is the reverse of this sequence. Adjust the hang of the door by means of the adjuster nuts and packing washers. Adjust the position of the door lock striker plate as necessary.

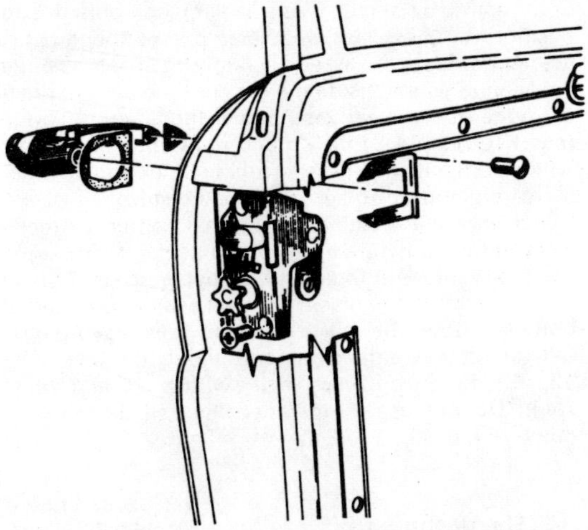

FIG 12:36 The door lock assembly

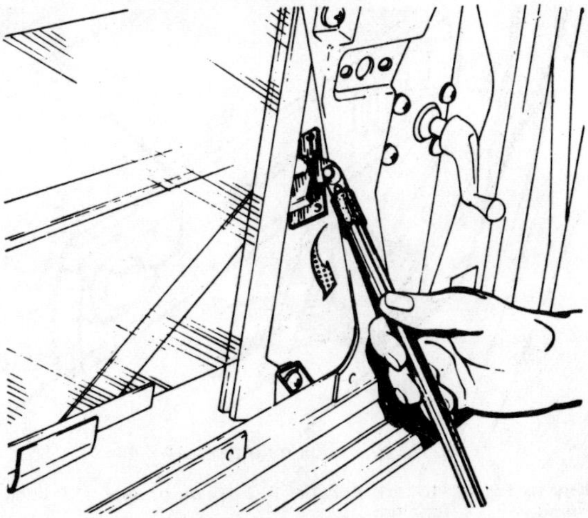

FIG 12:37 Removing the door lock remote control

DAF 44 and 46 door hinges:

Remove the door trim as described in **Section 12:7**.

Disconnect the door stay. Tap out both door hinge pins using a .276 inch (7 mm) diameter drift after removing their sealing caps. Lift off the door.

Fitment is the reverse of this sequence. Fit sealing caps to the hinge pins. Adjust the position of the door lock striker plate if necessary.

12:9 Windscreen, backlight and quarterlight glass

The procedure for replacing a windscreen, backlight or quarterlight glass is basically the same. If the original weatherstrip is being used, ensure that it is thoroughly clean of old sealing compound and that all particles of broken glass have been removed from it. Small particles of old glass left in the weatherstrip may induce breakage of the new glass.

Removing the original glass:

1. If the windscreen is being dealt with, remove the windscreen wiper arms. Run a thin-bladed tool round the aperture to break the seal between the weatherstrip and the body aperture.
2. Press the glass by hand from inside the car and dismount it complete with weatherstrip. If the glass was shattered, remove sections until the weatherstrip can be pulled away from the aperture.
3. Clean the body aperture and remove all traces of old sealing compound. Check that the aperture is undamaged. File away any bumps as these could induce breakage of the new glass. Apply metal filler to dents and smooth off.

Fitting new glass:

1. Clean the edge of the glass and fit the weatherstrip and ornamental surround to it (see **FIG 12:43**). Insert a draw cord in the inner lip of the weatherstrip. This must go completely round and finish with the ends overlapping near the top centre.

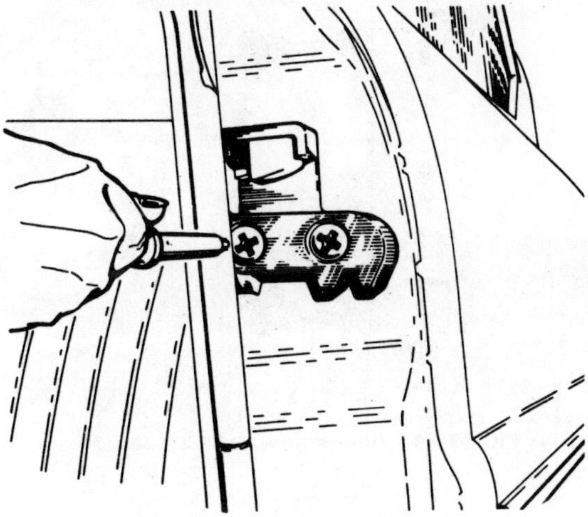

FIG 12:38 Door lock striker plate

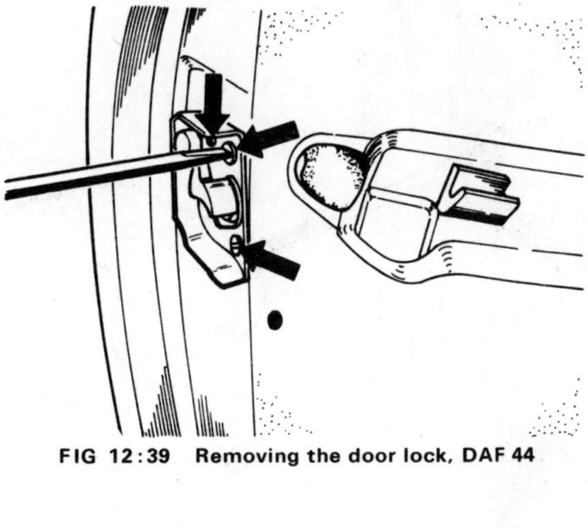

FIG 12:39 Removing the door lock, DAF 44

FIG 12:40 Lock cylinder, DAF 44

Key to Fig 12:40 1 Retainer 2 Nylon washer 3 Lock cylinder 4 Retainer

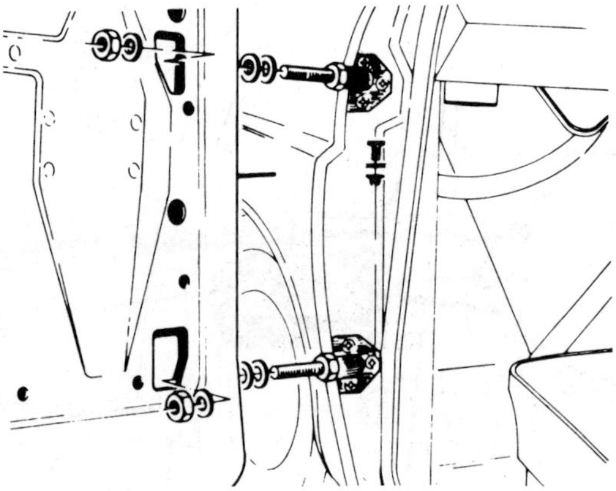

FIG 12:41 Door hinges, DAF 31, 32, 33

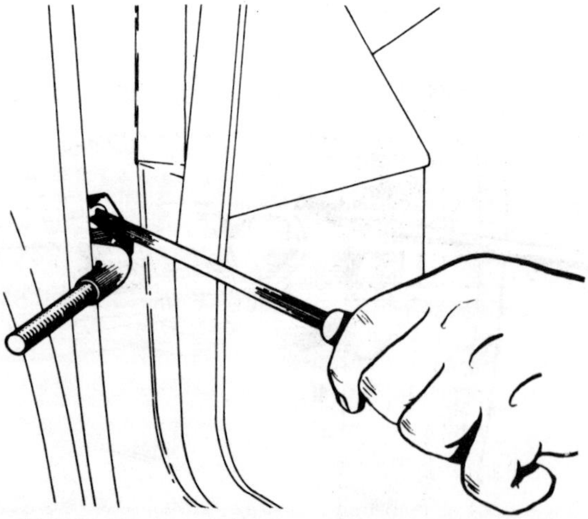

FIG 12:42 Removing door hinge retaining screws

2 Coat the body flange with sealing compound and position the glass and weatherstrip assembly against the flange. Press the assembly firmly against the flange while an assistant inside the car pulls the cord to draw the edge of the weatherstrip over the aperture flange (see **FIG 12:44**). Pull left and right ends alternately while, from outside the car, a rubber block and hammer are carefully used to seat the weatherstrip.

3 Check that the weatherstrip is finally fitted correctly all round the aperture inside and outside. If necessary, use a pressure gun fitted with a copper nozzle (which will not scratch the glass) to inject sealing compound between both the glass and the weatherstrip and between the weatherstrip and the body (see **FIG 12:45**). Remove excess sealer with a rag and white spirit. Do not use thinners as this will damage the paintwork.

12:10 The dashboard

DAF 31, 32 and 33 models, dashboard top panel removal:

1 Disconnect the battery earth cable. Remove the windscreen wiper arms. Remove the windscreen as described in **Section 12:9**.

2 Remove the lid of the glovebox. Remove eight screws and withdraw the fuse box. Carefully lift out the glovebox. From DAF 31 LE models, remove the retaining nuts and dismount the grab handle.

3 Remove the three attaching nuts and lift off the top panel.

DAF 31, 32 and 33 models, top panel fitment:

Fitment of the top panel is the reverse of the removal procedure. Installation of the windscreen is described in **Section 12:9**.

DAF 31 LE model, drain trough removal:

1 Remove the steering column as described in **Chapter 9**, **Section 9:6**. Remove the dashboard top panel as described earlier. Uncouple both drain hoses.

2 Release the instrument panel as described in **Chapter 11**. Remove the further two screws and release the centre panel. Move both panels aside.

3 Remove the steering column bracket, the demister nozzles and hoses (retained by two screws) and withdraw the windscreen wiper assembly after removing the four wiper motor support screws and, from outside the car, the nuts from the wiper arm pivots.

4 Dismount the water drain trough.

DAF 31 LE model, drain trough fitment:

Fitment of the drain trough is the reverse of the removal sequence. Fitment of the dashboard top panel is described earlier in this Section.

Dashboard removal, DAF 44 and 46:

Removal of the dashboard in DAF 44 models is undertaken as described in **Chapter 11**, **Section 11:10**, where instructions on the operations concerned are given in conjunction with obtaining access to the instruments.

12:11 Sliding sunroof

A sliding sunroof is provided as optional equipment on DAF 44 cars. An exploded view of the assembly is shown in **FIG 12:46**.

Removal of sliding roof:

Open the roof halfway, release the roof lining at the front and pull it back. Almost close the roof. Remove the front guide plates (two bolts to each). Swing the leaf springs inwards, remove the retaining bolts and take out the plates. Lift up the roof at the front and remove it.

Withdraw the attaching screws and remove the corner pieces 22 and 43. Withdraw three screws from each guide rail cover strip and remove the strips. Lift up the guide rails 15 and 44 and withdraw the roof lining.

Installation of the lining and roof is the reverse of this sequence.

Renewal of rear guide plates and operating cables:

Remove the sliding roof as described earlier. Remove the winding handle 29 and the escutcheon. Remove the front cover strips 37, 39 and 42. Lift up the guide rails and push the guide plates complete with operating cable off the rails.

Cables must be renewed as a set. Ensure that, when installing cables, the cable for the lefthand guide plate is fitted in the inner opening in the rails. Lubricate the cables with graphite grease and slide the guide plates carefully over the rails.

Check the cable drive gear for wear and renew it if necessary. **If a new drive gear has to be fitted, new operating cables must be installed at the same time**.

Slide the guide plates over the rails until they are just behind the stop. Fit the guide rail cover strips and the corner pieces. It should be possible to move the guide plates to and fro by hand. Fit the winding handle onto the gear shaft and turn the handle as far as it will go. Close the roof completely by hand and push up the rear guide plate lever. Turn back the gear by $\frac{1}{4}$ turn and install the escutcheon and gear. The remaining operations are the removal procedure in reverse.

Adjustment of sliding roof:

Remove the roof lining. Close the roof fully. Loosen the bolts which attach the front guide plates (two bolts to each). Adjust the roof by means of the milled nuts and retighten the bolts.

Open the roof, swing the leaf springs inwards and close the roof to the point **just before it rises**. Loosen the adjuster bolts (screwdriver slot in hexagon head), raise or lower the sliding roof so that it will be flush with the car roof when fully closed and retighten the adjuster bolts. Swing the springs into their operating position and install the roof lining. Ensure the indentation in the end of the spring is deep enough to prevent it becoming loose in service.

Renewal of velvet cording and rubber sealing strips on sliding roof:

Remove the sliding roof as described earlier. Pull off the velvet cording and rubber sealing strips. Use paraffin to remove all traces of old adhesive.

FIG 12:43 Windscreen details

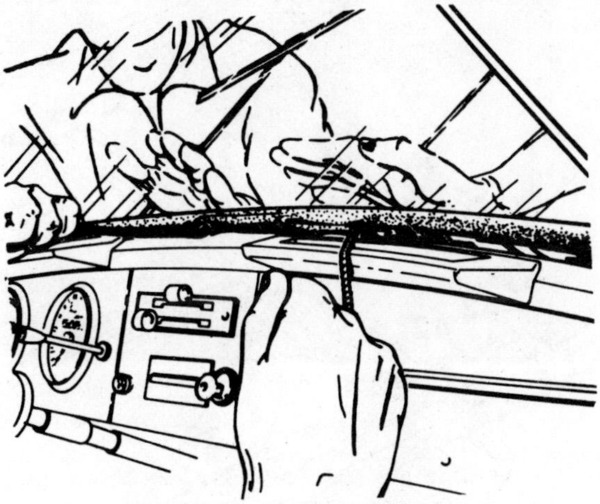

FIG 12:44 Fitting windscreen

FIG 12:45 Inserting sealing compound between weather strip and body

Apply fresh adhesive. Fit new cording with its ends passing round the corners of the roof and ensure that the top of the cording is flush with the roof. Fit the rubber sealing strips.

Renewal of velvet cording on car roof:

Open the roof fully. Remove the cording from the car roof. Use paraffin to remove all traces of old adhesive.

Apply fresh adhesive to the cording and to the roof. Fit the new cording. Ensure that the top of the cording is flush with the roof. Carefully close the roof to the point where the cording on the sliding roof and the cording on the car roof just touch. Cut the cordings parallel with the side of the opening so that the cording on the sliding roof will, when it is opened, just pass the cording on the car roof.

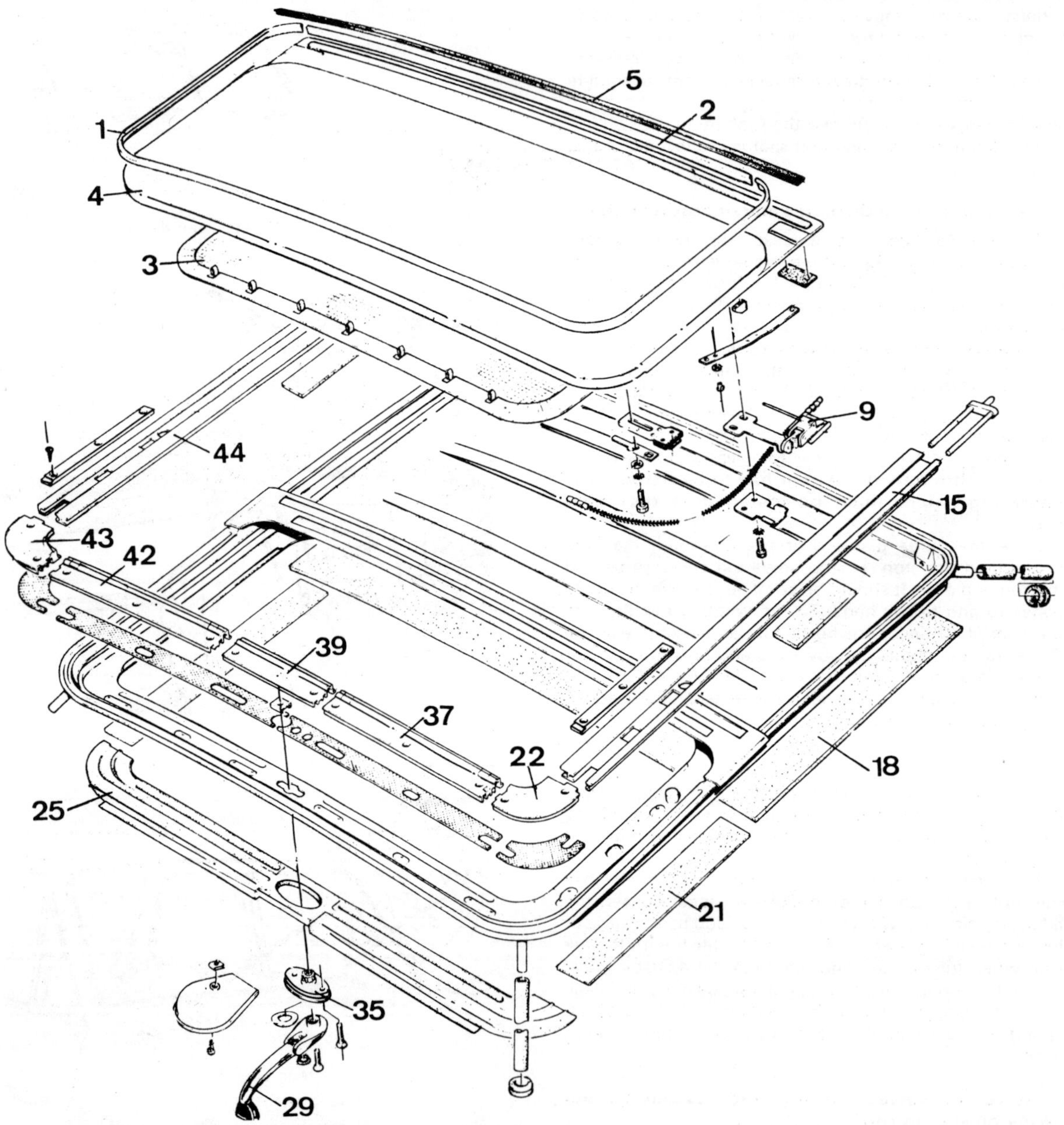

FIG 12:46 An exploded view of a sliding roof assembly

Key to Fig 12:46 1 Velvet cording 2 Velvet cording 3 Lining 4 Sliding roof 5 Rubber sealing strip 9 Cable mechanism 15 Guide rail 18 Insulation panel 21 Insulation strip 22 Corner piece 25 Crosspiece 29 Handle 35 Gear assembly 37 Cover strip 39 Cover strip 42 Cover piece 43 Corner piece 44 Guide rail

APPENDIX

Inches	Decimals	Millimetres	Inches to Millimetres: Inches	Inches to Millimetres: mm	Millimetres to Inches: mm	Millimetres to Inches: Inches
1/64	.015625	.3969	.001	.0254	.01	.00039
1/32	.03125	.7937	.002	.0508	.02	.00079
3/64	.046875	1.1906	.003	.0762	.03	.00118
1/16	.0625	1.5875	.004	.1016	.04	.00157
5/64	.078125	1.9844	.005	.1270	.05	.00197
3/32	.09375	2.3812	.006	.1524	.06	.00236
7/64	.109375	2.7781	.007	.1778	.07	.00276
1/8	.125	3.1750	.008	.2032	.08	.00315
9/64	.140625	3.5719	.009	.2286	.09	.00354
5/32	.15625	3.9687	.01	.254	.1	.00394
11/64	.171875	4.3656	.02	.508	.2	.00787
3/16	.1875	4.7625	.03	.762	.3	.01181
13/64	.203125	5·1594	.04	1.016	.4	.01575
7/32	.21875	5.5562	.05	1.270	.5	.01969
15/64	.234375	5.9531	.06	1.524	.6	.02362
1/4	.25	6.3500	.07	1.778	.7	.02756
17/64	.265625	6.7469	.08	2.032	.8	.03150
9/32	.28125	7.1437	.09	2.286	.9	.03543
19/64	.296875	7.5406	.1	2.54	1	.03937
5/16	.3125	7.9375	.2	5.08	2	.07874
21/64	.328125	8.3344	.3	7.62	3	.11811
11/32	.34375	8.7312	.4	10.16	4	.15748
23/64	.359375	9.1281	.5	12.70	5	.19685
3/8	.375	9.5250	.6	15.24	6	.23622
25/64	.390625	9.9219	.7	17.78	7	.27559
13/32	.40625	10.3187	.8	20.32	8	.31496
27/64	.421875	10.7156	.9	22.86	9	.35433
7/16	.4375	11.1125	1	25.4	10	.39370
29/64	.453125	11.5094	2	50.8	11	.43307
15/32	.46875	11.9062	3	76.2	12	.47244
31/64	.484375	12.3031	4	101.6	13	.51181
1/2	.5	12.7000	5	127.0	14	.55118
33/64	.515625	13.0969	6	152.4	15	.59055
17/32	.53125	13.4937	7	177.8	16	.62992
35/64	.546875	13.8906	8	203.2	17	.66929
9/16	.5625	14.2875	9	228.6	18	.70866
37/64	.578125	14.6844	10	254.0	19	.74803
19/32	.59375	15.0812	11	279.4	20	.78740
39/64	.609375	15.4781	12	304.8	21	.82677
5/8	.625	15.8750	13	330.2	22	.86614
41/64	.640625	16.2719	14	355.6	23	.90551
21/32	.65625	16.6687	15	381.0	24	.94488
43/64	.671875	17.0656	16	406.4	25	.98425
11/16	.6875	17.4625	17	431.8	26	1.02362
45/64	.703125	17.8594	18	457.2	27	1.06299
23/32	.71875	18.2562	19	482.6	28	1.10236
47/64	.734375	18.6531	20	508.0	29	1.14173
3/4	.75	19.0500	21	533.4	30	1.18110
49/64	.765625	19.4469	22	558.8	31	1.22047
25/32	.78125	19.8437	23	584.2	32	1.25984
51/64	.796875	20.2406	24	609.6	33	1.29921
13/16	.8125	20.6375	25	635.0	34	1.33858
53/64	.828125	21.0344	26	660.4	35	1.37795
27/32	.84375	21.4312	27	685.8	36	1.41732
55/64	.859375	21.8281	28	711.2	37	1.4567
7/8	.875	22.2250	29	736.6	38	1.4961
57/64	.890625	22.6219	30	762.0	39	1.5354
29/32	.90625	23.0187	31	787.4	40	1.5748
59/64	.921875	23.4156	32	812.8	41	1.6142
15/16	.9375	23.8125	33	838.2	42	1.6535
61/64	.953125	24.2094	34	863.6	43	1.6929
31/32	.96875	24.6062	35	889.0	44	1.7323
63/64	.984375	25.0031	36	914.4	45	1.7717

UNITS	Pints to Litres	Gallons to Litres	Litres to Pints	Litres to Gallons	Miles to Kilometres	Kilometres to Miles	Lbs. per sq. In. to Kg. per sq. Cm.	Kg. per sq. Cm. to Lbs. per sq. In.
1	.57	4.55	1.76	.22	1.61	.62	.07	14.22
2	1.14	9.09	3.52	.44	3.22	1.24	.14	28.50
3	1.70	13.64	5.28	.66	4.83	1.86	.21	42.67
4	2.27	18.18	7.04	.88	6.44	2.49	.28	56.89
5	2.84	22.73	8.80	1.10	8.05	3.11	.35	71.12
6	3.41	27.28	10.56	1.32	9.66	3.73	.42	85.34
7	3.98	31.82	12.32	1.54	11.27	4.35	.49	99.56
8	4.55	36.37	14.08	1.76	12.88	4.97	.56	113.79
9		40.91	15.84	1.98	14.48	5.59	.63	128.00
10		45.46	17.60	2.20	16.09	6.21	.70	142.23
20				4.40	32.19	12.43	1.41	284.47
30				6.60	48.28	18.64	2.11	426.70
40				8.80	64.37	24.85		
50					80.47	31.07		
60					96.56	37.28		
70					112.65	43.50		
80					128.75	49.71		
90					144.84	55.92		
100					160.93	62.14		

UNITS	Lb ft to kgm	Kgm to lb ft	UNITS	Lb ft to kgm	Kgm to lb ft
1	.138	7.233	7	.967	50.631
2	.276	14.466	8	1.106	57.864
3	.414	21.699	9	1.244	65.097
4	.553	28.932	10	1.382	72.330
5	.691	36.165	20	2.765	144.660
6	.829	43.398	30	4.147	216.990

TECHNICAL DATA

Dimensions are in inches unless otherwise stated

ENGINE, DAF 31, 32, 33, 44 and 46 models

Type	Aircooled, opposed twin cylinder (flat) ohv 4-stroke
Capacity:	
DAF 31, 32 and 33 models	746 cc
DAF 44 and 46 models	844 cc
Bore and stroke:	
746 cc engines	85.5 x 65.0 mm
844 cc engines	85.5 x 73.5 mm
Compression ratio, both engines	7.5:1
Connecting rods:	
Length between centres:	
746 cc engines	4.921
844 cc engines	5.256
Small-end bore (unbushed)	1.1024 to 1.1032
Small-end bush bore	.9845 to .9850
Big-end bore	2.1606 to 2.1614
Big-end bearing diameter, standard	2.0482 to 2.0495
Big-end bearing interference fit	Zero to .001
Big-end side clearance	.004 to .012
Crankshaft:	
Journal diameter	2.2823 to 2.2831
End float	.004 to .012
Radial clearance	.0024 to .004
Cylinder bores:	
Standard, blue marked	3.3661 to 3.3665
Standard, red marked	3.3665 to 3.3669
.5 mm oversize, blue marked	3.3858 to 3.3862
.5 mm oversize, red marked	3.3862 to 3.3866
1.0 mm oversize, blue marked	3.4055 to 3.4059
1.0 mm oversize, red marked	3.4059 to 3.4063
Piston diameters:	
Standard, blue marked	3.3644 to 3.3648
Standard, red marked	3.3648 to 3.3651
.5 mm oversize, blue marked	3.3840 to 3.3844
.5 mm oversize, red marked	3.3844 to 3.3848
1.0 mm oversize, blue marked	3.4037 to 3.4041
1.0 mm oversize, red marked	3.4041 to 3.4045
Piston rings:	
Clearance in ring grooves:	
Top compression	.0026 to .0036
Lower compression	.0018 to .0028
Oil control	.0010 to .0020
Ring gaps:	
Compression	.014 to .024
Oil control	.010 to .020
Gudgeon pin:	
Diameter	.9840 to .9843
Clearance	.0003 to .0010
Timing gears:	
Crankshaft	26 teeth
Camshaft	52 teeth

Camshaft:

Journal bore	.9843 to .9850
Journal diameter	.9831 to .9835
Cam lift:	
DAF 31 and 32 models	.2323
DAF 33, 44 and 46 models	.240
Tappet clearance in guide	.0005 to .0020

Valve timing:

DAF 31 and 32 models:	
Inlet opens	14 deg. after TDC
Inlet closes	26 deg. after BDC
Exhaust opens	26 deg. before BDC
Exhaust closes	14 deg. before BDC
DAF 33, 44 and 46 models:	
Inlet opens	13 deg. after TDC
Inlet closes	27 deg. after BDC
Exhaust opens	27 deg. before BDC
Exhaust closes	13 deg. before TDC

Valves:

Exhaust:	
Head diameter, both engines	1.240
Seat width, both engines	.063 to .075
Stem diameter, 746 cc engines	.3124 to .3128
Stem clearance in guide, 746 cc engines	.001 to .002
Stem diameter, 844 cc engines	.3129 to .3134
Stem clearance in guide, 844 cc engines	.0015 to .0025
Inlet, DAF 31 and 32 models:	
Head diameter	1.30
Seat width	.051 to .063
Stem diameter	.3134 to .3138
Stem clearance in guide	.001 to .002
Inlet, DAF 33, 44 and 46 models:	
Head diameter	1.378
Seat width	.051 to .063
Stem diameter	.3129 to .3138
Stem clearance in guide	.001 to .002
Seat angle, both valves, both engines	45 deg.

Valve spring load at 1.36 inch length:

DAF 31 and 32 models	36 to 40 lb
DAF 33, 44 and 46 models	42 to 46 lb

Valve clearance, cold engine:

Inlet, both engines	.004
Exhaust, both engines	.006

Rocker shaft:

Diameter	.7868 to .7871
Bush bore	.7874 to .7882
Clearance	.0003 to .0015

Oil pump:

Drive shaft bore clearance	.0005 to .0014
Idler gear bore clearance	.005 to .0015
Gear end clearance	.0008 to .004

FUEL SYSTEM

DAF model			31 and 32	33	
Solex 34 carburetter series			PICS	PICS 2	PICS 3
Venturi diameter			30 mm	34 mm	30 mm
Main jet			170	170	170
Air correction jet			170	150	140
Pilot jet (to end of 1964)			45	45	
Pilot jet (1965 onwards)			47	55	55 (electrically operated)
Float setting (± 1 mm)			17 mm	17 mm	

DAF 44 model:

Solex 40 carburetter series:					
Chassis number	50000-527600	527601-544999	545000-714457	714458-743500	as from 743500
Type of carburetter	PICS 1	PICS 2	PICS 4	PICS 5	PICS 6
Reference number	96 (1)	962	964	37	371
Jet calibrations					
Main jet	175	175	175	170	170
Air correction jet	140	140	140	120	120
Pump discharge nozzle	50	50	60	60	60
Pilot jet	52	60	62.5	65 (electrically operated)	65 (electrically operated)
Air correction jet (for idling; not removable)				150	150
Venturi dia.	34 mm	34 mm	34 mm	34 mm	34 mm
Secondary venturi	2.8 mm	2.8 mm	2.8 mm	2.8 mm	3.2 mm
By-pass passages	3	4	4	3	3
Float needle	2.1 mm	2.1 mm	2.1 mm	2.1 mm	2.1 mm
Float weight	5.7 g	5.7 g	5.7 g	5.7 g	5.7 g
End of stroke for throttle opening of accelerating pump	3.7 mm	3.7 mm	3.7 mm	11 mm*	12 mm*
Fuel level in float chamber	22.5 (±1) mm	22.5 (±1) mm	24 (±1 mm)	24 (±1) mm	24 (±1) mm

* At this position of the throttle valve, the fuel supply by the accelerating pump is stopped by means of a valve. The fuel level in the float chamber is measured from the edge of the gasket. First check the fuel pump pressure which should be between 1 and 2 lbs/sq inch (0.07-0.14 kg/cm²). Next allow the engine to idle. Then switch off the engine and disconnect the fuel hose from the carburetter, so as to allow the residual pressure to fall.

IGNITION SYSTEM

Distributor:	
DAF 31 and 32 models	Bosch 0.231.155.001
Ignition timing	4 deg. before TDC
DAF 33 models	Bosch 0.231.155.002 (224511)
Ignition timing	4 deg. before TDC
DAF 44 models, 6-volt	Bosch 0.231.155.001 (223422)
DAF 44 and 46, 12-volt	Bosch 0.231.155.004
Ignition timing	6 deg. before TDC
From July 1971, all models with EEC	5 deg. after TDC
Breaker gap, all distributors	.016 to .020
Coil:	
DAF 31 and 32 models	Ducellier 4033, 6-volt
DAF 33 and 44 models, 6-volt	Bosch 0.221.100.022 (224509)
12-volt	Bosch 0.221.123.005

Sparking plugs:

DAF 31 and 32 models	Autolite AE 32p
DAF 33 models	Bosch W200T35
DAF 44 and 46 models	Bosch W175T1 or equivalent

Sparking plug gap:

DAF 31, 32, 33, 44 and 46 models	.032 to .035

COOLING SYSTEM

Type	Finned cylinders air cooled through cowling by engine-driven blower

CLUTCH

Type	Automatic, centrifugal
Engagement speeds:	
Primary shoes:	
Without emission control	800 to 1000 rev/min
With emission control	975 to 1175 rev/min
Secondary shoes, fully engaged:	
Without emission control	1900 to 2200 rev/min
With emission control	2100 to 2300 rev/min

TRANSMISSION

Type	Variomatic, belt drive		
Drive unit:	*31, 32, 33*	*44*	*46*
Ratio	1.69 : 1	1.69 : 1	1.53 : 1
Fluid	SAE 80EP to specifications MIL-L2105 or MIL-L2105B without lead bearing additives		
Capacity:			
Initial fill	475 cc	475 cc	475 cc
Refill	400 cc	430 cc	430 cc
Sliding discs:			
Gap	1.5 to 2 mm between discs		
Fluid	Automatic transmission type A/A		
Capacity:			
Initial fill	100 cc	100 cc	100 cc
Refill	75 cc	75 cc	75 cc

Reduction gear:	*31, 32, 33*	*44 up to chassis number 743246*	*44 from chassis number 743246*	*46*
Ratio	4.75 : 1	3.65 : 1	3.643 : 1	4.51 : 1
Fluid	As for drive unit			
Capacity:				
Initial fill	180 cc	250 cc	250 cc	825 cc
Refill	140 cc	230 cc	230 cc	800 cc
Sliding discs:				
Gap	1.5–2 mm between discs			
Fluid	Automatic transmission type A/A			
Capacity	75 cc	75 cc	75 cc	75 cc

Drive shafts, DAF 46:

CV joints:	
Grease	Molykote BR2-S
Capacity	70 g

SUSPENSION

Front suspension:	
DAF 31, 32, 33, 44 and 46 models	Transverse multi-leaf spring
Rear suspension:	
Except DAF 46	Independent, one coil spring per wheel
DAF 46	De Dion type rear axle with single leaf semi-elliptic springs
Dampers, front and rear	Double-acting, telescopic hydraulic
Leaf spring:	
Type	4621, 4623
Number of leaves	1
Length	43.3 inch (1100 mm)
Width	2.36 inch (60 mm)

STEERING

Type	Rack and pinion	
DAF model	31, 32 and 33	44 and 46
Turning angle, max	40 deg.	38 deg.
Swivel incl. ($\pm\frac{1}{2}$ deg.)	$7\frac{1}{2}$ deg.	$8\frac{1}{2}$ deg.
Castor angle ($\pm\frac{1}{2}$ deg.)	Zero	$4\frac{3}{4}$ deg.
Camber angle ($\pm\frac{1}{2}$ deg.)	$1\frac{1}{2}$ deg.	$1\frac{1}{4}$ deg.
Toe-in (per wheel):		
Front wheels	Zero to .04	.08 to .16
Rear wheels (wheel vertical)	Zero to .02	Zero

BRAKES

Operation:	
DAF 31, 32, 33 and early 44 models	Single line hydraulic
DAF 44 (later) and DAF 46	Dual line hydraulic
Fluid specification:	
DAF 31, 32 and 33 models	SAE 70 R3
DAF 44 and 46 models	SAE J-1703
Type:	
Front and rear	Drum

ELECTRICAL EQUIPMENT

Battery:	
Type, up to 1972	6-volt, negative earth
From September 1972	12-volt, negative earth
Starter motor:	
Drive, all models	Positive pinion engagement
Type:	
DAF 31 and 32 models	Ducellier 6148A, 6-volt
DAF 33 and 44 models, 6-volt system	Bosch 0.001.209.14
12-volt system	Bosch 001.211.037
Generator:	
Type:	
DAF 31 and 32 models	Ducellier 7257G, 6-volt
DAF 33 and 44 models, 6-volt system	Bosch 0.101.206.148
12-volt system	Bosch 0.101.206.079
Voltage regulator:	
Type:	
DAF 31 and 32 models	Ducellier 8305A, 6-volt
DAF 33 and 44 models, 6-volt system	Bosch 0.190.215.011
12-volt system	Bosch 0.190.215.034

TORQUE WRENCH SETTINGS

Torques are in lb ft unless otherwise stated

The following list includes only leading torque wrench settings. Further settings are included in the chapter texts.

DAF 31, 32 and 33:

Cylinder head	14.5 to 16.3
Connecting rod	20 to 22
Flywheel	18 to 19.5
Crankcase halves:	
$\frac{1}{4}$ inch	5.1 to 6.5
$\frac{5}{16}$ inch	13.5 to 15.2
$\frac{3}{8}$ inch	21 to 22.5
Oil drain plug	25.3 to 29
Sparking plugs	13 to 16
Impeller	8.7 to 10
Rear axle shaft nut	130 to 150
Steering ball joints:	
At rack	20 to 22, all models
At steering arm	25 to 29, all models

DAF 44 and 46:

	Inch	*lb ft*
Cylinder heads	$\frac{3}{8}$	14.5 to 16.3
Connecting rod nuts	M9 × 1	25.3 to 27.5
	$\frac{5}{16}$	18 to 19.5
	M8 × 1	28.9 to 32.5
Flywheel	$\frac{1}{4}$	5.1 to 6.5
Crankcase halves	$\frac{5}{16}$	13.5 to 15.2
	$\frac{3}{8}$	21 to 22.5
Clutch housing	$\frac{5}{16}$	13.5 to 15.2
Clutch drum	$\frac{5}{16}$	19.5 to 21.7
Crankshaft pulley	$\frac{9}{16}$	58
Oil pump cover	$\frac{1}{4}$	6.5 to 8.0
Oil strainer cover	$\frac{1}{4}$	5.1 to 6.5
Oil drain plug	$\frac{5}{8}$	25.3 to 29
Oil pressure relief valve plug	$\frac{3}{4}$	40 to 43.5
Inlet manifold	$\frac{1}{4}$	8.7 to 10
Inlet manifold to crankcase	$\frac{5}{16}$	13.5 to 15.2
Exhaust pipe to cylinder head	$\frac{5}{16}$	13.5 to 15.2
Exhaust pipe to cross-brace	$\frac{5}{16}$	18 to 19.5
Fuel pump	$\frac{5}{16}$	13.5 to 15.2
Oil filler pipe	$\frac{5}{16}$	13.5 to 15.2
Spark plugs	14 mm × 1.25 pitch	13 to 16
Starter	$\frac{3}{8}$	21 to 22.5
Impeller	$\frac{1}{4}$	8.7 to 10
Valve covers	$\frac{3}{8}$	4.4 to 5.8
Oil cooler to oil pump cover	$\frac{1}{4}$	8.7 to 10
Oil cooler banjo bolt	$\frac{1}{2}$	13.5 to 15.2
Oil cooler union nipple	$\frac{1}{2}$	23.8 to 25.3
Oil cooler union nut	$\frac{1}{2}$	21 to 22.5
Front engine mountings	$\frac{3}{8}$	21 to 22.5
Rear engine mounting	$\frac{5}{16}$	13.5 to 15.2
	M10	29 to 32.5
Generator brace to engine	$\frac{5}{16}$	13.5 to 15.2
Impeller shroud to engine	$\frac{5}{16}$	13.5 to 15.2
Silencer to clutch housing	M10	21.7 to 25.3

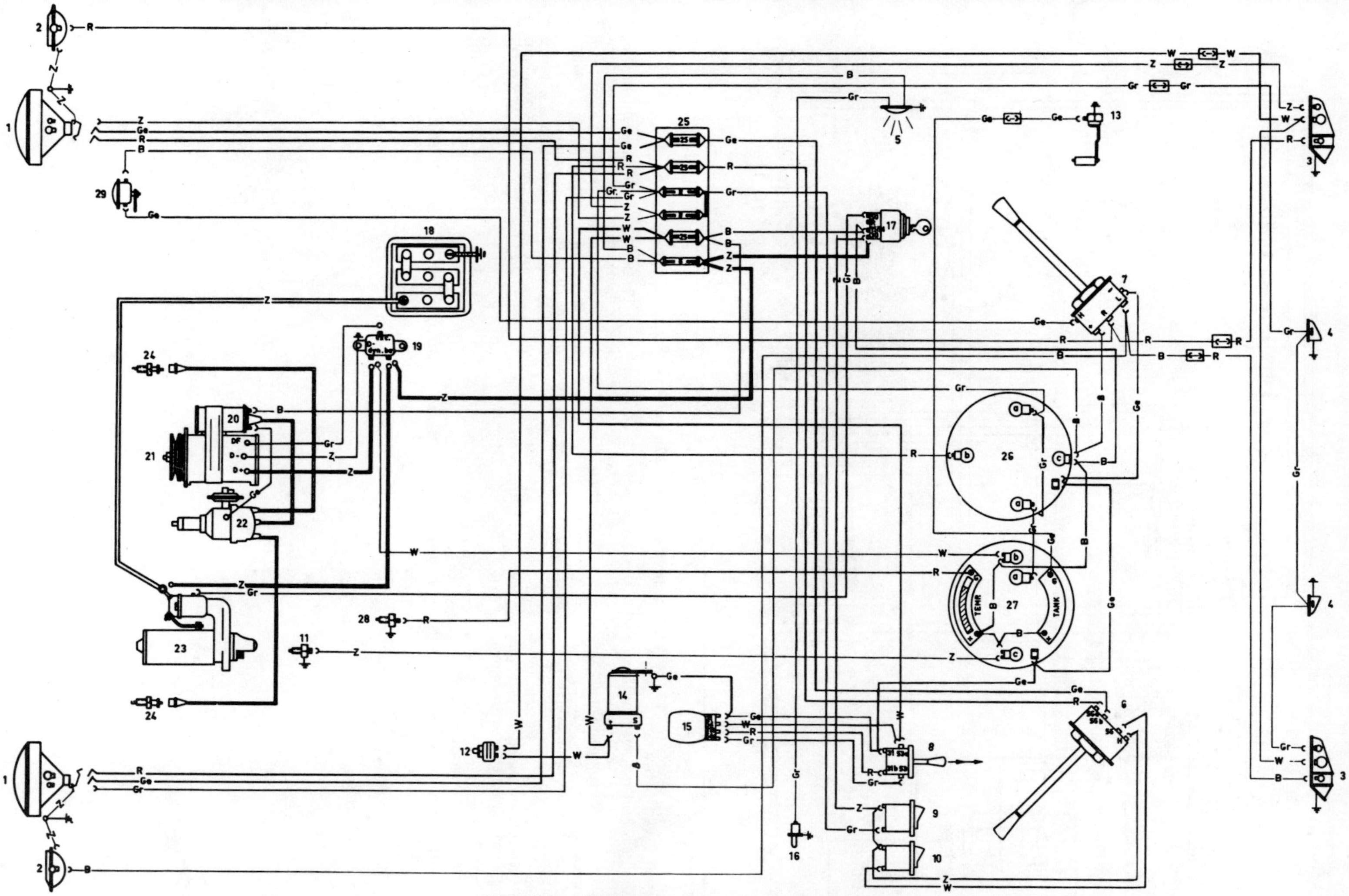

FIG 13:1 Wiring diagram, DAF 31 LE model

Key to Fig 13:1 1 Headlight, main beam/dipped beam 45/40 watt-4 watt (2x) 2 Direction indicator light 18 watt (2x) 3 Stop/tail/direction indicator light 18-4-18 watt (2x) 4 Number plate light 3 watt (2x) 5 Interior light 5 watt 6 Dipswitch 7 Direction indicator/horn switch 8 Windscreen wiper/switch 9 Parking light switch 10 Headlight switch 11 Oil pressure indicator light switch 12 Stop light switch 13 Fuel gauge tank transmitter 14 Flasher unit 15 Windscreen wiper motor 16 Courtesy light switch 17 Ignition switch 18 Battery 77 amp/20-hr 19 Voltage regulator 20 Ignition coil 21 Generator 240 watt 22 Distributor 23 Starter 0.4-0.5 hp 24 Spark plug (2x) 25 Fuse holder 3 x 8 amp-3 x 25 amp 26 Speedometer: a Instrument lighting (white) 2 watt b Main beam indicator light (blue) 2 watt c Direction indicator pilot light (green) 2 watt 27 Oil temperature and fuel gauge cluster: a Instrument lighting (white) 2 watt b Generator charge indicator light (red) 2 watt c Oil pressure indicator light (red) 2 watt 28 Oil temperature gauge transmitter 29 Horn

Colour code

Key to colour code **Z** Black sheathed wire **Gr** Green sheathed wire **Ge** Yellow sheathed wire **B** Blue sheathed wire **W** White sheathed wire

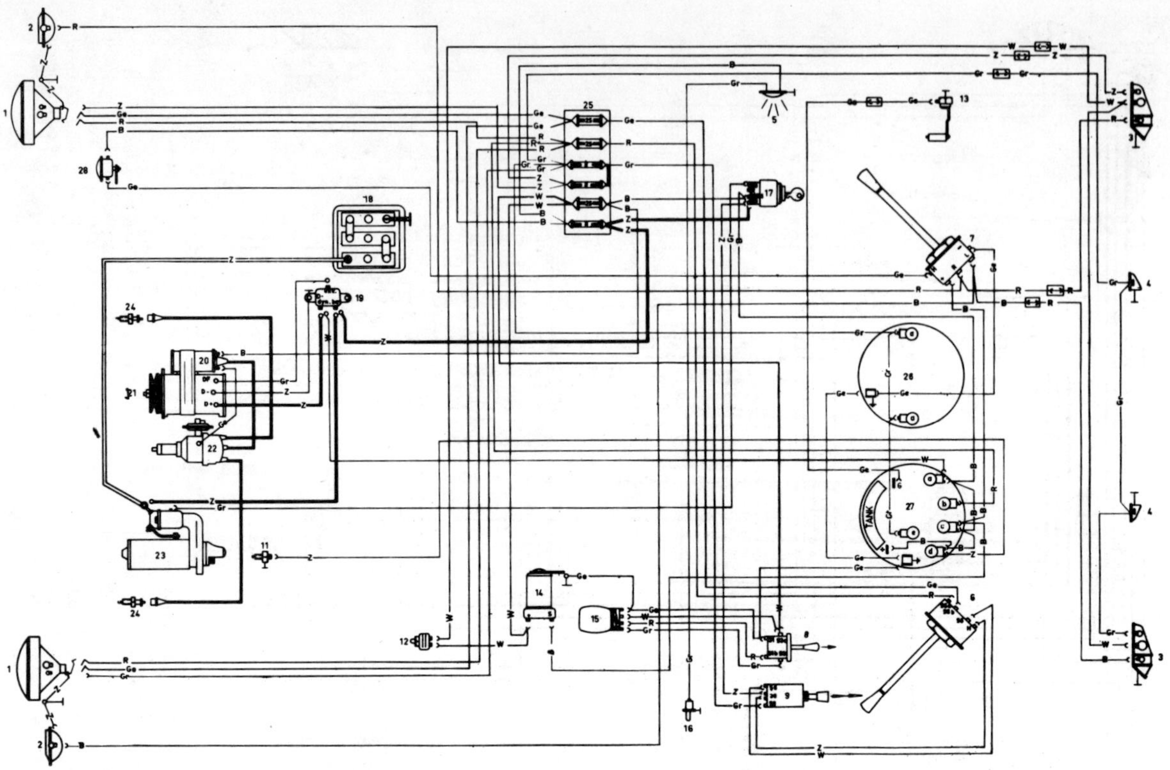

FIG 13 : 2 Wiring diagram, DAF 33 model, 6 volt

Key to Fig 13 : 2 1 Headlight, main beam/dipped beam/parking light 45/40/4 watt 2 Direction indicator light 18 watt 3 Stop/tail/direction indicator light 18/4/18 watt 4 Number plate light 5 watt 5 Courtesy light 5 watt 6 Headlight dipped beam/main beam switch 7 Direction indicator/horn switch 8 Windscreen wiper switch 9 Parking light/headlight main beam switch 11 Oil pressure warning light switch 12 Stop light switch 13 Fuel tank transmitter 14 Flasher unit 15 Windscreen wiper motor 16 Courtesy light switch 17 Ignition switch 18 Battery 66 amp/hr at 20-hr rate 19 Voltage regulator 20 Ignition coil 21 Generator 300 watt 22 Distributor 23 Starter 0.45 hp 24 Sparking plug 25 Fuse holder 3 x 8 amp 3 x 25 amp 26 Speedometer: a Instrument lighting 1.2 watt 27 Warning-light dial: a Generator charge warning light (red) 1.2 watt b Main beam warning light (blue) 1.2 watt c Direction indicator warning light (green) 1.2 watt d Oil pressure warning light (red) 1.2 watt e Instrument lighting 1.2 watt 28 Horn

Colour code

Key to colour code **Bl** Blue **Gr** Green **G** Grey **W** White **Br** Brown **Ge** Yellow **R** Red **Z** Black

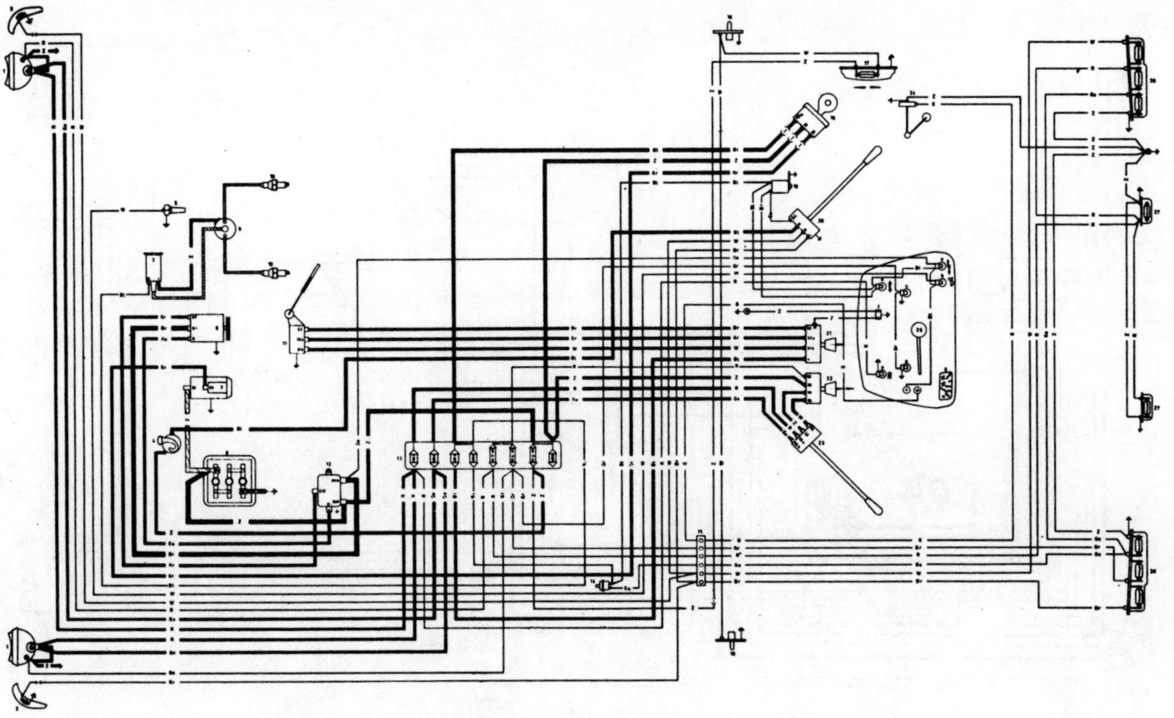

FIG 13:3 Wiring diagram, DAF 44 model, up to 1970

Key to Fig 13:3 1 Headlight, main beam/dipped beam/parking light 45/40/5 watt 2 Direction indicator light 18 watt 3 Ignition coil 4 Horn 5 Oil pressure warning light switch 6 Generator 240 watt 7 Starter 0.5 hp 8 Battery 66 amp/hr at 20-hr rate 9 Distributor 10 Sparking plug 11 Windscreen wiper motor 12 Voltage regulator 13 Fuse holder 3 x 8 amp 5 x 25 amp 14 Stop light switch 15 Wire connector, 6-pole 16 Courtesy light switch 17 Courtesy light 5 watt 18 Ignition switch 19 Flasher unit 20 Direction indicator/horn switch 21 Windscreen wiper switch 22 Parking light/headlight main beam switch 23 Headlight dipped beam/main beam switch 24 Fuel tank transmitter 25 Speedometer a Generator charge warning light (red) 1.2 watt b Oil pressure warning light (red) 1.2 watt c Instrument lighting 1.2 watt d Direction indicator warning light (green) 1.2 watt e Main beam warning light (blue) 1.2 watt f Earth g Fuel gauge '+'/'G' 26 Stop/tail/direction indicator light 18/5/18 watt 27 Number plate light 5 watt 28 Reversing light connection 29 Loudspeaker

(−) Female wire terminal
(o) Round wire terminal

Colour code

Key to colour code **Bl** Blue **Gr** Green **G** Grey **W** White **Br** Brown **Ge** Yellow **R** Red **Z** Black

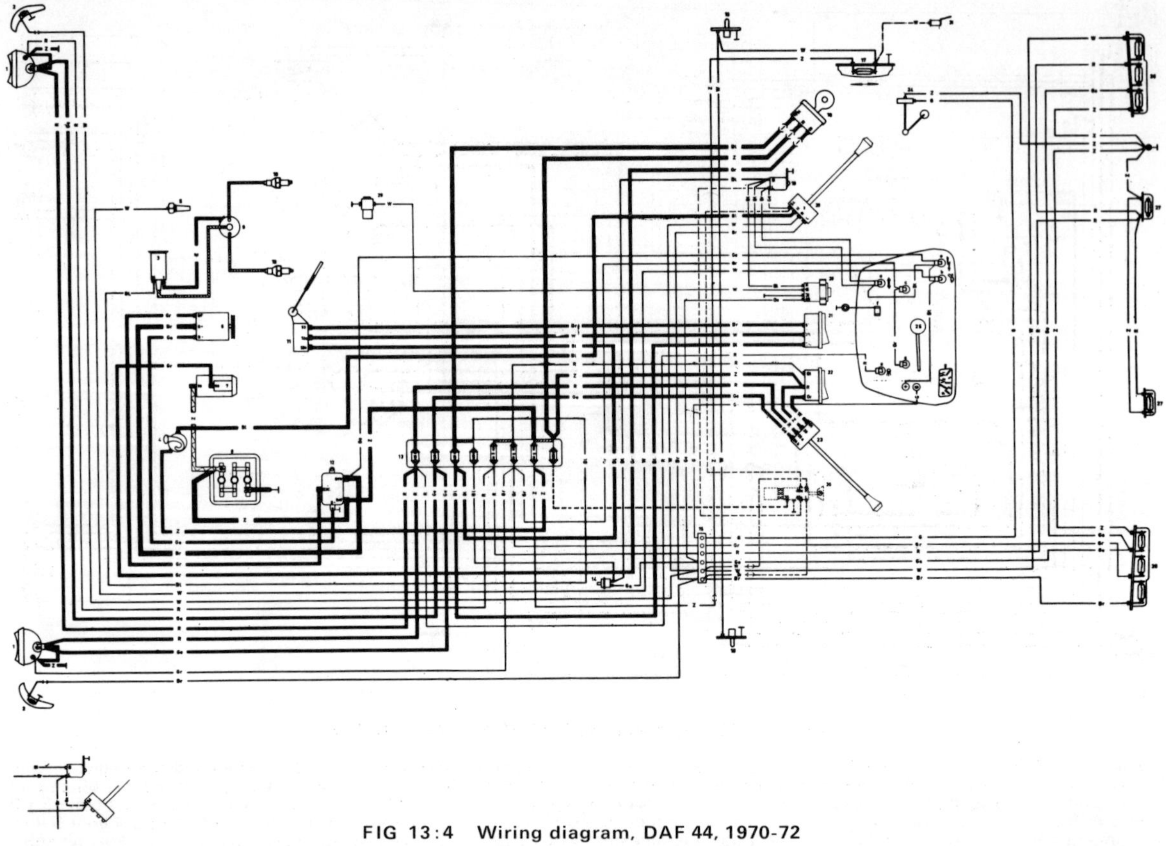

FIG 13:4 Wiring diagram, DAF 44, 1970-72

Key to Fig 13:4 1 Headlight, main beam/dipped beam/parking light 45/40/4 watt 2 Direction indicator light 18 watt 3 Ignition coil 4 Horn 5 Oil pressure warning light switch 6 Generator 240 watt 7 Starter 0.5 hp 8 Battery 66 amp/hr at 20-hr rate 9 Distributor 10 Sparking plug 11 Windscreen wiper motor 12 Voltage regulator 13 Fuse holder 3 x 8 amp 5 x 25 amp 14 Stop light switch 15 Wire connector, 6-pole 16 Courtesy light switch 17 Courtesy light 5 watt 18 Ignition switch 19 Flasher unit 20 Direction indicator/horn switch 21 Windscreen wiper switch 22 Parking light/headlight main beam switch 23 Headlight dipped beam/main beam switch 24 Fuel tank element 25 Speedometer a Generator charge warning light (red) 1.2 watt b Oil pressure warning light (red) 1.2 watt c Instrument lighting 1.2 watt d Direction indicator warning light (green) 1.2 watt e Main beam warning light (blue) 1.2 watt f Earth g Fuel gauge '+'/'G' 26 Stop/tail/direction indicator light 18/5/18 watt 27 Number plate light 5 watt 28 Transmission low ratio hold switch 29 Electromagnetic vacuum valve 30 Alarmswitch 31 Mercury switch (for DAF estate car and delivery van only)

(−) Female wire terminal
(o) Round wire terminal

Colour code

Key to colour code **Bl** Blue **Br** Brown **Gr** Green **Ge** Yellow **G** Grey **R** Red **W** White **Z** Black

When installing the alarmswitch, remove the yellow wire between pos. 19 and 20

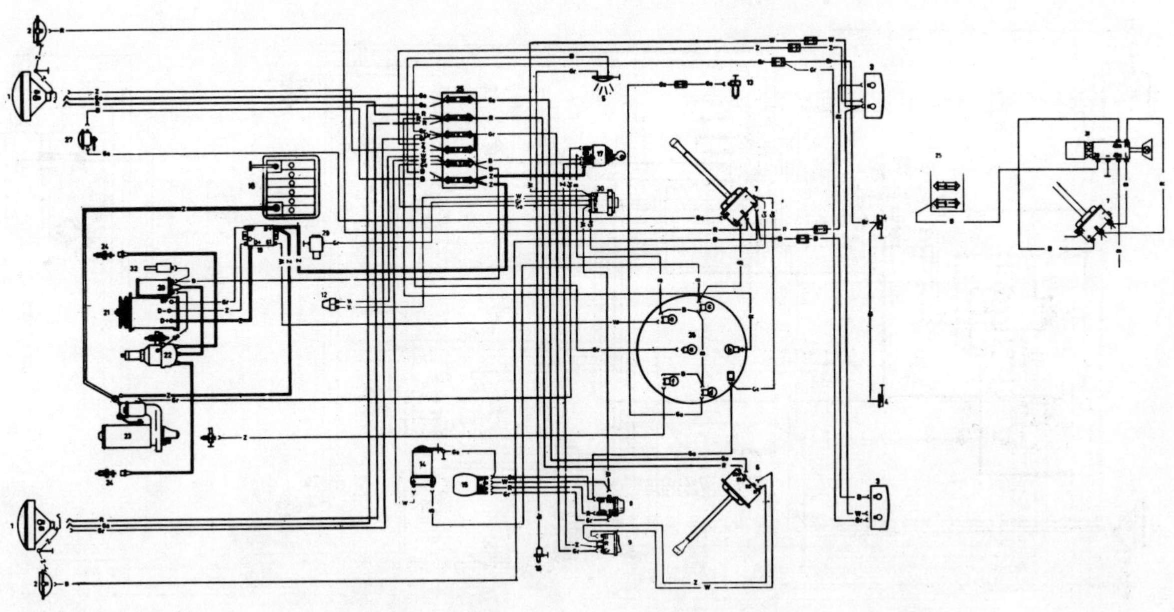

FIG 13:5 Wiring diagram, DAF 33 Comfort, 12 volt

Key to Fig 13:5 1 Headlight, main beam/dipped beam/parking light 45/40/4 watt 2 Direction indicator light 21 watt 3 Stop/tail/direction indicator light 21/5/21 watt 4 Number plate light 3 watt 5 Interior light 5 watt 6 Headlight dipped beam/main beam switch 7 Direction indicator/horn switch 8 Windscreen wiper/windscreen washer switch 9 Parking light/headlight main beam switch 11 Oil pressure warning light switch 12 Stop light switch 13 Fuel tank element 14 Flasher unit 15 Windscreen wiper motor 16 Interior light switch 17 Ignition switch 18 Battery 36 amp/hr at 20-hr rate 19 Voltage regulator 20 Ignition coil 21 Generator 22 Distributor 23 Starter 24 Sparking plug 25 Fuse holder 6 x 8 amp 26 Speedometer/distance recorder a Instrument lighting (white) 2 watt b Main beam warning light (blue) 2 watt c Direction indicator warning light (green) 2 watt d Fuel warning light (yellow) 2 watt e Generator charge warning light (red) 2 watt f Oil pressure warning light (red) 2 watt 27 Horn 29 Electromagnetic valve of low ratio hold 30 Low ratio hold switch 32 Slow running air jet (closeable)

Colour code

Key to colour code **Bl** Blue **Br** Brown **Gr** Green **Ge** Yellow **G** Grey **R** Red **W** White **Z** Black

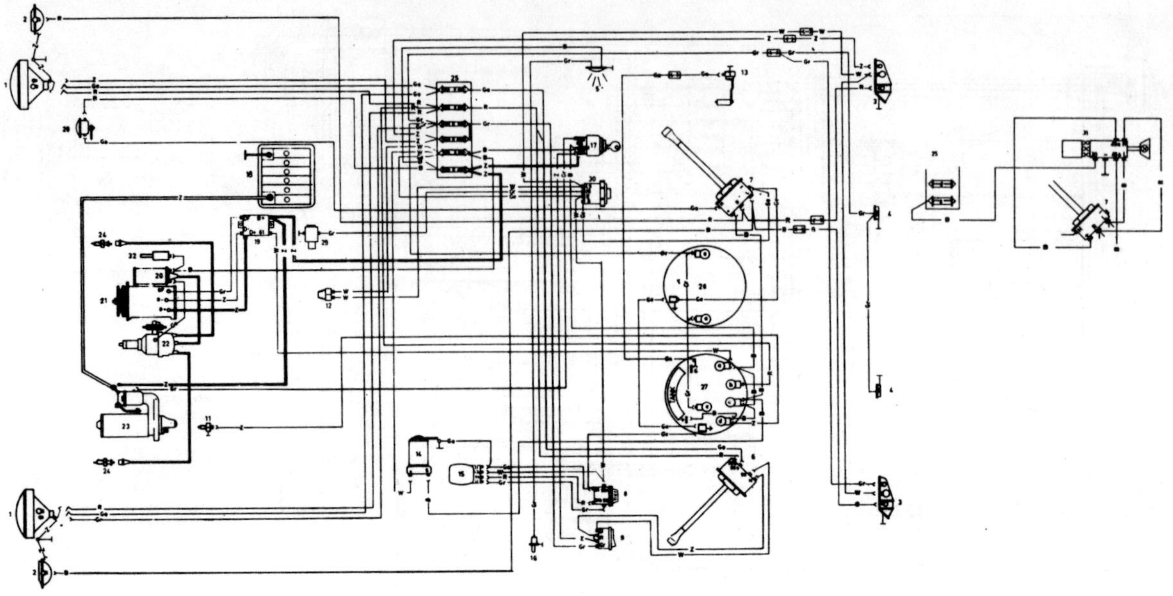

FIG 13:6 Wiring diagram, DAF 33 de Luxe, 12 volt

Key to Fig 13:6 1 Headlight, main beam/dipped beam/parking light 45/40/4 watt 2 Direction indicator light 21 watt 3 Stop/tail/direction indicator light 21/5/21 watt 4 Number plate light 3 watt 5 Interior light 5 watt 6 Headlight dipped beam/main beam switch 7 Direction indicator/horn switch 8 Windscreen wiper/windscreen washer switch 9 Parking light/headlight main beam switch 11 Oil pressure warning light switch 12 Stop light switch 13 Fuel tank element 14 Flasher unit 15 Windscreen wiper motor 16 Interior light switch 17 Ignition switch 18 Battery 36 amp/hr at 20-hr rate 19 Voltage regulator 20 Ignition control 21 Generator 22 Distributor 23 Starter 24 Sparking plug 25 Fuse holder 6 x 8 amp 26-27 Instruments: a/e Instrument lighting (white) 2 watt a Generator charge warning light (red) 2 watt b Main beam warning light (blue) 2 watt c Direction indicator warning light (green) 2 watt d Oil pressure warning light (red) 2 watt 28 Horn 29 Electromagnetic valve of low ratio hold 30 Low ratio hold switch 32 Slow running air jet (closeable)

Colour code

Key to colour code **Bl** Blue **Br** Brown **Gr** Green **Ge** Yellow **G** Grey **R** Red **W** White **Z** Black

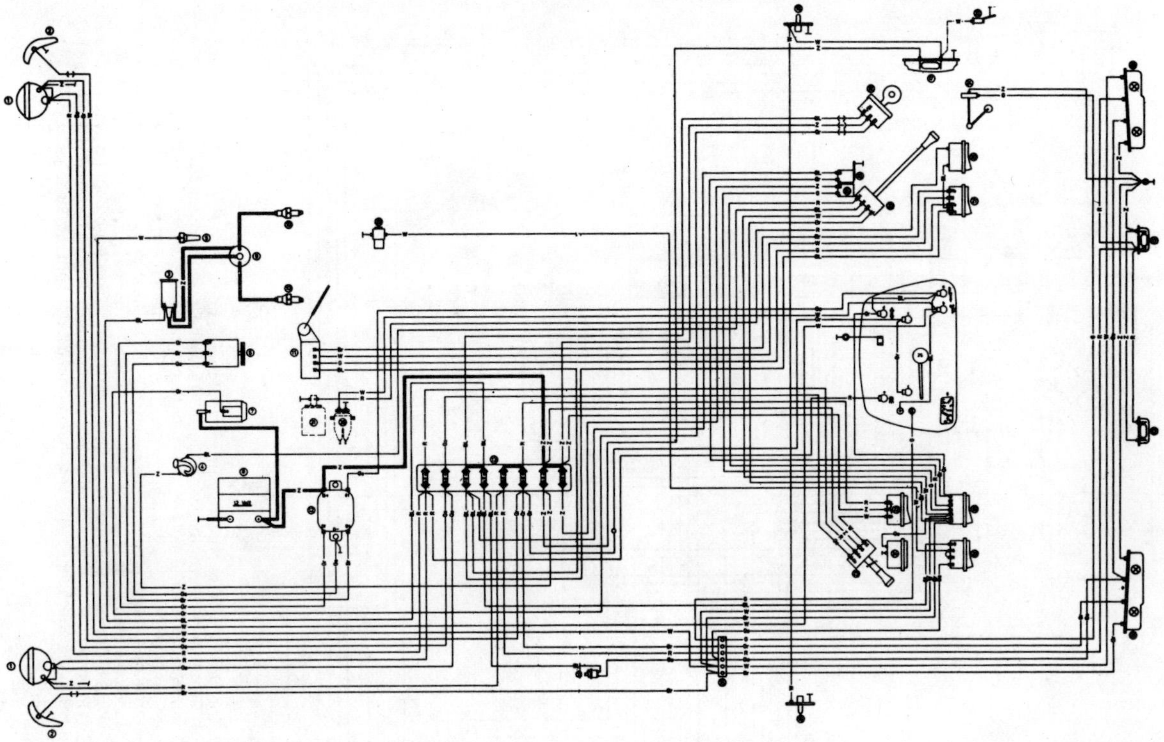

FIG 13:7 Wiring diagram, DAF 44, 12 volt

Key to Fig 13:7 1 Headlamp (2 x) Main beam/dipped beam 45/40 watt Parking light 4 watt 2 Direction indicator 21 watt (2 x) 3 Ignition coil 4 Horn 5 Oil pressure warning light switch 6 Generator 7 Starter 8 Battery 36 amp/hr 20-hr rate 9 Distributor 10 Sparking plug 11 Windscreen wiper motor 12 Voltage regulator 13 Fuse holder 8-pole Fuses 8 amp (8 x) 14 Stop light switch 15 Wire connector 9-pole 16 Courtesy light switch 17 Courtesy light 5 watt 18 Ignition switch 19 Flasher unit 20 Direction indicator/horn switch 21 Windscreen wiper switch 22 Parking light/ headlight main beam switch 23 Headlight dipped beam/main beam switch 24 Float 25 Speedometer a Generator charge warning light (red) 2 watt b Oil pressure warning light (red) 2 watt c Instrument lighting (2 x) 2 watt d Direction indicator warning light (green) 2 watt e Main beam warning light (blue) 2 watt f Earth g Fuel gauge '+'/'G' 26 Tail-lamps (2 x) Stoplight 21/5 watt Tail-lamp 21/5 watt Direction indicator light 21 watt 27 Number plate light 5 watt (2 x) 28 Engine brake switch 29 Electromagnetic valve 30 Windscreen washer switch 31 Reservoir/pump windscreen washer 32 Mercury switch 33 Alarm switch 34 Alarm switch control 35 Alarm flasher unit 36 Float brake fluid level control

When installing the alarmswitch, remove the yellow wire between pos. 19 and 20

(−) Flat wire connection
(o) Plug wire connection

Colour code

Key to colour code **Bl** Blue **Gr** Green **G** Grey **W** White **Br** Brown **Ge** Yellow **R** Red **Z** Black

Wire, 6 mm2 cross-section
Cable, 25 mm2 cross-section
Cable, anti-interference

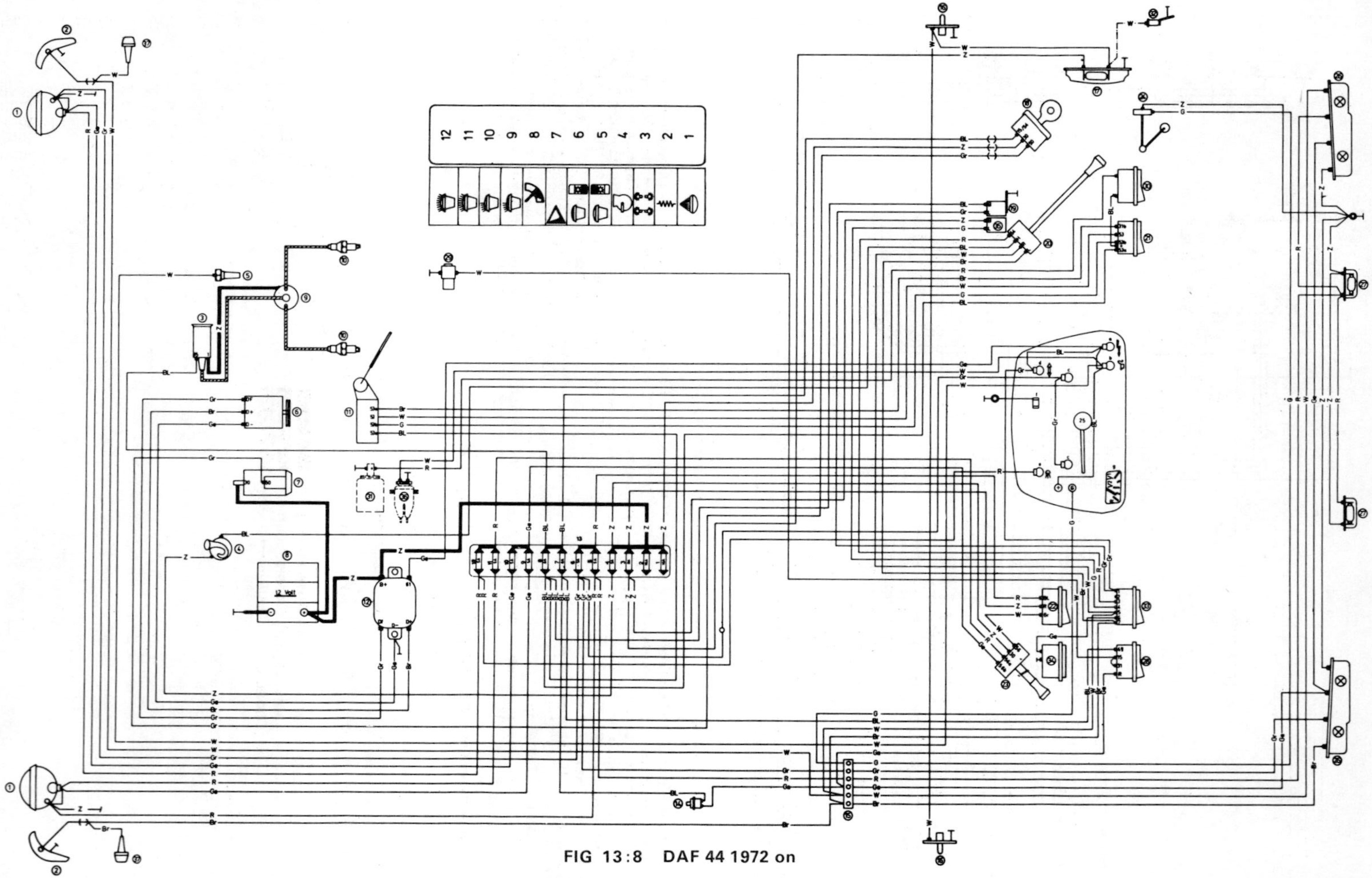

FIG 13:8 DAF 44 1972 on

Key to Fig 13:8 1 Headlight main beam/dipped beam/parking light 45/40/4 watt 2 Direction indicator light 18 watt 3 Ignition coil 4 Horn 5 Oil pressure warning light switch 6 Generator 7 Starter 8 Battery 66 amp/hr at 20-hr rate 9 Distributor 10 Sparking plug 11 Windscreen wiper motor 12 Voltage regulator 13 Fuse holder 7 x 5 amp; 3 x 8 amp; 2 x 16 amp 14 Stop light switch 15 Wire connector, 9-pole 16 Courtesy light switch 17 Courtesy light 5 watt 18 Ignition switch 19 Flasher unit 20 Direction indicator/horn switch 21 Windscreen wiper switch 22 Parking light/headlight main beam switch 23 Headlight dipped beam/main beam switch 24 Fuel tank element 25 Speedometer a Generator charge warning light (red) 2 watt b Oil pressure warning light (red) 2 watt c Instrument lighting 2 watt d Direction indicator warning light (green) 2 watt e Main beam warning light (blue) 2 watt f Earth g Fuel gauge '+'/'G' 26 Stop/tail/direction indicator light 21/5 watt; 21/5 watt; 21 watt 27 Number plate light 5 watt 28 Transmission low ratio hold switch 29 Electromagnetic vacuum valve 30 Windscreen washer switch 31 Windscreen washer reservoir and pump 32 Mercury switch (for estate car and delivery van only) 33 Hazard warning switch 34 Hazard warning switch warning light 35 Hazard warning flasher unit 36 Brake fluid level indicator float 37 Side direction indicator light 4 watt

Colour code

Key to colour code **Bl** Blue **Br** Brown **Gr** Green **Ge** Yellow **G** Grey **R** Red **W** White **Z** Black

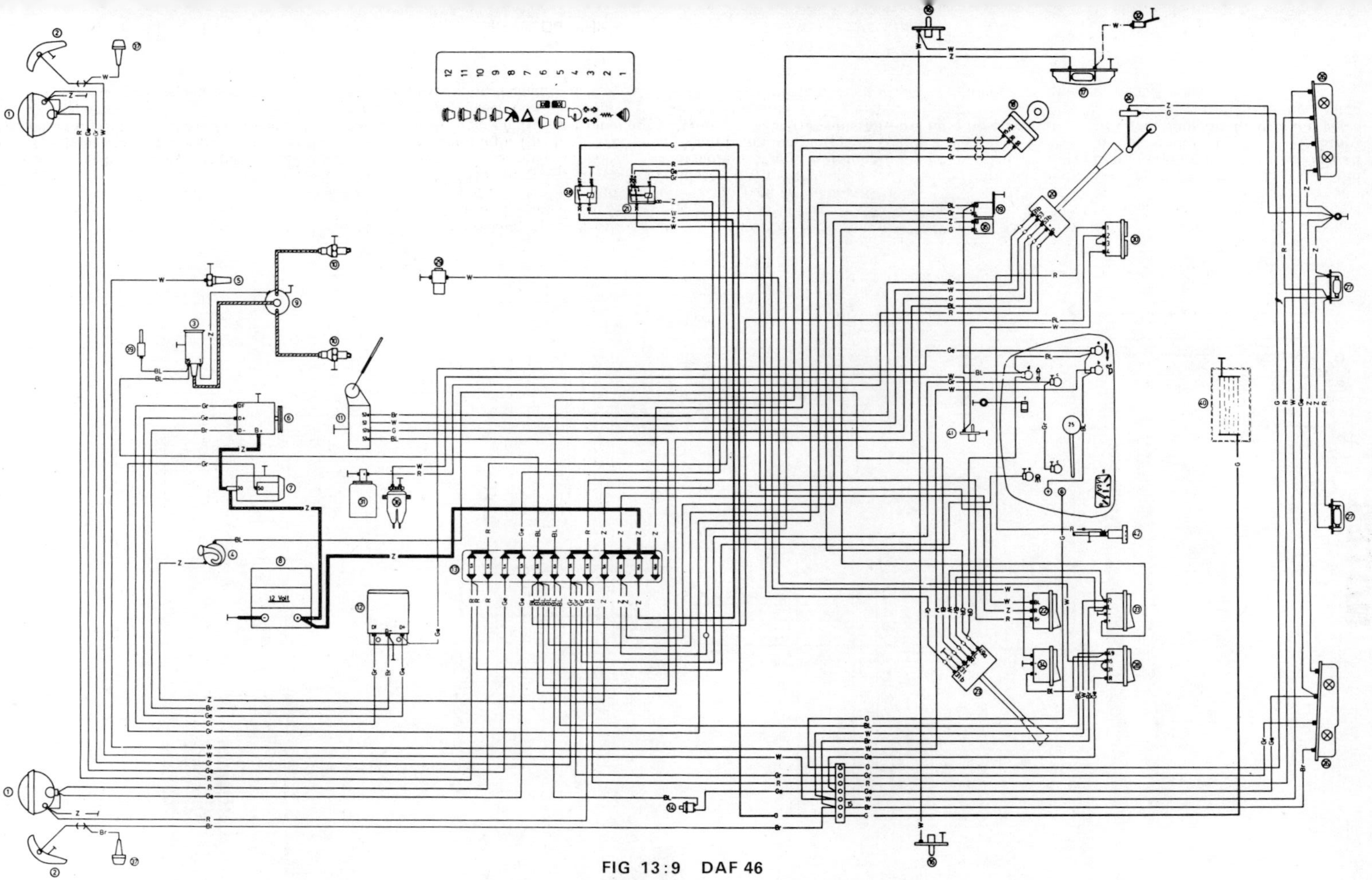

FIG 13:9 DAF 46

Key to Fig 13:9 1 Headlamp, main beam/dipped beam/parking light 45/40/4 watt 2 Direction indicator 21 watt 3 Ignition coil 4 Horn 5 Oil pressure warning light switch 6 Alternator 7 Starter 8 Battery 36 amp/hr at 20-hr rate 9 Distributor 10 Sparking plug 11 Windscreen wiper motor 12 Voltage regulator 13 Fuse holder 7 x 5 amp; 3 x 8 amp; 2 x 16 amp 14 Stop light switch 15 Wire connector 9-pole 16 Courtesy light switch 17 Courtesy light 5 watt 18 Ignition switch 19 Flasher unit 20 Windscreen wiper switch 21 Headlight dipped beam/main beam relay 22 Parking light/headlight main beam switch 23 Direction indicator/horn switch 24 Float 25 Instrument binnacle a Alternator charge warning light (red) 2 watt b Oil pressure warning light (red) 2 watt c Instrument lighting d Direction indicator warning light (green) 2 watt e Main beam warning light (blue) 2 watt f Earth g Fuel gauge '+'/'G' 26 Stop/tail/direction indicator light 21/5 watt; 21/5 watt; 21 watt 27 Number plate light 5 watt 28 Transmission low ratio hold switch 29 Electromagnetic vacuum valve 30 Handbrake, brake fluid level and choke warning lights 31 Windscreen washer reservoir and pump 32 Mercury switch 33 Hazard warning switch 34 Heated rear window switch 35 Hazard warning flasher unit 36 Brake fluid level indicator float 37 Side direction indicator light 4 watt 38 Relay for heated rear window

Colour code

Key to colour code **Bl** Blue **Br** Brown **Gr** Green **Ge** Yellow **G** Grey **R** Red **W** White **Z** Black

NOTES

HINTS ON MAINTENANCE AND OVERHAUL

There are few things more rewarding than the restoration of a vehicle's original peak of efficiency and smooth performance.

The following notes are intended to help the owner to reach that state of perfection. Providing that he possesses the basic manual skills he should have no difficulty in performing most of the operations detailed in this manual. It must be stressed, however, that where recommended in the manual, highly-skilled operations ought to be entrusted to experts, who have the necessary equipment, to carry out the work satisfactorily.

Quality of workmanship:

The hazardous driving conditions on the roads to-day demand that vehicles should be as nearly perfect, mechanically, as possible. It is therefore most important that amateur work be carried out with care, bearing in mind the often inadequate working conditions, and also the inferior tools which may have to be used. It is easy to counsel perfection in all things, and we recognize that it may be setting an impossibly high standard. We do, however, suggest that every care should be taken to ensure that a vehicle is as safe to take on the road as it is humanly possible to make it.

Safe working conditions:

Even though a vehicle may be stationary, it is still potentially dangerous if certain sensible precautions are not taken when working on it while it is supported on jacks or blocks. It is indeed preferable not to use jacks alone, but to supplement them with carefully placed blocks, so that there will be plenty of support if the car rolls off the jacks during a strenuous manoeuvre. Axle stands are an excellent way of providing a rigid base which is not readily disturbed. Piles of bricks are a dangerous substitute. Be careful not to get under heavy loads on lifting tackle, the load could fall. It is preferable not to work alone when lifting an engine, or when working underneath a vehicle which is supported well off the ground. To be trapped, particularly under the vehicle, may have unpleasant results if help is not quickly forthcoming. Make some provision, however humble, to deal with fires. Always disconnect a battery if there is a likelihood of electrical shorts. These may start a fire if there is leaking fuel about. This applies particularly to leads which can carry a heavy current, like those in the starter circuit. While on the subject of electricity, we must also stress the danger of using equipment which is run off the mains and which has no earth or has faulty wiring or connections. So many workshops have damp floors, and electrical shocks are of such a nature that it is sometimes impossible to let go of a live lead or piece of equipment due to the muscular spasms which take place.

Work demanding special care:

This involves the servicing of braking, steering and suspension systems. On the road, failure of the braking system may be disastrous. Make quite sure that there can be no possibility of failure through the bursting of rusty brake pipes or rotten hoses, nor to a sudden loss of pressure due to defective seals or valves.

Problems:

The chief problems which may face an operator are:

1 External dirt.
2 Difficulty in undoing tight fixings.
3 Dismantling unfamiliar mechanisms.
4 Deciding in what respect parts are defective.
5 Confusion about the correct order for reassembly.
6 Adjusting running clearances.
7 Road testing.
8 Final tuning.

Practical suggestions to solve the problems:

1 Preliminary cleaning of large parts—engines, transmissions, steering, suspensions, etc.,—should be carried out before removal from the car. Where road dirt and mud alone are present, wash clean with a high-pressure water jet, brushing to remove stubborn adhesions, and allow to drain and dry. Where oil or grease is also present, wash down with a proprietary compound (Gunk, Teepol etc.,) applying with a stiff brush—an old paint brush is suitable—into all crevices. Cover the distributor and ignition coils with a polythene bag and then apply a strong water jet to clear the loosened deposits. Allow to drain and dry. The assemblies will then be sufficiently clean to remove and transfer to the bench for the next stage.

On the bench, further cleaning can be carried out, first wiping the parts as free as possible from grease with old newspaper. Avoid using rag or cotton waste which can leave clogging fibres behind. Any remaining grease can be removed with a brush dipped in paraffin. If necessary, traces of paraffin can be removed by carbon tetrachloride. Avoid using paraffin or petrol in large quantities for cleaning in enclosed areas, such as garages, on account of the high fire risk.

When all exteriors have been cleaned, and not before, dismantling can be commenced. This ensures that dirt will not enter into interiors and orifices revealed by dismantling. In the next phases, where components have to be cleaned, use carbon tetrachloride in preference to petrol and keep the containers covered except when in use. After the components have been cleaned, plug small holes with tapered hard wood plugs cut to size and blank off larger orifices with grease-proof paper and masking tape. Do not use soft wood plugs or matchsticks as they may break.

2 It is not advisable to hammer on the end of a screw thread, but if it must be done, first screw on a nut to protect the thread, and use a lead hammer. This applies particularly to the removal of tapered cotters. Nuts and bolts seem to 'grow' together, especially in exhaust systems. If penetrating oil does not work, try the judicious application of heat, but be careful of starting a fire. Asbestos sheet or cloth is useful to isolate heat.

Tight bushes or pieces of tail-pipe rusted into a silencer can be removed by splitting them with an open-ended hacksaw. Tight screws can sometimes be started by a tap from a hammer on the end of a suitable screwdriver. Many tight fittings will yield to the judicious use of a hammer, but it must be a soft-faced hammer if damage is to be avoided, use a heavy block on the opposite side to absorb shock. Any parts of the steering system which have been damaged should be renewed, as attempts to repair them may lead to cracking and subsequent failure, and steering ball joints should be disconnected using a recommended tool to prevent damage.

3 If often happens that an owner is baffled when trying to dismantle an unfamiliar piece of equipment. So many modern devices are pressed together or assembled by spinning-over flanges, that they must be sawn apart. The intention is that the whole assembly must be renewed. However, parts which appear to be in one piece to the naked eye, may reveal close-fitting joint lines when inspected with a magnifying glass, and, this may provide the necessary clue to dismantling. Left-handed screw threads are used where rotational forces would tend to unscrew a right-handed screw thread.

Be very careful when dismantling mechanisms which may come apart suddenly. Work in an enclosed space where the parts will be contained, and drape a piece of cloth over the device if springs are likely to fly in all directions. Mark everything which might be reassembled in the wrong position, scratched symbols may be used on unstressed parts, or a sequence of tiny dots from a centre punch can be useful. Stressed parts should never be scratched or centre-popped as this may lead to cracking under working conditions. Store parts which look alike in the correct order for reassembly. Never rely upon memory to assist in the assembly of complicated mechanisms, especially when they will be dismantled for a long time, but make notes, and drawings to supplement the diagrams in the manual, and put labels on detached wires. Rust stains may indicate unlubricated wear. This can sometimes be seen round the outside edge of a bearing cup in a universal joint. Look for bright rubbing marks on parts which normally should not make heavy contact. These might prove that something is bent or running out of truth. For example, there might be bright marks on one side of a piston, at the top near the ring grooves, and others at the bottom of the skirt on the other side. This could well be the clue to a bent connecting rod. Suspected cracks can be proved by heating the component in a light oil to approximately 100°C, removing, drying off, and dusting with french chalk, if a crack is present the oil retained in the crack will stain the french chalk.

4 In determining wear, and the degree, against the permissible limits set in the manual, accurate measurement can only be achieved by the use of a micrometer. In many cases, the wear is given to the fourth place of decimals; that is in ten-thousandths of an inch. This can be read by the vernier scale on the barrel of a good micrometer. Bore diameters are more difficult to determine. If, however, the matching shaft is accurately measured, the degree of play in the bore can be felt as a guide to its suitability. In other cases, the shank of a twist drill of known diameter is a handy check.

Many methods have been devised for determining the clearance between bearing surfaces. To-day the best and simplest is by the use of Plastigage, obtainable from most garages. A thin plastic thread is laid between the two surfaces and the bearing is tightened, flattening the thread. On removal, the width of the thread is compared with a scale supplied with the thread and the clearance is read off directly. Sometimes joint faces leak persistently, even after gasket renewal. The fault will then be traceable to distortion, dirt or burrs. Studs which are screwed into soft metal frequently raise burrs at the point of entry. A quick cure for this is to chamfer the edge of the hole in the part which fits over the stud.

5 **Always check a replacement part with the original one before it is fitted.**

If parts are not marked, and the order for reassembly is not known, a little detective work will help. Look for marks which are due to wear to see if they can be mated. Joint faces may not be identical due to manufacturing errors, and parts which overlap may be stained, giving a clue to the correct position. Most fixings leave identifying marks especially if they were painted over on assembly. It is then easier to decide whether a nut, for instance, has a plain, a spring, or a shakeproof washer under it. All running surfaces become 'bedded' together after long spells of work and tiny imperfections on one part will be found to have left corresponding marks on the other. This is particularly true of shafts and bearings and even a score on a cylinder wall will show on the piston.

6 Checking end float or rocker clearances by feeler gauge may not always give accurate results because of wear. For instance, the rocker tip which bears on a valve stem may be deeply pitted, in which case the feeler will simply be bridging a depression. Thrust washers may also wear depressions in opposing faces to make accurate measurement difficult. End float is then easier to check by using a dial gauge. It is common practice to adjust end play in bearing assemblies, like front hubs with taper rollers, by doing up the axle nut until the hub becomes stiff to turn and then backing it off a little. Do not use this method with ballbearing hubs as the assembly is often preloaded by tightening the axle nut to its fullest extent. If the splitpin hole will not line up, file the base of the nut a little.

Steering assemblies often wear in the straight-ahead position. If any part is adjusted, make sure that it remains free when moved from lock to lock. Do not be surprised if an assembly like a steering gearbox, which is known to be carefully adjusted outside the car, becomes stiff when it is bolted in place. This will be due to distortion of the case by the pull of the mounting bolts, particularly if the mounting points are not all touching together. This problem may be met in other equipment and is cured by careful attention to the alignment of mounting points.

When a spanner is stamped with a size and A/F it means that the dimension is the width between the jaws and has no connection with ANF, which is the designation for the American National Fine thread. Coarse threads like Whitworth are rarely used on cars to-day except for studs which screw into soft aluminium or cast iron. For this reason it might be found that the top end of a cylinder head stud has a fine thread and the lower end a coarse thread to screw into the cylinder block. If the car has mainly UNF threads then it is likely that any coarse threads will be UNC, which are not the same as Whitworth. Small sizes have the same number of threads in Whitworth and UNC, but in the $\frac{1}{2}$ inch size for example, there are twelve threads to the inch in the former and thirteen in the latter.

7 After a major overhaul, particularly if a great deal of work has been done on the braking, steering and suspension systems, it is advisable to approach the problem of testing with care. If the braking system has been overhauled, apply heavy pressure to the brake pedal and get a second operator to check every possible source of leakage. The brakes may work extremely well, but a leak could cause complete failure after a few miles.

Do not fit the hub caps until every wheel nut has been checked for tightness, and make sure the tyre pressures are correct. Check the levels of coolant, lubricants and hydraulic fluids. Being satisfied that all is well, take the car on the road and test the brakes at once. Check the steering and the action of the handbrake. Do all this at moderate speeds on quiet roads, and make sure there is no other vehicle behind you when you try a rapid stop.

Finally, remember that many parts settle down after a time, so check for tightness of all fixings after the car has been on the road for a hundred miles or so.

8 It is useless to tune an engine which has not reached its normal running temperature. In the same way, the tune of an engine which is stiff after a rebore will be different when the engine is again running free. Remember too, that rocker clearances on pushrod operated valve gear will change when the cylinder head nuts are tightened after an initial period of running with a new head gasket.

Trouble may not always be due to what seems the obvious cause. Ignition, carburation and mechanical condition are interdependent and spitting back through the carburetter, which might be attributed to a weak mixture, can be caused by a sticking inlet valve.

For one final hint on tuning, never adjust more than one thing at a time or it will be impossible to tell which adjustment produced the desired result.

NOTES

GLOSSARY OF TERMS

Allen key	Cranked wrench of hexagonal section for use with socket head screws.
Alternator	Electrical generator producing alternating current. Rectified to direct current for battery charging.
Ambient temperature	Surrounding atmospheric temperature.
Annulus	Used in engineering to indicate the outer ring gear of an epicyclic gear train.
Armature	The shaft carrying the windings, which rotates in the magnetic field of a generator or starter motor. That part of a solenoid or relay which is activated by the magnetic field.
Axial	In line with, or pertaining to, an axis.
Backlash	Play in meshing gears.
Balance lever	A bar where force applied at the centre is equally divided between connections at the ends.
Banjo axle	Axle casing with large diameter housing for the crownwheel and differential.
Bendix pinion	A self-engaging and self-disengaging drive on a starter motor shaft.
Bevel pinion	A conical shaped gearwheel, designed to mesh with a similar gear with an axis usually at 90 deg. to its own.
bhp	Brake horse power, measured on a dynamometer.
bmep	Brake mean effective pressure. Average pressure on a piston during the working stroke.
Brake cylinder	Cylinder with hydraulically operated piston(s) acting on brake shoes or pad(s).
Brake regulator	Control valve fitted in hydraulic braking system which limits brake pressure to rear brakes during heavy braking to prevent rear wheel locking.
Camber	Angle at which a wheel is tilted from the vertical.
Capacitor	Modern term for an electrical condenser. Part of distributor assembly, connected across contact breaker points, acts as an interference suppressor.
Castellated	Top face of a nut, slotted across the flats, to take a locking splitpin.
Castor	Angle at which the kingpin or swivel pin is tilted when viewed from the side.
cc	Cubic centimetres. Engine capacity is arrived at by multiplying the area of the bore in sq cm by the stroke in cm by the number of cylinders.
Clevis	U-shaped forked connector used with a clevis pin, usually at handbrake connections.
Collet	A type of collar, usually split and located in a groove in a shaft, and held in place by a retainer. The arrangement used to retain the spring(s) on a valve stem in most cases.
Commutator	Rotating segmented current distributor between armature windings and brushes in generator or motor.
Compression ratio	The ratio, or quantitative relation, of the total volume (piston at bottom of stroke) to the unswept volume (piston at top of stroke) in an engine cylinder.
Condenser	See capacitor.
Core plug	Plug for blanking off a manufacturing hole in a casting.
Crownwheel	Large bevel gear in rear axle, driven by a bevel pinion attached to the propeller shaft. Sometimes called a 'ring gear'.
'C'-spanner	Like a 'C' with a handle. For use on screwed collars without flats, but with slots or holes.
Damper	Modern term for shock-absorber, used in vehicle suspension systems to damp out spring oscillations.
Depression	The lowering of atmospheric pressure as in the inlet manifold and carburetter.
Dowel	Close tolerance pin, peg, tube, or bolt, which accurately locates mating parts.
Drag link	Rod connecting steering box drop arm (pitman arm) to nearest front wheel steering arm in certain types of steering systems.
Dry liner	Thinwall tube pressed into cylinder bore
Dry sump	Lubrication system where all oil is scavenged from the sump, and returned to a separate tank.
Dynamo	See Generator.
Electrode	Terminal, part of an electrical component, such as the points or 'Electrodes' of a sparking plug.
Electrolyte	In lead-acid car batteries a solution of sulphuric acid and distilled water.
End float	The axial movement between associated parts, end play.
EP	Extreme pressure. In lubricants, special grades for heavily loaded bearing surfaces, such as gear teeth in a gearbox, or crownwheel and pinion in a rear axle.

Fade Of brakes. Reduced efficiency due to overheating.

Field coils Windings on the polepieces of motors and generators.

Fillets Narrow finishing strips usually applied to interior bodywork.

First motion shaft Input shaft from clutch to gearbox.

Fullflow filter Filters in which all the oil is pumped to the engine. If the element becomes clogged, a bypass valve operates to pass unfiltered oil to the engine.

FWD Front wheel drive.

Gear pump Two meshing gears in a close fitting casing. Oil is carried from the inlet round the outside of both gears in the spaces between the gear teeth and casing to the outlet, the meshing gear teeth prevent oil passing back to the inlet, and the oil is forced through the outlet port.

Generator Modern term for 'Dynamo'. When rotated produces electrical current.

Grommet A ring of protective or sealing material. Can be used to protect pipes or leads passing through bulkheads.

Grubscrew Fully threaded headless screw with screwdriver slot. Used for locking, or alignment purposes.

Gudgeon pin Shaft which connects a piston to its connecting rod. Sometimes called 'wrist pin', or 'piston pin'.

Halfshaft One of a pair transmitting drive from the differential.

Helical In spiral form. The teeth of helical gears are cut at a spiral angle to the side faces of the gearwheel.

Hot spot Hot area that assists vapourisation of fuel on its way to cylinders. Often provided by close contact between inlet and exhaust manifolds.

HT High Tension. Applied to electrical current produced by the ignition coil for the sparking plugs.

Hydrometer A device for checking specific gravity of liquids. Used to check specific gravity of electrolyte.

Hypoid bevel gears A form of bevel gear used in the rear axle drive gears. The bevel pinion meshes below the centre line of the crownwheel, giving a lower propeller shaft line.

Idler A device for passing on movement. A free running gear between driving and driven gears. A lever transmitting track rod movement to a side rod in steering gear.

Impeller A centrifugal pumping element. Used in water pumps to stimulate flow.

Journals Those parts of a shaft that are in contact with the bearings.

Kingpin The main vertical pin which carries the front wheel spindle, and permits steering movement. May be called 'steering pin' or 'swivel pin'.

Layshaft The shaft which carries the laygear in the gearbox. The laygear is driven by the first motion shaft and drives the third motion shaft according to the gear selected. Sometimes called the 'countershaft' or 'second motion shaft.'

lb ft A measure of twist or torque. A pull of 10 lb at a radius of 1 ft is a torque of 10 lb ft.

lb/sq in Pounds per square inch.

Little-end The small, or piston end of a connecting rod. Sometimes called the 'small-end'.

LT Low Tension. The current output from the battery.

Mandrel Accurately manufactured bar or rod used for test or centring purposes.

Manifold A pipe, duct, or chamber, with several branches.

Needle rollers Bearing rollers with a length many times their diameter.

Oil bath Reservoir which lubricates parts by immersion. In air filters, a separate oil supply for wetting a wire mesh element to hold the dust.

Oil wetted In air filters, a wire mesh element lightly oiled to trap and hold airborne dust.

Overlap Period during which inlet and exhaust valves are open together.

Panhard rod Bar connected between fixed point on chassis and another on axle to control sideways movement.

Pawl Pivoted catch which engages in the teeth of a ratchet to permit movement in one direction only.

Peg spanner Tool with pegs, or pins, to engage in holes or slots in the part to be turned.

Pendant pedals Pedals with levers that are pivoted at the top end.

Phillips screwdriver A cross-point screwdriver for use with the cross-slotted heads of Phillips screws.

Pinion A small gear, usually in relation to another gear.

Piston-type damper Shock absorber in which damping is controlled by a piston working in a closed oil-filled cylinder.

Preloading Preset static pressure on ball or roller bearings not due to working loads.

Radial Radiating from a centre, like the spokes of a wheel.

Radius rod	Pivoted arm confining movement of a part to an arc of fixed radius.
Ratchet	Toothed wheel or rack which can move in one direction only, movement in the other being prevented by a pawl.
Ring gear	A gear tooth ring attached to outer periphery of flywheel. Starter pinion engages with it during starting.
Runout	Amount by which rotating part is out of true.
Semi-floating axle	Outer end of rear axle halfshaft is carried on bearing inside axle casing. Wheel hub is secured to end of shaft.
Servo	A hydraulic or pneumatic system for assisting, or, augmenting a physical effort. See 'Vacuum Servo'.
Setscrew	One which is threaded for the full length of the shank.
Shackle	A coupling link, used in the form of two parallel pins connected by side plates to secure the end of the master suspension spring and absorb the effects of deflection.
Shell bearing	Thinwalled steel shell lined with anti-friction metal. Usually semi-circular and used in pairs for main and big-end bearings.
Shock absorber	See 'Damper'.
Silentbloc	Rubber bush bonded to inner and outer metal sleeves.
Socket-head screw	Screw with hexagonal socket for an Allen key.
Solenoid	A coil of wire creating a magnetic field when electric current passes through it. Used with a soft iron core to operate contacts or a mechanical device.
Spur gear	A gear with teeth cut axially across the periphery.
Stub axle	Short axle fixed at one end only.
Tachometer	An instrument for accurate measurement of rotating speed. Usually indicates in revolutions per minute.
TDC	Top Dead Centre. The highest point reached by a piston in a cylinder, with the crank and connecting rod in line.
Thermostat	Automatic device for regulating temperature. Used in vehicle coolant systems to open a valve which restricts circulation at low temperature.
Third motion shaft	Output shaft of gearbox.
Threequarter floating axle	Outer end of rear axle halfshaft flanged and bolted to wheel hub, which runs on bearing mounted on outside of axle casing. Vehicle weight is not carried by the axle shaft.
Thrust bearing or washer	Used to reduce friction in rotating parts subject to axial loads.
Torque	Turning or twisting effort. See 'lb ft'.
Track rod	The bar(s) across the vehicle which connect the steering arms and maintain the front wheels in their correct alignment.
UJ	Universal joint. A coupling between shafts which permits angular movement.
UNF	Unified National Fine screw thread.
Vacuum servo	Device used in brake system, using difference between atmospheric pressure and inlet manifold depression to operate a piston which acts to augment brake pressure as required. See 'Servo'.
Venturi	A restriction or 'choke' in a tube, as in a carburetter, used to increase velocity to obtain a reduction in pressure.
Vernier	A sliding scale for obtaining fractional readings of the graduations of an adjacent scale.
Welch plug	A domed thin metal disc which is partially flattened to lock in a recess. Used to plug core holes in castings.
Wet liner	Removable cylinder barrel, sealed against coolant leakage, where the coolant is in direct contact with the outer surface.
Wet sump	A reservoir attached to the crankcase to hold the lubricating oil.

NOTES

INDEX

NOTES

Alfa Romeo Giulia 1600, 1750, 2000 1962 on
Aston Martin 1921-58
Auto Union Audi 70, 80, Super 90, 1966-72
Audi 100 1969 on
Austin, Morris etc. 1100 Mk. 1 1962-67
Austin, Morris etc. 1100 Mk. 2, 3, 1300 Mk. 1, 2, 3 America 1968 on
Austin A30, A35, A40 Farina 1951-67
Austin A55 Mk. 2, A60 1958-69
Austin A99, A110 1959-68
Austin J4 1960 on
Austin Allegro 1973 on
Austin Maxi 1969 on
Austin, Morris 1800 1964 on
Austin, Morris 2200 1972 on
Austin Kimberley, Tasman 1970 on
Austin, Morris 1300, 1500 Nomad 1969 on
BMC 3 (Austin A50, A55 Mk. 1, Morris Oxford 2, 3 1954-59)
Austin Healey 100/6, 3000 1956-68
Austin Healey, MG Sprite, Midget 1958 on
Bedford CA Mk. 2 1964-69
Bedford CF Vans 1969 on
Bedford Beagle HA Vans 1964 on
BMW 1600 1966 on
BMW 1800 1964-71
BMW 2000, 2002 1966 on
Chevrolet Corvair 1960-69
Chevrolet Corvette V8 1957-65
Chevrolet Corvette V8 1965 on
Chevrolet Vega 2300 1970 on
Chrysler Valiant V8 1965 on
Chrysler Valiant Straight Six 1963 on
Citroen DS 19, ID 19 1955-66
Citroen ID 19, DS 19, 20, 21 1966 on
Citroen Dyane Ami 1964 on
Daf 31, 32, 33, 44, 55 1961 on
Datsun Bluebird 610 series 1972 on
Datsun Cherry 100A, 120A 1971 on
Datsun 1000, 1200 1968 on
Datsun 1300, 1400, 1600 1968 on
Datsun 240C 1971 on

Datsun 240Z Sport 1970 on
Fiat 124 1966 on
Fiat 124 Sport 1966 on
Fiat 125 1967-72
Fiat 127 1971 on
Fiat 128 1969 on
Fiat 500 1957 on
Fiat 600, 600D 1955-69
Fiat 850 1964 on
Fiat 1100 1957-69
Fiat 1300, 1500 1961-67
Ford Anglia Prefect 100E 1953-62
Ford Anglia 105E, Prefect 107E 1959-67
Ford Capri 1300, 1600 OHV 1968 on
Ford Capri 1300, 1600, 2000 OHC 1972 on
Ford Capri 2000 V4, 3000 V6 1969 on
Ford Classic, Capri 1961-64
Ford Consul, Zephyr, Zodiac, 1, 2 1950-62
Ford Corsair Straight Four 1963-65
Ford Corsair V4 1965-68
Ford Corsair V4 2000 1969-70
Ford Cortina 1962-66
Ford Cortina 1967-68
Ford Cortina 1969-70
Ford Cortina Mk. 3 1970 on
Ford Escort 1967 on
Ford Falcon 6 1964-70
Ford Falcon XK, XL 1960-63
Ford Falcon 6 XR/XA 1966 on
Ford Falcon V8 (U.S.A.) 1965-71
Ford Falcon V8 (Aust.) 1966 on
Ford Pinto 1970 on
Ford Maverick 6 1969 on
Ford Maverick V8 1970 on
Ford Mustang 6 1965 on
Ford Mustang V8 1965 on
Ford Thames 10, 12, 15 cwt 1957-65
Ford Transit V4 1965 on
Ford Zephyr Zodiac Mk. 3 1962-66
Ford Zephyr Zodiac V4, V6, Mk. 4 1966-72
Ford Consul, Granada 1972 on
Hillman Avenger 1970 on
Hillman Hunter 1966 on
Hillman Imp 1963-68
Hillman Imp 1969 on
Hillman Minx 1 to 5 1956-65
Hillman Minx 1965-67

Hillman Minx 1966-70
Hillman Super Minx 1961-65
Jaguar XK120, 140, 150, Mk. 7, 8, 9 1948-61
Jaguar 2.4, 3.4, 3.8 Mk. 1, 2 1955-69
Jaguar 'E' Type 1961-72
Jaguar 'S' Type 420 1963-68
Jaguar XJ6 1968 on
Jowett Javelin Jupiter 1947-53
Landrover 1, 2 1948-61
Landrover 2, 2a, 3 1959 on
Mazda 616 1970 on
Mazda 808, 818 1972 on
Mazda 1200, 1300 1969 on
Mazda 1500, 1800 1967 on
Mazda RX-2 1971 on
Mazda R100, RX-3 1970 on
Mercedes-Benz 190b, 190c, 200 1959-68
Mercedes-Benz 220 1959-65
Mercedes-Benz 220/8 1968 on
Mercedes-Benz 230 1963-68
Mercedes-Benz 250 1965-67
Mercedes-Benz 250 1968 on
Mercedes-Benz 280 1968 on
MG TA to TF 1936-55
MGA MGB 1955-68
MGB 1969 on
Mini 1959 on
Mini Cooper 1961-72
Morgan Four 1936-72
Morris Marina 1971 on
Morris (Aust) Marina 1972 on
Morris Minor 2, 1000 1952-71
Morris Oxford 5, 6 1959-71
NSU 1000 1963-72
NSU Prinz 1 to 4 1957-72
Opel Ascona, Manta 1970 on
Opel GT 1900 1968 on
Opel Kadett, Olympia 993 cc 1078 cc 1962 on
Opel Kadett, Olympia 1492, 1698, 1897 cc 1967 on
Opel Rekord C 1966-72
Peugeot 204 1965 on
Peugeot 304 1970 on
Peugeot 404 1960 on
Peugeot 504 1968 on
Porsche 356A, B, C 1957-65
Porsche 911 1964 on
Porsche 912 1965-69
Porsche 914 S 1969 on
Reliant Regal 1952-73

Renault R4, R4L, 4 1961 on
Renault 5 1972 on
Renault 6 1968 on
Renault 8, 10, 1100 1962-71
Renault 12, 1969 on
Renault 15, 17 1971 on
Renault R16 1965 on
Renault Dauphine Floride 1957-67
Renault Caravelle 1962-68
Rover 60 to 110 1953-64
Rover 2000 1963-73
Rover 3 Litre 1958-67
Rover 3500, 3500S 1968 on
Saab 95, 96, Sport 1960-68
Saab 99 1969 on
Saab V4 1966 on
Simca 1000 1961 on
Simca 1100 1967 on
Simca 1300, 1301, 1500, 1501 1963 on
Skoda One (440, 445, 450) 1955-70
Sunbeam Rapier Alpine 1955-65
Toyota Carina, Celica 1971 on
Toyota Corolla 1100, 1200 1967 on
Toyota Corona 1500 Mk. 1 1965-70
Toyota Corona Mk. 2 1969 on
Triumph TR2, TR3, TR3A 1952-62
Triumph TR4, TR4A 1961-67
Triumph TR5, TR250, TR6 1967 on
Triumph 1300, 1500 1965-73
Triumph 2000 Mk. 1, 2.5 PI Mk. 1 1963-69
Triumph 2000 Mk. 2, 2.5 PI Mk. 2 1969 on
Triumph Dolomite 1972 on
Triumph Herald 1959-68
Triumph Herald 1969-71
Triumph Spitfire, Vitesse 1962-68
Triumph Spitfire Mk. 3, 4 1969 on
Triumph GT6, Vitesse 2 Litre 1969 on
Triumph Stag 1970 on
Triumph Toledo 1970 on
Vauxhall Velox, Cresta 1957-72
Vauxhall Victor 1, 2, FB 1957-64
Vauxhall Victor 101 1964-67
Vauxhall Victor FD 1600, 2000 1967-72

Continued on following page

Vauxhall Victor 3300, Ventora 1968-72
Vauxhall Victor FE Ventora 1972 on
Vauxhall Viva HA 1963-66
Vauxhall Viva HB 1966-70
Vauxhall Viva, HC Firenza 1971 on
Volkswagen Beetle 1954-67
Volkswagen Beetle 1968 on
Volkswagen 1500 1961-66
Volkswagen 1600 Fastback 1965-73
Volkswagen Transporter 1954-67
Volkswagen Transporter 1968 on
Volkswagen 411 1968-72
Volvo 120 series 1961-70
Volvo 140 series 1966 on
Volvo 160 series 1968 on
Volvo 1800 1960-73

NOTES

NOTES

NOTES

NOTES